CANADA

AN ILLUSTRATED HISTORY | DEREK HAYES

CAN

AN ILLUSTRATED

ADA

HISTORY | DEREK HAYES

Douglas & McIntyre

VANCOUVER / TORONTO

Douglas & McIntyre Ltd.
2323 Quebec Street, Suite 201
Vancouver, British Columbia V5T 4S7
www.douglas-mcintyre.com

National Library of Canada Cataloguing in Publication

Hayes, Derek, 1947–
    Canada: an illustrated history / Derek Hayes.

Includes bibliographical references and index.
ISBN 1-55365-046-8

    1. Canada—History—Pictorial works. I. Title

FC174.H38 2004   971   C2004-901665-2

Design and layout by Derek Hayes
Image research and acquisition by Derek Hayes
Copyediting by Naomi Pauls
Printed and bound in China by C & C Offset Ltd.
Printed on acid-free paper

We gratefully acknowledge the financial support of the Canada Council for the Arts, the British Columbia Arts Council, and the Government of Canada through the Book Publishing Industry Development Program (BPIDP) for our publishing activities.

To contact the author:
www.derekhayes.ca
derek@derekhayes.ca

Other books by Derek Hayes:
Historical Atlas of British Columbia and the Pacific Northwest
First Crossing: Alexander Mackenzie
Historical Atlas of the North Pacific Ocean
Historical Atlas of Canada: Canada's History Illustrated with Original Maps
Historical Atlas of the Arctic
America Discovered: A Historical Atlas of Exploration

Acknowledgements

Many people helped with the tracking down and supplying of images for this book. In particular I would like to thank the following: artists Peter Rindlisbacher, Harry Heine, and Lewis Parker, all of whose paintings appear in the book, and Jean-Marc Carisse, photographer of Pierre Trudeau. The following individuals provided images, advice, or both: Jennifer Devine, Louis Cardinal, Natalie Stone, Henri Huard, and Sean Lancaster of the National Archives of Canada, now the Library and Archives of Canada; Jim Bowman, Glenbow-Alberta Institute Archives; Heather Gillis, Fortress of Louisbourg Photo Archives; Wayne Kerr and Regan Oliver, Environment Canada, Parks and Historic Properties, Halifax; Heather McNabb, McCord Museum of Canadian History, Montréal; Jackie Hillier and Debbie Edgecombe, Centre for Newfoundland Studies, Memorial University of Newfoundland, St. John's; Andre Guidon, Parks Canada, Hull; Anne-Marie Beaton, Canadian Press; Debra Moore, Hudson's Bay Company Archives, Winnipeg; Debbie Keffer, Hudson's Bay Company corporate office, Toronto; Carol Haber, City of Vancouver Archives; Kevin Joynt, National Library of Canada (Library and Archives of Canada); Raven Amiro, National Gallery of Canada; Maggie Arbour-Doucette, Canadian War Museum; Janet Lacroix, Armanda Tomei and Charles Rhéaume, Department of National Defence; Alan Walker, Toronto Public Library; Gillian Reddyhoff, Government of Ontario Art Collection; Jean-François Royal, Musée du Château Ramezay, Montréal; Mike Baker, Museum London, London, Ontario; Kelly-Ann Nolin, British Columbia Archives, Victoria; Carol Anderson, Ontario Society of Artists; Stewart Boden, Archives of Ontario; Ronald Whistance-Smith; Michelle Roy, Provincial Archives of Alberta; Tim Novak, Saskatchewan Archives Board, Regina; Janelle Reynolds, Provincial Archives of Manitoba; Richard Schofield, Heritage Scarborough; Kate Bird, Pacific Press (*Vancouver Sun*); Ken Hernden, York University Archives and Special Collections; Bob Kennell, Canadian Pacific Railway Archives, Montréal; Patrica Desjardins, Montréal *Gazette*; and all those archives, libraries, museums, art galleries, etc. that are acknowledged in the image credits (page 278). In addition I thank the following for permission to use images: Sister Pierrette Boulet; Garry Sheriff Scott; Joan Macpherson; Stewart B. Sheppard and Margaret H. Knox; Kiyoko Grenier Sago, designer of the Fort Anne Tapestry; and Empire Financial Group, Kingston. Finally I should acknowledge my debt to those anonymous artists and photographers who recorded images that make possible a book such as this, but whose names have unfortunately become detached from their work. Our history is richer due to their collective efforts.

Thanks are due to Naomi Pauls, my ever diligent copy editor, without whom the book would contain many more errors than it probably does now. Thanks too to my publisher, Scott McIntyre, for his continuing confidence. Last but not least, thanks to my wife, Carole Hayes, for her encouragement.

Half-title page.
For more than fifty years the British organization for homeless children, Dr. Barnado's, sent some of its charges to Canada, where, it was hoped, they would find a better life. Between 1882 and 1939 the organization sent about thirty thousand children to Canada. Most of these children were sent to help out on farms and to work as domestic servants; few were adopted. These "home children" were open to abuses, but many did do far better for themselves than they would have if they had not left Britain. Here a group of Dr. Barnardo's children have arrived at the dock at Saint John. The photograph is undated but was probably taken either just before or just after the First World War. (See also page 189.)

Title page.
A view of Montréal from the Custom House, about 1878. It was taken by a photographer from the renowned studio of William Notman.

Contents

1 *Since the World Began*

anada is a land of immigrants and their descendants. And, it seems, all of us are immigrants—some just very much earlier than others. The First Nations peoples have the longest history by far, so long that much of their own history and mythologies have attributed their origins to a creation in situ. Many accept some form or another of the Mi'kmaq belief that they have been living in the land that is now Canada "since the world began."

But the scientific evidence tells a different, perhaps less eloquent, story. It is generally accepted that the first people migrated from eastern Siberia, a region where humans had been living long before. They likely followed the animals on which they relied for food across Bering Strait when it was a land bridge caused by the reduction of sea levels by the great ice sheets during several periods from about 40,000 years ago. From Alaska they travelled south through an ice-free corridor formed between the Rocky Mountains to the west and the Laurentide Ice Sheet, which covered most of the rest of Canada. This ice-free pathway was created during cyclical retreats of the ice 35,000 to 40,000 years ago, and at several later periods.

Alternatively, recent research has suggested that people may also have migrated into North America by moving south along the fringes of the ice sheets down the West Coast, a possibility that might help to explain the relatively high density of native peoples on the margins of the Pacific.

Whatever the actual route, it seems that by about 30,000 years ago, people had reached as far south as Mexico, although there is no consensus as to the timing. By about 12,000 to 10,000 years ago, some hardy hunters were living in the land we now call Canada, as is evidenced by a few—so very few—fluted stone lance points used for hunting caribou and bison, and also mammoth and mastodon.

The climate of Canada slowly moderated until, about 3,500 years ago, it became similar to that we know today. Some would say—after a proverbial Canadian winter—that it is still not so moderate. But it was survivable, and Canada's first immigrants set about developing sophisticated societies in all regions of the country, highly adapted to the local living conditions. The peoples of the West Coast fed on salmon and whale meat; those of the Prairies hunted buffalo, driving the unfortunate beasts over cliffs in frenzies of killing.

Above.
A native arrowhead from White Rock, British Columbia, meticulously chipped to form a point and to fit a wooden shaft. Actual size.

Left.
This totem pole stood outside the house of Nuxalk chief Qomoqua at Qomq'-ts (Bella Coola) for many years. It is now in the Canadian Museum of Civilization in Ottawa.

Those of the Great Lakes hunted and learned how to grow crops of corn and squash, while their maritime cousins lived from land and sea. Later migrations populated Newfoundland with the Beothuk and the Arctic, more sparsely, with the Inuit. These diverse peoples living in their own tribal areas across Canada developed a multitude of cultures and languages.

The Iroquoian-speaking group of native peoples settled in the lands around Lakes Erie and Ontario, in a region stretching from the western shore of Lake Huron eastwards to the St. Lawrence. They developed a lifestyle based on slash-and-burn agriculture together with hunting. These peoples included the Laurentian Huron "Stadaconans" and "Hochelagans" of today's Québec and Montréal. They lived in a series of longhouses that could be as long as 45 metres and 13 metres wide. These were communal dwellings made of bent saplings covered with bark, with holes in the roof to allow smoke from the essential fires to escape. Closed tight in the winter, such dwellings were smoky affairs indeed. The longhouses were usually surrounded by a high stockade, a barrier against what seems to have been incessant aggression from other tribes.

Agriculture was the essential support for these peoples, producing half to three-quarters of their food requirements. An area was cleared—an arduous task with only stone axes, but larger trees were killed by stripping their bark, and then all the vegetation was burnt, providing excellent potash fertilizer for the new fields. Beans, squash, and especially corn could be cultivated for about ten years before yields declined, necessitating a move to a new area. Thus, every ten years or so, the entire village was moved.

Hunting and fishing provided the rest of their food, often with seasonal migrations to take advantage of local availabilities. It was the "Stadaconans" that Cartier first met in Gaspé Bay in 1534, when the native group was on one of these seasonal treks, coming to the Gaspé to fish (see page 19).

To the north, both west and east, lay the colder forests inhabited by the Algonquian-speaking peoples, including the Odawa (or Ottawa), the Montagnais, and the Cree. They lived in a region reaching from what is now north Saskatchewan east to the north shore of the Gulf of St. Lawrence. These people were largely hunters and fishers, hunting woodland bison, caribou, elk, moose, and small animals. Their eastern neighbours, in what is now the Maritimes, hunted moose and other animals, but obtained much of their subsistence from fishing, collecting shellfish, and hunting sea mammals, especially seals. As always, food was dictated by what was available. Habitations of both were less elaborate than those of the more sedentary Iroquoians, although the basic construction materials were the same, saplings and bark. They built smaller houses—wigwams—in which one or two families might live. Moving was thus relatively easy, following the animals they hunted on their seasonal migrations.

The most important method of transport for these peoples was the canoe, an invention that would be quickly adopted by European explorers and traders as the only practical means of travel in a land of rivers. Their light canoes were covered with the bark of the silver birch. They were in marked

Below and opposite, bottom.
The exterior and interior of an Iroquoian longhouse, made from saplings and bark, and an encampment. The modern reconstruction is in Québec, at the Cartier-Brébeuf National Historic Site, and the model is at the Musée du Château Ramezay, Montréal.

Opposite, top.
An Algonquian wigwam, again made from saplings and bark. This recontruction is at Fort William, Thunder Bay.

contrast to the canoes developed by the coastal peoples, whose heavy dugout canoes did not have to be portaged from one river system to the next. For travel in winter the sledge and the snowshoe were developed.

Group membership was somewhat flexible, so that in times when food was scarce the tribe might disperse, coming back together when better times returned. From spring to fall, a normally predictable food supply, especially of fish, allowed encampments of up to a hundred.

Farther west, on the southern prairie, a different lifestyle evolved, based on the abundance of one particular food source—the plains bison, commonly called the buffalo. Migration of the buffalo herd was quite predictable, enabling such tribes as the Blackfoot and the Piegan to follow their food supply. Here there were fewer trees but plenty of buffalo skins, and so the covering of their shelters—teepees—was not bark but skins, even easier to move. In winter the buffalo sought shelter in aspen woodlands, and the native people constructed enclosures (under the winter chief, or "poundmaker") and drove buffalo into them. Before the horse we know today (introduced into North America about 1519 by the Spanish) reached the prairie in the 1720s, an adaptation of pound construction was used to kill buffalo on a grand scale. The animals were driven and stampeded over cliffs where, if they did not die in the fall, they were easily dispatched at the cliff's base. The prairie is dotted with these "buffalo jumps," the most famous and perhaps the largest being Head-Smashed-In Buffalo Jump near Lethbridge, today a UNESCO World Heritage Site.

To the north, some of the Athapaskan peoples of the Barren Grounds, the Chipewyan, also built enclosures in which to trap animals, in this case the caribou. Here survival was more difficult and every edible animal, fish, and plant was utilized. Small mammals were an important food source, especially the beaver. Beaver pelts provided excellent winter clothing too, worn with the fur against the body. It was these used and thus slightly abraded pelts, the guard hairs having been lost, that became so prized by European traders. And it was the search for more and more beaver pelts that motivated the

European push towards the West and led to the founding of both the Hudson's Bay Company and the North West Company (see pages 51 and 103).

The principal food over the winter for many Athapaskan tribes was fish caught using hooks and lines, nets, and weirs. Some fish was preserved by drying or simply freezing once the weather was cold enough.

Farther north still is the Canadian Arctic, home of the Inuit, known by Europeans until quite recently as Eskimo. Here subsistence was even more difficult, requiring special adaptations to survive the long Arctic winter night. The most important food source for the Inuit was the seal, supplemented by walrus, whales, polar bears, and fish—especially Arctic char—as available. Beaver and muskrat were hunted by the Invialuit of the Mackenzie Delta, but these animals were not found elsewhere. The Ungava Inuit hunted caribou, and everywhere there were Arctic hares and foxes—if you knew where to find them. The Inuit, perhaps because of their fine adaptation to their environment, could read the subtle signs of life that others would miss. Inuit hunting equipment was of necessity not made from wood but from bone, and the Inuit became adept at carving this material. They often hunted using an atlatl, or spear thrower, designed to increase the thrust of a spear thrown from a sitting position, in a kayak. For the ubiquitous canoe had in the North become the

This model from the Manitoba Museum in Winnipeg shows a Cree encampment being set up on a riverbank.

kayak, a one- or two-person skin-covered canoe that in the hands of a skilled hunter virtually became part of his body as he silently crept up on his unsuspecting prey. For larger transportation needs, such as moving a family from winter to summer hunting grounds, or for hunting whales and polar bears, a larger skin-covered boat called an umiak was used.

Summer shelters were also skin-covered. Available driftwood was used as a framework, often giving a rather irregular-shaped structure. But it is the winter shelter for which the Inuit are best known, the cleverly constructed dome of ice blocks known as the iglu.

The greatest concentration of First Nations peoples prior to the coming of Europeans was to be found on the Pacific coast of Canada. Here also were the most different language groups and the largest number of tribes. This density was directly related to the abundance of resources of the land and sea. The principal food source for the coastal peoples was the salmon, which, like the buffalo of the prairie, had quite predictable behaviour, returning to the streams of their origin to spawn and die. Salmon could be caught at sea, but were fished in much larger numbers in the rivers, using a variety of methods. Intricate fish weirs and traps were a common sight on rivers, channelling the salmon into holding areas where they could easily be landed. Nets and spears were also used. Salmon would be caught in large numbers at the time of migration upriver and preserved by drying or smoking, providing a store for the winter. The salmon was revered, which was not surprising given its importance as a food source and how relatively easy it made the life of the coastal peoples. Nothing that had touched meat was allowed to touch the waters of a river for fear of offending the gods of the salmon.

The First Nations of the coast traded with those inland. One of the most important trade items other than salmon was the oil of the small oolichan (or eulachon) fish, which, transported in cedar containers on the backs of natives, created the so-called grease trails, named for the spilled or leaked oil to be found on them. It was one such trail that Alexander Mackenzie was shown in 1793, allowing him to cut across land from the Fraser River to the Pacific at Bella Coola (see page 103).

West Coast natives hunted whales and seals as well as the sea otter. The superbly fine fur of the latter started a rush of fur traders to the Northwest Coast in the years after the visit of Captain James Cook to Nootka Sound in 1778, and led through overhunting to the near demise of these creatures.

Varying estimates exist of the total First Nations population living in the country we now call Canada at the time when Europeans arrived to begin exploration and settlement, that is, at the beginning of the seventeenth century. The best estimate seems to be about half a million people. Of this number, perhaps 30 to 40 percent lived on the Pacific coast, 20 to 30 percent around the Great Lakes and in the St. Lawrence Valley, and 10 to 20 percent on the Prairies. Whatever the exact numbers, they demonstrate that, contrary to the belief of many Europeans—a belief that persisted until relatively recently—the land was by no means empty and by no means undiscovered when Europeans appeared on the scene.

Left, top.
A Kwakwa̱ka̱'wakw (Kwakiutl) wedding party approaches the bride's village at the northeastern end of Vancouver Island, about 1890. Another Edward Curtis photograph, the scene is likely staged for the camera. The Thunderbird at the bow of the dugout cedar canoe performs a wing-flapping dance.

Left, bottom.
Totem poles front Haida houses at Skidegate, Queen Charlotte Islands (Haida Gwaii), on 26 July 1878 in this photograph by George M. Dawson of the Geological Survey of Canada.

Totem poles fell and were reclaimed by the earth, but were replaced by new ones. But this fallen pole at Yuquot (Friendly Cove), Nootka Sound, has not been replaced. Yuquot today has no permanent settlement. The photograph was taken in 1998.

The Vikings Reach Canada

The first European explorers had almost no effect on the indigenous peoples of Canada, except those near their landing place. As far as we know for sure, the first Native-European contact was between the Beothuk of Newfoundland and Norse explorers who landed at the tip of Newfoundland's Northern Peninsula about 1000. Arguments still rage as to precisely where the Norse explorers landed in Canada, and recent evidence suggests that there were other contacts farther north, on Baffin Island—certainly later, perhaps earlier. But we do know that the Norse landed at the tip of Newfoundland's Northern Peninsula, for the remains of a settlement have been found there. In 1960, at L'Anse aux Meadows, archaeologists Helge Ingstad and Anne Stine Ingstad found the remains of eight sod houses and evidence of ironworking, carpentry, and needlework. Subsequent excavations have found hundreds of other artifacts.

It seems likely that this was the encampment of Leifr Eiríksson (often spelled Ericsson), who, according to the Norse sagas, made a voyage to the west in 1001. The Norse had reached Greenland from Iceland by 983, and in 985 or 986 Bjarni Herjolfsson had been blown farther westwards to a forested land. In 1001 Eiríksson retraced Herjolfsson's voyage to find the reported land. His first landfall was likely on Baffin Island, which he called Helluland, or "Slab-Land." He then sailed southwards to a forested land with sandy beaches, which he called Markland, or "Forest-Land." This was probably the southern coast of Labrador, forested at the time. Eiríksson then continued southwards to a place he called Vinland. This is today thought to be the region around L'Anse aux Meadows. "Vin" could have meant "green meadow" but probably meant "wine." Grapes perhaps grew in the area at this time—Cartier later found grapes on the shores of the St. Lawrence—but the name may have simply meant that grapes were gathered farther south and brought back to the settlement. Butternut or white walnut wood, which never grew this far north, has been found at the site; if this was brought north, grapes may have been as well.

Eiríksson stayed in Newfoundland two or three seasons at most. It would be another six centuries before Europeans would come to stay.

The Norse thought that Europe was connected to Greenland and to North America by land to the north. From a practical point of view this was not far wrong, for a wall of ice does indeed connect them, at least in winter. In the late sixteenth and early seventeenth centuries the king of Denmark dispatched several expeditions to attempt to find any of his subjects who might still be living in Greenland. He found none, but as part of this effort several maps were drawn, purportedly using information from yet older maps. This one, originally drawn in 1590, shows Britain at the right-hand margin, with the coast of Norway to the north. *Grönlandia* is Greenland, south of which is Eiríksson's *Helleland* (Helluland), *Markland,* and *Promontorium Winlandia* (thought to be Vinland Peninsula, the Northern Peninsula of Newfoundland and the site of L'Anse aux Meadows). *Below* is a modern reconstruction of the Norse buildings at L'Anse aux Meadows. At *far left* is a Norse runestone from Jelling, Jutland, Denmark, erected by King Harald Bluetooth about 965. Viking letters, or runes, proclaim the deeds of a heroic king.

Hym That Found the New Isle

Aside from the very brief Viking interlude, Canada—and, indeed, North America—was discovered by Europeans because it blocked the way to the East. The intended destination of most early explorers was not Canada but Cathay (China) or Cipango (Japan), where they thought they might find gold, or the Spice Islands (Moluccas), where they hoped to find the culinary gold that would make their unrefrigerated and often spoiled food edible. The way to the East had been barred to Europeans since 1453, when Constantinople (Istanbul, Turkey) fell to the Ottoman Turks. Thus there was a real incentive to find an alternative route.

Christopher Columbus, sponsored by the Spanish king, had sailed west in 1492 and found America—or at least some Caribbean islands—but he thought he had reached the East. Therefore, when a Genoese merchant, Giovanni Caboto, decided that he too would try sailing to the west, he found a ready backer in England's King Henry VII and the merchants of Bristol.

After changing his name to the English form John Cabot, he set sail—in 1496, it is thought—on an unsuccessful first voyage. The following year he tried again, leaving Bristol in May in his ship the *Matthew.* On 24 June 1497 he made a landfall in Canada. Where, exactly, is not known. It was likely in Newfoundland, but it could have been in Nova Scotia. For a re-enactment ceremony in 1997, Cape Bonavista in Newfoundland was chosen, and this is as good a guess as any.

Cabot found the seas near his new-found land to be swarming with fish. There were so many that they could be plucked from the sea with merely a weighted basket. This was not what Cabot had had in mind, but it was gold of a different kind to a Europe that ate no meat three days a week on papal edict. Cabot returned to England later that year and was rewarded by King Henry with £10 from his privy purse, given "to hym that found the New Isle."

Certain that he had found an eastern peninsula of Asia, Cabot convinced his backers to underwrite another expedition, this time on a grander scale. He sailed from England

in February 1498 with five ships under his command. But things did not work out the way he had hoped, for Cabot was never seen again. There is evidence of some contact with the Beothuk of Newfoundland on the 1498 voyage, however, for two years later, in 1500, when a Portuguese navigator, Gaspar Corte-Real, visited the island and kidnapped a number of native people, one of them had a broken Venetian sword hilt in his possession, while another had two silver earrings. And cartographic evidence suggests Cabot first visited Newfoundland and then sailed south along the coast, looking for the way east. We do know that in 1501 a brutal Spanish explorer, Alonso de Hojeda, who had visited the Caribbean in 1499, was given a gift by his king for "the stopping of the English," and Cabot was seemingly the only possible Englishman in the region at the time.

In 1500 the Portuguese king had also dispatched João Fernandes to search for islands to the west. Fernandes rediscovered Greenland and named it Tierra de Lavrador, because he was himself a *lavrador*, the Portuguese word for a small landowner. This name, slightly changed, was later transposed by mapmakers across Davis Strait to become part of Canada—Labrador.

An inconvenient continent may have obstructed the route to gold and spices, but the word quickly spread in Europe about the rich fishing grounds of Newfoundland's Grand Banks. By the first years of the sixteenth century fishing boats from England, Portugal, Spain, and France were all making the voyage across the Atlantic to fish.

John Cabot takes leave of the mayor of Bristol and receives the blessing of the bishop for his voyage in 1497. At *far left* is part of a Portuguese map drawn in 1502 showing Gaspar Corte-Real's *Terra del Rey de portuguall* (Land of the king of Portugal)—Newfoundland. The bold north-south line is the Tordesillas line, a division of the world according to a 1493 treaty between Spain and Portugal. An attempt has been made to place at least some of the new lands in Portugal's domain, east of the line. João Fernandes's *Lavrador* (Greenland) is the other land shown.

2 *The Land God Gave to Cain*

The first European attempt to settle in Canada—other than the Norse attempt five centuries before—came in 1521. A Portuguese adventurer, João Alvares Fagundes, who had explored the Gulf of St. Lawrence the previous year, landed colonists on Cape Breton Island, on a bay, it is thought, near Ingonish, at the island's northern tip. But Breton fishermen, who had by this time been fishing in the nearby waters for some years, did not like the idea of competition and harassed Fagundes's colonists, cutting fishing lines and burning houses. By 1526 the Portuguese settlement was abandoned.

Most of the early exploration of the eastern coasts of Canada was done by those looking for a strait through them to Cathay. In 1524 the Spanish king sent Estévan Gomez to try to find an easier passage than that which Ferdinand Magellan had found far to the south. Gomez sailed into the Gulf of St. Lawrence but in February 1525 decided there was too much ice for a practicable passage and tried farther south, where, of course, he had no luck either.

About this time the French sent the Florentine navigator Giovanni Verrazano to find the strait everyone was convinced must exist somewhere. Verrazano is better known for his explorations of the east coast of the United States than of Canada, finding New York Harbor (Verrazano Narrows) and famously misinterpreting the lagoons between the offshore islands of the Carolinas and the mainland coast as an entire sea stretching westwards to the Pacific. But he did name one region Acadia, a name that migrated north on maps and eventually became the French name for Nova Scotia. There were also English attempts to find the illusive strait at this time. In 1527 a groups of investors sent John Rut west, but he chose to ignore two opportunities to enter the Gulf of St. Lawrence. Had he done so the English might have laid claim to eastern Canada before the French.

A more substantial probe was made in 1534 by the French. In May of that year Jacques Cartier made a landfall at Cape Bonavista in Newfoundland and entered the Gulf of St. Lawrence through the Strait of Belle Isle (between Newfoundland and Labrador). Near the Îles de la Madeleine he correctly deduced that there must be a strait to the south of Newfoundland, which he noted for future use. Continuing southwards, Cartier visited Prince Edward Island, then followed the coast northwards, meeting Mi'kmaq people at

This pastel by George Agnew Reid shows Jacques Cartier erecting a cross on Gaspé Bay, claiming the land for France, while Laurentian Iroquois peoples look on.

When he first sighted mainland Canada Cartier was not impressed, for it was a particularly barren part of Labrador that he saw. "There is nothing but moss and short stunted shrub," wrote Cartier. "I am rather inclined to believe that this is the land God gave to Cain."

Baie de Chaleurs (Bay of Warmth), which he at first thought was his strait to Cathay. The Mi'kmaq wanted to trade, often considered a sign of previous European contact. Farther north in Baie de Gaspé—Gaspé Bay—Cartier met more native peoples. This time they were about two hundred Laurentian Iroquois led by their chief, Donnacona, on a fishing trip from their base farther up the St. Lawrence. Here Cartier had his men erect a large cross, taking possession of the country in the name of the king of France. This has been seen as the birth of French Canada. The native peoples looked on, not comprehending this usurpation of their lands. Could land be taken this easily? But, effectively, it was.

Cartier "persuaded" Donnacona to let the chief's two sons go with him, promising to return them the following year. Then he sailed into the St. Lawrence, getting as far west as Anticosti Island. Here he met a fierce current and decided it was too late in the season to proceed. So, with Donnacona's sons, he returned to France.

The following year, 1535, Cartier was back, "for the perfection," so his commission read, "of the navigation of lands by you already begun to discover beyond les Terre Neufes." The king of France thought, as Cartier did, that this must be the long-sought strait. Given the enormous width of the St. Lawrence, it was an understandable error. On 10 August Cartier anchored in a bay on the north side of his strait, naming it Baye sainct Laurens because it was the feast day of St. Lawrence, a Roman martyr. The name would come to be applied to both the river and the gulf.

On 7 September Cartier arrived "at the point where the province and territory of Canada begin." He named Île d'Orléans after the son of the French king and anchored in the St. Charles River, below Québec, then the native village of Stadacona, returning Donnacona's sons to him. Obviously by now Cartier had realized that this was not a strait, but he wanted to explore farther upstream to a much larger native city that he had heard about. Donnacona, wanting to preserve possible trade with the French for himself, refused to guide them. Cartier went anyway, taking his smallest ship and towing longboats. They

No one really knows what Jacques Cartier looked like, as no contemporary portrait of the famous navigator survives. This now famous later portrait by Théophile Hamel, which was based on an earlier sketch of unknown provenance, has come to be accepted as his likeness, and has been used on Canadian postage stamps.

Canada—The Origin of a Name

In 1535, on Cartier's return to the St. Lawrence, Donnacona's sons Domagaya and Taignogny told him that the river was the route to Canada, and he later found that their settlement, on the site of to-day's city of Québec, was also called Canada. Cartier appended to his book about the voyage a list of native vocabulary in which he noted that the word *kanata* meant "town." It seems likely that Domagaya and Taignogny were only telling Cartier that this was the way to their home, but it was the probably misinterpreted word *Canada* that stuck. The name appeared on a manuscript map in 1541 and on a printed map in 1560. Mapmakers at the time copied each other and so the name Canada became universally applied, although it was not "official" until 1791, when the British jurisdictions of Upper and Lower Canada were created.

reached Lac Saint-Pierre and then had to continue in the longboats. On 2 October Cartier arrived before Hochelaga, a large fortified Iroquois settlement, at a place he called Mont Réal. Cartier and his men put on a performance calculated to impress, wearing their finest clothes and sounding trumpets. And impress they did. The disabled were brought to be cured. "One would think that God had come down there to cure them," wrote Cartier.

Jacques Cartier at the large Iroquois settlement of Hochelaga, on the site of today's Montréal.

From the top of his Mont Réal Cartier could see that he could go no farther, for the river was barred by rapids. He returned to Stadacona and prepared to stay there for the winter. But Cartier had not foreseen the severity of the famous Canadian winter; he and his men had a bad time of it and only survived because Donnacona's people showed them how to use the bark of the arborvitae tree to avert scurvy.

Probably to cultivate Cartier's friendship, Donnacona embroidered tales of a King-dom of Saguenay filled with gold and precious stones. Cartier returned this favour by kid-napping Donnacona and taking him back to France when they left in 1536, once the ice had left the river. There Donnacona lived out his days regaling the French court with tales of the riches of Saguenay, riches which expanded to include oranges and pomegranates and the much-sought-after spices.

Saguenay came to be regarded as a new empire of gold in the same vein as the Aztec empire found by the Spanish farther south, and so a large expedition was organized to both explore and colonize these new lands. Cartier was nominally second-in-command

The Mapmakers of Dieppe

At the time of the first French attempts to establish a colony in Canada, the centre of French merchant shipping was the port of Dieppe, on the English Channel coast of France. Here lived the wealthy shipowners who needed maps of their expanding world with which to plan their next voyage. With a clientele like this, it is not surprising that there were also in and around Dieppe a number of expert mapmakers, and today a whole series of maps is attributed to this "Dieppe school."

One of these mapmakers was Pierre Desceliers. Around 1550 he produced a map of the world, part of which showed his knowledge of North America learned from Jacques Cartier and the Sieur de Roberval. The map was huge—2.15 m x 1.35 m—and arranged so that whichever side of it one stood, the information was always the right way up. Being at the "top," Canada is shown "upside down," so that south is at the top of the section shown here. In fact, many maps of this period had south at the top; having north at the top was a convention that developed later.

Stunningly and fantastically illuminated, the map was drawn and painted on animal hide. *Canada* is placed in central Québec and on the south shore of the St. Lawrence, *Terre des bretons* is Nova Scotia and New Brunswick, *Terre Neueve* is Newfoundland, *Mer de France* the North Atlantic. *Terre du Laborador* is not Labrador but Greenland; Labrador is the middle peninsula between Greenland and Newfoundland. The St. Lawrence River stretches far inland. On its northern shore (towards the bottom on this map) are *Sagne*, the Saguenay River, and *Ochelaga*, Cartier's Hochelaga (Montréal) applied to a wider region.

A wonderful combination of geography and art, fact and fiction is this map by Dieppe mapmaker Pierre Desceliers created about 1550. It is part of a map of the world showing Canada. South is at the top. The east coast is according to Jacques Cartier and earlier explorers and mapmakers. The north and west coasts are entirely fantasy, on a par with most of the illustrations.

Jean-François de La Roque, Sieur de Roberval.

to Jean-François de La Roque, Sieur de Roberval, but sailed before him, with five ships and several hundred colonists. In August 1541 he set up an encampment at Cap Rouge, just upriver from Québec, naming it Charlesbourg-Royal. Exploring westwards they were again stopped by the Lachine Rapids at Montréal.

The native people, under a new chief, Agona, were now less friendly, and over the winter Cartier lost thirty-five men to their attacks and to scurvy; he seemed to have forgotten the cure showed to him earlier by Donnacona. And so, as soon as he could, Cartier sailed back to France. On the way, in the harbour at St. John's, Newfoundland, he met Roberval on his outward voyage, a year late; Cartier refused to join him.

Undaunted, Roberval continued up the St. Lawrence, on the way marooning his niece or cousin, Marguerite de La Roque, on a small island in the middle of the river for having an affair with one of his men. Marguerite's maid went with her, and her amour jumped overboard to join them. Neither survived, but Marguerite did, undergoing various trials and tribulations until picked up by a French fishing boat. Her story went on to become one of the classics of French literature.

Roberval, meanwhile, continued upriver, and on the site of Cartier's Charlesbourg-Royal built a settlement with his colonists that he called France-Roy. His colonists had a worse winter than Cartier's men, for fifty of them died of scurvy. Belatedly, the next season (1543) they began their fruitless search for the gold and spices Donnacona had assured them abounded, and for the strait Roberval was convinced existed somewhere near. It did not take too long for them to realize that Donnacona had been vastly elaborating the truth, and in July Roberval gave up and sailed back to France. Thus ended the first attempt by the French to establish a colony in Canada.

The Illusion of a Strait

Roberval's pilot, Jean Alphonce, explored the Saguenay River, a little downstream from Québec, and became convinced that this was the elusive strait they had all been searching for. The river enters the St. Lawrence on the north shore, and postglacial drowning of the river's valley does indeed give the impression that the river is an arm of the sea. One can understand how Alphonce could have been so excited. "I estimate that this sea [the Saguenay River] leads to the Pacific Ocean or even to la mer du Cattay," Alphonce wrote. In fact the Saguenay's navigable waters end at the Chicoutimi Rapids, about 100 km upstream. This photograph is a midstream view of the Saguenay River today, taken from near the point where it joins the St. Lawrence, looking north, or upstream.

To Canada to Stay

The French soon realized that there was wealth to be gained from the lands that had blocked their attempts to find a passage to the East. Fish was the initial resource they had exploited; fur was the second. But not until 1600 was the first organized attempt made to formalize a trade in furs. The French king granted monopolies on trade to various private companies in return for promises that they would settle colonists in what he viewed as his domains, thus enhancing his claims to them.

In 1600, Pierre de Chauvin de Tonnetuit, with François Pont-Gravé and Pierre du Gua, Sieur de Monts, sailed from France with four ships, intending to start a little colony based on the fur trade. He selected a bay near the mouth of the Saguenay River, at a place the Montagnais called Totouskak (now it is Tadoussac), and built a house. This was the first European house and first fur-trading post in Canada. After a season of trading furs with the native people he left sixteen colonists to spend the winter and returned to France. Only five of those left behind survived. The rest died from the cold, scurvy, or depredations of the Iroquois, who were fighting their enemies the Montagnais. Chauvin sent ships to trade for two more years, and the house, now completely rebuilt and serving as a museum, still stands.

In 1603 more ships, now commanded by Pont-Gravé, arrived at Tadoussac. On board was a young Samuel de Champlain. He used a smaller ship, a pinnace, to explore inland, with the intention of finding new fur trade opportunities. Champlain sailed some way up the Saguenay and up the St. Lawrence as far as the rapids that had stopped Cartier at Montréal. But he saw little that Cartier had not already documented, and even less, in fact, because the native settlements of Stadacona and Hochelaga had by this time disappeared.

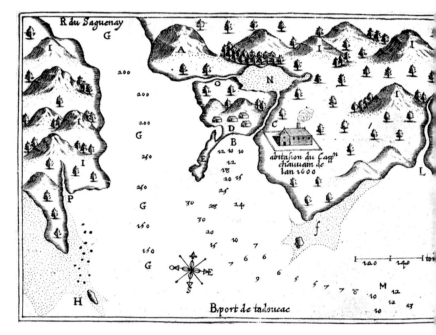

Right, top. Pierre Chauvin's house in Tadoussac is shown as it is today, rebuilt as a museum, on the original site. It is the earliest European house in North America, more or less continually occupied (except for a few winters after the first disastrous overwintering in 1600–1601).

Right, centre. This map is that published by Samuel de Champlain in 1613 and shows the location of Chauvin's house in a small bay close to the entrance to the Saguenay River. The modern view at left is taken from approximately where Champlain has marked the second *G* from the bottom on his map, looking upriver. Apart from being a fur-trading post in its own right, Tadoussac was the first port of call for ships arriving from France for nearly a century.

Right, bottom. Champlain's *habitation* at Port Royal (Annapolis Royal), Nova Scotia. This is a 1939 reconstruction, following a picture plan of the structure published by Champlain himself.

In April 1604 three ships sailed from France, carrying perhaps a hundred potential colonists. Two of the ships, with Pont-Gravé, Champlain, and de Monts, the latter now in charge of the enterprise, headed this time for Nova Scotia, where, de Monts thought, the climate might be more conducive to colonization. But they ended up spending the winter on an island in the St. Croix River, right on what is now the Maine–New Brunswick boundary,

and having a terrible time with the cold and scurvy; thirty-five out of seventy-nine men died. Here Champlain wrote his oft-repeated comment "Il y a six mois d'yuer en ce pays," "There are six months of winter in this country."

The following summer they found a new site on the north side of the Annapolis Basin, on the Fundy coast of Nova Scotia, and an elaborate *habitation* was built, a replica of which is shown on the previous page. Still men died; twelve more in the winter of 1605–06. In 1607 the settlement was abandoned, although renewed by others not long after. Champlain went back to France in September 1607.

The following year Champlain, as de Monts's agent, was back in the St. Lawrence again. This time he went farther upriver so as to be closer to sources of fur. On 3 July 1608 he arrived before Québec, which he selected for their settlement, and set his men to cutting down trees to clear a place for another *habitation* to be built. Thus began the French occupation of what was to become New France. But the first winter was again a trial. Out of twenty-four, only eight of his colonists still lived in the spring. Luckily, de Monts sent Pont-Gravé with reinforcements the following spring, or the new colony would not have survived.

Above. Champlain arriving at Québec, 1608, a painting by Henri Beau.

Below. Champlain firing his arquebus in battle with the Iroquois at Ticonderoga. This sketch, by Champlain himself, is the only known portrait of the founder of New France.

In June 1609 Champlain agreed to assist the Huron, Algonquin, and Montagnais in their ongoing battle with the Iroquois, and at Ticonderoga, on a large lake on the Richelieu River that he named Lake Champlain, a pitched battle was fought between the two groups in which the Iroquois were defeated largely because of the use by Champlain and his men of the arquebus, an early rifle-like firearm fired by a slow-burning match. This resulted in the Iroquois becoming the most deadly enemies of the French for almost a century thereafter, until 1701, when a peace treaty was signed (see page 38).

Champlain's little colony grew, and the fur trade prospered. Champlain, perhaps the first recorded snowbird, often returned to France in the fall, coming back to Québec the following spring. In 1610, while in Paris, he married twelve-year-old Hélène Boullé, although she did not join him in Québec for another ten years. She would tolerate Québec for only four years before returning to France. Champlain named Île Sainte-Hélène (in 1967 the site of Expo) in Montréal after her.

Champlain habitually collected information from native sources about the country to the west and north because he was charged with expanding the trade in furs. In 1613 he had ascended the Ottawa River and in 1615, with native guides, he found the route across the portage between the Ottawa and Mattawa Rivers and then the French River to Lake Huron. He had heard about this lake, which he thought was a sea that might open to the west, and called it Mer Douce ("Gentle Sea"). On a map Champlain drew in 1616, Lake Huron has been transformed into a strait leading to the west. There is no doubt that he was still looking for this, for in 1618, on one of his trips back to France for the winter, he told potential investors "one may hope to find a short route to China by way of the River St. Lawrence . . . It is certain that we shall succeed in finding it without much difficulty . . . The voyage could be made in six months."

Champlain always seems to have been a good promoter, for investment flowed in to the Québec enterprise, but the living was always tenuous due to the Iroquois threat. Récollet missionaries were brought to the colony in 1615, as Champlain thought that perhaps converting the Iroquois would make the settlers safer. The Récollets were not active enough proselytizers, however, and in 1625 the Jesuits were invited, and they proved much more active in their attempts at conversion (see page 32).

In 1627 the king of France's first minister, Cardinal Richelieu, created an organization known as the Cent-Associés, or Hundred Associates, to promote French trade and colonial expansion overseas. In New France this became the Compagnie de la Nouvelle France, with vast monopolistic powers. The company planned to send out four thousand new colonists in the next four years.

But these grand plans were cut short by a war between England and France. The Kirke family of Scotland was authorized to attack Québec. In 1628 they blockaded the St. Lawrence with three ships, capturing several ships of the Hundred Associates. A French relief fleet was defeated, and the Kirkes demanded the surrender of Québec. Champlain's colony held out through the winter but the following spring the Kirkes were back, and there were no relief ships from France. Champlain was forced to surrender; he and many others were shipped to England, although later they were allowed to return to France.

A peace, the Treaty of Saint-Germain-en-Laye, was signed on 20 March 1632 and provided for the return of Québec to the French. The French king agreed to pay an unpaid debt to the English, a dowry for his sister when she married Charles I of England. Thus Canada was retrieved from the hands of the English by paying a bad debt.

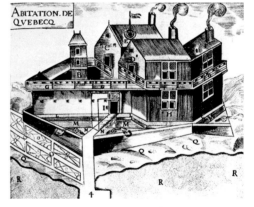

Champlain's Québec *habitation* under construction, *top*, in a painting by Charles Jefferys, and Champlains's own drawing of the completed structure.

Below. Québec today.

Champlain, called for good reason the "Father of New France," died on Christmas Day 1635 in the Québec he had created. Although his infant colony would struggle from time to time during the next few years, the French were now indelibly established in their new North American domains.

The Feuding French

It was bad enough for a pioneering seventeenth-century French entrepreneur that he had to fight the elements and perhaps the natives and the English, but the early history of French settlement in the Maritimes is dominated by a convoluted feud that developed between two Frenchmen, Charles Sainte-Étienne de La Tour and Charles de Menou d'Aulnay de Charnisay.

Charles La Tour had come to Port Royal with his cousin Jean de Biencourt de Poutrincourt in 1610, when the settlement was re-occupied by the French after being abandoned in 1607. In 1623 Biencourt died, and his affairs in Acadia passed to La Tour. In 1630 La Tour built a new fort, called Fort Sainte-Marie, at the mouth of the Saint John River, deep in rich fur country. During the war between England and France, La Tour held onto the only part of peninsular Nova Scotia left to the French, a fort at Cape Sable, on the southwestern tip of the peninsula. For this he was made governor and lieutenant governor of Acadia by the French king in 1631. Then, in 1632, as part of the peace treaty with England, all Acadia was given back to France. Isaac de Radzilly was appointed lieutenant general of all New France. He accepted the surrender of Port Royal, which had been taken over by Scottish settlers (see page 48), and brought three hundred colonists to the La Have River, on Nova Scotia's east coast. Radzilly was largely responsible for organizing a major influx of French colonists to Acadia over the next three years. In 1633, an arrangement was worked out whereby he was to share in the fur trade equally with La Tour. Each was authorized to inspect the other's warehouses. This plan worked as intended until 1635 when Radzilly died, and management of his affairs was given by his brother to Menou d'Aulnay.

D'Aulnay did not like La Tour, for the latter was not an aristocrat or a Catholic like himself—La Tour was a Huguenot. In 1640, when La Tour and his wife showed up at Port Royal to inspect D'Aulnay's store of furs, as was his right under the 1633 agreement, the two came to blows and La Tour was thrown into prison, although friars later obtained his release. D'Aulnay complained to the king, and La Tour was ordered to return to France to explain himself, but refused on the grounds of misrepresentation by D'Aulnay. This proved to be a bad move, for D'Aulnay was then able to convince the king that La Tour was a traitor. Now with royal authority, D'Aulnay attacked La Tour's fort at Cape Sable, burning it to the ground. La Tour found himself cut off from the necessary trade goods he needed to exchange for furs and instead went to Boston to buy them. At D'Aulnay's instigation La Tour was then ordered back to France in August 1642 to explain this apparent collusion with the English. But his wife, Françoise-Marie Jacquelin de La Tour, who was also his business partner, went back to France in his stead, where with the skill of a contortionist she managed to convince the authorities that it was D'Aulnay who was the traitor rather than her husband. She came back to Acadia in 1643 with a ship laden with supplies and soldiers but, attempting to get to Fort Sainte-Marie, the ship was blockaded by D'Aulnay with three ships in the Bay of Fundy.

In 1995, the *Fort Anne Heritage Tapestry*, designed by Kiyoko Grenier Sago, was completed by a group of volunteers. It has four panels depicting the history of the Annapolis Basin. This is the panel from the 5.5 m x 2.5 m tapestry showing Port Royal during the French regime.

Françoise-Marie managed to make contact with her husband, and the pair sailed to Boston, where La Tour mortgaged his property in order to raise the money for four ships and more soldiers. With these he attacked D'Aulnay's fort at Port Royal.

This was getting out of hand. D'Aulnay now went to France and himself convinced the king that, since he was now apparently in cahoots with the English, it was La Tour who was the traitor. The next year, when Françoise-Marie went back to France to obtain supplies, she was refused permission to leave the country. Unfazed, she escaped to England in disguise. There she contracted a ship to carry her precious supplies back to the Saint John. But the voyage took six months—not least because of a delay on the Grand Banks to fish—and the ship was stopped off Cape Sable by D'Aulnay's men. Françoise-Marie avoided detection only by hiding amongst the cargo in the hold. The captain decided that it was too risky to continue to the Saint John, where D'Aulnay still maintained a blockade, and he diverted to Boston. He had not reckoned on Madame La Tour, however. She successfully sued him both for the undue delay and for not taking her to the Saint John, as he was contracted. With money from a court award she hired three ships to run the blockade. By this roundabout method, Françoise-Marie arrived back at the fort on the Saint John at the end of 1644.

At about the same time, D'Aulnay had also returned from France, with yet more soldiers. In February 1645, learning that Fort Sainte-Marie was left in the hands of Françoise-Marie while Charles had gone to Boston for supplies, he attacked. But he had not reckoned on the fiery Françoise-Marie. She gathered her small band of defenders and repulsed D'Aulnay's men, many of whom were killed. D'Aulnay was furious. In April, when he learned that La Tour had once more gone to Boston for supplies, he attacked again. This time he was successful, despite a further spirited defence of the fort led by Françoise-Marie, ending with hand-to-hand fighting. But the La Tour defenders numbered only fifty-five, whereas D'Aulnay had two hundred men. On D'Aulnay's promise to "give quarter to all," Françoise-Marie, realizing the position hopeless, ordered her men to lay down their arms. A revengeful D'Aulnay forced her to watch as he hanged her surviving defenders in contravention of all the rules of war, then or now. Françoise-Marie died a few weeks later, some think poisoned on the orders of her adversary.

D'Aulnay himself did not live much longer. He died in 1650, and Charles La Tour returned to France to clear his name and re-establish himself in the royal favour. One would have thought the king might be a little confused by now, but La Tour succeeded in once again reversing the animus. In 1653 La Tour returned to Acadia with more colonists, sailing into Port Royal and presenting D'Aulnay's widow, Jeanne Motin, a royal order restoring the fort on the Saint John to him. She did better, becoming La Tour's new wife that same year. Both, it seems, were fed up with the continuous fighting, not to mention broke, and the marriage effectively brought the feud to an end.

But it was not the end of the story, for the following year Fort Sainte-Marie was attacked again, this time by English soldiers—Oliver Cromwell's men—and being outnumbered five hundred to seventy, La Tour was forced to surrender his fort once more. He never got it back. Forced into a partnership with two English merchants, he sold his interest to them and retired to Cape Sable, where he died in 1666.

Françoise-Marie Jacquelin de La Tour pleads with a merciless Charles de Menou D'Aulnay as her men are hanged after the surrender of Fort Sainte-Marie in April 1645.

There is considerable confusion over the names of the various forts in Acadia at this time. La Tour's fort at Cape Sable was originally Fort Lomeron but later the name was changed to Fort La Tour. To add to the confusion, Fort Sainte-Marie, now in Saint John, is often referred to as Fort La Tour.

The Vast Designs of Heaven

Both Jacques Cartier and Samuel de Champlain had visited the location that was to become Montréal. Champlain had noted its suitability for settlement and had in 1611 cleared a spot that he named Place Royale and planted a garden to check the fertility of the soil.

Late in 1640 the Cents Associés granted most of the island of Montréal to Jérôme Le Royer de la Dauversière and Pierre Chevrier, Sieur de Fancamp, on condition that they in turn grant land only to people currently in France. Thus it was hoped to encourage new population growth in the colony. The pair were part of a group called the Société de Notre-Dame de Montréal that was planning to establish a religious community in New France. To lead their venture they interested a devout "gentleman of virtue and courage," Paul de Chomedey, Sieur de Maisonneuve.

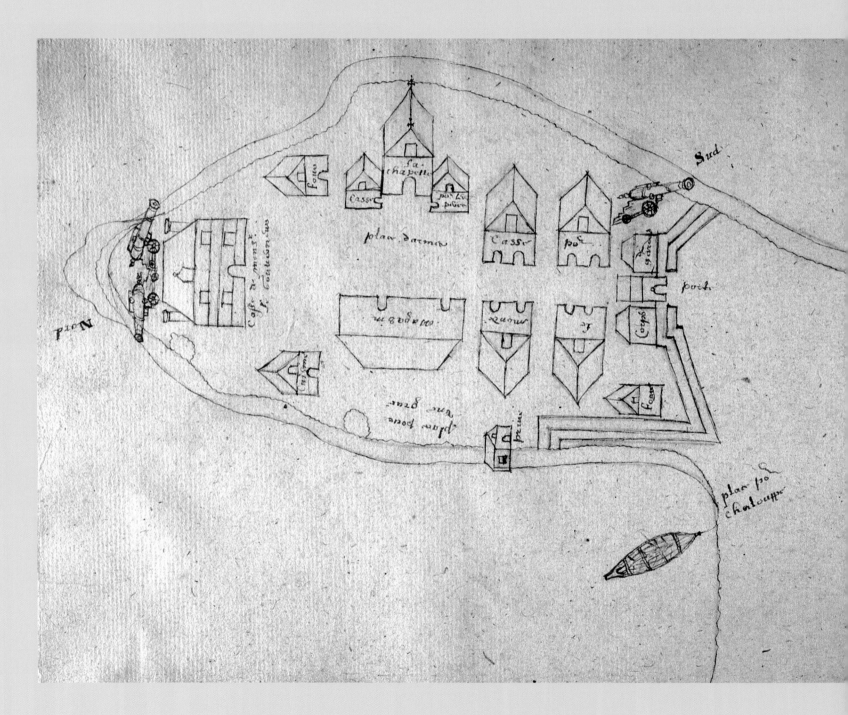

The settlers left France in three ships in 1641. They were met with little enthusiasm in Québec, because the colony's still small population (about two hundred at this time) were being threatened by the Iroquois and had hoped that the ships were carrying reinforcements. The Iroquois menace was so bad that there was even talk of abandoning Québec.

The governor of New France, Charles Huault de Montmagny, not wanting to disperse the population, opposed Maisonneuve's plan to settle on the island of Montréal and offered him instead Île d'Orléans, close to Québec. Maisonneuve would have none of it. He famously told Montmagny that it was a matter of honour that he go where he was sent, "even if all the trees on the island were turned into as many Iroquois." In any case it was too late in the season to do anything that year.

The settlers finally left Québec on 8 May 1642, accompanied by Montmagny and Father Bartholémy Vimont, the Jesuit superior. They reached the chosen site on 17 May. The governor formally gave Maisonneuve possession of the place and Father Vimont said Mass. "What you see is but a grain of mustard seed," he said, "but it is sown by hands so pious . . . that Heaven must doubtless have vast designs . . . and I have no doubt that the seed will grow into a great tree, one day to achieve wonders." The new settlement was christened Ville-Marie, a name which had been carefully considered before leaving France.

The trees of Ville-Marie were not yet Iroquois, but nevertheless the threat was very real, and the men quickly set to work to build a protective stockade. The Iroquois, who could have overwhelmed the tiny colony at any time, were away, giving the settlement a little time to get organized.

As if the Iroquois threat were not enough, in late December the waters of the St. Lawrence began to rise, endangering the little settlement in a different way. Maisonneuve, hoping to restrain the flood, Canute-like erected a cross and promised to carry another to the top of Mont Royal if the waters receded. At the last moment they did just that, and so Maisonneuve a few days later made good on his promise. A stained glass window in Notre Dame Basilica today shows him toiling up the mountainside with his heavy cross.

In June 1643 came the first major Iroquois attack, and five of the settlers were killed. Luckily reinforcements arrived in September 1643, and by the following March the colonists felt strong enough to attack Iroquois that were constantly lurking in the nearby forest, using dogs to warn and flush. But for many more years the settlers of Ville-Marie would have to tend their fields with their muskets at the ready. In 1653, a hundred more settler reinforcements arrived, financed by the so appropriately named Marquise de Bullion, and this instantly doubled the population of the town. Montréal was here to stay.

Above.
The stained glass window of Notre Dame Basilica shows Maisonneuve carrying a cross to the summit of Mont Royal on 6 January 1643 in thanks for the saving of Ville-Marie from flooding.

Opposite.
Five years after the founding of Montréal by Maisonneuve, the French engineer Jean Bourdon drew this plan of the little settlement called Ville-Marie. The original site has been rediscovered and some of the ruins can be seen in the basement of the Pointe-à-Callière Museum.

To Sow and to Gather

The Jesuits first came to Canada in 1625, invited because it was thought they would devote themselves to the conversion of the natives to Christianity, which in turn would make the natives less inclined to attack French settlements. The Jesuits applied themselves to their task with zeal. Jesuit explorations in search of souls brought vast tracts of the Canadian hinterland into European knowledge. Other exploration was done by traders, searching not for souls but for fur. And it was still expected that the way through the continent to Cathay would be found. One trader, the Cent-Associés agent Jean Nicollet, travelled to Lake Superior to start a trade with the Winnibago people of that region. So certain was he that he would find the way to China that he took with him a splendid damask robe. He did not find China, but no doubt made a fine impression on the Winnibago.

The Huron country between Lakes Ontario and Huron was explored by Jesuits who built missions at strategic points for snagging souls. The most famous of these was the Ste. Marie Mission, built at the mouth of the Wye River in 1639, a major stockaded base from which the missionaries could reach many Huron. Unfortunately the mission had to be burned in 1649 to prevent its desecration by attacking Iroquois, who in that year carried out their long-planned annihilation of their Huron enemies. The missionaries from Ste. Marie took refuge on an island in Georgian Bay—now called Christian Island—but it proved too small to support the Huron who had accompanied them and many died over that winter. As elsewhere, the Iroquois attacks on the Huron were extensive, coordinated, and deliberate—and utterly ruthless. The once proud Huron Nation, already weakened by smallpox and other European diseases, were decimated by their enemies and trade competitiors, the Iroquois. And the fury of the Iroquois was also turned on many of the Jesuit missionaries, who suffered egregious tortured deaths at their hands. The French public learned of these atrocities though the publication of Jesuit diaries, the *Relations.*

In 1672, Louis de Buade, Compte de Frontenac et de Pallau, then newly appointed as governor of New France, recognized the potential value of a new route into French territory that would be open all year. He sent Louis Jolliet and Father Jacques Marquette to find a large river reported to flow south. This, of course, was the Mississippi. Jolliet and Marquette found the river and descended it as far as the Arkansas River, far enough to know that it had to empty into the Gulf of Mexico. Ten years later, René Robert Cavelier, Sieur de La Salle, established fur-trading posts down the length of the river and reached the Mississippi Delta, which he claimed for France; in 1703 it became Louisiana.

In 1688 Jacques de Noyon found the pathway, much less well defined, to the west. This was the route from the western end of Lake Superior up the Kaministiquia River to Rainy Lake and Lake of the Woods, allowing, by the 1730s, for the establishment of fur trade posts by Pierre Gaultier de Varennnes et de La Vérendrye as far west as Lake Winnipeg and onto the Prairies (see page 99). The French fur trade also expanded northwards, where it came into conflict with the English on Hudson Bay (see page 51).

A Royal Province

In 1663 Louis XIV took over the administration of New France from the Cent-Associés and made it a royal province of France. Louis and his new minister Jean-Baptiste Colbert had decided to become much more aggressive in asserting France's position in Europe, and this required the accumulation of wealth, including making the French colonies contribute more to the king's coffers. Under the beneficence of the Sun King and the able administration of Colbert, New France was to grow from the Iroquois-terror-stricken compact colony on the St. Lawrence to cover 40 percent of North America.

Louis—really Colbert—appointed a new governor, Daniel de Rémy de Courcelle, and an able local administrator—the intendant—Jean Talon. Colbert was determined to free the colonists of New France from the constraint of the Iroquois threat, realizing that the colony could not grow without settlers—habitants—being able to freely cultivate their own land. They could not do this while bottled up in tight villages for defence. To deal with the Iroquois, Alexander de Prouville, Marquis de Tracy, was sent to New France with an army. First sent to the West Indies to drive out the Dutch, Tracy and the army, mostly men of the Carignan-Salières regiment, arrived at Québec in the summer of 1665. By the end of the year they had built three forts along the main Iroquois pathway, the Rivière Richelieu. The following year Courcelle and Tracy with an army of a thousand men and four hundred habitants—equivalent to half the entire population of New France before Tracy's arrival—went on a punitive expedition. Faced for the first time with a French force capable of destroying them, the Iroquois fled, but Tracy burned villages and winter food supplies to the

Jesuit fathers Jean de Brébeuf and Gabriel Lalemant are martyred by their Iroquois captors in this horrific scene drawn by another Jesuit father, Francesco Giuseppe Bressani, who accomplished the drawing and a large map that it illustrates despite the fact that he had only one finger, the result of Iroquois torture. At left are smaller depictions of other Jesuit deaths.

Diaries kept by Jesuits were published under the title *Relations of the Most Remarkable Events* and served to inform the public back in France of these atrocities, encouraging—amazingly enough—recruitment and, more credibly, donations to the cause.

extent that the following July the Iroquois accepted peace terms. A fragile balance of power had been achieved—for the time being. The Iroquois would prove to be a difficult force to contain and would harry the French many more times up to the turn of the century.

One of the most able of the administrators of New France was intendant Jean Talon, whose tenure lasted, with a short break, until 1672. He had been specifically instructed by the king to expand New France and work towards self-sufficiency for the colony. One of the most pressing issues was immigration, generally to be done without bringing people from France, an impossible job in the short term. Talon persuaded many officers and soldiers of the Carignan-Salières regiment to stay, setting up officers as seigneurs along the St. Lawrence where their men could settle with them. This policy was seen as an easy way of ensuring the longer-term security of the colony against the Iroquois. In all about eight hundred soldiers settled, from the Carignan-Salières and other regiments sent later.

To obtain the required growth in population, more women were needed. Colbert and Talon arranged for the transport of more than a thousand young women to the colony, many of whom were poor and destitute, and saw to it that they had a small dowry in the form of household goods. These were the so-called *filles du roi* (daughters of the king). Needless to say, most received offers of marriage within a few days of disembarking, helped along, after 1671, by an ordinance requiring bachelors to marry them, under penalty of being deprived of hunting and fishing rights. The colony was going to grow whether its inhabitants liked it or not!

Talon also made fathers with marriagable-age sons or daughters appear before him to explain themselves. Marriage became the duty of all. As a carrot to complement the stick Talon offered considerable bonuses to those with large families. The measures worked. According to the censuses—another Talon innovation, although they are not completely reliable—the population of New France increased from 3,215 in 1666 to 7,605 in 1673, an astonishing 136 percent growth in seven years.

The hard-working Talon also encouraged agriculture and industry. He introduced hemp, flax, and hops to the country and interested farmers in breeding cattle. He distributed looms to encourage textile manufacture and bestowed monies on other industries: hat-making, tanning, and, most famously, Canada's first brewery. Most of his work was undone when he left for France in 1672, as the colony was left without an intendant for three years. Frontenac, the new governor who replaced Courcelle in 1672, was more concerned with the military and the expansion of empire and the fur trade than he was with the more mundane minutiae of making a colony grow.

Frontenac's passion was the fur trade. Against the will of Colbert, Frontenac established Fort Cataracoui, usually known as Fort Frontenac, at the location that is now Kingston, Ontario. The fort was intended to protect against the Iroquois and act as a western trading post for the fur trade. No less than four hundred men from Montréal were seconded to assist in its construction, quite an insult, since the position of the new fort threatened the pre-eminent position of their own city in the fur trade at that time. They need not have worried. Fort Frontenac soon proved to be a bit of a white elephant, as it was

Above, top.
Jean Talon, intendant of New France.
Above.
Jean-Bapiste Colbert, minister of Louis XIV.
Above, right.
Filles du roi arriving. This painting probably overdoes the finery, though certainly the women may have dressed up when leaving the ship in order to impress potential husbands.

expensive to supply. Even as a defensive post it was not a success, as it could easily be bypassed.

A man of his own mind, Frontenac did not get on with Jacques Duchesneau, a new intendant send out in 1675, and quarrelled with the sovereign council, an executive governing body under the governor. For this Frontenac was recalled to France in 1682. Military minds do not always make good diplomats, it seems.

The Iroquois were again becoming troublesome, aided by a supply of muskets from the English, who had taken over the Dutch territory in New York. A failed punitive raid in 1684 led to the Iroquois dictating terms to the French. In 1687 a new governor, Jacques-René de Brisay de Denonville, led an attack against the Seneca, one of the Iroquois Five Nations. He could only attack one tribe because he lacked the resources to launch a bigger offensive. The Seneca melted away into the forest, and Denonville had to be satisfied with the destruction of their villages and winter food supplies.

At this point England and France were again at war (in Europe the War of the Grand Alliance, called King William's War in North America), so that there were inevitable reprisals from the English-supplied Iroquois. The most bloody was the raid on Lachine in 1689. Under cover of a hailstorm some fifteen hundred Iroquois fell on the unsuspecting outlying village (today incorporated within Montréal), killing at least twenty-four and taking perhaps another ninety prisoner—often a fate worse than outright death. Fifty-six of the seventy-seven houses at Lachine burned to the ground.

From the Mouths of My Cannon

Denonville knew that he had to have more men to control the Iroquois and in 1688 he had sent Louis-Hector de Callières, the governor of Montréal and his second-in-command, to France with a bold plan for a fleet to attack New York; this, it was thought, would cut off the Iroquois supply lines. After the Lachine raid, the western posts (which by now included Fort Conti, later Fort Niagara, founded in 1679) became untenable and Denonville ordered them abandoned. At Fort Frontenac the structure was blown up and the harried garrison retreated to Montréal.

The expedition against New York was delayed by contrary winds and did not arrive in Québec, from where the foray would be launched, until 12 October 1689, too late in the season to continue. But, perhaps luckily for the fortunes of New France, in command of this fleet was none other than Frontenac, returned to bring his superior military skills to bear on the situation and become governor of New France once more.

Above.
René Robert Cavelier, Sieur de La Salle, inspects Fort Frontenac, under construction in 1673. La Salle is famous for his 1683 exploration of the Mississippi to the Gulf of Mexico, which led to the founding of a new French colony in America, Louisiana.

Below.
All that is left of Fort Frontenac today is one of the bastions, which has been excavated and now sits on a traffic island in Kingston.

This superb picture-map of the New England fleet before Québec in October 1690 was drawn three years later by French mapmaker Nicolas de Fer. It is probably more accurate than the contemporary engraving of the attack shown in the inset. Here, using artistic licence, the engraver has placed Phips's fleet far closer to the cannon of Québec. In 1994, the wreckage of one of Phips's ships, *Elizabeth and Mary*, was found at Baie Trinité, where the St. Lawrence first begins to narrow.

Although Frontenac had 1,400 regular troops under his command, his army was not considered large enough to attack Fort Albany, the main English supply post for the Iroquois. Instead, Frontenac's army attacked Schenectady, a much smaller frontier village. Many of its inhabitants were killed and houses were burned, but apart from raising the level of fear among the English settlers, the raid had little effect. However, it did bring reprisal once more, in the form of a New England fleet led by Sir William Phips, until recently provost marshal general of the Dominion of New England, a short-lived consolidation of the New England colonies.

Phips had first plundered Port Royal, an enterprise that was found so profitable by the Boston men that they organized an attack on Québec largely as a commercial venture. A simultaneous land-based attack on Montréal was also planned, but was abandoned largely due to an outbreak of smallpox. This was lucky for the French side, for it meant that all their forces could be concentrated for the main English attack against Québec. Phips appeared before Québec on 16 October 1690 with a fleet of thirty-four ships and 2,300 soldiers and militia. He immediately dispatched an envoy, Major Thomas Savage, to Frontenac to demand the surrender of the city. When he reached the shore, Savage was blindfolded and led up the steep steps to where Frontenac and his commanders were waiting. During his ascent, Savage was subjected to a carefully orchestrated illusion. A group of men pressed in on him, making him think that he was being led through a dense crowd, to which the laughter of ladies was added. This show was a deliberate attempt to make Savage think that the people of Québec were not in the least concerned about the English. And it worked. Savage meekly handed over the English demands for surrender. Regaining some confidence during the period it took to translate the document, Savage demanded an answer, in writing, within the hour, to which Frontenace made his famous response: "I have no reply to make to your general other than from the mouths of my cannon and muskets."

In fact the balance of power was with Frontenac's forces. The English did not have the luxury of waiting for the best time for an attack, because of the lateness of the season. It would have been disaster for Phips's fleet to have become trapped by ice. And that evening Frontenac's defenders were reinforced by Callières with another five or six hundred men who had marched from Montréal. Two days later the New England attack began, but it was poorly orchestrated, requiring precise timing to get troops across the St. Charles River at low tide while at the same time landing troops above Québec and bombarding the city from the ships. Phips was not up to the task, and the attacks were repulsed. Disillusioned by the difficulty of what had originally been thought to be an easy victory, and harassed yet more by outbreaks of smallpox, on 25 October Phips gave up and the fleet sailed away.

A Peace and an Empire

The war with England continued until 1697, and attacks from the English in Fort Albany continued. Before the war was over the conflict had reached the shores of Hudson Bay (see page 51). But the main adversary for the French was not the English but the Iroquois, who, in the last years of the seventeenth century—often with English incitement and supplies—harried the French in Canada mercilessly.

Approaching the end of the century even the Iroquois were exhausted. The years of constant warfare with their neighbours and the French had reduced their population and they had finally grown weary of conflict. Thus when the French in 1696 first suggested a peace treaty, the Iroquois chiefs were receptive. It took a while, but the new governor, Louis Hector de Callières—Frontenac had died in office in November 1698—reached an initial peace agreement with the Iroquois in September 1700 in Montréal. In order to make the treaty all-encompassing and more binding, Callières invited the representatives of the native groups then in Montréal to another peace conference the following summer. At the same time he dispatched messengers to the Great Lakes region and

Below.
Part of a French map drawn in 1699 showing Montréal and the surrounding area. The locations of some redoubts are shown. These were mini-forts designed to provide a place of refuge for settlers if they were attacked by the Iroquois.

east to the Maritimes to invite all the other native groups who had been allied with the French against the Iroquois.

In the summer of 1701 some 1,300 representatives of about forty native groups met in Montréal to ratify the peace treaty. Some came from considerable distances away; the Mi'kmaq and the Abernakis from the Maritimes, the Cree from west of Lake Superior, and the Illinois from south of Lake Michigan, for example.

Some of the delegates brought illness with them, which killed many of their numbers, some without even reaching Montréal. One chief central to the peace ratification process was a Huron leader, Kondiaronk. The contemporary French historian Claude-Charles de La Potherie wrote of him that he "had the sentiments of a beautiful soul, and was a savage only in name." But Kondiaronk came down with a violent fever while meeting with Callières on 1 August and died the following day. On 3 August he was buried after a solemn funeral. Luckily for the French the peace process was far enough along that Kondiaronk's death did

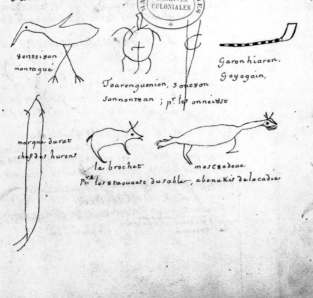

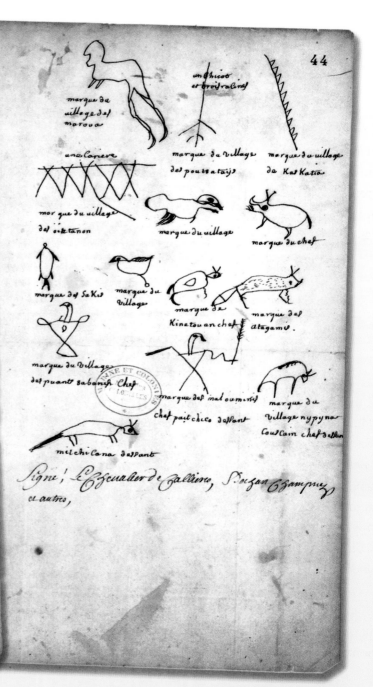

not stop the treaty from being signed the following day. Some pages from the Great Peace of Montréal, as it has become known today, are shown here, with the iconographic signatures of the native chiefs. The conference ended with the exchange of gifts, intended to seal a mutual commitment. This peace did largely endure until the fall of New France in 1760, despite a number of attempts by the British to turn native groups against their enemy. The Iroquois war cry was finally muted.

Louis XIV changed French policy in a big way the same year the Great Peace was signed. He agreed to the permanent establishment of the new colony of Louisiana and allowed the French *coureurs du bois* to go there to trade their furs. This was a deliberate attempt to counter any expansion of the English colonies inland. With the founding of Louisiana the French now laid claim to a vast empire in North America from the St. Lawrence to the Gulf of Mexico.

The Beginning of the End for the French

Peace with the Iroquois proved to be more long-lasting than peace with the English. By 1702 England and France were again at war, squabbling over the successor to the Spanish throne, and the conflict soon spread to North America, where it was known as Queen Anne's War. The growth of the English colonies meant that they readily jumped at the chance to fight their continental competitors the French. After the French attacked the village of Deerfield in 1704, killing fifty New Englanders and taking more than a hundred prisoners, an attack on Acadia was planned in reprisal. A New England force laid waste to a considerable area, breaking dikes, slaughtering cattle, and burning settlements. Only the fortified and garrisoned Port Royal was able to withstand the onslaught. The French carried out a similar despoilation along the east coast of Newfoundland the following year.

Another attack on Acadia came in 1707, but Port Royal, now commanded by a vigorous new commander, Daniel d'Auger de Subercase, again withstood the assault. However, the English—strictly now the British, after the union of England with Scotland in 1702—maintained an economic blockade of Acadia and life for the French became more difficult. Subercase reputedly sold his best silverware to finance repairs to his fort. French forces in Newfoundland retaliated in 1708, raiding from their base at Plaisance (Placentia) and capturing three forts at St. John's and burning most of the town.

In 1710 Subercase was unable to repulse a third attack on Port Royal. The assault was planned by an aggressive Scot named Samuel Vetch—whose goal was nothing less than to drive both France and Spain from North America. A combined British and New England fleet of thirty-six ships and two thousand men pounced on the French. Subercase, with only about three hundred men, to his credit held out for a week but was then forced to surrender due to the overwhelming odds. French Acadia became British Nova Scotia, and such it would remain.

Left.
Part of the Great Peace of Montréal, signed in August 1701, showing some of the signatures of native chiefs, and that of the governor of New France, Louis Hector de Callières. The treaty is written as if spoken by Callières. Translated from the French, it begins:

Ratification of the Peace concluded in the month of September last, between the Colony of Canada, its Indian allies, and the Iroquois in a general assembly of the chiefs of each of those nations convened by the Chevalier de Callières, governor and Lieutenant-General of the King in New France. At Montreal the Fourth of August 1701.

As there were only delegates of the Huron and the Odawa here last year when I concluded peace with the Iroquois for myself and all my allies, I considered it necessary to send [emissaries] to visit all the other nations that are my allies who were absent to tell them about what had occurred, and to invite a chief from each nation to come [to Montréal] with the Iroquois prisoners they had in order that they might all, together, hear my words. It is with extreme joy that I see all my children assembled here now . . .

The church of Notre-Dame-des-Victoires in Québec's Lower Town. The date of construction, 1688, is over the door. The church was given its singular name Notre-Dame-de-la-Victoire in 1690, after the defeat of Phips; the name became plural after the defeat of Walker in 1710.

What was supposed to be the grand finale for the British came the next year, 1711. This was a seaborne assault on Québec by a huge combined British and colonial fleet of seventy-one ships and twelve thousand men, led by British admiral Sir Hovenden Walker. In addition, a land force under Francis Nicolson was to advance on Québec via Lake Champlain. With such enormous forces rallied against New France, the fall of the French empire in North America appeared imminent. Nevertheless, the attack failed monumentally due to the bungling incompetence of Walker.

Walker underestimated everything: labour, ammunition—and pilots and charts. When the fleet was at the point where the Gulf of St. Lawrence narrows to become the river—but is still 100 km wide—Walker gave orders that sent many of his ships onto the

Above.
The royal coat of arms of France, carved in wood and painted, 1728.

Right.
A reminder of the French empire in Canada. This old wet-plate photograph (see page 170) of Fort Chambly, on the Rivière Richelieu near Montréal, was taken by William Notman in 1863, a hundred years after the official loss of Canada to Britain. The fort was originally built on this site in 1665 to help control incursions by the Iroquois, who frequently came down the Richelieu to the St. Lawrence. But it has a poor history of holding out against aggressors. It was burned by the Iroquois in 1702 after the declaration of war against the French by their allies the British, despite the Iroquois signing of a peace treaty the year before. The fort was rebuilt in stone in 1709–11. It was captured by the British in 1760 and by the Americans in 1775 and again in 1812. It was garrisoned by the British until 1855 and was restored as a historic site in 1921.

54—FORT CHAMBLY—NEAR MONTREAL

rocks. Walker had thought that he was in midstream, but he was not. Eight ships were wrecked, with the loss of more than a thousand lives. At this, Walker abandoned all hopes of attacking Québec and ordered the fleet home. Nicolson, leading the land force, realized that he could not take Québec alone, and so also gave up.

But Britain, not France, won the War of the Spanish Succession. As a result, in the Treaty of Utrecht, signed in 1713, France officially lost Acadia, Newfoundland, and Hudson Bay (see page 52), retaining, with New France and Louisiana, Prince Edward Island (Île St. Jean) and Cape Breton Island (Île Royale). To guard the approaches to Québec the great fortress of Louisbourg was built by the French, starting in 1719. It was to give the British much trouble (see page 57).

From 1713 onwards, it was all downhill for the French empire in North America. From thenceforth territory would only be lost.

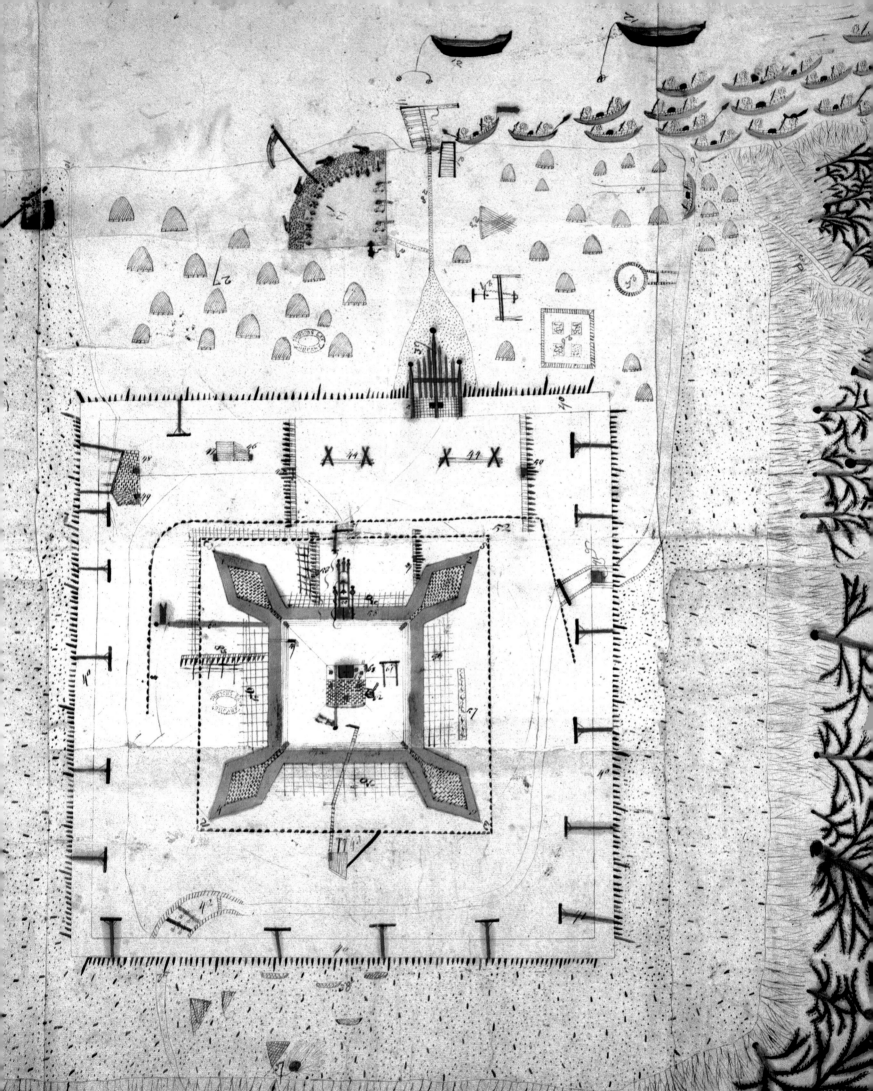

3 *The English Interest*

The first real English interest in Canada itself, as opposed to simply wanting to find a way through it to the East, occurred in 1577. It resulted from the discovery of what was thought to be gold, found as an apparent side benefit to an attempt to find a Northwest Passage the year before. Perhaps, thought the London investors, riches can be found without the long voyage to Cathay.

At the extreme tip of South America the Spanish had in 1519 discovered a strait connecting the Atlantic with the Pacific—the Straits of Magellan. Popular wisdom at the time held that there had to be a similar strait at the northern tip of the continent to somehow "balance" the southern one; everything in the Elizabethan world had to be symmetrical or, it was thought, the earth's rotation would be upset. It was to find this essential northern strait, and to pass through it to China, that a group of London investors came together to finance an expedition. The experienced sea captain they chose to lead their venture was Martin Frobisher, who had previously been accused of piracy, but was nevertheless a man of boldness and panache.

Frobisher left England in June 1576 with three ships and sailed to the west and north. He found a "greatte gutte, bay, or passage, deviding as it were, two maynelands or continents asunder," a channel that he thought was the passage to Cathay and which was subsequently named Frobisher Strait. Still named after the illustrious explorer, it is today Frobisher Bay, on which the capital of Nunavut, Iqaluit, stands. After sailing "fyftie leagues" to the west, Frobisher returned to an island called Hall's Island, after his sailing master Christopher Hall, where some of his crew were lost during an encounter with the local Inuit people. On this island some black stones were picked up—the first souvenirs of Canada. On his return to England these stones, which were actually iron pyrites, were determined by assayers to be gold. Why this happened is clear to no one, but what is certain is that after this point the Frobisher expeditions took on a new life of their own.

The search for a strait was forgotten, and the search for gold was on. Investors piled in. Even Queen Elizabeth invested in a new Company of Cathay formed to retrieve the gold piles of the Canadian barrens. In 1577 three ships, one much larger than any used in 1576,

A picture plan of the Hudson's Bay Company's York Fort, on the north shore of the Hayes River, on the western side of Hudson Bay. It was drawn by James Isham, factor at the fort, about 1740. It shows a group of native canoes arriving to trade. Native tents are pitched in front of the fort, and cannon line the wharf.

Pistol at the ready, Martin Frobisher looks every bit the marauding sea dog in this contemporary portrait, painted by Cornelius Ketel in 1577 and now in the Bodleian Library at Oxford.

sailed to Frobisher's strait with a hundred and twenty men, thirty of whom were miners. They returned to England at the end of the year piled to the gunnels with two hundred tons of the black stones they had been assured were gold.

Assayers again declared the rocks to be gold ore, although it is clear with hindsight that some skulduggery was going on, likely at the instigation of promoters interested in lining their own pockets. The venture now became what was by Elizabethan standards truly spectacular. In 1578 a fleet of fifteen ships was assembled and three hundred miners were transported back to Frobisher's Eldorado, where the summer was spent mining and filling the ships with no less than 1,350 tons of rock. Only when this massive cargo was returned to England was it discovered that the rocks so carefully gathered were not gold at all. The Company of Cathay fell apart and many of its investors were bankrupted.

This also ended the first attempt by the English to found a colony in any part of North America. On this last voyage materials had been transported to build a house and volunteers selected to overwinter. This scheme was only abandoned when the ship carrying part of the prefabricated house foundered. Since there were no more English voyages back to Frobisher Bay, the change of plans was likely just as well for the volunteers.

One enthusiast of English colonization in the New World and the search for a Northwest Passage was Humfrey Gilbert. In 1576 he had published a treatise called *A Discourse of a Discoverie for a New Passage to Cataia*, which had been used to promote Frobisher's first voyage. Then in 1578 Gilbert was granted a charter by Queen Elizabeth "to discover, searche, finde out and view such remote heathen and barbarous lands . . . not actually possessed of any Christian prince or people." He sailed off with nine ships to found a new English colony in September 1578, but the enterprise was so poorly organized that three ships defected almost immediately and one turned to piracy—the line between piracy and defence of the realm being remarkably difficult to discern in those troubled times of conflict with Spain. The result was that he was forbidden to sail again until five years later.

In June 1583 Gilbert set sail with five ships and two hundred and sixty men, intending to found a colony in Norumbega, today New England. But it was in Newfoundland, not New England, that he landed. There, in St. John's Harbour on 5 August 1583, he planted on the shore a wooden pillar with the "Armes of England ingraven in lead." Some historians consider this act the birth of the British Empire. Gilbert did not put his colonists ashore at St. John's, however. Two of his captains refused to go any farther and he sent them back to England, while he cruised southwards to his intended New England destination. Then one of his remaining ships was wrecked off Nova Scotia's Sable Island, with the loss of eighty-five men. With so few remaining, Gilbert decided to return to England and try again the following year, but his ship, a pinnace named the *Squirrel,* was swamped in a storm. Legend has it that he went to the bottom of the sea calling out "we are as neare to Heaven by sea as by land."

At the same time that Humfrey Gilbert had received his patent from the Queen to found colonies and search for a passage, his brother, Adrian, had received a similar dispensation. Adrian Gilbert sent out an experienced captain, John Davis, with two ships, the delightfully named *Sunneshine* and *Mooneshine,* with the sole purpose of finding a Northwest Passage. Davis sailed in 1585 to the northwest and into the strait between Greenland and Baffin Island that bears his name today. In a series of three voyages in that year and the following two, Davis explored as far north as what is now Upernavik, Greenland. This is at the same latitude—but on the eastern shore of Baffin Bay—as the true entrance to the Northwest Passage, Lancaster Sound. Perhaps Davis's most important discovery was a "whirling and overfalling" at the entrance to Hudson Strait. He concluded that it was caused by a "meeting of tydes," which others would later become convinced marked the entrance to a passage between seas. It does, of course, but the sea is Hudson Bay, not the Pacific Ocean. It is surprising that Davis did not investigate further at the time. The search for a Northwest Passage would not be seriously taken up again until 1610 (see page 48).

To Builde, Set and Sowe

By the beginning of the seventeenth century boats of a number of European nations were regularly crossing the Atlantic to fish in Newfoundland's rich fishing grounds. Sometimes drying racks, or "stages," were set up onshore to dry the catch, but no one stayed in Newfoundland over the winter.

Above.
Humfrey Gilbert.

Below.
The Northwest Passage that everyone was looking for is shown clearly in this 1570 map by Dutch mapmaker Abraham Ortelius. But if the passage was so obvious why then could no one find it?

A choice of beach space for these stages, and the ability to start fishing earlier, would await anyone who braved the winter. In 1608 John Guy wrote a *Treatise to animate the English to plant there,* and two years later a group of Bristol merchants formed the Newfoundland Company and set up a "plantation" at Cupids, on the western shore of Conception Bay, with Guy as governor. This first English colony in Newfoundland lasted until about 1630. In 1613 Guy left for England never to return and was replaced by John Mason. He was an experienced sea captain and the company felt he would be better able to deal with the pirates that plagued early settlers.

Other settlement attempts were made by a group called the Bristol Society of Merchants Adventurers beginning about 1616. They included three "gentleman proprietors" of benevolent disposition: William Vaughan, a Welsh scholar who thought colonization a way of helping his poor Welsh countrymen; Henry Cary, who as Viscount Falkland became lord deputy of Ireland and who had the same idea for the Irish; and George Calvert, later Baron Baltimore, whose emigrants would be English. The Avalon Peninsula was subdivided between them and the Newfoundland Company. One would think that big plans were afoot, and indeed they were, but they all came to very little in the end.

It was Calvert who gave this earternmost peninsula of Newfoundland its name, after the Avalon of King Arthur fame. In 1623 the Charter of Avalon granted Calvert, who, "being exited [excited] with a laudable, & pious Zeale, to enlarge the extentes of the Christian World," a territory "scituate in the Westerne partes of ye World. Commonly called Newfound Land not yet husbanded or Planted, though in some partes thereof Inhabited by certain Barbarous people wanting the knowledge of Almighty God." He was "to Transport thither a very Greate and ample Colony of the English Nations."

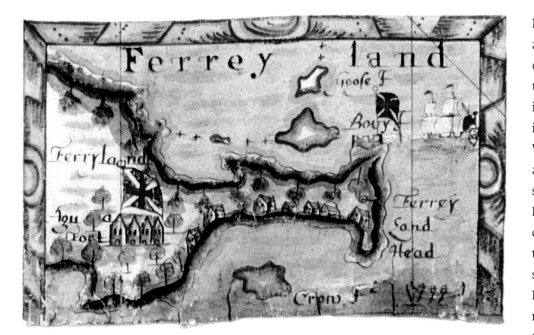

Calvert had already sent colonists to Newfoundland in 1621, and they had settled at Ferryland, a little south of St. John's. A charter made little difference to the realities of life. The colony struggled. To Calvert it was a place to "builde, set and sowe," but it proved to be too exposed to the "furious Windes" of the Atlantic coast and miserably cold in winter in houses almost impossible to keep warm. Calvert, after 1625 Lord Baltimore, to his credit actually visited his colony in 1627 and again the following year, this time with his family and intending to settle himself. By 1630 he had decided that Newfoundland was too far north and moved most of his settlers to a new location far to the south, today Baltimore, Maryland.

The orphaned Newfoundland colony lived on in much reduced form, and those who remained found that for effective fishing they needed to be scattered along the coast rather than in a single place, a pattern that continues to this day. By 1660 only about a hundred and fifty families remained on the Avalon Peninsula.

Nova Scotia Gets Its Name

William Alexander, Earl of Stirling, was a man of many talents. An advocate of colonial emigration, he was a poet, author, and scholar. At the same time that Calvert sent his first colonists to Newfoundland, Alexander suggested to the King that a New Scotland, comparable to New France or New England, should be created to persuade the Scots to emigrate. This had already been done in Northern Ireland, where knight baronetcies had been created; the new barons then imported colonists. In 1621 James VI of Scotland (who was also James I of England) granted Alexander the territory that is today the provinces of Nova Scotia, New Brunswick, and Prince Edward Island, together with the Gaspé Peninsula. The fact that this was already French territory did not matter a wit. Somehow Alexander was to deal with this minor problem. Knight baronetcies were offered to those who would settle colonists in the new land, but although the titles attracted, nobody was very keen to go there, and there were few takers.

A sad attempt to take colonists to New Scotland—in Latin, Nova Scotia—was made in 1622–23, at which time the grand total of ten settlers made it to the shores of the new colony. In 1624 Alexander published an advertising pamphlet called *An Encourageement to Colonies,* which included the map of the land grant illustrated below. Alexander's fiefdom has been divided into two provinces, Alexandria and Caledonia. A new king, Charles I,

Above.
William Alexander, Earl of Stirling.

Below.
New Scotlande joins *New France* and *New Englande* on William Alexander's map of his domains published in 1624. The English king James I (James VI of Scotland) had no problem granting lands already claimed (as Acadia) by the French. He could ignore that claim just as easily as he ignored that of the native peoples already living in the region. The rivers *Tweede* and *Solway* separate the new Scotland and the new England just as they do the original ones.

granted Alexander armorial bearings and a flag, both of which remain as Nova Scotian emblems today. But despite the grand schemes Alexander was still not able to attract much interest, and by 1627 war had broken out between England and France. James Stewart did manage to establish a colony briefly at Baleine in Cape Breton, but it lasted all of two months before being attacked by marauding French. Alexander's son, also named William, finally established a colony of about seventy Scots at a deserted Port Royal in 1629, which he named Charlesfort. This, however, was lost three years later when the Treaty of Saint-Germain-en-Laye restored peace and all of France's colonies in North America were returned. Samuel de Champlain had his Québec restored under the same treaty (see page 27). Québec would remain French until 1763, but Nova Scotia—the French Acadia—would be lost in 1711 (see page 52).

A Sea—But Not the South Sea

After John Davis's abortive attempts to find a way through Canada, the English did not try again until 1602, when George Waymouth entered Hudson Strait, but was forced to turn back by a mutinous crew. The ice-choked waters of Canada's North were to prove to have a mutinous effect on others as well.

Henry Hudson, a name forever linked with mutiny, was an experienced navigator by the time he came to Canada. He had sailed to the Arctic in 1607 and 1608, and to North America in 1609, the latter voyage being under the auspices of the Dutch East India Company. His discovery of the Hudson River in today's New York state led to the Dutch founding of New Amsterdam—today the city of New York. In 1610, again back in the English fold, he set out on his final, fatal voyage to find the Northwest Passage. By August Hudson had sailed right through his eponymous strait and into a "spacious sea" he was sure was the South Sea, or Pacific. One can imagine his disappointment a few weeks later when, having turned south, he reached the "bottom of the bay" and came to the realization that this could not after all be the ocean he sought.

Worse was to come. Trapped by the ice, he was forced to overwinter, and the following June, as they were attempting to escape the bay's icy grip, the ship became stuck once more. After Hudson issued orders to enforce sharing of food came the mutiny. Hudson, his son, and a few of his closest followers were set adrift in the ship's longboat, with few provisions and no hope of survival. They were never seen again. Hudson's South Sea became his grave, forever bearing the tombstone marker "Hudson Bay."

It was rumoured by the ever-optimistic in England that Hudson had been killed to protect a secret: the discovery of a passage to Cathay. A new company, called the Company of the Merchants Discoverers of the North-West Passage, or Northwest Company, was formed and Welshman Thomas Button was dispatched, ostensibly to search for Hudson but also to complete "ye full and perfect discovery of the North-West Passage." Button did not look for Hudson at all, but did find and chart the west side of Hudson Bay, where he thought an outlet to the west would be. Part of Canada became known as New Wales.

The Northwest Company next dispatched Robert Bylot, who had been with both Hudson and Button, first through Hudson Strait in 1615 and north through Davis Strait the following year. His navigator, William Baffin, mapped the northern extent of Davis Bay—Baffin Bay—in detail not exceeded for two centuries. Included on his map was *Sir James Lancaster's Sound,* today Lancaster Sound, the eastern entrance to the true Northwest Passage. But such were the ice conditions that Baffin did not realize the sound continued westwards. This was a mistake that would be repeated as late as 1818 (see page 111).

The English investors had had enough, for now. The torch of the Northwest Passage passed to the Danes, whose king was worried that the English might actually find

Jens Munk produced a series of delightful picture-maps of his travels in Canada. This one shows the two ships overwintering at the mouth of the Churchill River. Men are cutting wood, and—ominously—some are already preparing to bury one of their dead.

something. The top Danish navigator, Jens Munk, was sent to try his luck for Denmark. Of course, rather predictably when the objective doesn't exist, he also failed—rather spectacularly in fact. Munk left Denmark in 1619 with two ships and sixty-four men; he returned in late 1620 with one ship and only two men—the latter representing astonishing sailing skills, three weakened men sailing a large ship. Munk was trapped over the winter at the mouth of the Churchill River on the west side of Hudson Bay, and his crew, unclear on how to use medicines they had with them, were decimated by that scourge of sailors, scurvy. The Danes never ventured into Canada again.

It was not until 1629 that the English tried once more. Not one but two expeditions were sent off that year. The first was that of Luke Foxe, organized by a group of London merchants, and the other was a rival effort from Bristol merchants afraid that the London group would discover a passage and gain a commercial advantage over them. The Bristol group sent Thomas James. Both did as well as they could have been expected to given the fact that they both were trying to penetrate the dead end of Hudson Bay. Both found a certain immortality in that their names became part of the Canadian landscape: Foxe Channel and Foxe Basin to the north of Hudson Bay, where Foxe tried to find a passage (and where there is one, but unnavigable without modern ice-breakers), and James Bay (which was marked *James his Baye* on James's map), in the southern part of Hudson Bay. And part of what is now northern Manitoba was New Yorkshire for centuries, named after Foxe's home county in England.

Wealth from an Inland Sea

Prince Rupert.

Below.
The *Nonsuch* in heavy seas en route
to Hudson Bay in 1668.

English attempts to find a Northwest Passage lapsed for a hundred years after Foxe and James, and in the meantime the English interest turned to a commercial one. For there was a real treasure waiting to be exploited without having to go to the East—furs. Finally English investors were to get a return from their voyages to Canada.

But it was not the English who found the furs; the furs found the English, or, rather, they were brought to them by two French traders disillusioned with the restrictions that the French government had placed on them, since the French were more interested in concentrating their population for defensive reasons than exploring the West. The two traders were the "Mr. Radishes" and "Mr. Gooseberry" of English children's history books, Pierre Esprit Radisson and Medart Chouart des Groseilliers.

The pair arrived in London in 1665 to tout their plan at the worst possible moment; the Great Plague was raging and when it ended London burnt to the ground. But this merely delayed matters. The plan proved irresistibly attractive none the less. Ships were to sail into Hudson Bay and take out furs, completely avoiding the French territory on the St. Lawrence. A trial voyage was arranged; two little ships, the *Nonsuch* and the *Eaglet,* sailed from London in June 1668. The *Eaglet* was turned back by storms, but the *Nonsuch* ploughed on to a worthy place in Canadian history, and the investors were rewarded in September 1669 when the ship returned laden with furs.

The success of this trial led directly to the formation of the Hudson's Bay Company—"The Governor and Company of Adventurers of England tradeing into Hudson's Bay"—with Prince Rupert, cousin of King Charles II, as governor. The adventurers were made "Lordes and Proprietors" of 40 percent of modern Canada, some 3.9 million km², the entire drainage area of Hudson Bay, unknown to Europeans at the time but granted anyway. This gift of Rupert's Land was the most breathtaking example of a European monarch granting land that did not belong to him in the first place.

The first governor on the ground in Hudson Bay was Charles Bayly. He was a rather eccentric Quaker known for an attempt to convert the Pope to Protestantism. He had been imprisoned in the Tower of London for seven years before being released to the Hudson's Bay Company. Hudson Bay, it seems, was seen as a place of exile suitable for a man persecuted for his religious beliefs.

But Bayly did a good job. It was he who set up the system of land-based forts on the shores of the bay that was to prove more

Left.
The *Nonsuch* being loaded at a London wharf in 1668 prior to sailing for Hudson Bay. This full-scale reconstruction is in the Manitoba Museum in Winnipeg and features the *Nonsuch* replica built by the Hudson's Bay Company to commemorate its tercentenary in 1970.

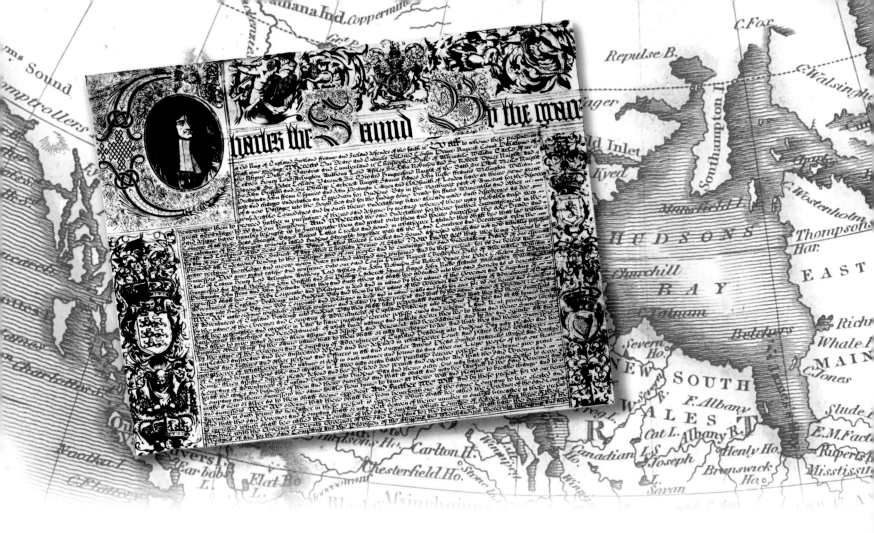

workable for the company than trading from ships. This system of trade would continue until competition from an upstart North West Company in the 1770s forced the Hudson's Bay Company to move inland (see page 101).

The one exception to this was the journey of Henry Kelsey in 1690. He was dispatched inland essentially to drum up business by encouraging natives to travel to the Bayside forts to trade. Kelsey seems to have gone about 1 000 km to the west, reaching Cedar Lake, just west of Lake Winnipeg. He is often said to have been the first European to have seen the Prairies, but there is little real evidence for this. It was a one-time exploration and was not followed up by the company.

Life was not dull, however, at times towards the end of the seventeenth century, for the French were challenging, culminating in a war between England and France, known as King William's War (see page 35). This severely interrupted the company's business for many years. In 1686 Pierre de Troyes was sent with a force of ninety or a hundred men to the bay to seize English forts. The French ascended the Ottawa River, portaged to Lake Abitibi, and descended the Abitibi River to James Bay, where

Above.
The Hudson's Bay Company charter, superimposed on an 1817 map of Canada. The original charter remains in the possession of the company and is kept at its corporate headquarters in Toronto, in a special climate-controlled case. The charter performs the same legal function for Canada's oldest company as do articles of incorporation for other companies, but is also a prized cultural artifact and work of art.

Right.
The charter required that the English monarch be presented with a rent of two elks and two black beavers if he or she visited Rupert's Land, an event that occurred only in the twentieth century. When Queen Elizabeth II visited Winnipeg on a royal tour in 1959 she was presented with two mounted elk heads and two black beaver skins by William Johnston Keswick, the governor of the company.

they surprised the English at the bottom of the bay, taking three posts from them, Moose Fort, Rupert House (Charles Fort), and Fort Albany. De Troyes left one of his officers, Pierre Le Moyne d'Iberville, in charge, and left for Québec in a captured English ship.

What may be the longest sea battle ever took place in 1688. D'Iberville was leaving Fort Albany in September with a shipload of furs and only sixteen men when he was blockaded by two armed English ships with eighty-five men. The onset of winter froze all three vessels in place, prolonging the conflict until the spring. D'Iberville refused to let the English hunt for game and even captured their surgeon; as a result, scurvy killed twenty-five of them, and they were forced to surrender. It was a victory, but not the most honourable.

The swashbuckling d'Iberville continued to be a major scourge to the Hudson's Bay Company. In August 1694 York Fort was besieged, and it surrendered in October. Such were the logistics of doing battle in the bay that both captives and captors had to spend the winter together in the fort. Renaming it Fort Bourbon, the French operated what had been the company's most lucrative post the next season. But the English were not going to let this last. In 1696 five ships and four hundred men wrested control back again.

D'Iberville's attention then focused on Newfoundland, where the French were trying to expel the English; St. John's was captured in November 1696. Then d'Iberville sailed north once more to Hudson Bay, where they intended to regain York Fort. Separated from other ships by fog, he alone attacked three ships, the *Hampshire*, a British Royal Navy frigate, and two armed company ships. Despite the fact that his ship, the *Pélican*, was vastly outgunned, he sank the *Hampshire* and captured one of the company ships. Then, with the aid of other French ships, York Fort was again captured.

D'Iberville's *Pélican* battles with the English naval frigate *Hampshire* off York Fort, on the west side of Hudson Bay, on 5 September 1697.

Below. Pierre Le Moyne d'Iberville, thorn in the side of the Hudson's Bay Company.

At this point the 1697 Treaty of Ryswick (properly Rijswijk) intervened, when the French in Europe capitulated. One of the terms of the treaty was the return of York Fort to the English, but with all the forts at the bottom of the bay remaining French. In fact Fort Albany was retained by the English while York (the French Bourbon) remained in French hands until yet another war, the War of the Spanish Succession—Queen Anne's War in North America—was terminated by another peace treaty, this time much less favourable to France. The Treaty of Utrecht, signed in 1713 (see page 41), gave the English all "the bay and streights of Hudson" to be "possessed in full right forever." Most importantly for the Hudson's Bay Company, York Fort, its most productive post, was regained.

The English Take Over Nova Scotia

The treaty also gave the English Newfoundland and "all Nova Scotia or Acadie, with its ancient boundaries." Since no one really knew what was meant by "ancient boundaries," the treaty would lead to more conflict, culminating in the French losing their entire empire (see page 57). For now, it meant that the French retained Cape Breton Island and the English had at least nominal control over what is now peninsular Nova Scotia.

The English control was incomplete not only because of the French, who soon installed themselves in their new fortress at Louisbourg, on Cape Breton, but also because of the native people, who had not been consulted by either France or England.

Encouraged by French priests, the Mi'kmaq attacked and seized fishing boats, driving the English out of Canso in 1720. Retaliation from New England was not long forthcoming, and the conflict escalated. In 1724 Mi'kmaq attacked Annapolis Royal and burnt part of the town. A treaty with the natives was worked out late in 1725 and ratified the following summer. The Mi'kmaq were promised fishing and hunting rights, and they in turn promised to recognize the sovereignty of Britain over "Nova Scotia or Accadie." The terms of this treaty were to feature late in the twentieth century in native land-claims negotiations.

As for the French, they would fare worse, for, starting in 1755, the English would finally decide that the Acadian population posed too much of a risk to English security in Nova Scotia and elsewhere in the Maritimes, and order them all deported (see page 64).

Once in Nova Scotia the British strengthened the defences of selected places, notably the French Port Royal, renamed Annapolis Royal after the British Queen Anne. They would later create a new fortress at Halifax, to counteract more substantially the one the French had built at Louisbourg.

The fort at Annapolis Royal, shown here in a map from 1753, had its defences improved; it was renamed Fort Anne. The earthworks were originally built by the French in 1702 and represent the earliest Canadian example of a fort designed on the fortification principles of the French military engineer Sebastien le Prestre de Vauban.

The photograph shows the officers' quarters at Fort Anne, constructed in 1797. Today the fort is a National Historic Site.

To Find an Illusive Passage

"Canada with a haircut." This strange-looking map was reputedly drawn for Northwest Passage promoter Arthur Dobbs in the dirt on the floor of a London tavern by a disaffected *coureur de bois* (backwoods trader) named Joseph La France. Passages from the northwestern part of Hudson Bay are shown as having direct access to the northwest coast of the continent. No doubt La France, aided by a few sips of gin, was giving his sponsors what they wanted to see. But maps like this were enough to convince investors to finance another voyage.

James Knight was placed in charge of the Hudson's Bay Company's forts in the bay in 1713, just in time to receive York Fort back from the French the following year, according to the terms of the Treaty of Utrecht. Knight assiduously gathered information from the native population about the geography of the region, which he managed to misinterpret in a way that convinced him there was a passage to the west somewhere to the north of the fort. In 1719 he persuaded a reluctant company to allow him to sail north to find this outlet. It was the worst mistake of his life; Knight's two ships were wrecked on Marble Island, just south of Chesterfield Inlet, and he and all of his men perished.

This maladventure underlined to the governor of the Hudson's Bay Company, Bibye Lake, the wisdom of sticking to the business he knew: collect furs, ship furs, and pay a healthy dividend to the stockholders. Lake's tenure at the company, which lasted from 1712 to 1743, was later famously described by one ex-employee as being the period when the company "slept at the edge of a frozen sea."

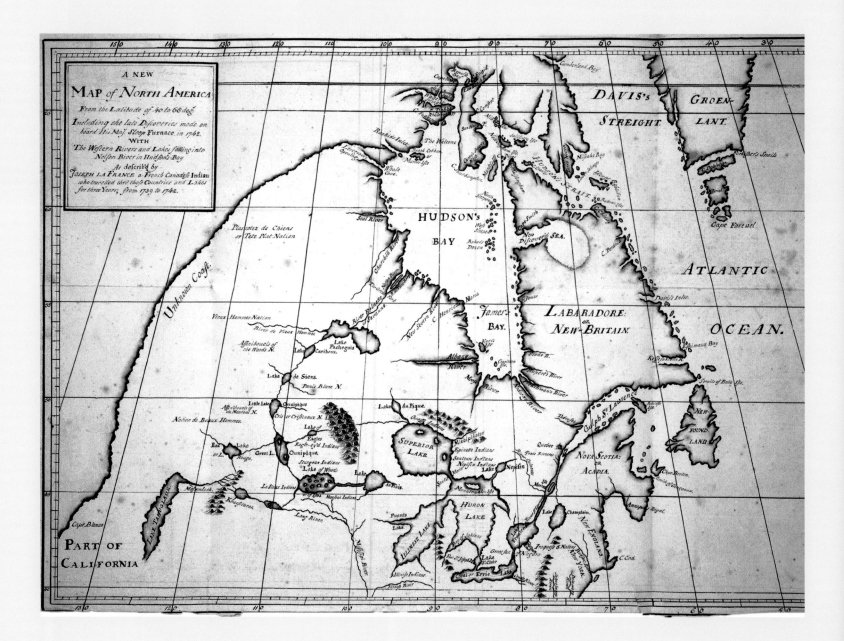

But some in England were dissatisfied with this approach. The company's charter, they argued, required more active exploration of the vast region over which it had been granted a monopoly. Particularly persuasive was one Arthur Dobbs, an Ulster landowner and member of Parliament who had convinced himself that a Northwest Passage awaited British discovery. By gaining the approval of King George II, who thought that "the expence was such a trifle," and aided much by the prodding of Dobbs, a naval voyage was organized. In 1741 two ships left England under the command of Christopher Middleton, a former company captain.

After a difficult winter at the mouth of the Churchill River, Middleton sailed north, finding Wager Bay—which he called Wager River—but not investigating its western end. Then he passed a point where the land turned west, naming it Cape Hope, for it "gave him great joy and hopes of it's being the extream Part of America." But it turned out to be a large bay that finally frustrated his attempts to go west or north. Middleton named it Repulse Bay.

When Middleton returned to England in October 1742 he was viciously attacked by Dobbs, who thought he should have probed farther, especially in Wager Bay, and accused him of concealing information and falsifying his logs and maps. Dobbs's belief in the existence of a Northwest Passage bordered on the religious. He managed to get Parliament to authorize a £10,000 reward for a finder of such a passage, then organized another voyage, this time financed by private backers, including the Earl of Chesterfield, whose only reward would be his name on the map of Canada.

Two ships under the command of William Moor (who had been Middleton's second-in-command on the first voyage) left England in 1746. The following year the northwest part of Hudson Bay was again examined. Wager Bay, where Dobbs had been sure was his passage, was explored to its western end. Henry Ellis, Dobbs's agent, wrote that they "had the Mortification to see clearly that our hitherto imagined Strait ended in two small unnavigable rivers."

The principal discovery of the Moor expedition was the finding of Chesterfield Inlet. The indefatigable Arthur Dobbs seized on this as his new passage, but was unable to interest more investors to throw good money after bad. Instead Dobbs turned his attention to discrediting the Hudson's Bay Company, against which he seemed to be conducting a personal vendetta. But his challenge to the company's renewal of its monopoly in 1749 fell on deaf ears, the credibility of his arguments having been dissipated by the two fruitless voyages.

The search for a passage through Canada to the East lapsed for seventy years after Dobbs's efforts. When it was renewed, in 1818, the search would not be by privately financed ventures but by the full force of the British Royal Navy (see page 111).

A Hudson's Bay Company vessel similar to Christopher Middleton's modified bomb ketch *Furnace* surges westward to Hudson Bay.

4 *Clash of Empires*

Britain's North American colonies in 1713 had about 375,000 people, almost eighteen times the 20,000 of New France, and they were growing faster. It was inevitable that there would be mounting pressure on the French as the British wanted more and more land. Although the period to 1744 was nominally one of peace, there were a number of struggles as the French sought to contain the British and protect their fur trade.

In preparation for the war they knew would come one day, the French built the fortress of Louisbourg on the northeast coast of Cape Breton Island (Île Royale). It would become the principal target of the British. Louisbourg had been built to be impregnable from the sea, but would be taken twice from the landward side.

In March 1744 France declared war on Britain, this time over an Austrian succession. In North America, where all the various wars seem to have different names, this one was called King George's War. At first the British colonies were reluctant to get involved in a European war, and most did not. But New England, finding its fishing fleet harassed by privateers operating out of Louisbourg, was persuaded to take action. The governor of Massachusetts, William Shirley, in turn had to persuade militia colonel Sir William Pepperrell to lead an army to attack Louisbourg. Pepperrell was a successful merchant with much to gain from a British victory. Shirley also managed to secure the help of the British navy, which diverted ships from Antigua, commanded by Peter Warren.

When the French got wind of the New Englanders' plan to attack them, the governor of Île Royale, Louis Duchambon, set about readying the town's defences. Fire ships were made so that they could be used to prevent British ships forcing their way into the harbour through its relatively narrow entrance. Unfortunately for Duchambon, he never seemed to consider that the British forces might simply lay siege by land. This is doubly strange, for Duchambon was at the same time advocating a pre-emptive French attack on Annapolis Royal in which ships would transport soldiers for a land assault.

Six armed colonial vessels were dispatched in late March 1745 to begin a blockade of the fortress. The main contingent of 2,800 New England militia sailed on 4 April in fifty-one ships. After a rendezvous of the attackers at Canso, they moved to Gabarus Bay, a spacious

New England troops landing at Kennington Cove, on Gabarus Bay, just south of Louisbourg, on 11 May 1745.

bay a short distance south of Louisbourg itself, and landed on 11 May in a flotilla of whale-boats at Kennington Cove. A procrastinating Duchambon, who had time to send a substantial force out to combat the New Englanders, sent none. The small number of French soldiers who were already on the shore at Flat Point Cove, close to Kennington—twenty in total—did in fact turn back boats attempting to land in that location. Duchambon lost his chance to repel the invaders from a better military position. Now he would suffer the consequences.

The New England troops laid siege to Louisbourg. The separate Grand Battery was soon taken. This was a fortified gun emplacement strategically placed to cover the harbour entrance, but like Louisbourg itself, vulnerable to a land attack. Its commander had sensibly suggested that it be abandoned, leaving the cannon spiked to prevent their use against the town, but the decision to allow this was delayed. Thus when the attack came and the battery was over-whelmed, its defenders had so little time to render the cannon unusable that the New Englanders soon got them working again, turning them on the unfortunate townsfolk of Louisbourg.

On 30 May Warren's fleet intercepted a large French warship, the *Vigilant*, making a run into the harbour. The ship was carrying five hundred men and a thousand barrels of powder, with forty cannon and a quantity of food. This had a considerable demoralizing effect on the defenders of Louisbourg.

It is an interesting comment on the lack of communications at this time that War-ren's fleet was augmented in June by more British warships—*that just happened to be passing by*. They had not been specifically sent. Warren now had eleven ships under his command. Viewed from inside Louisbourg, the situation was beginning to look hopeless. On 20 June

Below.
View from a Warship, a painting by Lewis Parker, depicts the harbourfront at Louisbourg during the summer of 1744.

Opposite, top.
The capture of Louisbourg, 1745.

Opposite, bottom.
A map of Louisbourg harbour produced for a British magazine shortly after the capture of the fortress. The Grand Battery is at centre left, with lines of fire to the harbour entrance. The battery at the harbour entrance is the Island Battery, which was attacked by the British during the siege but repulsed.

two Swiss mercenaries sprinted away from the city, deserting to the New Englanders. With them they carried the information that the French had only a hundred and fifty barrels of powder left and that many of the soldiers would be "Glad To Come Out and Deliver themselves." Pepperrell, sensing an end, instructed his gunners to "Fire Smartly att ye Citty," the object being to get the French to use up the small amount of powder they had left. The same day Warren's fleet was again augmented by another British warship, this time actually sent to join him, as the Admiralty thought that French ships that had broken through a blockade of the French port of Brest were on their way to help Louisbourg; in fact they were headed to the West Indies. The new British ship was soon to be joined by two others following.

But while plans were being made for a final assault, the merchants of Louisbourg pressured Duchambon to surrender so as, they thought, to preserve some of their wealth. And so terms were agreed on 28 June, and the French surrendered to Pepperrell.

The New England forces remained at Louisbourg over the next winter. About 1,200 of them died of disease, far more than had perished during the siege. Louisbourg remained in Anglo-American hands for only three years. Much to the disgust of the Americans, the Treaty of Aix-la-Chapelle, which ended the war in 1748, returned the fortress to the French. It was one of those things that, come 1776, they would not forget. They would also not forget that the American citizen soldier had proved himself against European regulars.

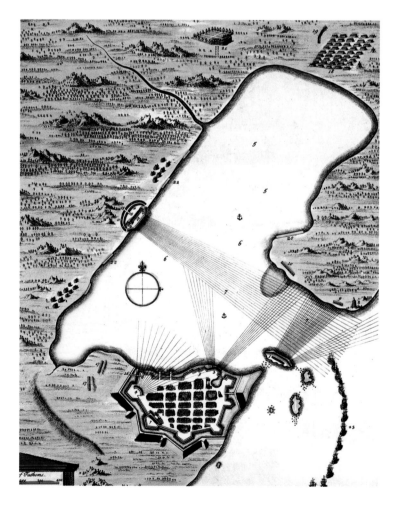

A New British Stronghold

After the return of Louisbourg to the French in 1748, the British made plans to build an equivalent fortress to neutralize the menace of the French stronghold and to guard the approaches to New England. In March 1749, George Dunk, Earl of Halifax, wrote a report suggesting that the British government establish a town on Chebucto Bay. The main reason was to redress the grievances of the New England colonies over the return of Louisbourg. Chebucto Bay, called Kjipuktuk by the Mi'kmaq, had been the site of a French proposal for a fortified town and plans had been drawn up in 1711, but with the loss of Acadia this plan did not proceed.

With the help of newspaper advertising, settlers were recruited from England, not the American colonies, to populate the new town. Settlers were promised free transportation, free food for a year, and military protection. Lieutenant Colonel Edward Cornwallis was appointed governor of Nova Scotia, and he sailed from England with 2,576 colonists in May 1749.

The first task was to choose a site for the new town, and, after much deliberation, the slope of the hill overlooking the harbour, now Citadel Hill, was selected. Originally named Chebucto, the name of the new settlement was soon changed to Halifax. Cornwallis had trouble getting his colonists to help build fortifications—they wanted to build their own houses first—and this problem was only solved when troops arrived in July from Louisbourg, after its transfer back to France had taken place. The first walls were to protect against the Mi'kmaq rather than any European power. The initial settlers received free building

Below.
A view of Halifax soon after its founding, from a map of Halifax Harbour published in England in 1750.

Opposite, top.
From the same map comes this detail of Halifax. St. George's Island is marked *where the Transports first Landed.*

Also from the same map comes the decorative embellishment, *above.*

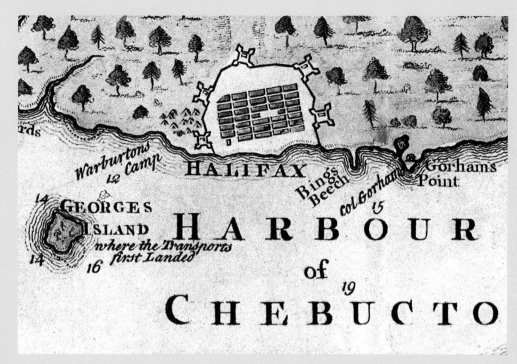

lots, but only a few houses were constructed before the onset of winter. Many of the colonists spent the first winter aboard the ships, and about a thousand of them decided not to stay, moving south to Boston and other parts of New England. Nevertheless, merchants from the American colonies, sensing an opportunity, soon opened businesses in the new town. In fact, the location of Halifax on such a superb harbour virtually assured its success.

Below.
The construction of Halifax during the summer and fall of 1749, shown in a painting by Charles Jefferys. A sentry keeps a wary eye out for lurking Mi'kmaq.

NOVA-SCOTIA. No. 1.

THE

Halifax GAZETTE.

MONDAY, *March* 23. 1752.

AS many of the Subscribers to the Proposals for publishing of this PAPER, may be desirous of knowing the Cause why it hath been *so long de-*layed; the Printer begs Leave to inform them, That the Gentleman who is possess'd of the origi-nal, whenever desired, will give them a sa-tisfactory Account. And as the Letter-Press is now commodiously fixed for the Printing Business, all such Gentlemen, Merchants, and others, as may have Oc-casion for any Thing in that Way, may depend upon being served in a reasonable and expeditious Manner, by their

Most Obedient,

Humble Servant,

John Bushell.

By the last Papers, &c. from London, by the Way of Boston, we have the following Intelligence, viz.

FOREIGN ADVICES.

ROME, *September* 24.

A Few Days ago, as the Pope was going in his Coach to the Qui-rinal, an ordinary man kneeled in the Street upon his Knees as if he wanted to receive a Blessing from him, which as he was going to give, the Man threw a Stone at his Holiness's Head, which narrowly missed: He proved to be a Madman lately escaped from the Hospital forLunaticks, to which Place he was remanded, with strict Orders to the Officers, to take more Care for the future of the unhappy People committed to their Charge.

Venice, Octo. 7. They write from Constantinople, That the Inhabitants who retired into the Country to avoid the Plague, are far from being secure, as the Air is infected for twenty Leagues round.

FROM THE BRITISH PRINTS.

LONDON, *September* 18.

This Day came on the Election for Lord Mayor of this City, when Thomas Winterbottom, Esq; Alderman of Billingsgate-Ward was elected for the Year ensuing. At the same Time, Slingsby Bethel and Marsh Dickenson, Esqrs; were chosen into the Office of Sheriffs for the Year ensuing.

On the 13th of May last, an Act passed for regulating the Com-mencement of the Year, and for correcting the Kalender now in Use; to extend throughout all his Majesty's Dominions. [The Par-ticulars of which will be published in our next.]

On the 14th of June, two Bills passed the Hon. House of Com-mons, which have since obtain'd the Royal Assent, viz. One for continuing the Bounty on the Importation of Masts, Tar, &c. The other for encouraging the making of Potashes and Pearlashes in A-merica. And on the 25th of the same Month, his Majesty closed his most gracious Speech to both Houses of Parliament, as follows, viz.

" My Lords and Gentlemen,
----- " I Have nothing to desire of you, but effectually to consult your " own true Interest and Happiness. Let it be your Care " to maintain in your several Countries, the publick Peace and good Or-" der; to encourage and promote a just Reverence for Government and " Law, and not to suffer those good Laws, which are enacted here, to " loose their Effect for want of a due Execution."

His Majesty has been pleased to require and command, that all Vessels arriving from the Levant should perform Quarantine.

November 2. We hear that a Report has been sent up by his Ma-jesty's Officers at Portsmouth, to the Hon. the Commissioners of the Navy, and by them to the Lords of the Admiralty, of the Success of the Experiment made by Mr. George Bridges, on several Pieces of Planks, to prevent Worms eating Holes in Ships Bottoms; The Advantages that will accrue to his Majesty's Dominions, are many: First, It will save the Expence of Sheathing, and cause the

ship to last twice as long. Secondly, Will save Numbers of Seamen, as well as preserve the Cargoes. Thirdly, All such Ships, that make use of it, require but little Ballast, so consequently, will hold more Stowage. Fourthly, The Ship will answer the Helm much better, and sail faster by some Knots in an Hour, &c. &c. &c.

Nov. 13. Last Saturday Night died, in the 78th Year of his Age, that great Mechanic Mr. George Graham, F. R. S. Watch-maker in Fleet-street, who may truly be said to have been the Father of the Trade, not only with Regard to the Perfection to which he brought Clocks and Watches, but for his great Encouragement to all Artificers employ'd under him, by keeping up the Spirit of Emu-lation among them.

Nov. 19. Last Week happened a very melancholy Accident, which, we hear, is as follows, viz. Mr. Dubuy, Confectioner to his Royal Highness the Prince of Wales, in Norris street, in the Hay-Market, being on Friday Evening at a Tavern near Pall-Mall, with an eminent Chymist, who was his intimate Friend and Neighbour, of a sudden complained of a violent Pain in his Side, which he fre-quently labour'd under; his Friend endeavoured to perswade him, that he would soon get the better of it, if he would go immediately to Bed, and take in the Morning a Dose of Physick that he would send him for that Purpose, accordingly the Draught had it's desired Effect; and on Saturday Morning about Eight o'Clock, he was seemingly quite recovered, and at his own Door. His Friend, who was glad to find him so much better when he came in the Morning, thought it adviseable to order him a second Dose, which one of his Servants being left to prepare, (and at the same Time several Chests of Medicines being packing in the Shop for Exportation) by some unhappy Means, a Phial, containing a Liquid of a poisonous Na-ture, was sent instead; which, on the Patient's swallowing, he was immediately taken Speechless, and in two Hours after died in great Agony, to the inexpressible Grief of all who knew him.

Nov. 19. A few Days ago, as some Workmen were digging up a Terrace at Sion-House, the Seat of the Right Hon. the Earl of Northumberland, about ten Feet from the Surface under the Walls, they found twenty-seven human Skulls, one of them of a most enor-mous Size, with the Teeth all fix'd and sound in the Jaws of them all; and seven Barrels fill'd with humane Bones; which are suppo-sed to have been there same Ages.

Nov. 30. On Thursday Night, about Ten o'Clock, as a Gen-tleman, who had been drinking pretty freely with some Friends, was going thro' Holborn, and seeing a Mob, his Curiosity led him to en-quire into the Cause of it, which he unfortunately mistook to be a Apprentice, for Treatment too severely inflicted by them upon an Apprentice, for using too much Liberty with his Tongue. The Gentleman taking Compassion of the young Man, very officiously interposed his Endea-vours to appease the exasperated Mob, and to rescue the Offender, which at length, by pressing Instances and mollifying Speeches, he accomplished; and it had been lucky for him if his Generosity had ended there; but not contented with having rescued him, he after-wards took him to a publick House to refresh him, where being in a private Room, and before a great Fire, the Gentleman fell asleep; In the mean Time, the supposed Apprentice pick'd his Pocket of Eighteen Shillings, and three new Silk Handkerchiefs, stripp'd him of his Hat and Cane, and made clearly off. As this ungrateful Be-haviour verifies the old Proverb, *Save a Thief from the Gallows, and he'll cut your Throat,* it is hoped it will be a Warning to Gentlemen, not to thrust themselves rashly into Mobs, where, though their Pur-ses escape, they seldom come off without some Damage.

Dec. 31. According to private Advices from Paris, the Com-missaries that have been so long conferring together in that City, a-bout a new Regulation of Limits in America, have already made so surprising a Progress, that the Publick in general begin to be per-swaded the Affair will ere long be brought to a happy, tho' not a surprizing Conclusion.

Jan. 1. Yesterday was held a Board of Trade, when James Oswald, Esq; took his Seat accordingly; at the same Time the seve-ral Dispatches brought by Commodore Pye and Capt. Hutchinson concerning Nova-Scotia were laid before them.

The same Day ------ Cornwallis, Esq; was appointed an Agent for that Colony.

Jan. 2. They write from Copenhagen, That, on the Occasion of the Death of the Queen of Denmark, his Danish Majesty has issu-ed an Edict, forbidding for a whole Year all Plays, Balls, Operas, Concertos, &c. ------ *Heaven preserve us from such Mourning, which would send at least one half of our gay, polite Gentry to the Grave!*

HALIFAX: Printed by John Bushell.

Canada's First Newspaper

In June 2002, the National Library of Canada announced that it had purchased, from the Massachusetts Historical Society, a copy of the first newspaper to be published in Canada. It was the *Halifax Gazette,* dated 23 March 1752 (shown at left). An important historical artifact had been returned to Canada.

The *Gazette* was an uninspiring paper by modern standards. Just one sheet of paper, printed front and back, it was printed by the newly established king's printer, John Bushell, in less than three-year-old Halifax. So low was its circulation—perhaps fifty or a hundred copies at most—that it had to be subsidized by the British government as a means of disseminating information in that slow age of sail and horseback. The paper mainly carried shipping news, advertisements (beginning a long tradition!), and extracts of information from British newspapers, with very little local news. This was because the people of Halifax likely already knew the local news because their community was then so small and isolated; the news they *really* wanted to know came from the outside world.

The *Halifax Gazette* lasted until 1767, when Bushell's successor as king's printer was dismissed for having the audacity to criticize the government's Stamp Act, the law under which Britain taxed its colonists for part of the costs of garrisoning troops in the colony. So much for newspapers being an organ of free speech.

But the situation was worse in New France, where the government would not allow the establishment of printing presses and so there were no newspapers at all. Québec did not get its first newspaper until 1778, when Fleury Mesplet—who had just got out of prison for trying to persuade his countrymen to join the American Revolution—started *La Gazette de commerce et littéraire* in Montréal. It survived only a year but was revived in 1785, still with Mesplet at the helm. It survives today as the Montréal *Gazette,* now Canada's longest continuously published newspaper.

Other noteworthy early newspapers include the *Upper Canada Gazette,* started in 1793 at the behest of John Graves Simcoe, the governor of the then new Upper Canada; this was the first newspaper in what is today Ontario. Later newspapers were often mouthpieces for special interest groups such as merchants. Firebrand and rebel-to-be William Lyon Mackenzie's *Colonial Advocate,* first published in 1824, became an important vehicle for change, as did Joseph Howe's *Novascotian,* first published in Halifax the same year.

Left.
The front page of the first issue of Canada's first newspaper, the *Halifax Gazette,* published on 23 March 1752. The paper measured about 36 x 22 cm. It has been reproduced here large enough to be read, at about 70 percent of its original size.

Below.
A copy of the *Quebec Gazette* for 4 June 1829. Published by John Neilson and his family from 1793 to 1848, the *Gazette* was one of the more established colonial newspapers. As early as 1810 it had a circulation of more than a thousand. By 1829 the paper was bilingual, as is the issue shown here.

The Quebec Gazette.
PUBLISHED BY AUTHORITY.
PUBLIÉE PAR AUTORITÉ.
Gazette de Quebec.
VOLUME VI.—No. 33.
TOME VI.—No. 33.
THURSDAY, JUNE 4, 1829.
JEUDI, 4 JUIN, 1829.
[New Series.]
FIERI FACIAS.
ALIAS FIERI FACIAS.
W. S. SEWELL, Sheriff.
JAMES KEMPT.

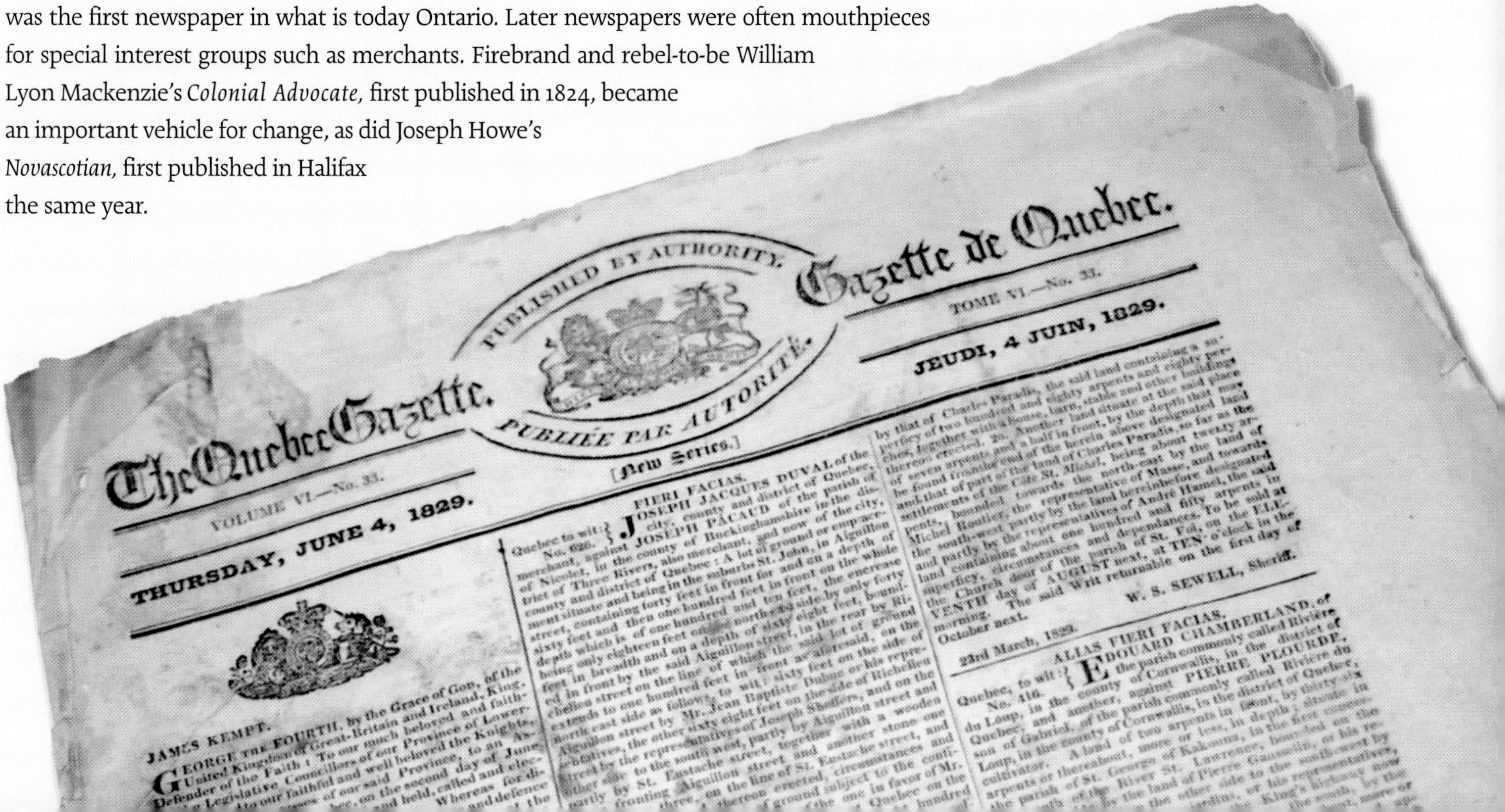

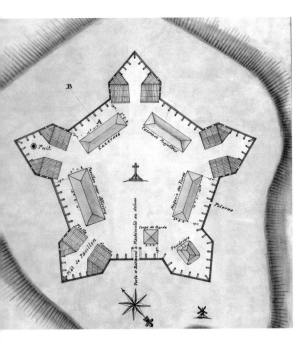

Forfeited All Title to Their Lands

Although the period from 1748 to 1756 was nominally one of peace between Britain and France, there was constant jockeying for position in Nova Scotia, France's erstwhile Acadia. The Treaty of Utrecht in 1713 had stated that "all Nova Scotia or Acadie, with its ancient boundaries" was to be "possessed alone hereafter by British subjects." This seemingly clear statement was in fact problematical, for nobody knew where those "ancient boundaries" actually were.

One of the grey areas was the neck of land at the head of Chignecto Bay, itself at the head of the Bay of Fundy, right on what is today the boundary between Nova Scotia and New Brunswick. Here, in 1750 and 1751, the French built Fort Beauséjour and the British Fort Lawrence almost within shooting distance of one another.

By 1754 the tensions between the American colonies and the French had risen to the point that skirmishes took place on the Ohio frontier, and the British decided to attack the French in several disputed locations. The only assault that succeeded was one against

Fort Beauséjour in June 1755 by Colonel Robert Monckton and 2,500 men. The fort had only 460 defenders, but 300 of them turned out to be militia—Acadians.

This Acadian defence made the British even more aware that the Acadians could be a potential problem to them. The governor of Nova Scotia, Charles Lawrence, summoned the Acadian leaders and gave a last chance "to such of them as had not been openly in Arms"—take an unqualified oath of allegiance to the British Crown. They refused to a man. At a meeting on 28 July attended by a newly arrived vice admiral, Edward Boscawen, a decision was made to expel the Acadians. Lawrence has generally been credited (if credited is the right word) with the idea, but recent research has suggested that Boscawen may have had an important influence. Lawrence obtained a legal opinion from his chief judge. Not surprisingly, the judge ruled that since the Acadian leaders had refused to take an oath of allegiance they were now "rebels" and could be dealt with accordingly. "If they would presume to do this [that is, refuse allegiance]," wrote Lawrence on 11 August, "when there is such a large fleet of Ships of War in the Harbour, and a considerable Land force in the Province, what might not we expect from them when the approaching winter deprives us of the former, and when the troops . . . have returned home. By this behaviour the Inhabitants have forfeited all title to their Lands."

Monckton ordered several hundred Acadians to assemble at Fort Cumberland, as the seized Fort Beauséjour was renamed. Then he arrested them as rebels. For the next several months British soldiers roamed the countryside as far south as Annapolis Royal rounding up Acadians, declaring them rebels who had forfeited their land, burning their houses, and seizing their cattle. Boats were also seized to prevent escape. Most Acadians were taken to Fort Lawrence, and from there they were mainly shipped to the American colonies, where, it was thought, they would be assimilated in the overwhelming British majority. To this day there are many Acadians—now termed Cajuns—in the American South.

In the fall of 1755, 6,000 to 7,000 Acadians were expelled from Nova Scotia. Some managed to escape and more than a few died from diseases and other causes before they reached their destinations. Smaller numbers were deported over the next few years. Some 3,100 Acadians were expelled from Île St. Jean (Prince Edward Island) in 1758. Estimates vary, but in all, perhaps 11,000 people were exiled, out of a total Acadian population in the Maritimes of 15,500.

The Acadian deportation has been described as the cultural genocide of its time. But heartless as it seems to us today, it is important to assess it in the context of the day. To the British, trying to consolidate their hold on Nova Scotia, the Acadians appeared as a dangerous insider element that could rise up against them without warning. And the British did not overtly kill Acadians, but deported them. This was considered humane treatment in the eighteenth century, although too many died trying to find a new place to live. In 2003, a Royal Proclamation officially acknowledged the sufferings of the Acadians during the deportations.

Opposite, top.
A plan of Fort Beauséjour, drawn in 1751 by French military engineer Louis Franquet.

Opposite, bottom.
This watercolour by Charles Jefferys shows the expulsion order being read to the Acadians at the church at Grand Pré, a settlement on the Minas Basin.

Below.
This painting by Canadian artist Lewis Parker shows the expulsion of the Acadians, in this case those from Île St. Jean (Prince Edward Island) in 1758, repeating a scene from the 1755 expulsions from Acadia (Nova Scotia) itself. The Acadians are shown leaving Fort Amherst, across the bay from today's Charlottetown.

Above.
Louisbourg reconstructed, as it is today. The view is from the harbour to Porte Frédéric, the large gateway. Ships had to anchor away from the Louisbourg wharf, for the water there was too shallow.

Opposite, top.
James Wolfe leads his men ashore at Kennington Cove.

Opposite, bottom.
This dramatic oil painting by Richard Paton shows the burning of the *Prudent* and the capture of the French flagship *Bienfaisant* by British sailors in small boats on the night of 25–26 July 1758. The sailors are towing the *Bienfaisant* (at right) out to sea and away from the guns of Louisbourg.

The European Seven Years War, from 1756 to 1763, though as yet undeclared was underway in North America by 1754, when skirmishes between the British and French and their various native allies began. The taking of Fort Beauséjour was one of these battles. In North America the war became known as the French and Indian War. Britain wanted to eliminate France as a commercial rival and aimed to destroy its navy and seize its merchant fleet—and its colonies. A major force behind this policy was William Pitt, who became British prime minister in July 1757. He was convinced that the future wealth and glory of Britain lay in the establishment of an empire and he convinced King George II to allow a major switch in resources from the European to North American theatres of war.

By 1756, the French had appointed the man who was to prove pivotal in the war on their side. He was Louis-Joseph de Montcalm, Marquis de Montcalm, made *maréchal de camp* (major general), and the overall commander of the French forces, subject only to the governor of New France, Pierre de Rigaud de Vaudreuil. Montcalm orchestrated some stunning early French successes. In the strategic Hudson River–Lake Champlain corridor he defeated the British at Fort William Henry in 1757 and at Fort Carillon in 1758. At the former fort, Montcalm was unable to control his native allies after the British surrendered, leading to carnage that enraged the British and was to lend a heightened viciousness to the war.

The British commander, Major General John Campbell, Earl of Loudon, was the strategist who devised the military plan that would ultimately lead to the demise of New France, although he was himself unable to achieve this goal. Loudon's plan was three-pronged: an attack up the Ohio Valley, Lake Ontario, and the St. Lawrence to Montréal; another up Lake Champlain and the Rivière Richelieu to the St. Lawrence; and another by sea, to take Louisbourg, then Québec, then Montréal.

After some initial failures Pitt managed to replace Loudon with an upstart new military commander, Jeffrey Amherst, who was given the special but local title of "Major General in America." At the same time, one of his immediate subordinates, James Wolfe, was given the title "Brigadier in America." Vast new resources were committed to the war. Some thirty-eight warships under Admiral Edward Boscawen and a hundred troop transports carrying 12,000 soldiers sailed from England in early 1758. The first objective was Louisbourg.

The plan was to take Louisbourg and Québec in a single season, but, as it turned out, the French were able to hold Louisbourg for longer than expected, and Québec had to wait until the following year. Unlike in 1745, Louisbourg was now commanded by a highly competent naval officer, the Chevalier Augustin de Drucour. He had assumed command in 1754 and set about repairing the defences badly damaged during the 1745 assault. Instead of Duchambon's mercenary mixture with their doubtful loyalties, Drucourt had about 6,000 men under his command, including a garrison of 3,500 regular soldiers. And he had learned from history; the possible landing places along Gabarus Bay had been fortified with the assistance of military engineer Louis Franquet, the designer of Fort Beauséjour.

The British, for their part, also now had mainly regular soldiers rather than the New England militia of 1745, but, perhaps more significantly, they had overwhelming numbers. After a rendezvous at Halifax, the fleet sailed north to Gabarus Bay, where the assault began on 8 June. The hero of the landing was James Wolfe. The entrenched French troops on the shore had for a time a distinct advantage over the British flotilla in small boats in a heavy surf. The boats had difficulty pulling in to shore, but Wolfe spotted an inexplicable temporary hole in the French defences and waded ashore, rallying his men. This

decisive action saved the day and was noted by Amherst, who would need a bold leader for the later attempt on Québec.

The British lost no time is mounting a classic siege of Louisbourg's defences. They advanced to just outside cannon range and proceed to dig a series of trenches, dragging cannon along the trenches until they were in a position where they could pound at the walls of the fortress. The Grand Battery, which had been captured and turned on the town in 1745, was once more overrun to repeat effect.

By 6 July the British trenches were so close to the fortress walls that mortar bombs and incendiaries were falling onto the town itself. On 21 July a red-hot cannonball struck one of the French ships in the harbour, setting it and its neighbouring ships on fire. Four days later, Boscawen ordered sailors in boats into the harbour under cover of darkness, where they attacked two remaining French warships, burning one, the *Prudent,* and audaciously towing another, the sixty-four gun French flagship *Bienfaisant,* out to sea, all the while under fire from the town.

The end was now not long in coming. Drucour now had a third of his men out of action and only four of his cannon still serviceable. British ships were preparing to enter the harbour and shell the town from its undefended side. Drucour had done all he could; he raised a flag of truce and asked for terms. But Amherst refused. The legacy of Fort William Henry the year before had triggered Amherst's more ruthless streak. He allowed the town's civilians to retain their belongings, but the entire population, along with the military, were shipped to England as prisoners. All the French inhabitants of Île Royale and Île St. Jean (Cape Breton and Prince Edward Islands) were deported back to France. From now on, civilians would also suffer the consequences of opposition to the British.

Prelude to a Finale

When Drucour signed the capitulation of Louisbourg at midnight on 26 July, he had held the British at bay for exactly seven weeks, far longer than the British had anticipated. Because of the resupply and regrouping required it was now considered too late in the season to launch an attack on Québec, as had been intended. Instead, Amherst dispatched James Wolfe to destroy French sources of food in the Gaspé, and James Murray, another of his officers, to so the same in the Miramichi. Moses Hazen was sent to burn St. Anne's—Fredericton—for the same reason. This was a cruel and heartless task that inflicted widespread hardship on the civilian population, and one the British have been well criticized for. Amherst saw it only as a military necessity, to soften up his foe for the coming battle.

Not everywhere had things gone the way the British desired, however. Even while the siege of Louisbourg was continuing, James Abercromby, who had assumed overall North American command from Loudon in March 1758, amassed the largest army ever before fielded in North America at Fort Carillon (later Ticonderoga), south of Lake Champlain. Abercromby had an astonishing 16,000 men at his command, but he was repulsed by Montcalm with only 3,500, cleverly using defence works and *abatis* (felled trees to break up

enemy formations). It was hard to argue about a victory as decisive as that. Montcalm was later that year made a lieutenant general, the second highest rank in the French army, and given overall command of the French forces in North America, over the objections of governor Vaudreuil. This setback for the British further confirmed that there could be no assault on Québec that year.

With the permission of Abercromby following this defeat, James Bradstreet put into action a plan to capture Fort Frontenac, on Lake Ontario, destroy ships, and take control of the lake. With 3,000 men Bradstreet approached the fort in August in 218 small boats. The fort's commander, Pierre-Jacques Payen de Noyan, had only 110 men in the fort, which was in poor repair anyway. Suddenly faced with such an overwhelming force he had little choice but to surrender. The way to Montréal from the west had been opened.

Above.
Louis-Joseph de Montcalm, Marquis de Montcalm, commander of the French forces in North America.

Right.
Montcalm's first offensive against the invading British fleet at Québec was to unleash a number of carefully prepared fire ships. On the night of 28–29 June they were released on the turning tide to drift into the fleet. But they were lit too soon; the British saw them coming, and with their boats managed to tow them out of the way of the fleet.

The Fall of Québec

After the fall of Louisbourg, it was obvious that an attack on Québec itself was coming. The French were also aware that they could not hope to hold New France against the resources that the British now seemed willing to amass against it. One of Montcalm's senior officers, Louis-Antoine de Bougainville, thought the situation "utterly hopeless." Urgent appeals were sent to France for massive reinforcements, but the French government planned an invasion of England and thought that this would surely distract the British from North America. Montcalm thought the situation so bad that he even asked what terms of capitulation he should seek. In any event, the reinforcements he sought were denied, although twenty or so supply ships did make it to Québec in May 1759 complete with the grand total of 331 soldiers accompanying a returning Bougainville, who had taken the appeals to France. Montcalm's great victory at Carillon had come back to haunt him; he had defeated the British against overwhelming odds once, the French government reasoned, so why not again?

James Wolfe was selected to lead the British assault. Vice Admiral Sir Charles Saunders arrived off Île d'Orléans on 26 June 1759, with a huge fleet of warships and troop transports, a hundred and eighty in all, with thousands of men. The first action of the drama was Montcalm's. He had a number of fire ships prepared—old ship hulks filled with combustible material—and on the night of 28–29 June he sent them drifting towards the British fleet on the ebb tide. Unfortunately for the French they were lit too soon and the British had enough time to tow the blazing hulks towards the river bank, away from their ships.

Montcalm was convinced that the British attack would come on the Beauport shore, a flatter area just east of the fortress city, and he had fortified entrenchments and other defensive works built along this stretch of the shoreline. Wolfe, of course, knew that the French army was waiting there. On 31 July he ordered a frontal assault on the shore just west of the Montmorency waterfall, where there are low cliffs, but it failed miserably largely because a chance heavy thunderstorm made the cliffs unscalable.

Wolfe spent the next five weeks vacillating, all the while ordering his men to raze the surrounding countryside. To attack or not to attack, and more importantly, where? He knew that he would have to make a decision soon or the encroaching winter would make it for him. On 29 August Wolfe's three subordinate officers, Brigadiers Robert Monckton, George Townshend, and James Murray, suggested an attack from above the town, in the vicinity of Cap Rouge, but Wolfe, who did not get on very well with his officers in any case, was not in a receptive mood. Slowly he hatched a plan of his own, telling no one until a few hours before it was put into operation. A British captain, Robert Stobo, who had been a prisoner of war in

This contemporary map shows the action of the battle for Québec in 1759 and was published in England soon after the event. As is usual in maps like this, drawn up to be sold to a public thirsting for information on a major news event of the day, it shows a sequence of events. The French fire ships, marked *rafts,* with an arrow, are in midstream just off the city. The initial failed British attack of 28–29 June is shown at top right. There is ongoing bombardment of the city from cannon on the Lévis shore opposite, and at left are British ships (*Admiral Holmes's Division*) that had drifted downstream to release the flotilla of boats filled with troops towards L'Anse-au-Foulon on the night of 12–13 September. The yet later formations of the battle lines to the west of the city on the Plains of Abraham are also shown.

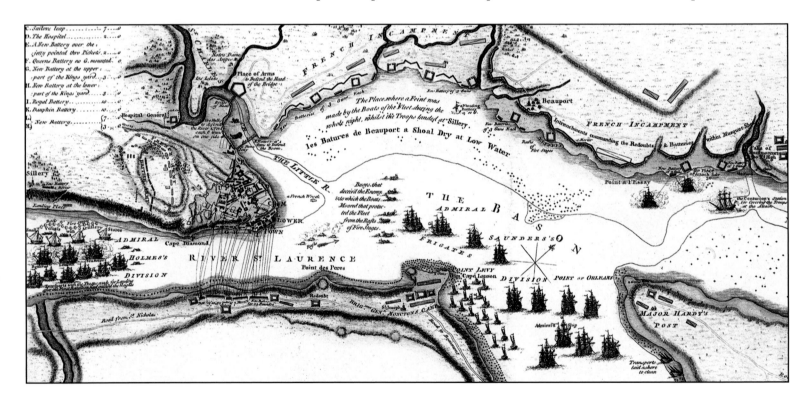

Québec until escaping earlier that year, told Wolfe of a chink in the French armour, a narrow defile up the steep cliff at L'Anse-au-Foulon, below the flat area just west of the city known as the Plains of Abraham. The evidence is that Wolfe thought an attack via this route was probably hopeless, but he was now ill and thought he would die before returning to England in any case, so he preferred to die what he considered a glorious death leading his troops into battle. And if the attempt failed, at least he would have been seen to try.

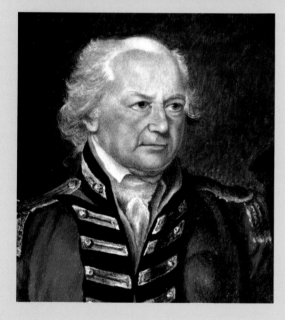

Military officers, perhaps, wanted to preserve their likeness in case they were killed in battle. At any rate, these superb portraits of James Wolfe and his officers give us some insight into the characters of these men who changed Canadian history forever. Clockwise from top left they are Robert Monckton, Wolfe's second-in-command; James Wolfe, the vacillating primadonna who orchestrated the battle for Québec; Vice Admiral Sir Charles Saunders, in command of the fleet (and in an especially classical pose); James Murray, Wolfe's junior brigadier; and George Townshend, third in command.

In this multi-sequence engraving designed to illustrate the Battle of Québec, British troops arrive in boats at L'Anse-au-Foulon and climb to the Plains of Abraham, where the battle is depicted well underway.

On the night of 12–13 September, troops were packed into boats. Between one and two o'clock, at a signal light from the command ship *Sutherland,* the landing at L'Anse-au-Foulon began. Some advance boats were heard by French guards, but a quick-thinking officer replied to their challenge in French, making them think they were ferrying supplies to the city under cover of darkness. Led by a nimble lieutenant colonel, William Howe, the British troops scrambled up the cliff and overpowered astonished French guards at a post at the top, by chance commanded by the very same officer who had surrendered Fort Beauséjour in 1755.

In the early hours of 13 September more and more British troops made the ascent, until as dawn broke seven battalions were lined up facing Québec. Wolfe, who had not planned on getting this far, seemed unsure what to do next. But the next move was surely Montcalm's. He had spent the night at Beauport, where he had thought an attack was coming, but the noise of rowing that he heard was in fact sailors rowing up and down, sent by Saunders to create precisely the illusion Montcalm fell for. In the light of day Montcalm could see his mistake, though he hardly believed the messenger who told him what had happened. He rushed all his available men over to the city, and by nine in the morning two armies, each of 4,500 to 5,000 men, faced each other on the Plains of Abraham.

Then Montcalm made a classic mistake. He had previously sent 2,000 men upriver under Bougainville to deal with any possible British landing farther west, and Montcalm had sent for them to return poste-haste; they were on their way. But Montcalm thought that the British were entrenching, that is, digging themselves in to begin a conventional siege of the city, and he thought they would have more and more cannon—they already had two, manhandled by sailors up the cliff—as time went on. So Montcalm thought he had better attack immediately.

Montcalm had one big disadvantage compared to his foe: the ranks of his army included a large number of militia, who were not as disciplined under fire in a battlefield situation. Instead of advancing, firing, and reloading as was the standard technique, the militia ran forward when the order to advance was given, and the French lines soon broke down. Wolfe ordered his men to stand firm until the enemy were very close, and he told them to load their muskets with two balls instead of one. The result was a withering fire that halted the French in their tracks. It was a stroke of genius by Wolfe, and his last, for he was an early casualty of the melee, dying on the battlefield. Montcalm fared little better. Ripped apart, he was carried back to the city, where he died the following night.

Bougainville arrived an hour after the fighting, which itself had taken only an hour, was over. Seeing what had happened he decided to retreat and save his army for a counteroffensive. Had he been somehow able to move his army the 15 km from Cap Rouge an hour earlier, it would almost cetainly have made a critical difference, for the British would have suddenly found themselves sandwiched between two armies.

The senior officer in Québec was now its town-major, the Sieur de Ramezay. Governor Vaudreuil had been with the remnant of the French troops at Beauport and had taken them north and west to join up with Bougainville. Ramezay saw the town's position as hopeless and, wishing to avoid further civilian casualties, signed the formal capitulation of the city on 18 September. François-Gaston de Lévis, Duc de Lévis, who had been in command of an army at Montréal, hastened to Québec, but once again, by the time the French army arrived, it was too late; Québec had surrendered.

James Murray was left in command of Québec that winter, a hard one by all accounts. The British must have wished they had not been as thorough in their destruction of the countryside around the city the previous summer.

This watercolour sketch of the death of James Wolfe surrounded by only two or three others is a far more accurate portrayal than the more famous allegorical painting by Benjamin West. Painted by James Barry, this painting was recently acquired by the National Archives of Canada.

Montréal was now all that stood between the British and New France. Over the winter, Lévis, now in command of the army, and Vaudreuil, still governor, planned to take back Québec. Their plan, however, could not succeed without reinforcements from France, and France was too preoccupied with the war in Europe to care about the lost cause of Canada, which Voltaire had famously dismissed as a "few acres of snow."

Lévis conscripted all available men for his militia, under pain of death if they did not report. Then his army made its way to Québec on barges. As they landed upstream of the city, one of his men fell into the St. Lawrence. He was saved a little later by the British as he floated past Québec. Lucky for him, but unlucky for Lévis, for the soldier revealed the presence of the French army, and thus Murray could ready himself for the coming encounter. But Murray repeated the error made by Montcalm the year before and suffered the same consequences. He attacked too soon, hoping to prevent the French army from becoming too entrenched. This resulted in the Battle of Sainte-Foy, fought on 28 April 1760, on almost the same spot as the battle the year before.

Murray retreated within the walls of Québec, and Lévis laid siege to the city. But the French army was so critically short of ammunition that Lévis had to limit his gunners to

Above.
The ruins of Québec, drawn by a British officer in 1760.

Below.
François-Gaston de Lévis, Duc de Lévis, victor of the Battle of Sainte-Foy in April 1760.

twenty shots a day. Both forces were essentially stalemated. The war would be decided by whichever nation sent reinforcements first and, of course, it was the British. On 9 May a single ship, HMS *Lowestoft*, appeared in the river bearing, among other supplies, newspapers. Murray sent some over to Lévis in case he was bored. The French still hoped against hope that the next ships would be French, but they were not. More British ships appeared on 15 May; Lévis realized that the game was up and retreated back to Montréal.

With the French forces now concentrated at Montréal, Lévis intended to make a last stand, but as it happened, the British were able to bring overwhelming numbers to their advantage. Finally the three-pronged master plan of Loudon would come to fruition. Murray advanced up the St. Lawrence with his army, now resupplied by ships from England. He bypassed Trois-Rivières and arrived at Varennes, across the river from the northern tip of the island of Montréal, on 1 September.

Another British army, led by William Haviland, advanced up the Lake Champlain–Rivière Richelieu corridor, pausing only to take the island fortress at Île-aux-Noix (later Fort Lennox) held briefly by Bougainville and 1,400 men, who retreated to Montréal. Haviland's army joined with Murray's at Varennes on 5 September.

The third army, led by Jeffrey Amherst himself, advanced from the west, down the St. Lawrence. In a similar fashion to Haviland he was held up for a week by a small island fortress in the St. Lawrence, Fort Lévis, but arrived at Île Perrot, at the southern end of the island of Montréal, on the same day Haviland arrived at Varennes. The following day Amherst moved his army to Lachine, about 6 km from

Montréal's walls, and Murray's and Haviland's armies moved across the river opposite.

The cast was now in position for the final act. Murray had about 2,200 men, Haviland 3,500, and Amherst almost 11,000. Lévis had at most 4,000 in Montréal, which was essentially indefensible, having been built to withstand Indian raids, not vast European-style armies. Vaudreuil, the realist, knew he had to negotiate a surrender. Lévis, a firebrand concerned about his honour, was all for fighting to the last man. In the end, common sense prevailed and much bloodshed was averted.

On 7 September Bougainville arrived at Amherst's camp with a list of articles for the surrender of the city. Amherst agreed to many, but would not agree to the French troops being granted the "honours of war," that is, being allowed to return to France with their regimental colours to fight on. Instead Amherst insisted that they must simply surrender, to punish them for the part they had played "in exciting the savages to perpetrate the most horrid and unheard of barbarities." This was a deliberate insult. Lévis snapped his sword rather than surrender it to the British and that night ordered his regiments to burn their colours.

But Vaudreuil was in no position to dictate terms. On Sunday, 8 September 1760, he did the only thing he could and signed the articles of capitulation. With his signature all of New France was surrendered; Canada passed to Britain.

Above.
The surrender of Montréal, a painting by Adam Sheriff Scott.

Below.
The two chief protagonists in the climactic stages of the collapse of the French empire in North America. At left is François-Pierrre de Rigaud de Vaudreuil, last governor of New France, and at right the ruthless but brilliant British military commander Jeffrey Amherst.

5 *The British in Canada*

Vaudreuil's surrender at Montréal in 1760 was confirmed by the Treaty of Paris, signed in 1763. France lost all of New France, including Île Royale (Cape Breton Island), Île St. Jean (Prince Edward Island), Newfoundland (except for some ill-defined fishing rights and the islands of St. Pierre and Miquelon), and its posts in the west such as Detroit and those in the Illinois country. France also lost Louisiana; it had been ceded to Spain the year before to stop it falling into British hands.

The French empire in North America had crumbled, and in its place was a new British domain stretching from Hudson Bay in the north to Florida in the south, and west to the Mississippi. It would very soon prove too big for the British to handle, and much of this huge swath of territory would be lost to a new United States.

After the fall of New France in 1760, James Murray was appointed first military governor of New France and then civilian governor of a newly created province—Québec. Murray had been James Wolfe's fourth in command, and it was he who had been left to govern Québec during the first winter after its fall, when all the other high-ranking officers left for better climes.

The British government seriously debated handing back much of New France to the French, as the country was widely considered of doubtful value. It was only the arguments of William Pitt, that long-time advocate of a British Empire, and Benjamin Franklin, then living in London, that forestalled this possibility.

The British for a time faced a new threat: a newly militant native population to the west. Pontiac, war chief of the Ottawa, led a coalition of tribes, capturing once-French forts such as Fort Pitt (Pittsburgh) and laying a savage siege to Fort Detroit in 1763. British commander-in-chief Jeffrey Amherst, who had always despised the natives of North America, suggested that the Indians could be subdued by spreading smallpox among them. It had already been done. In one of the low points of North American history and perhaps the first recorded use of biological warfare, the disease had been spread to the natives by distributing cut-up infected blankets. In many native camps this new weapon was devastatingly effective. Pontiac signed a peace treaty with the British in 1766, a peace that notably did not include recognition of British sovereignty over native lands.

In June 1813, during the War of 1812, the British warship HMS *Shannon* captured an American frigate, the *Chesapeake,* and is shown here amid much jubilation leading her prize into Halifax Harbour on 6 June.

A Royal Proclamation in 1763 had already recognized native title outside of a newly defined Province of Québec, specifying that all areas outside of the new province were to be Indian reserve, and allowed treaties to be negotiated with native peoples. This continues to the present day; the 1982 Constitution (see page 271) allows no diminution of native rights from those in the 1763 proclamation.

At first there was a determined effort to anglicize Québec. The Royal Proclamation applied British law. "All Persons Inhabiting in or resorting to our Said Colonies may confide in our Royal Protection for the Enjoyment of the Benefit of the Laws of our Realm of England," it stated. This helped the flood of British merchants who came to Québec after 1763 take over the commerce of the colony, in particular the profitable fur trade. Murray's main difficulties arose over his insistence on recognizing the French nature of the majority of the inhabitants, without whose co-operation he knew he could not rule. He interpreted his instructions to allow the *Canadiens* to keep their own civil laws. But the merchants, whom Murray referred to as "Licentious Fanaticks," wanted the upper hand. A newly appointed magistrate, a wealthy Montréal fur trader named Thomas Walker, who wanted everything done the "British way," was particularly shrill in his criticism of Murray and his supporting military. One night, apparently in reprisal for a harsh ruling against an officer, Walker was

The Royal Proclamation of 1763 established narrow boundaries for the newly created "Province of Québec," outside of which was Indian reserve. The 1763 boundaries are shown on this map. The Quebec Act of 1774 extended Quebéc's territory well into what is now the United States, and also included Labrador, Île d'Anticosti, and Îles de la Madeleine.

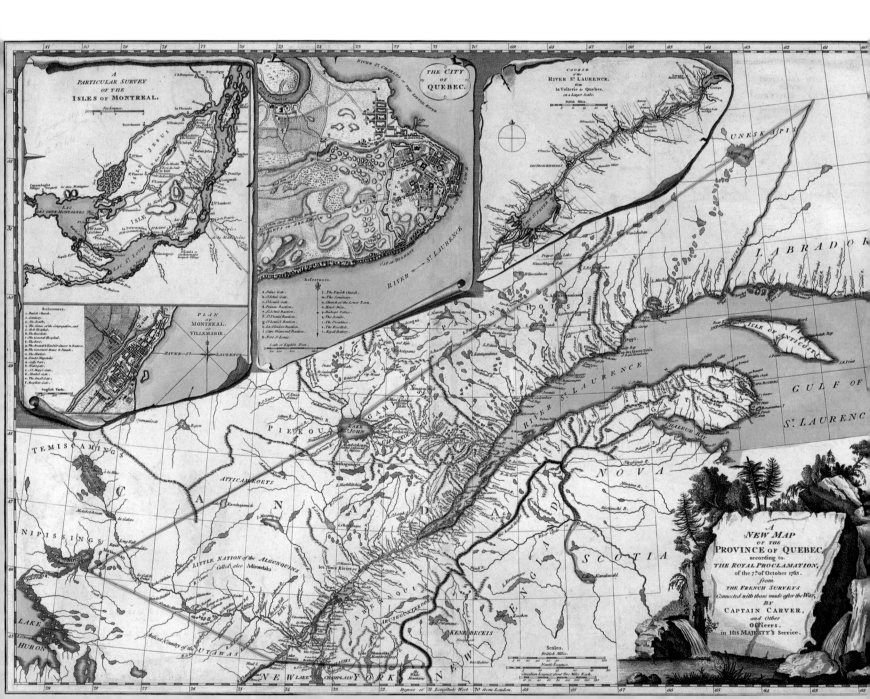

attacked by a group of masked men—probably military men—who cut off his ear. The incident caused an uproar. Although no one was convicted for the attack, it led to Murray's recall to England in 1766 to explain himself; he did not return and was dismissed as governor in 1768. Murray reported that he gloried "in having been accused of warmth and firmness in protecting the King's Canadian Subjects and of doing the utmost in my power to gain to my Royal Master the affection of that brave hardy People, whose Emigration, if it ever shall happen, will be an irreparable Loss to this Empire."

Murray's enlightened administration of the new colony served as a prototype for other British colonies, and his melding of the French and English legal systems was enshrined in a later act, the Quebec Act.

More Effective Provision

Murray was replaced by Guy Carleton, later Baron Dorchester, who had been Wolfe's quartermaster, always a good training for an administrator. Carleton was lieutenant-governor until 1768, then governor. But if the merchants thought they would gain the upper hand, they were mistaken. Carleton continued the integration of the French colonial and English systems initiated by Murray, which culminated in the Quebec Act of 1774. By this time the British government was aware of the coming storm in its American colonies and moved to placate the Canadiens, hoping to ensure their loyalty.

Guy Carleton, Baron Dorchester, the second governor of British Québec.

The "Act for making more effectual Provision for the Government of the Province of Quebec in North America," called the Quebec Act, guaranteed the religious freedom of Catholics. This was a tremendous leap for a government whose king had taken coronation vows to uphold the Protestant religion. The French language was allowed. French civil law was enshrined with British criminal law and the seigneurial system of land holdings continued. The governor was to be assisted by an appointed council whose members could be Catholic. And Carleton appointed many Catholics.

The merchants were furious, petitioning the British government with a document called *The Case of the British Merchants trading to Quebeck, and others of his natural-born Subjects, who have been induced to venture their Property in the said province on the Faith of his Majesty's Proclamation.* But their appeal was to no avail; the government's mind was made up. It would soon have other far more significant revolts to consider than that of a few English merchants.

For the American colonists saw the Quebec Act as one of the five so-called Intolerable Acts that led them on the path to revolution. This was because the act also extended the boundaries of the province to encompass the Indian territory south of the Great Lakes between the Mississippi and Ohio Rivers, recognizing that the 1763 Royal Proclamation had left vast areas with no legal system. The American colonists, whose numbers had grown to about 2.2 million at this time (compared to about 85,000 in Canada), coveted this land as a "natural" expansion of their territories and did not want to see it pre-empted as part of Québec. This part of the Quebec Act led to disastrous consequences for the British.

A British 38-gun frigate, about 1770.

A map published in London in September 1776 to inform the public about the American Revolutionary War. *American Forces under Genl. Arnold* are at left, with lines of fire into Québec. At bottom centre-right is the marker *L*, which is the place Richard Montgomery landed to begin his abortive attack on 31 December 1775.

You Are a Small People

When the first American Continental Congress met in Philadelphia in 1774 to assert the rights of America, it was assumed by many that Nova Scotia and Québec would join forces with the other American colonies to confront Britain, and delegates from the two had been invited. But they failed to show. The Congress sent out a warning, in a tactless form which could be calculated to have an opposite effect from that desired. "You are a small people," it began, "compared to those who with open arms invite you into fellowship." Surely the northern colonists would want to be in a North America of their friends rather than next to their enemies. The appeal was reprinted in Canadian newspapers and had some effect, especially in Montréal, but in general met with no response.

In answer to an appeal from Major General Thomas Gage, Carleton dispatched two of his five battalions to Boston, leaving him short of men. Calling up the militia, Carleton was disillusioned by the lack of response from the Canadiens, whose rights he had championed. In 1776 he wrote of them in a letter: "I think there is nothing to fear from them, while we are in a state of prosperity, and nothing to hope for when in distress."

The first incursion into Canada was essentially an amateur affair, unsponsored by Congress: a Vermont land speculator, Ethan Allen, and his ragtag little army known as the Green Mountain Boys. Amateur or not, Allen, allied with Benedict Arnold and a group of Massachusetts militiamen, succeeded in capturing Fort Ticonderoga in a daring midnight raid in May 1775. They followed it up by capturing two other forts, and then Arnold raided Fort St. John (at Saint-Jean-sur-Richelieu). But they retreated after squabbling among themselves. The next month Congress, persuaded that an invasion of Canada would be an easy one, authorized a much larger force to march north.

Commanded initially by New York Major General Philip John Schuyler and then by Richard Montgomery when Schuyler went home ill, an army advanced up Lake Champlain and took the fort at Île-aux-Noix in September. At this point the impetuous Ethan Allen led a raid on Montréal, which was repulsed by Carleton. This minor victory sent men running

to join the militia, so that Carleton had perhaps 2,000 men under his command, although because of inaction, many of them went back to their farms.

Fort Chambly fell to Montgomery's army on 18 October, and St. John on 3 November, after its commander had heard of the failure of a relief effort. A thousand of Carleton's men had tried to land at Longueil, opposite Montréal, but had been prevented from landing by American fire.

Carleton knew that Montréal was indefensible, and so on 11 November he took his army out of the city and retreated towards Québec. The Americans, unopposed, occupied Montréal on 13–14 November. Carleton's army could not get past American batteries at Sorel, where the Richelieu joins the St. Lawrence, and Carleton himself was only slipped by on a dark night with the help of ingenious Canadiens paddling with their hands to avoid any noise.

Montgomery advanced on Québec, where he arrived on 3 December. Meanwhile, Benedict Arnold had with small boats and not much else brought another small American army over the mountains and along the Chaudière River, which meets the St. Lawrence slightly upstream from Québec. He had arrived in early November, although by the time he got to Québec he had only six hundred men, half the number he had started out with. Arnold joined up with Montgomery, and the pair considered how to best attack the city.

It was certainly not the best season to carry out such operations. On 31 December, in a snowstorm, Montgomery led an attack designed to take the Lower Town. His attack, which Carleton knew from deserters was coming, was stopped at a barricade and Montgomery was killed. Arnold, only injured, took over command, but lacking heavy artillery, launched no more attacks. Instead the city was besieged. But on 6 May Arnold met with a surprise—literally. HMS *Surprise,* the first of a relieving British fleet carrying 10,000 troops, anchored before Québec. It was 1760 all over again. Arnold had little choice but to lift his siege.

The Americans in Montréal heard of the new British force and abandoned the city on 9 May. Arnold retreated to Sorel, wavered, anticipated reinforcements, and moved downstream again as far a Trois-Rivières, where his troops were opposed by a much larger British army. At this the Americans retreated back down the Richelieu Valley.

Guy Carleton was knighted for his defence of Québec, but chastised for not pursuing the fleeing American army, and for this he resigned. Because of this, when a British army did

The scene at the barricades in Québec's Lower Town on the night of 31 December 1775. *Below* is the same spot today. Marker plaques on the side of a house at the now appropriately named *Rue de la Barricade* commemorate the event.

finally advance on to what is now American territory, it was led not by Carleton but by Major General John Burgoyne. Burgoyne ended up disgraced when he was forced to surrender his entire army at Saratoga on 19 September 1777 to a large American army led by Horatio Gates —and including Benedict Arnold. The battle ended what had been a British plan to cut the colonies in two by an invasion from Canada, the purpose of all those troops that had arrived at Québec in the spring of 1776 to the dismay of Arnold.

The Loyalist Tide

On 17 March 1776, the British army, after suffering its first major defeat of the War of American Independence, evacuated Boston and sailed for Halifax. With them they took a thousand or so colonists who were still loyal to the British cause and whose lives would have been in jeopardy had they remained in Boston. When they arrived in Halifax, there was not enough accommodation for them all, and a severe strain was placed on the resources of the town. The city became a sea of tents.

It was a warning of things to come. As the war progressed, more and more of those still loyal—the Loyalists—migrated one way or another to the north, to the only area that seemed safely in British hands. In 1783 came a massive tide of humanity fleeing to Canada, which was that year confirmed as British territory by the defining of a boundary to the American colonies—soon to become the United States—in the Treaty of Paris, which ended the war. In the years 1783 and 1784, 50,000 Loyalists came to Canada. Nova Scotia was the destination for 32,000 of them.

Land had to be found quickly. In Nova Scotia previous land grants to now absentee landlords were cancelled, and Governor John Parr was appointed surveyor to survey and

Below.
Québec in 1788, viewed from across the St. Lawrence.

Opposite, top.
Shelburne, Nova Scotia, formerly Port Roseway, as it has been restored today.

allocate land. One major destination for the Loyalists was Port Roseway, south of Halifax, where a rapidly growing town was established that may have reached a population of 16,000, rivalling Halifax in size. Renamed Shelburne, after Parr's patron the Earl of Shelburne, the town proved to be a flash in the pan, however, for in the haste to build the town the harbour had not been surveyed and was soon found inadequate. Most of the Loyalists migrated elsewhere. During the mid-1780s, the population of Nova Scotia doubled.

Due to the rapidly growing population and the difficulties in administration that this brought with it, Nova Scotia was divided. In 1784 the new colony of New Brunswick was created, as was Cape Breton Island (though the latter rejoined Nova Scotia in 1820). The Island of St. John (renamed Prince Edward Island in 1799) had already been created as a separate colony in 1769.

In August 1783 Robert Campbell led nearly two hundred Loyalists up the Saint John River—which he referred to as "this re-mote part of Nova Scotia"—where the small

Below.
Part of a surveyor's map dated 1792 showing the layout of the lots along the St. Lawrence with the names of the military officers to whom the land has been granted. A town has been laid out—the divided square. This is Johnstown, which never grew due to a shoaling shore, but the village still exists, close to the junction of the Trans-Canada and the highway to Ottawa.

Below.
Loyalists camped on the banks of the St. Lawrence in 1784. The artist, James Peachy, was himself a Loyalist, trained as a draftsman in New England.

Opposite, top.
John Graves Simcoe, first lieutenant-governor of Upper Canada.

Opposite, bottom.
A 1798 broadsheet regarding the conditions under which land is granted on Yonge Street, which leads northward out of Toronto.

previously French settlement of Sainte-Anne became Fredericstown, today the provincial capital of Fredericton. In 1784 Thomas Carleton, younger brother of Guy, became the governor of the new colony of New Brunswick, and a town named after him was laid out at the mouth of the Saint John River, where there was already another settlement, called Parrtown after the previous governor when all was Nova Scotia. The following year both settlements were amalgamated to form the city of Saint John, the first incorporated city in Canada.

Québec already had about 10,000 Loyalists in the form of soldiers who had been brought to the province to defend it. About eight hundred of these stayed, taking up seigneurial lands. But most wanted land that was their own, without having an obligation to a higher landowner, as the seigneurial system demanded.

The governor of Québec, Frederick Haldimand, who had replaced Guy Carleton in 1778, decided that the Loyalists should be settled farther west, along the shores of the St. Lawrence and Lake Ontario. First Haldimand had to negotiate with the native peoples, for the region was all officially an Indian reserve under the terms of the 1763 Royal Proclamation. The land a day's march back from the river or lakefront was usually what was purchased.

In this way the Loyalists were spread out along the frontier with the new United States and could, it was hoped, provide a defensive barrier against it. Haldimand devised a way around the tenure problem by making the Crown the nominal seigneur, and this allowed the subdivision of vast tracts of land for the Loyalists. In 1784, while surveying continued apace, thousands of Loyalists left Montréal and made their way upriver on barges and whatever other floating transportation they could muster. With their land, each Loyalist family was to be provided with clothing, provisions, and tools for a period of three years. It was a good deal for these displaced American colonists, and one unmatched in its generosity.

But the new colonists wanted to change their tenures. A petition in 1785 from Sir John Johnson, a prominent Loyalist leader, noted that "the Tenure of Lands in Canada is such as to subject them to the rigorous Rules, Homages and Reservations, and Restrictions of the French Laws and Customs, which are so different from the mild Tenures to which they had ever been accustomed." He proposed a new district, "distinct from the Province of Quebec" in the same manner as Cape Breton Island had been created separate from Nova Scotia, with English-style tenures. Johnson's petition stated that "the Inhabitants of this Territory, already amounting to several Thousands, conceive with all Humility that they have the strongest grounds to hope for such an exempt Jurisdiction as they ask for."

It took a while, but Johnson got what he and his fellow settlers wanted. In 1791, the British Parliament passed the Constitutional Act. It divided Québec into two provinces. The new one was called Upper Canada, and the rest of the old province of Québec was renamed Lower Canada; it was the first official use of the name Canada. The new province was to be governed by a lieutenant-governor, John Graves Simcoe, who would report to Guy Carleton, now returned as Lord Dorchester, in Québec. The system of land tenure was to be along English lines and distinct from that of Lower Canada. It provided for reserves of land to support a Protestant clergy, which would later lead to discontent. The act also provided for a Legislative Council (and a small Executive Council) appointed by the lieutenant-governor, and the appointees would hold office for life. There was also to be an elected assembly, but no law could pass without the approval of the Legislative Council. This measure would concentrate power in the hands of a few council members and the lieutenant-governor, an arrangement that would ultimately lead to a rebellion (see page 115). But the British government, having just faced the consequences of representative assemblies in the American colonies, was in no mood to be generous with its authority in the Canadas.

The Loyalists continued to arrive in Upper Canada. In 1791, at its inception, the province had about 30,000 people. Twenty years later the population had tripled to about 90,000. Simcoe was an energetic lieutenant-governor, in contrast to those who would follow him. He seconded troops to build roads to open up the country, established a judiciary, and abolished slavery, but was frustrated with the lack of support he got from Britain. He resigned in 1798. Nevertheless, a framework had been laid for what would grow into Canada's most populous and economically dynamic province.

98

Council-Office, Dec. 29, 1798.

YONGE-STREET.

NOTICE is hereby given to all persons settled, or about to settle on *YONGE-STREET*, and whose *locations* have not yet been confirmed by order of the PRESIDENT in council, that before such locations can be confirmed it will be expected that the following CONDITIONS be complied with :

First. That within *twelve months* from the time they are permitted to occupy their respective lots, they do cause to be erected thereon a good and sufficient dwelling house, of at least 16 feet by 20 in the clear, and do occupy the same in *Person*, or by a substantial *Tenant.*

Second, THAT within the same period of time, they do clear and fence *five* acres, of their respective lots, in a substantial manner.

Third, THAT within the same period of time, they do open as much of the Yonge-Street road as lies between the front of their lots and the middle of said road, amounting to one acre or thereabouts.

JOHN SMALL, C. E. C.

Giving and Taking

Under the terms of the Royal Proclamation of 1763, all of the British territories outside of the Province of Quebec, narrowly defined as the region either side of the St. Lawrence (see the map on page 80), were retained by the British Crown as Indian "hunting grounds." In recognition of the fact that "Great Frauds and Abuses" had occurred in the past, private individuals were forbidden from buying land directly from the native people.

Once a decision had been made to settle the Loyalists, government negotiators commenced to purchase lands as required. One of the areas purchased was the land on which Toronto now stands (see *right*), and which was occupied (in very small part) by Fort York at the time. The price paid for such lands was a pittance compared to their current worth, and whether the native peoples were fairly compensated, given values at the time, is a matter of ongoing debate. And it is not at all clear whether the native peoples' idea of the sale of their lands was the same as that of the purchasers. But the fact that the lands were negotiated and compensated for, rather than just taken, was a factor in the relative peace in Canada between Europeans and native peoples as compared to the situation in the United States, where not inconsequential Indian wars occurred in the 1790s.

Not all the land purchased and granted was for Euro-American loyalists. After 1783, when the land south of the Great Lakes became part of the American colonies, and later that decade the United States, Frederick Haldimand, governor of Québec, arranged for land to be purchased from the Mississauga and granted to some of the Six Nations Mohawk led by their chief, Thayendanegea, or Joseph Brant, in compensation for war losses. Brant had been one of the native chiefs most loyal to the British cause during the War of Independence. So valued were his services that he had been made a captain in the British army, although he fought as a war chief.

The land granted to Brant and his followers was 2 million acres (809 400 ha) in the Grand River Valley, 6 miles (10 km) from the river on each side. Brant thought the land would have to be farmed, being too small for hunting, and so sold off some of the land. This created a problem for the British, who at that time did not want to see native-owned land sold. But Brant considered that the terms of the Royal Proclamation did not apply to his tribe since they were not the original owners. Some of the European colonists welcomed by Brant settled at a place on the river they called Brant's ford, today Brantford, Ontario.

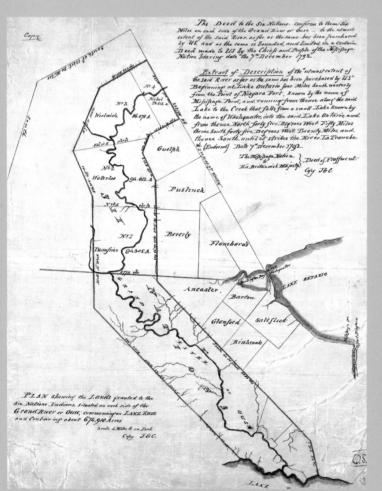

Left, top.
Mohawk chief Thayendanegea, known as Joseph Brant.

Left, bottom.
The grant of land to the Six Nations in 1784 is shown in this map, part of a deed of land drawn up in 1792. The Grand River flows into Lake Erie (at bottom). Lake Ontario is shown at right.

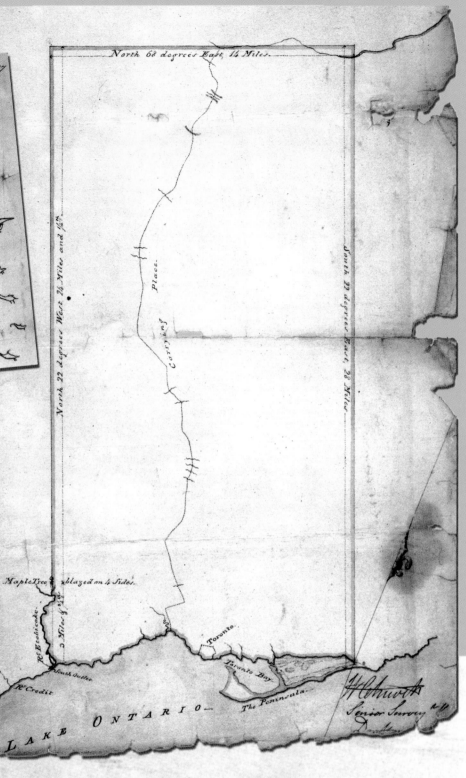

The front and back of the map accompanying the agreement with the Mississauga for the purchase of the land on which Toronto now stands. The original agreement was made in 1787 but no survey was made. The price was £1,700 and goods such as flour and cloth. In 1805, after the land had been surveyed, another agreement, shown here, was signed. The document was signed for the government by William Claus, deputy superintendent of Indian affairs, and by Chechalk and other chiefs for the Mississauga. *Below* is a view of Fort York in 1804.

Time Loyal Canadians to Shew Yourselves Worthy

Revolutionary France declared war on Britain in 1793, beginning a major European conflict that was to last, with a one-year hiatus in 1802, until the final fall of Napoleon in 1815. Since France had been allied with the American cause in the War of American Independence, the British authorities in Canada were immediately concerned that the Americans could join the war on the side of France, exploiting the fact that Britiain was necessarily preoccupied in Europe.

In fact it was the British who provoked the Americans. After Horatio Nelson's resounding victory over the French navy at Trafalgar in 1805, Britannia did indeed rule the waves and used naval superiority at any opportunity. In June 1807 HMS *Leopard* attacked USS *Chesapeake* after the latter refused to submit to a search for deserters. The attack caused outrage in the United States, and almost led to immediate war. Preparations were made on both sides. A recruiting broadsheet for the Canadian Fencibles Regiment (*fencible* was a term used for soldiers for de*fence*) in 1807 declared: "Now is your time loyal Canadians to shew yourselves worthy of the glorious constitution under which you enjoy so much happiness."

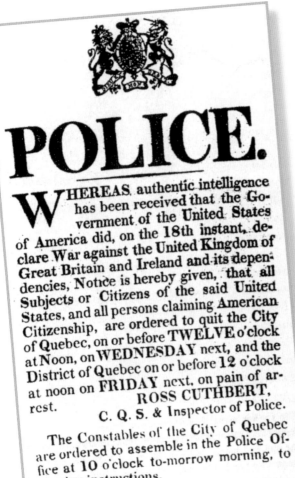

The British next declared that all neutral ships—that is, American—carrying supplies to Napoleon would be regarded as enemies, which infuriated the Americans and led them to impose a total trade embargo. By 1812, the level of outrage in the United States had risen to boiling point. A group of politicians, the so-called war hawks, demanded action. The Maritimes were not a potential target, because of British sea power, but Upper and Lower Canada were. It seemed to some (perhaps not those to heed history) that the Canadas were "ripe for the plucking." And what could be easier? In Thomas Jefferson's famous words, it was "a mere matter of marching." He ought to have known better. Nevertheless, on 18 June 1812, the United States declared war on Britain.

On the face on it, the odds look overwhelmingly in the American favour. A nation by this time of seven and a half million, the United States had an immediate army of 35,000 men. The Canadas and the Maritime provinces, by comparison, had a population of perhaps 600,000 and an army, to start, of only about 5,000 men, although 1,500 of them were redcoats, experienced soldiers hardened from the almost continuous war in Europe. The Americans had many inexperienced militia, and they had not fought a war, except against native people, for thirty years. And the British had Brock.

Major General Isaac Brock was a man in the right place at the right time. Possessed of nerves of steel and a brilliant military mind, he believed the best defence was attack. And attack he did, right away, for he knew it was essential to encourage natives to join the British side to compensate for small numbers. The best way of doing this was to provide quick evidence that the British would win the war. Brock dispatched an order to the commander of the British Fort St. Joseph, close to where the three largest Great Lakes meet, telling him to attack the American fort at Michilimackinac nearby. The early morning operation, on 17 July, was carried out so fast that the American commander woke up to find his fort besieged and infilrated before he had even heard that war had been declared. The scheme worked; native warriors streamed to the British side.

Then Brock pulled off an even bigger coup. On 12 July an American army under General William Hull crossed the Detroit River from his fort at

Detroit, the first invasion of Canadian soil. Expecting the population, which contained many Americans, to rush to his side, Hull issued a proclamation offering "freedom from oppression and tyranny." But few rushed to join him and, worried about his supply lines, he retreated back across the river to his fort. Brock's army, accompanied by native warriors under their chief, Tecumseh, crossed the river and laid siege to Detroit. Brock carefully made his small army look much larger than it was and, knowing Hull to be terrified of a native massacre, fed him threats. "You must be aware," he wrote in a note to Hull, "that the numerous body of Indians who have attached themselves to my troops will be beyond control the moment the contest commences." On 16 August, an intimidated Hull surrendered. It was a stunning victory for Brock. Hull surrendered not only Detroit and his army, but all of Michigan Territory.

Brock, guardian of too many frontiers, hurried back to the Niagara Peninsula, where the next American attack was expected. Troops had massed on the east side of the Niagara River, and on 13 October, they crossed near Queenston, easily taking a defensive position above the village, Queenston Heights. Brock's army had been dispersed along the

Above.
The Battle of Queenston Heights. The heroic Brock lies dying as he urges his troops onward.

Opposite, top.
A portrait of Isaac Brock.

Opposite, bottom.
A broadsheet issued in Québec at the beginning of the War of 1812, warning Americans to leave.

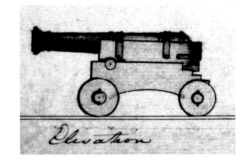

river, since he did not know exactly where the Americans would attack. Brock was at Fort George, a British fort at the mouth of the Niagara, when news of the attack came. Hurrying to Queenston, he impetuously attempted to retake the Heights without waiting for reinforcements that were on their way. He was killed by an American sniper. The Heights were retaken later that day by troops now led by Roger Hale Sheaffe, Brock's second-in-command, taking a thousand American prisoners. But the British, and Canada, had lost their inspiring leader. He would be worshipped as a hero and saviour for a century, and to this day Queenston Heights is topped by a tall monument bearing aloft his statue. Brock became an enduring Canadian legend.

Fort York was chronically short of armaments during the War of 1812. Old cannon which had been moved to the fort by Lieutenant-Governor Simcoe in 1793 had by 1807 been condemned as unserviceable and had their trunnions and buttons cut off. Yet in 1813, with the army desperate for firepower, several cannon were resurrected for service. The two old cannon pictured here, known as the Simcoe guns, were used against the American invaders in 1813 and survive today. One (*above*) was made about 1657 for Oliver Cromwell; the other (*right*) was made in England between 1737 and 1754. *Below* is a view of Fort York today.

Both the British and the Americans recognized that control of the lakes could be crucial, and throughout the war an arms race of sorts took place, with ships being built as fast as possible. An American fleet was constructed at Sackets Harbor at the east end of Lake Ontario. On 10 November 1812 the little fleet, commanded by Isaac Chauncey, chased the British ship *Royal George* into Kingston Harbour, all the while fighting a pitched battle with the shore defences.

On 22 April the following year Chauncey embarked 1,700 men under General Henry Dearborn on fifteen armed ships and sailed for York, arriving in the afternoon of 26 April. The next day at dawn, a force led by Brigadier General Zebulon Pike, of western exploration fame, attacked the British, under Roger Sheaffe. The British were outnumbered and Sheaffe it seems did a poor job of directing the defence. By early afternoon he decided to evacuate

and withdrew his troops east, towards Kingston. During the retreat Sheaffe ordered the destruction of a ship that was nearing completion on the stocks, in order to prevent it falling into American hands, and the blowing up of the powder magazine. This dealt the Americans a devastating blow. Casualties rose to 322 killed and wounded. York was sacked and the Parliament buildings burned.

The next offensive was a similar British attack, this time on the American base at Sackets Harbor. A newly arrived commodore, James Lucas Yeo, led the attack with a contingent of Royal Navy men rather than the less well trained provincials. Much damage was done, but Chauncey's fleet was not there and so the damage was not critical.

The next part of the American plan was the taking of the Niagara Peninsula. In May 1813, American troops under Lieutenant Colonel Winfield Scott attacked Fort George. The British under Brigadier General John Vincent were defeated and retreated west, but after a three-day delay were pursued by the Americans. The same day Fort Erie was abandoned by the British. On the night of 5–6 June Vincent turned on his pursuers with a plan to attack the American encampment at night. Although outnumbered, a force led by Lieutenant Colonel John Harvey managed to inflict heavy losses on the confused American force at Stoney Creek. Both of their commanding brigadier generals were taken prisoner.

On 23 June an American force was sent from Fort George to attack Vincent's advance post now at Beaver Dams (Thorold), just to the west of the fort. A Queenston woman, Laura Secord, overheard talk of the raid and set off across country to warn the British force. In fact,

Opposite, bottom.
The American attack on York, 27 April 1813, a painting by Owen Staples. The flag is flying above Fort York as Chauncey's ships bombard it. The tiny settlement of York is farther away, beyond the fort.

Above.
The dramatic and decisive engagement of Oliver Perry's force with that of Robert Barclay at Put-in-Bay on Lake Erie on 10 September 1813. The victory gave the Americans control of southwestern Upper Canada, as no supplies could then reach Colonel Henry Proctor at Amherstburg. This modern depiction of the battle is by Ontario artist Peter Rindlisbacher.

although forewarned, the British still did not know when the assault might come, and not until native scouts discovered the American force could anything be done. When they did, a Caughnawaga force of three hundred under Captain Dominique Ducharme of the Indian Department attacked the Americans. They were later joined by a hundred Mohawk, and later still by fifty regular troops. The Americans hastily surrendered to the regulars, under Lieutenant James Fitzgibbon, in order, they hoped, to avoid brutal treatment by the natives. The American commander Henry Dearborn lost his job over this defeat, and another enduring legend entered Canadian consciousness, that of Laura Secord bravely risking all by trekking overland to warn of the American advance.

By the end of 1813, the American position on the Niagara Peninsula had become untenable. In December they withdrew across the river after burning, quite unnecessarily, the little town of Newark, now Niagara-on-the-Lake. The British advance continued on to American territory with the taking of Fort Niagara, the one-time French fort at the mouth of the Niagara River on Lake Ontario. It would remain in British hands until war's end.

In the west, the war did not go so well for the British. The Americans, under naval commander Oliver Hazard Perry, built a number of ships at Presqu'Ile (Erie, Pennsylvania) and managed to launch then, unarmed, into the lake without attack. The British fleet, under Captain Robert Barclay, was woefully underequipped, despite using cannon from Fort Malden, but nevertheless engaged the Americans at Put-in-Bay, just south of Pelee Island, now Canada's southernmost point, on 10 September 1813. Despite putting up a brave fight, the British were defeated, and with their defeat went the control of the entire lake—and western Upper Canada.

The British land commander in the area, Colonel Henry Proctor, realizing his position was now hopeless, retreated east along the Thames River valley with his regular troops, supported by native warriors under their chief, Tecumseh, who did not want to retreat. They were pursued by a much larger American force under Major General William Harrison, governor of Indiana Territory. Near Moraviantown on 5 October, the two sides fought a short battle during which Tecumseh was killed. Harrison could have now pressed farther east, but instead he chose to be safe and withdrew to Detroit.

In the east the Americans mounted the third prong of their attack on the Canadas that year. A force led by Major General James Wilkinson was to descend the St. Lawrence towards Montréal, while at the same time Major General Wade Hampton was to advance north along the Lake Champlain–Rivière Richelieu route.

Hampton's force crossed into Lower Canada on 20 September, but met with resistance at the Lacolle River and so turned westwards to the Châteauguay River, which flows into the St. Lawrence just above Montréal. They were met near Ormstown by a native and Voltigeur force led by Lieutenant Colonel Charles-Michel d'Irumberry de Salaberry. The latter force, formed by Salaberry, were a light infantry, near-guerilla group of Canadiens. Although vastly outnumbered by the Americans, they succeeded in turning them back. This was the Battle of Châteauguay, fought on 25 October 1813.

Wilkinson's army, meanwhile, had moved down the St. Lawrence, passing Fort Wellington, at Prescott, by landing his troops on the American side and floating their boats down the river under cover of darkness. A short distance downstream he was stopped on 11 November by a British force, again much smaller than their opposition, under Lieutenant Colonel Joseph Morrison. This Battle of Crysler's Farm, together with that of Châteauguay, had saved Montréal from the invaders.

The American government intended that the next objective of the war should be Kingston, but through mismanagement this was not conveyed to the new field commander, Major General Jacob Brown. Instead, in 1814 the Americans again focused on the Niagara Frontier. But this was not to be the Americans' year, for the war in Europe was winding down and Britain would be able to commit many more battle-experienced troops to North America.

On 3 July 1814 another American invasion began. Brown took his army across the Niagara just above the falls while a force under now Brigadier General Winfield Scott crossed near Fort Erie, which was taken later that day. Scott advanced northwards and defeated Major General Phineas Riall, moving south from Fort George, at the Chippewa River on 5 July. The Americans now intended to retake York, but planned naval support from Chauncey did not materialize, and this gave the British time to regroup. Lieutenant General Gordon Drummond rushed from York to command a now reinforced army.

The American army under Major General James Wilkinson comes ashore on the north bank of the St. Lawrence above Prescott in preparation for the battle that would be named after John Crysler's farm, fought on 11 November 1813, by coincidence the eleventh day of the eleventh month that would become the Armistice Day of a much larger war in the next century. In 1813 an Anglo-Canadian force of only 800 turned back 4,000 Americans. The painting is by Peter Rindlisbacher.

Above.
The death of Tecumseh at the Battle of the Thames or Moraviantown, fought 5 October 1813.

Below.
This idyllic scene is the site of the battle of Châteauguay, fought on 25 October 1813.

The armies met once near Niagara Falls late in the afternoon of 25 July. A hard-fought battle took place at Lundy's Lane in which there were heavy casualties on both sides, and Generals Drummond, Riall, Brown, and Scott were all wounded. Riall was captured when his stretcher-bearers, unable to see in the smoke and the twilight, carried him into the American lines. Although the Americans captured the British artillery in hand-to-hand fighting, the battle was not conclusive; there are arguments today as to who won. The Americans withdrew after midnight, but the British were too exhausted to pursue them.

British reinforcements were on their way to Niagara, however, whereas the Americans had none. The American offensive had stalled. In November the Americans recrossed the river, abandoning Fort Erie.

The initiative now passed to the British, who, vastly reinforced by troops from the European front, landed in Chesapeake Bay and marched to Washington in August, setting afire the Capitol and the presidential residence, making President James Madison flee for his life. The latter, when rebuilt, was whitewashed to hide the effects of the fire, and thus became the "White House." In September Baltimore was attacked, though successfully defended by the Americans. It was here, at Fort McHenry, that Francis Scott Key penned the words that became the American national anthem; the "rocket's red glare, the bombs bursting in air" were British. The invaders re-embarked two days later and sailed for Halifax.

At the same time as the coastal attacks on the United States, the British had been planning an invasion south via Lake Champlain. Led by a cautious Sir George Prevost, governor general of the Canadas and commander-in-chief of British North America, a force of more than ten thousand got as far as Plattsburgh, New York, on the west side of Lake Champlain. However, after a naval defeat on the lake on 11 September Prevost retreated to Lower Canada, having been told "not to prejudice his lines of communication by too extended a line of advance."

In Europe, the British and American governments had been trying to negotiate a peace settlement since July. An agreement was finally reached in December, and the Treaty of Ghent, ending the war, was signed on Christmas Eve 1814. But, as always, communication was slow, and fighting continued. A British offensive against New Orleans had begun on 1 December, although by Christmas it had stalled. In January 1815 more than two thousand British soldiers were killed or wounded in another attack, and on 11 February the British besieged Fort Bowyer, at the entrance to Mobile Bay, east of New Orleans. It was then that news of the peace reached North America. War, more often than not a senseless squandering of lives, had for the previous six weeks been a particular waste.

When the peace negotiations had started in July 1814, the British commissioners had been instructed that "retention of conquered territory" should be demanded. After the failures of the August and September invasions, however, the British position softened. On the advice of the Duke of Wellington the British decided that a simple retention of the pre-war boundaries would be acceptable, and this was agreed to in the treaty.

In 1817 an understanding was signed by both countries to limit any future arms race on the Great Lakes, which, it was thought, probably correctly, would make it impossible for either side to gain a military advantage. This agreement has been hailed by some as the beginning of the so-called undefended border, although much distrust and defensive building would later occur in Canada to ensure no American attack could succeed. The final act of the War of 1812 occurred in 1818, when a convention further defined the boundary between the two countries and, in particular, defined the boundary between Lake of the Woods and the Rockies as the forty-ninth parallel, where it remains to this day.

Above.
The signing of the Treaty of Ghent, 24 December 1814. This painting by Amedee Forestier in entitled *A Hundred Years of Peace.*

Below.
The boundary between the United States and British territory as shown on an American map of 1818, the year this guesswork was replaced by a boundary of the forty-ninth parallel between Lake of the Woods and the Rocky Mountains. The boundary's extension to the Pacific would not be agreed upon until 1846. The Selkirk Grant, land given to Lord Selkirk by the Hudson's Bay Company in 1816 for the establishment of the Red River Colony (see page 109), is also shown.

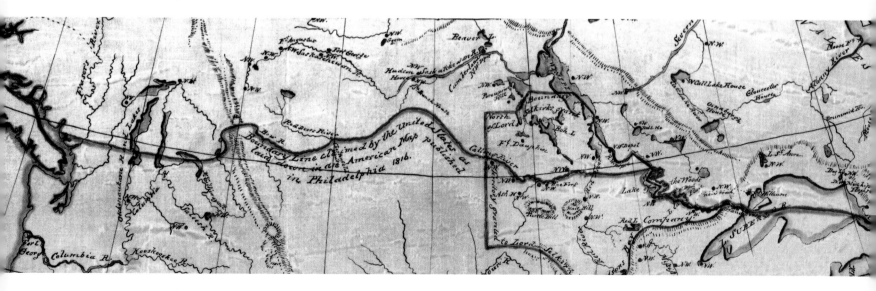

6 *Fur Trade and Exploration*

From the time Europeans reached Canada, they pursued the promise of wealth. After Canada made its presence felt as a formidable barrier to those who would sail west, the wealth of the wilderness—fur—was quickly discovered. Until Alexander Mackenzie actually reached a western sea overland in 1793, explorers and fur traders expected the ocean to appear momentarily over the next horizon. Men pushed west to find always more furs, and finally to find an easier way to ship them out, trying to get around the Hudson's Bay Company's monopoly of its inland sea.

Left.
Portaging a York boat. This photograph was taken at the Mountain Portage on the Slave River, between Lake Athabasca and Great Slave Lake, in 1901.

By the time the British took over the French fur trade out of Montréal in 1763, the boundaries of that trade had already been extended far to the west. The French had little option. After 1713 the Treaty of Utrecht had given Hudson Bay to the British and so a network of trading posts was established, with Montréal as their anchor. At its western end, a fort was built in 1713 at Kaministiquia, at the western end of Lake Superior, and strengthened and rebuilt in 1717. A post was built at Rainy Lake in 1718, but not continuously occupied, and smaller outposts were established at Nipigon and Michipicoten.

In 1728 Pierre Gaultier de Varennes et de La Vérendrye was given the task of exploring to the west, finding a River of the West or the Western Sea and establishing more fur trade posts. Together with his sons and a nephew, La Vérendrye vastly expanded the region known to the French, although considerably more would likely have been achieved if the French government had not made La Vérendrye finance his own explorations from his fur trading. Naturally enough, he did not find the River of the West or the Western Sea, although he did find Lake Winnipeg and, as he put it, "a sea of beaver."

Hunting beaver, painted by James Isham while governor of the Hudson's Bay Company's Fort Churchill in 1743.

In 1731 Fort St. Pierre was established at Rainy Lake and the following year Fort St. Charles was built on Lake of the Woods. In 1734 Fort Maurepas (named after the French Minister of Marine) was constructed on the lower Red River, which flows into Lake Winnipeg. At the urging of the French government the La Vérendryes struck out farther west, establishing

Fort La Reine on the Assiniboine River near today's Portage la Prairie in 1738. An exploration in 1738–39 is thought to have taken La Vérendrye to the Mandan villages on the Missouri, but, for him, the river flowed in the wrong direction. This was the very same river that Americans Meriwether Lewis and William Clark would follow on their successful trek to the Pacific in 1803–06.

In 1741–42 Fort Dauphin was established on Lake Dauphin and another fort (Fort Bourbon) where Cedar Lake meets Lake Winnipeg. In 1742–43 La Vérendrye's sons made a far-ranging exploration that may have reached as far west as the Big Horn Mountains, an outlying range of the Rockies. It seems certain that they were in the vicinity of Pierre, North Dakota, for a lead plate proclaiming possession for Louis XV was unearthed in 1913, and is thought to be genuine.

During this period, the British fur traders working for the Hudson's Bay Company were largely content to stay on the shores of the bay and let natives bring furs to them (see page 54). But with the fall of New France in 1763, British—actually mainly Scottish—traders moved into Montréal and took over the existing French fur trade empire. Lacking governmental control they could be much more aggressive than the French, and they soon moved to cut off the flow of furs moving to Hudson Bay by establishing themselves farther upstream. By 1775 traders were operating in groups to better finance the long time frame required to buy trade goods and exchange them for furs. This led to the emergence in 1783–84 of the North West Company, which until 1821 would prove to be the bane of the Hudson's Bay Company.

Certain of Its Being the Sea

The Hudson's Bay Company made few attempts to explore inland. Anthony Henday was dispatched in 1754 and may have reached the vicinity of Red Deer, Alberta, but there is considerable doubt about his route. In December 1770, after two failed attempts, Samuel Hearne was sent into the interior to look for copper—and the Northwest Passage. He was dispatched by Moses Norton from Prince of Wales Fort to follow up reports collected from native sources, and he took with him the Chipewyan chief Matonabbee and an entourage that included the chief's wives and two hundred others. It was just as well that Matonabbee came along, for Hearne would have become hopelessly lost had he not.

After a meandering trek across the maze of lakes and rivers of the Barren Lands, Hearne arrived at the Coppermine River on 13 July 1771. A few days later the reason Matonabbee had taken along such a large number of his fellow warriors became obvious. An Inuit encampment was found, and despite Hearne's protestations he could do nothing but watch as the Chipewyan proceeded to attack and massacre the Inuit, whom they considered their natural enemies. Hearne noted that the natives, normally an "undisciplined rabble,"

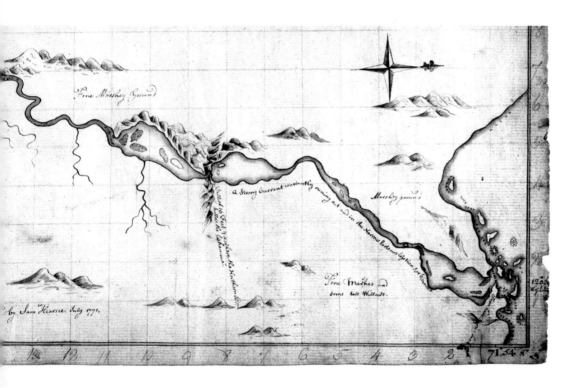

Above.
Samuel Hearne and part of his map of the Coppermine River and the Arctic Ocean, which he reached on 17 July 1771. The place where the Inuit were massacred is shown with the notation *Fall of 16 Feet & is where the Northern Ind[ia]ns killd the Eskamaux.* Hearne called it Bloody Falls.

suddenly became "united in the general cause" of the attack. Hearne was shocked; "The terror of my mind at beholding this butchery," he wrote, "cannot easily be conceived, much less described."

Later that day, 17 July, Hearne arrived at the edge of the Arctic Ocean, at Coronation Gulf. "The tide being out, the water in the river was perfectly fresh," he noted, "but I am certain of its being the sea, or some branch of it, by the quantity of whalebone and seal-skins which the Esquimaux had at their tents, and also by the number of seals I saw on the ice."

Hearne incorrectly calculated his latitude. He was at 67° 49′ N but he thought he was at 71° 54′ N (shown on the map at left). This discrepancy of about 450 km did not alter the fact that there could not be a Northwest Passage south of this latitude.

In 1772 and 1773 Matthew Cocking journeyed west from York Fort to encourage natives to come down to the bay to trade. He may have reached as far west as the current Alberta-Saskatchewan boundary. On his travels he kept meeting rival "pedlars" (independent fur traders) from Montréal and realized that the Hudson's Bay Company was losing a considerable amount of trade to these interlopers who traded with the natives inland, saving them the long journey to the bay. The result was that in 1774 Samuel Hearne was sent to establish the company's first inland trading post, Cumberland House, on the Saskatchewan River.

Above.
Hudson's Bay Company fur bale stamp.

Below.
The fur storage room at the North West Company's Fort Carlton, on the North Saskatchewan River.

To Russia with Love

The trespassers on the Governor and Company of Adventurers' monopoly were to become much more troublesome. In 1778, one of them, Peter Pond, became the first European to cross into the Mackenzie watershed, which opened up a vast new fur region. The furs here were better, because of the winter cold, and were thus worth more. However, the distances from Montréal were becoming greater and greater. It was the financing benefits that could accrue to a large organization in such endeavours that encouraged the disparate traders to band together, loosely at first. The large partnership called the North West Company, formed in 1783–84, quickly established a network of trading posts where wintering partners spent that season collecting furs, and a collection staging point at Grand Portage, at the western end of Lake Superior. They created an efficient transportation system consisting of large canoes between Montréal and Grand Portage, and smaller "north canoes" for use west of that point. Suddenly the Hudson's Bay Company had some real competition.

Peter Pond was by all accounts an extraordinarily good fur trader, the one who always seemed to gather the most and the best furs—and make the most money. Semi-literate, he had a knack of communicating with natives, and in addition to making the best deals this enabled him to elicit knowledge from them about the geography of the country beyond his location at the time. In this way, over several years, Pond composed maps of the river and lake system of the Northwest that were remarkably accurate for someone without surveying equipment or knowledge—except in one important

regard. Pond did not know how to measure longitude, which was difficult even for a trained surveyor in those days, involving long astronomical observations and calculations. But Pond did find out about James Cook's voyage to the west coast of Canada in 1778, likely from an American book published by one of Cook's crew before publication of the official account in 1784. From this he discovered the correct longitude of the west coast; Cook had the knowledge to survey accurately and also had the then new and experimental chronometers on board. Putting together the accurate west coast with his own accurately mapped but incorrectly positioned map, Pond drew another map that showed that the rivers and lakes of the Northwest were remarkably close to the Pacific.

Pond left the Northwest in 1788, under suspicion of murdering another fur trader, but not before he had spent the previous winter with an upcoming young partner with an adventurous spirit, one Alexander Mackenzie. Pond drew a map for Mackenzie to deliver to Catherine, Empress of Russia. For Mackenzie was off to the Pacific Ocean, where he thought he would surely find Russian fur traders who would take him back to Russia.

Above.
North West Company emblem, a reproduction photographed at Grand Portage, now in Minnesota.

From Canada by Land

Following Pond's map, Mackenzie set off for the Pacific in 1789 from his base at Fort Chipewyan, on Lake Athabasca. He followed the river that the map (*below*) showed flowing out of the western end of Great Slave Lake. This he expected to lead to Cook's River, actually Cook Inlet, Alaska, which James Cook had partially explored in 1778 (shown on the map at the extreme left). But the river he was descending, which would come to be known as the Mackenzie, flowed not to the Pacific but to the Arctic, and this is where Alexander ended up; on 12 July he reached what he initially thought was a lake but which he soon determined was indeed the Arctic Ocean. He continued as far north as Garry Island, which he called Whale Island, off the Mackenzie Delta, where one morning his equipment was soaked by rising water. This he recognized as the tide.

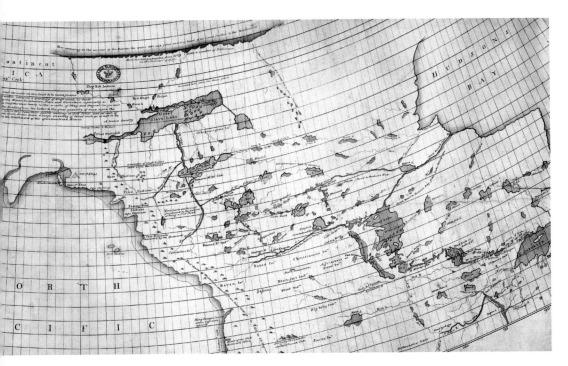

Left, centre.
The Methye Portage, or Portage La Loche, showing the Clearwater River, which flows into the Athabasca and ultimately into the Mackenzie and the Arctic Ocean. It was this entrance to the Mackenzie watershed that Peter Pond found in 1778. The view was painted by George Back, with John Franklin on his second land expedition in 1825.

Left.
Part of a contemporary copy (the original is lost) of Peter Pond's map of the Northwest that he gave to Alexander Mackenzie in 1788 to guide him to Russia. The longitude of the west coast is correct; Pond's delineation of the rivers and lakes is also reasonably accurate, but the relationship of the two is wrong, giving the impression of an easy journey from one to the other. This is the map that would inspire Mackenzie in 1789.

It had become obvious to Mackenzie that he needed better navigating skills, and so he went to England in 1791–92 to buy instruments and learn how to use them. He had come to realize during his 1789 expedition that he should have "turned left" somewhere along his original route. Now he knew where: it was the Unjigah, or Peace River. He was back at Fort Chipewyan by the end of the summer of 1792. In October he left the fort for a temporary one on the Peace River, Fort Fork, where he would overwinter in order to give himself a head start in the spring. He still expected to meet Russians on the west coast. He wrote to his cousin Roderick McKenzie, "I send you a couple of Guineas. The rest I take with me to traffick with the Russsians."

Mackenzie left Fort Fork in May and, following native advice, took the southern branch when the Peace River split into two. This was the Parsnip River, and at its headwaters he found a short portage to water flowing in the opposite direction. It was a tributary of the Pacific-bound Fraser River. But what waters they were. It took Mackenzie and his crew a wet week to descend the short tributary, which he called the Bad River. Then he was on the Fraser, but soon learned that this river was nearly impossible to canoe farther downriver, and so was persuaded to set off overland to the west, following a native "grease trail," used for the trade in oolichan oil. On 20 July 1793, Mackenzie reached Pacific waters at Bella Coola, on tidewater though quite far inland from the open ocean. After borrowing a sea-going canoe from the Nuxalk (Bella Coola), two days later he reached a rock on Dean Channel, which, since he was now harassed by Heiltsuk (Bella Bella), proved to be his farthest west. Here he left his famous

Sir Alexander Mackenzie Crossing the Rockies, 1793, a painting by Arthur Heming. This scene shows the Bad River, or James Creek, which took Mackenzie a week to descend.

inscription: "Alexander Mackenzie, from Canada, by land, 22nd July 1793." It is amazing how many people today do not understand this inscription, not realizing that the Canadas in 1793 stopped at the Great Lakes; beyond this was merely doubtful British territory claimed by Spain as well as Britain and still in reality in the hands of the native people.

Claims, Clashes, and Co-operation

The first European claim to what is now the west coast of Canada was Spanish, not British, as is often thought. Spanish navigator Juan Josef Pérez Hernández arrived on the coast four years before James Cook, sent to investigate reports received in New Spain (Mexico) of Russian incursions southward into what the Spanish regarded as very much their own territory.

Pérez sailed as far north as Dixon Entrance and Langara Island, at the northern tip of the Queen Charlotte Islands. This location would later be used to fix the southern extent of the Alaska Panhandle when the latitude, 54° 40´ N, had come to be accepted as the southern limit of Russian claims against the Spanish before the American purchase of Alaska in 1867. Pérez's map of the west coast was the first of coastal British Columbia from actual exploration, rather than guesswork, of which there had been plenty.

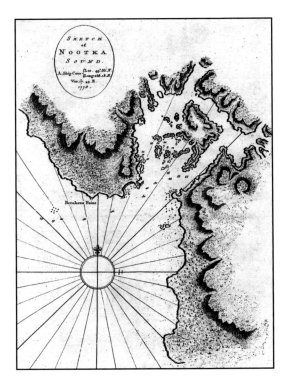

In 1778 James Cook arrived on the Northwest Coast on his way to probe Bering Strait for a western entrance to the Northwest Passage. He spent a month at Resolution Cove (named after his ship), on Bligh Island in Nootka Sound, a spacious harbour on the west coast of Vancouver Island. During that time, Cook very accurately determined his longitude; this for the first time fixed the location of Canada's west coast and established the width not only of Canada but also of the North American continent.

Not to be outdone by Cook, the French dispatched Jean-François Galaup, Comte de La Pérouse, on a round-the-world scientific voyage, and as part of this venture La Pérouse visited the Northwest Coast in 1786. He produced a considerably better map of the coast than had Cook, but it was not published until 1797, the year before George Vancouver's detailed survey was published. Thus the French work received less recognition than it deserved.

In the wake of Cook's voyage a number of British fur traders appeared on the coast, seeking to cash in on the fur of the sea otter. Cook had traded for the latter and later sold the pelts in Canton for a very high price, for the fur is very dense and fine. Thus began a search for the unfortunate sea otter that would lead almost to its extinction.

Above.
Britain's greatest navigator, James Cook, whose third voyage brought him to the west coast of Canada.

Right.
Cook's published map of Nootka Sound. Resolution Cove is shown by an anchor at a point marked *A* and keyed as *Ship Cove.*

Below.
In 1790 a Spanish flag flies above the fort at what they called Puerto de la Santa Cruz de Nuca, or Cala de Los Amigos, "Friendly Cove," today Yuquot, on Nootka Sound, on the west coast of Vancouver Island.

First to arrive on the coast, in 1785, was James Hanna, sailing from Macao. He traded many sea otter pelts, but when he returned the following year he had less success, finding other traders ahead of him. The rush was on. Many of Cook's ex-officers persuaded investors that they could make them a fast buck.

Bombay merchants with the East India Company sent two ships in 1786 under the overall direction of James Strange. He decided to leave an assistant surgeon, John Mackay, on the coast when they departed, with orders to foster a trading relationship with the natives and record vocabulary and customs. Unfortunately for Mackay, Strange's ships never returned, but he was rescued in June 1787 by another trader, Charles Barkley.

Nathaniel Portlock and George Dixon were also on the coast in 1786 and 1787, on behalf of the King George's Sound Company, which took its moniker from Cook's name for Nootka Sound. Dixon found and mapped the Queen Charlotte Islands and his name survives as Dixon Entrance, that rough passage at the northern end of the Islands. Another trader, Charles Barkley, Mackay's rescuer, found the Strait of Juan de Fuca, which "long lost strait" he named after the Greek pilot said to have discovered the strait for the Spanish in 1592, although De Fuca's account has never been substantiated.

Perhaps the most colourful character in this coastal fur trade was British naval captain John Meares. He was responsible for aggrandizing an international incident that led Spain and Britain to the brink of war in 1790. Meares first came to the coast in 1786, but made the big mistake of trying to overwinter with his ship in Alaska; only nine of his crew had survived the ravages of scurvy and cold by the time they were rescued by Portlock and Dixon in May 1787.

In 1788, Meares was back. With him was William Douglas, and their two ships flew Portuguese colours to try to circumvent an East India Company monopoly on the sale of furs in China. In May, Meares built a house at Friendly Cove, the first European settlement of any sort in western Canada, and also left one of his officers, Robert Funter, to build a forty-ton shallow-draft boat; this was the first European boat ever constructed on the west coast of Canada.

In 1789 the Spanish, moving northwards once again to investigate reports of Russian incursions, briefly established themselves in Nootka Sound. The Spanish commander, Estéban José Martínez, picked a fight with William Douglas and, maintaining that Douglas was trespassing on Spanish territory, seized his furs and trade goods, charts and journals. Martínez later confiscated the ship of another trader in the Meares group, James Colnett. When Meares, now back in England, heard of Douglas's mistreatment, he resolved to cause some mischief for the Spanish.

Meares presented a "memorial" to the British Parliament in which he listed so-called insults to the British flag. The prime minister, William Pitt (the younger), appropriated the issue to force Spain—under threat of war—to recognize the British right to occupy areas claimed but not actually settled by Spain. In other words, sovereignty would now follow not from mere discovery and claim but only from actual occupation. This principle would work to Britain's advantage since Spain had claimed vast amounts of territory that had never actually been occupied—the entire Pacific Ocean, for example. It would also remove the Spanish claim to the Northwest Coast north of the Strait of Juan de Fuca—the region that would one day be Canada. Two years later, under this new pact, called the Nootka Convention, George Vancouver would arrive at Nootka Sound charged with receiving back the territories seized from British subjects—Meares

James Cook's ship *Endeavour*, with *Discovery* behind, is approached by native canoes in Nootka Sound. This 1778 scene was painted by British Columbia artist Harry Heine in 1978 as part of a bicentennial commemoration of the famous navigator's visit.

and the other traders in his group—which amounted in fact to only a small plot of land on which Meares had built a house, but the size of which he had exaggerated.

While fur trading continued, the Spanish were interested in bigger things, for they considered it possible that this part of the coast hid the western entrance to the Northwest Passage, although the British knew this was unlikely because of Samuel Hearne's journey in 1771 (see page 100). Between 1790 and 1792 the Spanish mounted an all-out effort to ensure there was no passage in this region that the British might find before them.

Francisco de Eliza arrived at Nootka Sound in April 1790 and proceeded to build a settlement and a fort, manned by seventy-five soldiers under Pedro Alberni, who is remembered in British Columbia as being its first gardener. Eliza sent Salvador Fidalgo to Alaska to check out the Russians and dispatched Manuel Quimper into the Strait of Juan de Fuca. Deceived by the San Juan Islands, Quimper thought that the strait had a closed end.

The following year Eliza himself sailed into the Strait of Juan de Fuca, accompanied by a smaller boat for exploring shallow waters, the *Santa Saturnina,* commanded by José María Narváez. From Esquimalt Harbour a longboat, under ensign José Verdía, was sent to explore northwards into Haro Strait. Verdía was attacked by natives and hastily returned, but trying again, this time better armed, he found that the narrow channel opened out into a large body of water. Following up on this discovery, Narváez was sent north in the *Santa Saturnina.* He entered the Strait of Georgia and for three weeks sailed northwards, reaching beyond Texada Island, and in the process becoming the first European to explore the area that is now the city of Vancouver. At the end of the season, Eliza drew a map of southern Vancouver Island and the adjacent coasts called the *Carta que comprehende* ("map of what is known"), which stands as a remarkable testament to Spanish knowledge *before* George Vancouver arrived on the scene the following year.

The meeting of Spanish commander Juan Francisco de la Bodega y Quadra with British emissary George Vancouver at Friendly Cove in 1792 to negotiate a conclusion to the Nootka Convention of 1790. This stained glass window was presented to Canada by the Spanish government in 1957 and is now in the church at Yuquot.

The last Spanish voyage of exploration in what is now Canada took place in 1792. Two officers were detached from the Spanish round-the-world scientific voyage of Alejandro Malaspina (the Spanish counterpart to the voyages of Cook for Britain and La Pérouse for France). They were Dionisio Alcalá Galiano and Cayetano Valdes, in command of the *Sútil* and the *Mexicana,* respectively, small *goletas* suitable for shallow water. After taking their commanding officer, Juan Francisco de la Bodega y Quadra, to Nootka Sound, where he was to meet with Vancouver, Galiano and Valdes set off on a major survey that would take them completely around Vancouver Island, which (because they started and ended at Nootka) they were the first to circumnavigate.

They entered the Strait of Georgia in June 1792 and met the *Chatham,* under William Broughton, George Vancouver's second-in-command. Later they met also with Vancouver at a location close to today's city of the same name, commemorated locally in the name Spanish Banks, and from there co-operated with Vancouver in a survey of the northern part of the Strait of Georgia.

George Vancouver's epic survey of the Northwest Coast from California to Alaska took him three years, and in 1792 he was just beginning. Vancouver was charged with determining once and for all whether a western entrance to the Northwest Passage existed south of Bering Strait. Thus he examined in minute detail, usually using boats, what he referred to as the "continental shore"—the mainland coast. And he had to penetrate to the end of every one of the hundreds of inlets that line the British Columbia coast. It was a mammoth undertaking requiring infinite patience.

Vancouver sailed into the Strait of Juan de Fuca with his two ships, *Discovery* and *Chatham,* and first explored Puget Sound to the south before turning northwards, naming the strait he found—and initially thought a gulf—Georgia, after his king. When he met Galiano near the city of Vancouver, Galiano showed him Nárvaez's map of the previous year. Vancouver admitted to his journal that he "experienced no small degree of mortification in finding the external shores of the gulf had already been visited, and already examined." Vancouver also learned from Galiano that Bodega y Quadra was waiting for him at Nootka to transfer lands as agreed in the Nootka Convention. What he did not realize was that Bodega y Quadra intended to transfer the small area once occupied by John Meares's house, whereas Vancouver was expecting the transfer of the entire Northwest Coast, based on the prior claims of Francis Drake in 1579. As gentlemen, they would agree to disagree, and refer the matter to their respective higher authorities.

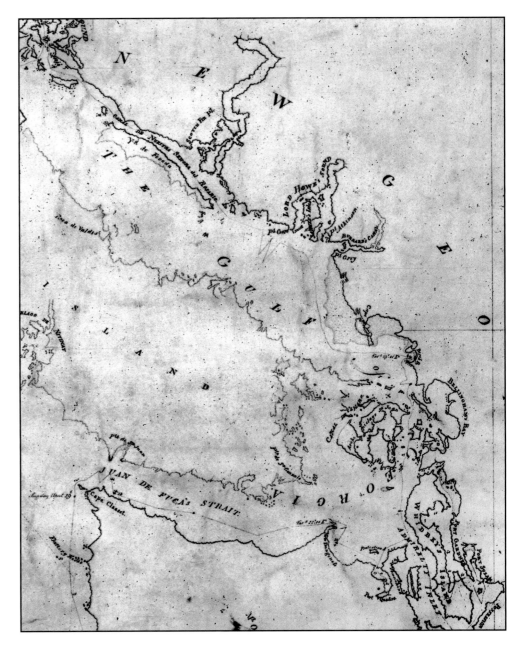

Part of the original manuscript of George Vancouver's map of the southwestern coast of British Columbia, from his 1792 survey. The coastlines shown in red are copied from the Spanish and are almost entirely non-mainland coasts. The "continental shore" was surveyed by Vancouver's men because he did not want to trust the Spanish, who might conceivably hide a Northwest Passage if they found one. This map was sent to England with William Broughton at the end of the 1792 surveying season.

On one of Vancouver's boat surveys one of his officers, James Johnston, discovered a channel that led northwards, not to a Northwest Passage but back to the Pacific. What they had thought mainland was in fact a large island. Vancouver named it Vancouver and Quadra's Island in honour of his meeting with the Spanish commander; sadly today the Spanish part has been dropped and it is just Vancouver Island.

Vancouver retreated to Hawaii at the end of the 1792 season and returned again the following year to continue his survey at the point he had left off. He would spend half of 1793 surveying the coast of what is now British Columbia, and another year and a half in Alaska. The result was a stunning map of the Northwest Coast that once and for all dispelled the chimera of a low-latitude Northwest Passage.

No more British or Spanish voyages of exploration came to the coast after Vancouver, but the fur trade continued, largely being taken over by American ships from Boston. However, where the relationship of naval personnel with the native peoples had generally been good, this was not always the case with the fur traders, who were on occasion overtaken by greed. Sometimes the native people retaliated. This was the case in 1803, when the American ship *Boston* was attacked by Nuu' chah'nulth warriors in Nootka Sound. The entire crew was killed, except for the armourer, John Jewitt, and the sailmaker, John Thompson. The pair were assimilated into the tribe, likely because of their skills, and were trusted enough to be made the chief's bodyguards. They were rescued two years later by another Boston trader. Jewitt was a keen observer, and his journal, later published as the *Narrative of the Adventures and Sufferings of John R. Jewitt,* became a best-seller and is an invaluable record of native life and customs of the time.

Down Mighty Rivers

Ever since Alexander Mackenzie had reached the Pacific in 1793, the North West Company had wanted to extend its fur-gathering domain to the lands on the other side of the Rocky Mountains. In 1805 one of the company partners, Simon Fraser, followed Mackenzie's route up the Peace and Parsnip Rivers but found a small tributary, the slow-moving Pack River, which led to a much easier portage across the divide. That year Fraser established a post at McLeod Lake, the first permanent European settlement west of the Rockies. A year later he built another post on Stuart Lake, later called Fort St. James, which was thought to connect via the Nechako River with the Columbia. In fact it connected with the Fraser River, as Simon Fraser found out to his dismay in 1808. That year he descended the river David Thompson would name after him, traversing the difficult Fraser Canyon only with native help using steps and ladders on the canyon sides. "We had to pass where no human being should venture," he famously wrote. Despite many trials, Fraser reached the sea at Vancouver on 2 July. He wanted to see what he called "the main ocean," but had to retreat hastily when threatened by natives from the village of Musqueam. Importantly, however, Fraser had established that the Fraser and the Columbia were not connected.

Above.
Simon Fraser.

Below.
Simon Fraser's canoes on his eponymous river. Fraser's difficulties proved to the North West Company that they could not use the Fraser River as a trade route to the Pacific.

David Thompson, another North West Company partner, was at this time exploring farther south. A meticulous master surveyor, Thompson is renowned for his extensive mapping of the West. He descended the Columbia River, by a more convoluted but much easier route than Fraser. On 15 July 1811 he finally reached the mouth of the river only to find Americans already ensconced in Fort Astoria, a fort belonging to John Jacob Astor's Pacific Fur Company. Two years later, when news of the War of 1812 reached the fort, the Americans agreed to sell it to the North West Company, but it was unnecessarily seized instead by a British naval officer from the warship *Racoon,* sent to ensure the fort ended up in British hands. This seizure rather than sale would weaken later British claims to the territory.

A Grant of Land

It was inevitable that eventually the fur trade would run afoul of settlement. The former, requiring vast wilderness areas, was at odds with the needs of the colonist and his agriculture. But the conflict happened sooner rather than later.

Thomas Douglas, Earl of Selkirk, was a Scottish philanthropist who concerned himself with the plight of dispossessed tenant farmers. In 1803 he had brought eight hundred Scottish Highlanders to settle on Prince Edward Island. In 1808, casting his eyes around for new lands to colonize, his attention turned to the apparently wide open Rupert's Land, chartered to the Hudson's Bay Company. By buying up blocks of stock he gained enough influence to persuade the company to grant him lands for settlement; the notion was that the colony could be a food supplier for the company.

On 12 June 1811, for the princely sum of ten shillings, Selkirk was granted 300 000 km² of land. (The area granted is shown on the map on page 97.) The land stood in the path of the rival North West Company's supply lines to the Athabasca country, and a colony was almost bound to cause problems for it. Selkirk appointed a governor for his Red River Colony, Miles Macdonell. After overwintering at York Fort, Macdonell and 115 colonists arrived near the confluence of the Red and Assiniboine Rivers on 29 August 1812.

The settlers had a hard time of it at first. In 1814, Macdonell, fed up with seeing the North West Company ship off pemmican (dried buffalo meat strips mixed with berries), he forbade the sending of food out of the colony and seized one shipment. It was 1815 before the Nor'Westers retaliated (due to the War of 1812), when they arrested Macdonell and took him to Montréal, charged with theft of pemmican. The settlers were persuaded to leave, and much of the colony was burned. But the Hudson's Bay Company's Colin Robertson, who had been bringing supplies to the colonists, retrieved the fleeing colonists (they had only reached Lake Winnipeg) and rebuilt the colony, harvesting grain still in the fields. The next month the regrouped settlers were joined by ninety more and a new governor of Assiniboia, Robert Semple, was appointed. By 1816 the situation was out of control. The Métis were upset at the loss of their buffalo hunting lands and a group of them, led by Cuthbert Grant and egged on by the Nor'Westers, attacked Semple and about thirty colonists, killing twenty of them, including Semple. This has come to be known as the Seven Oaks Massacre.

Lord Selkirk, who had come to Canada late in 1815 to try to control the situation, arrived at the

Above.
The Seven Oaks Massacre, 19 June 1816. Cuthbert Grant leads about sixty Métis horsemen against Robert Semple and the colonists. The encounter took place about 5 km from the confluence of the Red and Assiniboine Rivers—now Winnipeg—as Grant and his men were attempting to circle the Hudson's Bay Company's Fort Douglas.

Below.
The Red River Colony in 1820.

Above.
George Simpson, the Hudson's Bay Company's energetic governor.

Below.
A Hudson's Bay Company York boat, shown in a painting by Arthur Heming.

North West Company's Fort William in August 1816 with a force of discharged mercenaries from the War of 1812, arresting company luminaries such as William McGillivray, Simon Fraser, and John McLoughlin. The following year he reached his Red River Colony, but all possible offenders had already fled.

The arrest of the North West Company's leaders marked a watershed in the company's affairs from which it never recovered. In 1821 the company was taken over by the Hudson's Bay Company. With the stroke of a pen the Hudson's Bay Company became master of the fur trade to the Pacific and to the Arctic, a supremacy that would remain intact until the purchase of Rupert's Land by the new Canadian government in 1870.

A new governor, George Simpson, was appointed to oversee the company's expanded operations. He was charged with maximizing the profits from the Northern Department, which covered most of western Canada. For many years Simpson himself visited most trading posts in his bailiwick, instilling dread in the incompetent and excellence in the capable. In 1828 he even went down the Fraser River, just to make sure that Simon Fraser's assessment was correct. It was, even to the fearless Simpson.

The fur trade network was extended west and north, into the Yukon and up the Mackenzie, with company traders such as Robert Campbell carrying out valuable explorations in the process. What would become western Canada was in the fifty years from 1821 to 1870 almost the sole domain of the Hudson's Bay Company.

Exploring the North

Little interest had been shown in the icy wastes of the northernmost parts of Canada for almost a hundred years when the British navy in 1818 turned its attention once more to the achievement of a Northwest Passage, that elusive way through or around Canada to the East.

With the end of the Napoleonic wars in Europe the navy had many men on its hands and nothing for them to do. What better, then, but to put them to work to capture for Britain the laurels that would go with the finding of the Northwest Passage. In 1817 there had been reports of unusually easy ice conditions so it seemed like a fine time to try. But good ice one year does not necessarily mean good ice the next.

John Ross was dispatched in 1818. With William Edward Parry he sailed far to the north of Baffin Bay, but although he located Lancaster Sound, the western entrance to the Northwest Passage, Ross thought it merely a large bay ending in a mountain range. It was the biggest mistake of his career, for the very next year, Parry was sent north again and he sailed right through Ross's mountains. In a bold attack on the icy ocean Parry sailed more than a thousand kilometres westward, adding a vast swath of (what is now) Canada to the map. Parry spent the winter of 1819–20 in a bay he called Winter Harbour, on Melville Island, with his two ships covered and winterized as much as possible. This was the first time Europeans had overwintered in the Canadian Arctic, and much was learned from the experience that would be put to use time and time again in the future. Although he tried the following summer—it was August before his ships were freed—Parry was unable to force a way farther west to complete a passage, for he had reached the point where the multi-year ice, which was to defeat many others after him, pushes ever southeastwards.

Parry himself would return to the Arctic three times, twice still searching for other possible ways through the ice. His second voyage, in 1821–23, took him through Hudson Strait and into the Foxe Basin, but he was stopped by year-round ice in Fury and Hecla Strait, named after his ships. A third voyage, in 1824–25, was foiled by ice but would have been impossible anyway, as he sailed south down Prince Regent Inlet, a dead end. This time he lost one of his ships but left most of its supplies on the east side of Somerset Island, at Fury Beach. They would prove a lifesaver for a later expedition.

While Parry was probing the icy seas, another promising young naval officer was probing the icy land. John Franklin was sent to find the northern coast of mainland Canada, which he did in two broad-ranging

Above.
Artist Peter Rindisbacher was aboard this ship in Hudson Strait in June 1821 en route to Hudson Bay and the Red River Colony when it struck an iceberg.

Below.
The rescue of John Ross and his men in Lancaster Sound in August 1833 by his old ship *Isabella*, by this time a whaler.

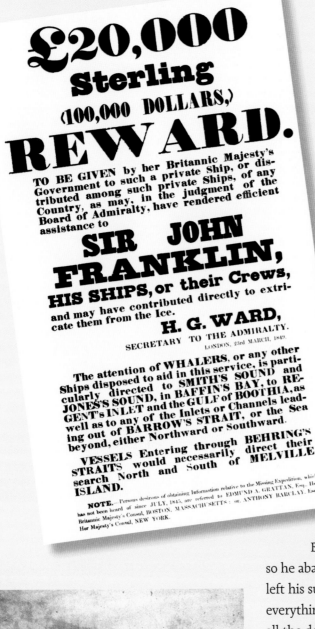

£20,000 Sterling (100,000 DOLLARS,) REWARD.

TO BE GIVEN by her Britannic Majesty's Government to such a private Ship, or distributed among such private Ships, of any Country, as may, in the judgment of the Board of Admiralty, have rendered efficient assistance to

SIR JOHN FRANKLIN, HIS SHIPS, or their Crews,

and may have contributed directly to extricate them from the Ice.

H. G. WARD,
SECRETARY TO THE ADMIRALTY.
LONDON, 23rd MARCH, 1849.

The attention of WHALERS, or any other Ships disposed to aid in this service, is particularly directed to SMITH'S SOUND and JONES'S SOUND, in BAFFIN'S BAY, to REGENT's INLET and the GULF of BOOTHIA, as well as to any of the Inlets or Channels leading out of BARROW'S STRAIT, or the Sea beyond, either Northward or Southward.

VESSELS Entering through BEHRING'S STRAITS would necessarily direct their search North and South of MELVILLE ISLAND.

NOTE.— Persons desirous of obtaining Information relative to the Missing Expedition, which has not been heard of since JULY, 1845, are referred to EDMUND A. GRATTAN, Esq. Her Britannic Majesty's Consul, BOSTON, MASSACHUSETTS : or, ANTHONY BARCLAY, Esq. Her Majesty's Consul, NEW YORK.

surveys in 1819–22 and 1825–27. During the first, in which he explored the coast east of the mouth of the Coppermine River (found by Samuel Hearne in 1771), the going became so tough that Franklin became known as "the man who ate his shoes." The second land expedition was a much better organized affair as a result—Franklin learned from his mistakes—and succeeded in surveying the coast from the mouth of the Mackenzie River both east and west. As a result a considerable length of the northern coastline of mainland North America became known.

In 1829 John Ross set off to find the Northwest Passage in a steamship, the *Victory*, which he thought better suited to ice navigation. His venture was privately financed by gin merchant Felix Booth; his failure to find Lancaster Sound in 1818 had made the Admiralty unwilling to give him another command. This is how a huge peninsula in northern Canada, the northernmost tip of mainland North America (the Boothia Peninsula), came to bear the name of a brand of gin.

Ross's steam engine soon caused him more trouble than it was worth, and he took it out. Parts of it are still lying on a northern Canadian beach today. Ross, like Parry on his second voyage, turned south down Prince Regent Inlet but was soon trapped in the ice. His ship would never be able to free itself again, and Ross was destined to set a record for his length of time in the Arctic. Between 1829 and 1833 Ross overwintered no fewer than four times. During this period his nephew James Clark Ross discovered the location of the North Magnetic Pole, and much of King William Island was surveyed.

By 1832 it had become obvious to Ross that *Victory* was not going to be released, and so he abandoned her, marching and rowing north to Fury Beach, the place where Parry had left his supplies in 1825. Luckily for Ross and his men, the Arctic refrigerator had preserved everything very well. After a failed attempt to row out that year, they built a shelter from all the debris available and overwintered once more. Finally, in August 1833, they managed to row out to Lancaster Sound, where they were picked up by a whaling ship that by the most amazing coincidence turned out to be the *Isabella,* the very same ship that Ross had commanded in 1818. Ross's return from the dead caused a huge sensation in Britain and Ross became an instant Arctic hero.

Much the same sort of predicament as that of Ross was faced by the much better equipped naval expedition of John Franklin fourteen years later, but with a less happy ending. By the time Franklin set off in 1845 more coastline had been mapped and Franklin, it was thought, would have an easy time sailing all the way to Bering Strait. But it was not to be. Franklin's ships were seen by whalers in northern Baffin Bay in late July 1845; then he disappeared. Franklin overwintered at Beechey Island, at the southwest corner of Devon

Above, left.
Poster offering a reward for information about the lost expedition of Sir John Franklin.

Left.
A ship stuck in the ice, a scene that was repeated many times in the nineteenth century. This was Henry Stephenson's ship *Discovery*, one of two with the Nares expedition of 1875–76, a British naval expedition towards the North Pole. The location is Lady Franklin Bay, on Ellesmere Island.

Island, and in 1846 sailed south down the western side of Somerset Island and the Boothia Peninsula. But his ships were trapped near King William island by the multi-year ice surging southeast down M'Clintock Channel, and were never released. By 1848, with Franklin dead, the survivors tried to escape to the south, dragging boats laden with all sorts of unnecessary baggage such as the officers' silver tableware, and died in the attempt.

A massive search was mounted for Franklin over twelve years, from 1848 to 1859, involving thousands of men, many sledge search parties, and at least fifty ships. The searches were organized by the Admiralty, by private individuals, and notably by Lady Franklin, who badgered anyone who might help, and monies were raised through public subscription.

The searchers did not find Franklin, though Leopold M'Clintock did in 1859 find evidence as to what had happened to him. But vast expanses of the Canadian North were explored and mapped as a result of this unprecedented search.

As part of a large multi-ship search organized by the Admiralty in 1850, Robert M'Clure sailed his ship *Investigator* through Bering Strait to begin the search from the west. After a first winter near the Princess Royal Islands in Prince of Wales Strait, M'Clure sailed round the western side of Banks Island and in September 1851 became trapped in Mercy Bay, on its northern coast. It was nearly Franklin all over again. By March 1853 M'Clure was planning an overland escape southwards when, on 6 April, Lieutenant Bedford Pim, with a sledge party from the *Resolute,* found him. The *Resolute* had been part of another wave of search ships sent out in 1852 and had made it westwards to Dealy Island, on the south coast of Melville Island. Thus it was that M'Clure's expedition became the first to traverse the Northwest Passage, albeit without his ship, and from west to east. In fact one of M'Clure's officers, Lieutenant Samuel Gurney Cresswell, was really the first person, because *Resolute* became trapped in the ice in Barrow Strait later in 1853; Cresswell had transferred to the supply ship *Phoenix* in order to carry the news of M'Clure's triumph back to England, and thus escaped that fall.

The tragedy of the Franklin expedition had in a few years been translated into an explosion of geographical knowledge of the Arctic, leaving only the far northern parts of the Canadian Arctic Archipelago remaining completely unknown. And the British exploration also laid claim to sovereignty; in 1880 this would be transferred from Britain to her new Dominion, Canada.

Above.
A macabre discovery of skulls of Franklin's men found on King William Island and photographed before being buried. This group of men huddled on the remains of a sledge encapsulates in a single photograph the tragedy of the Franklin expedition.

Right.
One of a series of paintings published by Samuel Gurney Cresswell, one of M'Clure's officers, who was an accomplished artist. This scene shows the abandonment of the *Investigator* in Mercy Bay, Banks Island, on 3 June 1853.

7 *Rebellion and Union*

After the War of 1812, the British withdrew most of their armies, the demand for all manner of goods suddenly plummeted, and the people were thrown back on their own resources, leading to a post-war economic depression. Although continued immigration fuelled continued growth, discontents began to surface, fundamentally arising from the policies of a far-distant mother country trying to dictate to its loyal colonists, most of whom saw themselves as independent and equal to Britain. The imposed system of government on a people with no direct say in the way things were run was in stark contrast to the American system just across the border. Indeed, the ideals of the French and American Revolutions were still echoing round the globe and would lead to similar uprisings in disparate places, such as South America, Mexico, Belgium, and Texas.

The Canadas were developing. Roads, such as passed for them, were being built. In 1817 the first steamboat appeared on Lake Ontario, a tremendous improvement in comfort for those who could afford it. Canals were planned. And the first bank, a vital element of commerce, was founded the same year—the Bank of Montreal.

Immigration was seen as a way to fill the colonies with those loyal to the British Crown, and also as a way to get rid of the poor and otherwise unwanted from Britain, its "superfluous population," as land agent Samuel Strickland termed them. "The lower class of Highlanders" of which pioneer Canadian novelist Catharine Parr Trail wrote were a major component of British emigration at the time because they had been dispossessed of their tenant farms in their native land. Canada, with its free land—heads of families could be granted one hundred acres (40 ha)—was seen as another chance at a good life. Strickland, though he was hardly an unbiased observer, maintained that the population passed "from a state of poverty to one of comfort." Initially there was even a free-passage scheme. Ships had to be sent out to pick up troops returning from the war, so why not fill them up with emigrants on the way?

Not all immigrants were satisfied. Some land agents were despotic. The ruthless Archibald McNab, for example, who left Scotland to escape his debts, set himself up in the Ottawa Valley and enticed his clansmen to settle there. But he did not tell them that the

The heavy artillery of the British army is brought to bear on the rebel *Patriotes* of Lower Canada, holed up in a church at Saint-Eustache, a short distance west of Montréal, on 14 December 1837. It was the final battle of the rebellion in that province.

land he allotted them was theirs, instead letting them believe they were tenants on his land, as they would have been in Scotland, ruling over them as a tyrannical local magistrate, and grabbing improved land back as often as he could. Then there was the reclusive Colonel Thomas Talbot, who had been building up his own lands on Lake Erie—though he was only a land agent—since before the war. He autocratically ruled his fiefdom, the Talbot Settlement, missing no opportunity to add to his own wealth. During the War of 1812 he had only escaped reprisals from defected settlers by being away when they came calling. By 1830 Talbot owned a massive slice of the Erie lands, 26 000 ha in all.

A farm carved from the bush near Chatham, Upper Canada, in 1838. Like all pioneer farms it was a small clearing in the forest, with any expansion representing years of back-breaking toil.

In Upper Canada, settlement tended to be scattered due to the preponderance of land reserves; when the original land-granting system had been set up for the Loyalists, two-sevenths of all surveyed land had been put aside to support the clergy and the government, and now it was proving to be a nuisance; with so much undeveloped land it was farther to market, farther to the mill, and farther even to your neighbour. The land-granting system was changed in 1826 to an open market for land, and that same year the Canada Company was chartered. Set up as a way to compensate residents of Upper Canada for war losses, it used land instead of cash for payment; the former the government had much of, the latter, very little. All the Crown reserves, half of the clergy reserves, and a large swath of land in the west (the Huron Tract), a million hectares in all, were purchased by the company for about $7.40 per hectare. By reselling this land, profits would be made to pay out claims, and the government would convert land into cash. John Galt, who had lobbied for the company, was soon appointed its superintendent, and he applied himself to the task in a practical fashion, tramping the land and planning settlements, including those of Guelph and Goderich.

With growth came demands for a voice in government. This fundamental tenet of the British system—in Britain—was denied to the colonies of British North America. Although they had an elected assembly, all resolutions had to be approved by the governor, and they were frequently rejected, in Lower Canada, in Upper Canada, and in Nova Scotia. In the latter colony a newpaper proprietor, Joseph Howe, used his *Novascotian* to lambaste the system where a few of the rich and privileged ran the affairs of government. In 1835, taken to court on a charge of seditious libel, Howe turned the tables on his accusers and the jury acquitted him. The trial made him famous and popular, however, so he went into politics. Yet it would take another eleven years for the colonies to achieve responsible government. Nova Scotia achieved this is 1846 (though it was not fully operative until 1848) at much the same time as Canada, but without, Howe proudly proclaimed, "a blow struck or a pane of glass broken." But this was partly made possible by the experiences the British government had had by this time in Lower and Upper Canada, where many blows had been struck before the goal was attained.

Taming the Waters

Since the beginning, rivers provided the easiest means of transportation in Canada. Where there were rapids and waterfalls, there were portages. But here the carrying of large amounts of goods, or large numbers of people, especially armies, became especially difficult. In a country attempting to develop its commerce, the elimination of the portages became essential, and led to the undertaking of a number of canal projects in the 1820s and 1830s.

The first of these, on the critical St. Lawrence, was the Lachine Canal. Circumventing the Lachine Rapids at Montréal, it was built between 1821 and 1825.

Three short canals on the Ottawa River, built between 1819 and 1834, and the Rideau Canal, built between 1827 and 1832, were military in origin, enabling avoidance of the St. Lawrence where the southern bank was United States territory.

The strategic value of the Rideau River had been recognized long before the canal was built. In 1816 military and Scottish settlers had been encouraged to locate in townships laid out west of the river, as a sort of first line of defence. Lieutenant Colonel John By was sent to Canada in 1826 to plan and build the canal, and during its construction he enlarged parts of it to accommodate the steamships he saw would soon take over. When the canal opened in May 1832, By was the first through it—on a steamboat. The Rideau Canal is today much the same as when it was completed and is a major attraction for pleasure boats in the summer months.

In 1817 the Americans began work on a canal that would connect Buffalo, at the eastern end of Lake Erie, with the Hudson River at Albany. Named the Erie Canal, it opened in 1825. From a commercial point of view this was a potential disaster for Montréal, for it would enable ships to completely bypass that city, diverting the business to New York instead. Hence in 1824, with the support of the merchants of Montréal, work was begun on a canal to remedy this situation, the first Welland Canal, built to connect the Welland River (which flows into the Niagara above the falls) with Twelve Mile Creek, which flows into Lake Ontario.

The private Welland Canal Company was taken over by the government in 1841 and a more direct route through to Port Colbourne, on the Erie shore, was cut, opening in 1845. Two additional canals were cut later, opening in 1887 and 1932, giving a 100-m lift with just eight locks, as compared to the original forty. Today the Welland Canal is an integral part of the St. Lawrence Seaway system, which allows large ships to reach deep into the continent at the western end of Lake Superior.

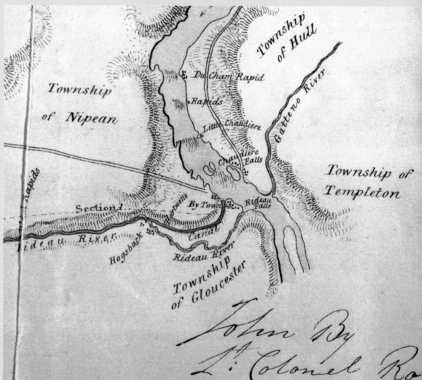

Above, top.
Lieutenant Colonel By oversees the building of the locks in Ottawa—originally Bytown—down to the Ottawa River. Today they are between the Parliament Buildings and the Château Laurier Hotel.

Above.
An 1830 map of the Rideau Canal and the site of Bytown. It is signed by John By.

The Last of the Beothuk

When Europeans started to settle in Canada, they occupied not an empty space but one already inhabited by First Nations peoples. European expansion of the settled parts of the country, competition for sometimes limited food supplies, and in particular the spreading of diseases to which the natives had no natural immunity led in many cases to a precipitous decline in the native population. Nowhere was this more marked than in Newfoundland, where the native Beothuk, eking out a living from meagre resources and never very numerous to start with, were decimated to the point of extinction by 1829.

The Beothuk were the original "Red Indians," so named because they covered their faces with a red ochre. When Europeans arrived the Beothuk retreated into the interior of Newfoundland and were rarely seen. They never really learned to trade, it seems, and took to acquiring what they needed, especially iron items, by theft. Needless to say, this trait did not find favour with the settlers, who often hunted down the Beothuk like animals.

Above. Demasduit.

Right. A distinctively shaped Beothuk canoe.

Below. A map drawn by Shanawdithit for William Epps Cormack in 1828 or 1829. It shows "2 different scenes & times," illustrating the visit of David Buchan in 1810 on the southern shore of Red Lake, and "The Taking of Mary March" (Demasduit) in 1819 on the north. The red figures are the Beothuk, "Red Indians." The red figure in front of the group of settlers is Nonosgawut, Demasduit's husband, who is also shown lying on the ice after being shot. The two semicircles with red figures are Beothuk hiding in the woods.

In 1810, realizing rather belatedly that Beothuk numbers were dwindling, the British issued a proclamation protecting them and began trying to establish contact. In an expedition that year led by Lieutenant David Buchan, two men were killed by the Beothuk when he left them with the natives overnight as a gesture of goodwill. Deplorable as this was, at this time European settlers were still shooting the Beothuk on sight.

Absurd though it seems to us today, in the winter of 1818–19 the governor of Newfoundland commissioned a group of settlers to capture a Beothuk, with the intention of using the captive to somehow establish friendly relations with the tribe. This led to the capture of Demasduit, called Mary March, after the settlers shot her husband when he tried to prevent them taking her away, a senseless act most certainly not likely to promote any friendliness.

In 1823 another Beothuk woman, Shanawdithit, was captured. She spent the next six years at the house of William Epps Cormack. This well-intentioned man had established a "Beothuk Institution," which had as its goal the "opening of communication and promoting the civilization of the Red Indians." Shanawdithit's written communications with Cormack provided the last information on the Beothuk, for in 1829, like Demasduit before her, she died of tuberculosis. Shawnawdithit was the last Beothuk; no more were ever found.

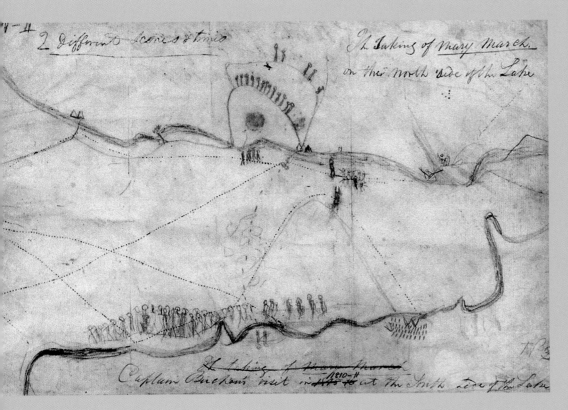

Steam across the Atlantic

For a hundred years *the* way to cross the Atlantic was by steamship. And the name most bound up with that grand era of luxurious ocean travel is that of Samuel Cunard, a Halifax-born entrepreneur par excellence, a man who was always alert for an opportunity to turn a profit.

The invention of the steamship promised to end an Atlantic crossing at the whim of the weather, bestormed or becalmed as nature saw fit. Even in coastal navigation the weather played a major role; contrary winds had been known to make even the relatively short voyage from Halifax to Québec take over three weeks. Cunard wanted to put an end to this and, together with two hundred shareholders in his Quebec and Halifax Steam Navigation Company, he took advantage of subsidies offered by the government to have a steamboat built in Québec.

The 50-m-long *Royal William* was launched at Québec on 27 April 1831 and steamed to Halifax in August. Unfortunately for Cunard and his shareholders, the ship was caught up in the outbreak of cholera at Québec the next year (see next page) and ended up quarantined at Miramichi and Halifax for much of the year, incurring heavy losses. Cunard bailed out, selling the ship to its mortgagees.

The new owners wanted to sell the ship but could find no buyers in North America, and so decided to try their luck in Britain. On 5 August 1833 the *Royal William* departed from Québec. After a stop at Pictou, Nova Scotia, for coal, the steamship arrived at Gravesend, England, on 11 September, twenty-five days later. It was the first ship to cross the Atlantic entirely under steam power (if a couple of pauses for boiler scraping are not taken into account). Crossings by steamships up to this date had always included periods of sailing.

Although the *Royal William* had gone, Samuel Cunard had seen the potential for steam in the Atlantic. Bigger ships would be needed, so that a load beyond the coal needed for fuel could be carried. Although Cunard was not the first to initiate regular steam crossings of the Atlantic—that honour went to British engineer Isambard Kingdom Brunel's *Great Western,* in 1836—he was the first to secure a British government mail contract, in 1840. With this guarantee of viability, Cunard set about attracting investors and building ships. The first scheduled ship of the "Cunard line of steam packet ships" (later the Cunard Steamship Company) arrived in Halifax at two in the morning on 17 July 1840, with Cunard on board, and reached Boston two days later. The reign of scheduled and reasonably safe Atlantic crossings—with increasing style as the years went on—had begun.

The *Royal William* at Québec in 1833.

Found in America But a Grave

Canada is a country principally peopled by immigrants. After the end of the Napoleonic Wars in Europe in 1815, many poor people saw emigration to North America as a way out of their desperate situation. But, unable to afford more than the cheapest possible passage, immigrants were crammed into crowded and unsanitary ships that became festering grounds for all manner of deadly diseases. By 1830 some 30,000 immigrants a year, 20,000 of whom were from Ireland, were arriving at Québec, the main entry port for Canada.

Cholera arrived in Canada in June 1832 aboard an emigrant ship from Ireland, hitting the port of entry, Québec, hard. Little was understood about how such diseases spread; people placed smouldering fires at their doorways, for instance, an essentially useless exercise. But if disease-ridden ships could be kept from landing in the first place, then, it was thought, spread of the contagion could be prevented.

A quarantine station was hastily set up on Grosse-Île, a verdant island in the St. Lawrence 60 km downstream from Québec. It would last more than a hundred years, and through it would pass huge masses of immigrants bound for Canada. But in 1832 many died there. The quarantine efforts met with very limited success, for over nine thousand, both immigrants and citizens, died that year from the dreaded cholera. Many blamed Britain for the disaster, claiming that misguided emigration policy was the problem. This contributed to the air of unrest that would lead, in 1837, to open rebellion (see next page).

In 1847, an even bigger tragedy struck. When the ice went from the St. Lawrence in the spring of that year the first of the ships bearing Irish emigrants fleeing the great potato famine arrived off Grosse-Île. Typhus, another scourge of the nineteenth century, was aboard. And it was the first of 224 ships that season that would arrive from the blighted Emerald Isle, many carrying typhus. That year, over five thousand immigrants died during the Atlantic crossing, more than this on Grosse-Île, and yet more again near Montréal. The doctor in charge at Grosse-Île, George Douglas, had seen it coming. Early in the year he had read of the famine in Ireland and knew that this would translate into considerably increased immigration, though even he had not realized the extent of the epidemic it would bring with it.

Grosse-Île, from 1832 to 1937 Canada's quarantine station in the St. Lawrence.

At first the authorities buried the men, women, and children in rough coffins, but as the numbers slowly overwhelmed them, they resorted to stacking the dead like cordwood in mass graves. Rats unearthed the corpses, gnawing on flesh and further spreading the disease. More earth had to be piled on to prevent this.

By mid-July the line of ships awaiting inspection stretched 3 km down the river. More and more poor immigrants were transferred to hastily-thrown-up sheds on Grosse-Île, where, if they were not sick already, they stood a very good chance of becoming so. For medical knowledge about such diseases as typhus was still primitive, and the sheds were constructed without sanitation; straw from the bed of a dead person was not changed before the bed was occupied by the next sickly immigrant. Such conditions fostered other diseases, with smallpox also rearing its ugly head.

That summer, the situation at Grosse-Île got so out of control that Douglas was ordered to allow the "healthy" to go on to Québec or Montréal without the customary two-week quarantine period. This was a mistake. Québec dealt with the situation relatively well, hospitalizing many of those landing right away. But in Montréal, the situation was much worse. Thousands of pitiful sick immigrants, the old, the destitute, were left on the waterfront with nowhere to go.

By August, citizens of Montréal, outraged that their city could be visited by such a plague, demanded and got some action; the sick were transported to a hospital at Pointe Saint-Charles. But hospitals in 1847 rarely did anybody any good; some six thousand persons died there. Those that seemed still well were transported by barge to Kingston and Toronto. Many of the survivors, less than pleased with the reception Canada had given them, found their way into the United States.

Grosse-Île remained a quarantine station for Québec, long the main entry point into Canada, until 1937. On the island is a memorial marker to the medical staff and immigrants who died in that terrible summer of 1847. "In this secluded spot lie the mortal remains of 5,424 persons who flying from Pestilence and Famine in Ireland in 1847 found in America but a Grave."

Above, right.
Grosse-Île in 1838, in a painting by Henry Percy.

Right.
In 1909 the Ancient Order of Hibernians erected a cross to commemorate the Irish immigrants who died on Grosse-Île in 1847. Here it is being unveiled.

Québec's Lower Town marketplace from MacCullum's Wharf, 4 July 1829, in a detailed painting by James Pattison Cockburn. The boat in the foreground is propelled by horses turning in an endless circle, hence the unusual width of the deck. Lieutenant Colonel James Pattison Cockburn, a highly proficient artist, was the commander of the Royal Artillery in Canada, and was based in Québec from 1826 to 1832.

Resolutions and Revolt

In the 1830s, physical and political factors combined to produce discontent. There was bad weather and crops failed due to a rust disease. Immigration increased, reaching 66,000 in 1832, and the cholera epidemic swept the country the same year. This was blamed on the British government for sending immigrants with the disease.

The two main political parties at this time were the English Party, representing Québec's English-speaking elite, and the Parti Patriote of the Canadiens, with Louis-Joseph Papineau as its leader. The Patriotes had a majority in the House of Assembly, but most of its resolutions were blocked by the executive and legislative councils, appointed by the governor.

In May 1832, after a fight at a polling station, soldiers opened fire on a crowd, killing three Patriotes. Papineau wrote to the governor: "The troops sent to protect His Majesty's subjects shot them. No such tragedy has ever before afflicted Canada." It turned out to be the first shot of a rebellion.

Two years later, as moderates were gradually replaced by extremists, the Patriotes drew up a long list of grievances, at the top of which were the demands that the legislative council be elected and that control over finance be given to the House of Assembly. It also pointed out, in a veiled threat, that "the neighbouring States have a form of government very fit to prevent abuses." This document, called the "Ninety-two Resolutions," was taken to London. But, after three years pondering it, the British

Above.
Patriote leader Louis-Joseph Papineau.

Below.
The Patriote flag, complete with shell holes from British cannon.

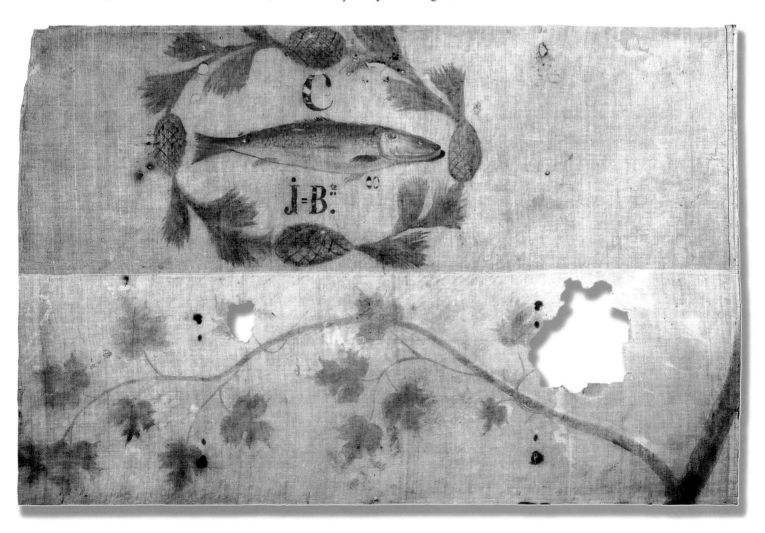

Lieutenant Charles Beauclerk was an officer in the British army and an accomplished artist. When he returned to Britain he published his memoirs and a set of lithographs of his paintings. Two of them are shown here, with a third on page 114. At *right, top* is a view of the battle at Saint-Charles, on 23 November 1837, while *right, below* is a view of the battle at Saint-Eustache on 14 December 1837. The attack on the church at Saint-Eustache is shown on page 114.

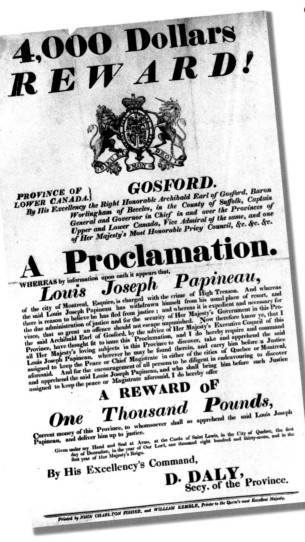

The reward poster for Louis-Joseph Papineau issued by Governor General Gosford on 1 December 1837. There was also a French version.

government, with ten resolutions of its own drafted by Lord John Russell, rejected it out of hand, instead dispatching troops to ensure any insurrection could be dealt with. In 1836, to escape the coming storm and to avail themselves of that very government fit to prevent abuses, at least five hundred Canadiens had left Québec for Michigan and other part of the United States.

Russell's resolutions were the last straw. Throughout the summer of 1837 discontent rumbled through Lower Canada. On 3 October, at a large gathering at Saint-Charles, in the Richelieu Valley, called the assembly of the six counties, the speaker of the House of Assembly, Wolfred Nelson, told an enthusiastic crowd that the time had come "to melt down our dishes and tin spoons to make bullets."

The British forces since May 1836 had been commanded by General John Colbourne, who had been Upper Canada's lieutenant-governor for eleven years prior to that time. He was a disciplined military man credited with a critical move during the Battle of Waterloo in 1815 that had ensured Napoleon's downfall. To his direction of the British side can be attributed the failure of the rebellion in Lower Canada in 1837. Colbourne decided upon a pre-emptive strike against the Patriotes. He wanted, as he wrote, "to drag the leaders of the revolt from their meeting places." Troops were dispatched to rebel strongholds in the Richelieu Valley. On 23 November, after marching all night, three hundred soldiers led by Colonel Charles Gore approached Saint-Denis-sur-Richelieu, where they ran into heavy opposition. Some eight hundred Patriotes, under Wolfred Nelson, outnumbered the British troops. Gunfire was exchanged for six hours, at which point Gore's men were running out of ammunition. He had little choice but to order a retreat. The Patriotes, naturally enough, celebrated their victory. But now that the conflict was merely a matter of military manoeuvres, the Patriotes were in a situation they could not win in the long run.

Two days later, at Saint-Charles-sur-Richelieu, a little upriver from Saint-Denis, another British force of over four hundred, led by Lieutenant Colonel George Wetherall, attacked two hundred and fifty Patriote defenders. It was a battle between one of the toughest regiments in the British army and inexperienced civilians, and the outcome was never in doubt. The Patriotes put up a brave resistance, but the relentless, disciplined advance of the army regulars could not be halted. At least one hundred and fifty Patriotes died, and Papineau and some of the other Patriote leaders fled for their lives to the United States.

Martial law was declared in Montréal district. There was only one other rebel stronghold left, at Saint-Eustache, to the west of the city. It was here that Colbourne now turned his attention. On 14 December, unwilling to take any chances as to Patriote strength, Colbourne himself led an army of about fifteen hundred men to Saint-Eustache. The show of force worked; most of the rebels realized that the situation was hopeless and fled. A hard core of two hundred and fifty Patriotes remained, determined to fight to the last.

Led by Jean-Oliver Chénier, the rebels holed up in the local church, which resisted the British cannon for two hours. They were only driven out near nightfall when the church was set on fire by British soldiers who had found a way in through a back door. Chénier and many other were shot as they tried to escape. In the next few days, nearby villages were searched, houses set on fire, and rebel leaders rounded up, including Wolfred Nelson. The rebellion in Lower Canada had been crushed.

An Improbable Revolution

The rebellion in Upper Canada was by comparison a somewhat more genteel affair and was inextricably bound up with one person, William Lyon Mackenzie. He was a colourful Scottish newpaper proprietor and erstwhile malcontent who had come to Upper Canada in 1820. He had a meticulous mind, which made him a formidable debating opponent. An idea of his personality is gained from the fact that between 1806 and 1820 he listed by year and type all of the 958 books he read. But systematic as he was in small affairs he was impulsive in larger ones. Anyone with any power was immediately suspect.

In May 1824 Mackenzie started up his *Colonial Advocate,* giving voice to his critical side. It was a popular hit, and in November Mackenzie moved from Queenston to York to be nearer those he was criticizing. He also overdid it. The following year, after he had published some particularly scurrilous pieces, his shop was broken into and his press smashed. Mackenzie took the perpetrators to court and won a settlement, which put him back in business with a new press paid for by his antagonists.

Mackenzie is often credited with coining the term "Family Compact" to describe the group of people against whom he railed. Under the lieutenant-governor Peregrine Maitland until 1825, then John Colbourne until 1836, then Francis Bond Head, was the close-knit group of advisors he placed on his executive council plus some senior officials and the judiciary. In short, these were the privileged few who actually wielded the power in the province. That was Mackenzie's view of it; to Bond Head they were merely the "social fabric" that existed in any civilized society. Virtually everything they did was subject to Mackenzie's critical scrutiny; they in turn hated him. John Beverley Robinson, the attorney general, called Mackenzie a "reptile."

Mackenzie was able, by his vociferous and aggressive nature, to become the de facto leader of the reform movement in Upper Canada, even though he was not. He fell out with many, even from among his own supporters, notably Egerton Ryerson, the leader of the Methodists. But he was popular with the public. When York was made a city in 1834—and the name changed to Toronto—Mackenzie was elected its first mayor.

As Papineau had done with Lower Canada's "Ninety-two Resolutions," Mackenzie wrote a list of grievances and recommendations, called the *Seventh Report on Grievances,* and sent them to England in 1835 to demand that the Colonial Office implement them. "This country is now principally inhabited by loyalists and their descendants, and by an accession of population from the mother country, where is now enjoyed the principles of a free and responsible government," he wrote, "and we feel the practical enjoyment of the same system in this part of the empire to be equally our right . . . There should be an entire confidence between the Executive and the Commons House of Assembly; and this confidence cannot exist while those who have long and deservedly lost the esteem of the country are continued in the public offices and councils."

Like Papineau's, Mackenzie's calls for representative government were rejected. The British government, however, fully aware that trouble was brewing, appointed a new lieutenant-governor to sort it all out. But the man they chose, Francis Bond Head, could hardly have been a worse choice. Head was sent out with instructions to reconcile the differences between the Assembly and the executive, but he did precisely the opposite, making the situation worse than it was before. For Head, in a position where he was supposed to be neutral, joined with those who opposed the reformers, even leading an election campaign in 1837 against them. He was a reactionary, not a conciliator. If he was, as he put it, "sentenced to contend on the soil of America with Democracy," he was convinced that if he "did not overpower it, it would overpower [him]." Head dissolved the legislative assembly in May 1837 and called an election. Due in no small part to Head's intervention in this election, and in particular his persuasion of new immigrants who still closely identified themselves with Britain, Mackenzie and some of the other reform leaders lost their seats.

But a muted radical is a dangerous one. At the end of July Mackenzie's supporters met in Doel's brewery in Toronto and adopted a declaration modelled quite closely on the 1776 American Declaration of Independence. Mackenzie then set off around the countryside north of the city to drum up support. Some of his meetings were broken up by Orangemen and other opponents, with the result that Mackenzie's supporters began to arm themselves for protection. Before long Mackenzie was arguing that a show of force might work to convince the government it needed to grant some reform.

Then, in October, Head, determined to show that all was well in his domain, dispatched almost all of his troops to Lower Canada to assist the governor general with the uprisings there. This proved to be a big mistake, for it encouraged the radicals to think they should act immediately. Mackenzie in particular called for the seizure of arms and ammunition stored in Toronto's city hall. Many of his less-fervent supporters backed away from this open revolution. Mackenzie's inner circle became convinced—probably by Mackenzie's deliberately similar wording of his previous declaration—that Upper Canada would be better off after their rebellion as a state of the United States. Mackenzie even produced a draft constitution for the State of Upper Canada, which he published on 15 November, and he set a date for the coming uprising, 7 December. Towards the end of the month news arrived of the rising in Lower Canada, reinforcing Mackenzie's resolve. He distributed a handbill with a call to arms: "Brave Canadians! Do you love freedom? . . . Do you hate oppression? . . . Do you wish perpetual peace? . . . Then buckle on your armour, and put down the villains who oppress and enslave our country."

Two events disrupted the rebels' plans. They thought Head had wind of their activities, and then they heard of the failure of the rebellion in Lower Canada. An attempt to speed up the timetable created confusion. Nevertheless, on the evening and night of 4–5 December, seven or eight hundred gathered at Montgomery's Tavern, about 3 km north of Toronto, and at midday on 5 December moved south down Yonge Street, a motley band with

Above.
Francis Bond Head, lieutenant-governor of Upper Canada during the critical years from 1836 to 1838. He was totally unsuited for his job, and did not even follow his instructions. British prime minister Lord Melbourne was heard to call Head "a damned odd fellow."

Left, top.
William Lyon Mackenzie, newspaper publisher extraordinaire, reformer, mayor of Toronto, rebel, parliamentarian, and one of Canada's more colourful historical figures.

Left, below.
The masthead of the *Colonial Advocate*, published by Mackenzie from 1824 to 1834.

A.D. 1837.

PROCLAMATION.

BY His Excellency SIR FRANCIS BOND HEAD, Baronet, Lieutenant Governor of Upper Canada, &c. &c.

To the Queen's Faithful Subjects in Upper Canada.

In a time of profound peace, while every one was quietly following his occupations, feeling secure under the protection of our Laws, a band of Rebels, instigated by a few malignant and disloyal men, has had the wickedness and audacity to assemble with Arms, and to attack and Murder the Queen's Subjects on the High-way—to Burn and Destroy their Property—to Rob the Public Mails—and to threaten to Plunder the Banks—and to Fire the City of Toronto.

Brave and Loyal People of Upper Canada, we have been long suffering from the acts and endeavours of concealed Traitors, but this is the first time that Rebellion has dared to shew itself openly in the land, in the absence of invasion by any Foreign Enemy.

Let every man do his duty now, and it will be the last time that we or our children shall see our lives or properties endangered, or the Authority of our Gracious Queen insulted by such treacherous and ungrateful men. MILITIA-MEN OF UPPER CANADA, no Country has ever shewn a finer example of Loyalty and Spirit than YOU have given upon this sudden call of Duty. Young and old of all ranks, are flocking to the Standard of their Country. What has taken place will enable our Queen to know Her Friends from Her Enemies—a public enemy is never so dangerous as a concealed Traitor—and now my friends let us complete well what is begun—let us not return to our rest till Treason and Traitors are revealed to the light of day, and rendered harmless throughout the land.

Be vigilant, patient and active—leave punishment to the Laws—our first object is, to arrest and secure all those who have been guilty of Rebellion, Murder and Robbery.—And to aid us in this, a Reward is hereby offered of

One Thousand Pounds,

to any one who will apprehend, and deliver up to Justice, WILLIAM LYON MACKENZE; and FIVE HUNDRED POUNDS to any one who will apprehend, and deliver up to Justice, DAVID GIBSON—or SAMUEL LOUNT—or JESSE LLOYD—or SILAS FLETCHER—and the same reward and a free pardon will be given to any of their accomplices who will render this public service, except he or they shall have committed, in his own person, the crime of Murder or Arson.

And all, but the Leaders above-named, who have been seduced to join in this unnatural Rebellion, are hereby called to return to their duty to their Sovereign—to obey the Laws—and to live henceforward as good and faithful Subjects—and they will find the Government of their Queen as indulgent as it is just.

GOD SAVE THE QUEEN.

Thursday, 3 o'clock, P. M.
7th Dec. 1837

☞ The Party of Rebels, under their Chief Leaders, is wholly dispersed, and flying before the Loyal Militia. The only thing that remains to be done, is to find them, and arrest them.

R. STANTON, Printer to the QUEEN'S Most Excellent Majesty.

pitchforks and the like, with perhaps thirty or forty riflemen as their vanguard. After halting to negotiate with a group sent out by Head, they approached the city as dusk was falling. As it became dark they were opposed by a small group of volunteers commanded by the sheriff, who fired at the rebels and then turned and ran. The front row of rebel riflemen, commanded by Samuel Lount, returned the fire, then dropped down to allow those behind to fire. But in the darkness those in the second row thought that the front row had been killed, and they turned and ran. Those left behind had little choice but to follow.

That evening militia, led by Colonel Allan Napier MacNab, arrived by steamer from Hamilton, and the next day they marched north to do battle. Near Montgomery's Tavern a battle, if it can be called that, took place, with predictable results. Within half an hour the poorly armed rebels were dispersed.

Mackenzie escaped to Niagara and installed himself on Navy Island, an island of modest size on the Canadian side of the Niagara River upstream of the falls, almost directly across from the Chippewa battlefield of 1814. Here he declared a Republic of Upper Canada and offered free land to all who would join him.

Colonel MacNab and his small army of militia had followed Mackenzie to the Niagara. MacNab saw that the rebels on Navy Island were being openly supplied by the Americans, from the American side of the river, using the steamer *Caroline,* and so he ordered naval commander Andrew Drew to destroy the ship. With a small raiding party, Drew slipped across to Navy Island during the night of 29 December but, not finding the ship there, continued to the American side where the *Caroline* was moored. They killed a watchman, set the ship afire, and sent it drifting towards the falls. With it went Mackenzie's hope for a republic.

The Americans were outraged that an attack had been made on their soil, but the British claimed it was a pre-emptive attack in self-defence. Secretary of State Daniel Webster argued that this was only justified if there was a necessity, "instant, overwhelming, leaving no choice of means and no moment for deliberation." This statement became incorporated into international law. This law, with the *Caroline* incident, has been revisited in the twenty-first century with the American "pre-emptive attack" on Iraq in 2003.

In 1838, with the patent failure of reform attempts, many reformers simply uprooted and moved to the United States, where the political system was more to their liking. The Mississippi Emigration Society was formed to aid the emigrés. A new lieutenant-governor, George Arthur, arrived from a previous similar position in the convict settlement of Van Diemen's Land (Tasmania). He was no less conservative than his predecessor, though more experienced. One of his first acts was to permit the execution of two unfortunate rebels, Samuel Lount and Peter Matthews, guilty no doubt, but singled out as an example to the others.

The burning remains of the American steamship *Caroline* go over Niagara Falls on 29 December 1837 in this dramatic contemporary painting by George Tattersall.

Left.
A call to duty and a price on the head of William Lyon Mackenzie and other rebel leaders. This handbill was issued by lieutenant-governor Francis Bond Head as the rebel forces were being attacked by MacNab's militia north of Toronto on 7 December 1937.

A Report and One Canada

Some of the Frères chasseurs, Patriote rebels, at Beauharnois, painted by Katherine Jane Ellis between 4 and 10 November 1838 after the rebels had attacked her father's house and held her prisoner. She was freed by government troops on 10 November.

Opposite, centre. Lord Durham.

Opposite, bottom. The title page of Durham's 1839 report recommending the union of the Canadas.

Mackenzie's cause, so near to their own, had fired up many Americans, and there were several incursions into Canada to assist the rebel cause. In June 1838 Americans crossed into the Niagara Peninsula and in December some crossed the river from Detriot, but both invasions were easily repulsed. Later that year Patriotes, in the form now of a secret society called the Frères chasseurs (Hunting Brothers), invaded Lower Canada in another rebellion, notably seizing the manor at Beauharnois, just upriver from Montréal, that belonged to Edward Ellice, a wealthy landowner. The new rebellion failed after a thousand Glengarry Highlanders attacked, laying waste to the entire Beauharnois region, burning houses of guilty and innocent alike.

On 11 November, a little farther upriver, in Upper Canada, about four hundred Patriotes crossed the St. Lawrence between Johnstown and Prescott. They were resisted by the local militia; many Patriotes escaped back across the river, but about half holed up in a large stone windmill, where they were later forced to surrender. Thirty were killed and 160 taken prisoner. The engagement was later dubbed the Battle of the Windmill.

Into this foment for a brief interval came John George Lambton, the Earl of Durham. Made governor general of all the British colonies in America, he was given sweeping powers to quell the discontent. He arrived at Québec on 29 May 1838; unlike Arthur, one of his first acts was to exile to Bermuda some imprisoned Patriote leaders, including Wolfred Nelson. It seemed the right thing to do; a French jury would have acquitted them while an English one would have hanged them. But he was unsupported in this by a harder-line British government—for Bermuda was not a penal colony—and Durham resigned and left Canada only five months later.

During his brief tenure, however, Durham travelled widely and talked to many people, trying to determine what should be done about the unrest in the Canadas. The result was a report, written after he had returned to Britain, entitled *Report on the Affairs of British North America,* universally referred to today as the Durham Report. It analyzed the reasons for the unrest and made extensive recommendations for the future. In one famous phrase, Durham wrote: "I expected to find a contest between a government and a people: I found two nations warring in the bosom of a single state: I found struggle, not of principles, but of races." He had encapsulated the ongoing central theme of the Canadian political and national dichotomy, the differences between the French and English-speaking populations. Durham referred to it as the "fatal feud."

The Durham Report had two main recommendations. The first was for a responsible government in the form of an executive council elected by the people, the demand of the reformers for many years. The government, he wrote, should be administered "on those principles which have been found perfectly efficacious in Great Britain."

The second was for a union of the two Canadas under a single legislature, which he hoped would be English-dominated and would lead eventually to French Canadians "abandon[ing] their vain hopes of nationality." It was not the first time such a union had been proposed. A bill to unite the two provinces had been introduced into the British Parliament in 1822, only to fail. Mackenzie and others on occasion had advocated a union.

Durham's recommendations were in large part acted upon. The Canadas were to be united, but only if the two legislatures agreed. A skilled politician, Charles Edward Poulett Thomson (after August 1840 Lord Sydenham), was sent to Canada in 1839, and he persuaded the legislatures to agree. But Thomson had instructions from Lord John Russell, now colonial secretary, that responsible government was not to be implemented as such, for, argued Russell, how could a governor take orders from the British government and also from his colonial legislature? Nevertheless, it was made clear that normally the British government would have no desire to thwart the will of the representative assembly. Responsible government was coming, but it would have to wait a few more years.

The united Province of Canada, comprised of Canada West and Canada East, came into existence on 10 February 1841. Its capital was at Kingston.

The site of the Battle of the Windmill today.

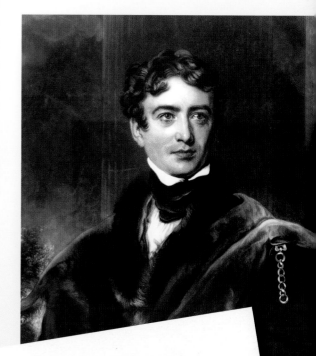

REPORT

ON

THE AFFAIRS

OF

BRITISH NORTH AMERICA,

FROM

THE EARL OF DURHAM,

HER MAJESTY'S HIGH COMMISSIONER,

&c. &c. &c.

8 *The Road to Nationhood*

The union of the Canadas in 1841 might have been expected to run quickly into trouble, for the Act of Union provided for equal representation for Canada West, the old Upper Canada, and Canada East, the former Lower Canada. This provision had been made despite the fact that out of a total population of about 1,150,000, French Canadians in Canada East alone outnumbered the entire population of Canada West. The writers of the act, as had Lord Durham, deliberately intended to suppress the French fact within a wider majority, which, it was hoped, would soon be enlarged by continued immigration. But the reformers in both Canada West and Canada East quickly realized that by working together they could achieve their aim of responsible government, and the union produced a series of co-operative majorities in the legislative assembly that foresaw the collaborative nature of the Canadian federation to come.

The first of these was the collaboration of Canada West reformers Robert Baldwin and Francis Hincks with Canada East Liberal leader Louis-Hippolyte La Fontaine. This co-operation got off to a good start in 1841 when La Fontaine lost his seat due to polling day violence and Baldwin got him re-elected in a riding in Toronto. In 1842 La Fontaine and Baldwin were taken into the government of a new governor general, Charles Bagot, when it became clear that his ministry could not survive without them. Since Bagot was defying his instructions from Britain to keep the reformers and the French Canadians out of his government, he was acceding to popular demand, the first concession to responsible government.

In 1846, in response to the Irish Famine, Britain repealed the Corn Laws, which ended an era of protectionism that favoured Britain's colonies. As a result the British government became less concerned with controlling the internal politics of its colonies. Thus in 1847 a new governor general, James Bruce, Earl of Elgin (of marbles fame), was sent to Canada with instructions from a new colonial secretary, Henry George Grey, Earl Grey (son of the earl after which the tea is named), to implement responsible government, now considered the best means of ending the political troubles in Canada.

After the reformers had won a parliamentary majority in 1848, Elgin called on La Fontaine to form a government, the first responsible government in Canada, of which

The parliamentary library and part of the original Parliament Buildings, built in 1863–66 and, except for the library, destroyed by fire in 1916. The buildings were designed by Thomas Fuller in a neo-Gothic style that was considered "Canadian" at the time. The photograph was taken by Samuel McLaughlin soon after the completion of the Parliament Buildings in 1866. McLaughlin was the official government "photographist" from 1861 to 1893.

Above.
Saint John, New Brunswick, in 1847.

Below.
The Parliament building in Montréal burns on 25 April 1849. This dramatic painting, attributed to Joseph Légaré, is an oil painted on wood, now in the McCord Museum in Montréal.

Baldwin was also a member. The same year Britain allowed a fully responsible government to take office in Nova Scotia, after an election returned the reformers in that province; responsible government came to the other British colonies in turn: Prince Edward Island in 1851, New Brunswick in 1854, and Newfoundland in 1855. Britain retained the right to set foreign ("imperial") policy, but for all other matters the lieutenant-governors and governor general were to follow the wishes of the elected body. The governors would only retain from now on what Elgin described as "a moral influence."

A test of the new order came soon enough. When La Fontaine's government attempted to atone for past injustices by passing the Rebellion Losses Bill in 1849, Elgin signed it, even though he knew that by so doing he would antagonize the English-speaking population. The bill had been passed by a majority in the Parliament, and thus Elgin thought he had no right to block it. "The Disgrace of Great Britain Accomplished!" blared the headlines in the Montreal *Gazette.* "Canada Sold and Given Away!" On 25 April 1849 Elgin arrived to sign the bill into law and was attacked by a stone- and egg-throwing mob. That evening a riot broke out. Agitators whipped the crowd into a frenzy, and its fury turned on the Parliament building, which since 1844 had been in Montréal. In an outrage clearly more organized than it seemed, the doors were broken down and the gas pipes were set on fire in at least a dozen places. In an instant, Canada lost all its historical parliamentary records, many paintings, and most of the books in the library. Luckily no lives were lost. The mob also de-

stroyed several reformers' houses, including that of La Fontaine. Elgin went home with a souvenir—a rock weighing nearly a kilogram that had been thrown at him.

In the aftermath of this turmoil arose a call for annexation to the United States, an idea born of the moment but which lasted until the signing of a reciprocal trade treaty in 1854. This Reciprocity Treaty aided Canada's prosperity—and the prosperous tend not to be rebellious. The economy was in an expansion phase during the 1850s, which included a railway-building boom (see page 140).

By the early 1850s the reformers found they had another problem—they were not radical enough for some. Left-leaning sectional interests emerged, the Parti Rouge in Canada East and the Clear Grits in Canada West, both of which advocated full parliamentary democracy and a written constitution, as in the American model. In 1851 La Fontaine and Baldwin retired and were succeeded by Augustin-Norbert Morin and Francis Hincks. In 1854 the government was replaced by a new Liberal-Conservative coalition, the Liberal Morin now allied with the Conservative Allan Napier MacNab, the colonel who had arrived with his militia in Toronto by steamer in the nick of time to put down the rebellion of 1837 and later chased William Lyon Mackenzie to Navy Island.

In 1856 the leadership of the Canada West (Conservative) part of the coalition passed to a man who was to have more than a passing influence on Canada—John Alexander Macdonald. He became co-premier of Canada with Étienne-Paschal Taché as prime minister, who had taken over from Morin in 1855. Taché retired in 1857, and John A. Macdonald became prime minister in a coalition with George-Étienne Cartier, another man who was to have a lasting effect on Canada.

At this time a decision was made as to the location of a capital city. So as to appear to have been above party politics the alternatives were submitted to Queen Victoria, who on the last day of 1857 selected Ottawa, and construction of the Parliament Buildings was begun in 1859.

The principal opposition to Macdonald's government was that of George Brown, editor of the Toronto *Globe,* and the Clear Grits, allied with the Rouges of Canada West, under Antoine-Aimé Dorion. In 1858 Brown and Dorion formed a government—for two days. Governments, in fact, came and went through the revolving door of politics many times in the period from 1858 to 1864, for the union of the dual Canadas was simply not working. Reformer John Sandfield Macdonald, who formed a government between May 1862 and March 1864, tried to govern on the principle of requiring a double majority, from east and west, but this also failed. By June 1864, the united Province of Canada was politically deadlocked. It was time for a bold new design.

Above.
"The man wot fired the Parliament House," by famous cartoonist John Wilson Bengough, published in a short-lived magazine, *Punch in Canada,* in 1849. It shows Louis La Fontaine—who looked like Napoleon—as the culprit.

Below.
John A. Macdonald, the "ruling genius" of Canadian Confederation.

Oil!

The discovery of oil in the middle of the nineteenth century transformed life at night. The whale or seal oil, fat, or tallow used in lamps and candles up till then yielded but a smokey and flickering flame. In 1854 Halifax physician Abraham Gesner patented a process that he had first demonstrated in 1846 for refining what he called kerosene from a coal-like deposit found in Nova Scotia. The new lamp fuel was called coal-oil by most who came to use it. Gesner found, however, that a Scottish chemist, James Young, had patented a similar oil he called "parafinne-oil" in 1850, so Gesner ended up paying royalties to Young to use his own invention.

The first oil company in North America was founded in Hamilton in 1854 by Charles Tripp. This company was taken over by James Miller Williams, a carriage maker, in 1856, and he started drilling for oil at Black Creek, near Oil Springs, just east of Sarnia, where, as the name suggests, oil had been seen at the surface for some time. This well went into production in 1858, becoming the first commercial oil well in North America. Williams's discovery was large enough to justify the construction of a refinery at Hamilton in 1860, to which oil was transported in barrels. Further oil discoveries in the mid-1860s led to the emergence of Petrolia, just north of Oil Springs, as the major oil-producing area.

The first western oil well was drilled at Oil City, now within Waterton National Park in Alberta, in 1901, again at a place oil had been seeping to the surface for centuries. But production proved erratic, and the well only produced a total of 32 000 litres before being shut down. The oil and gas industry of Alberta was born in May 1914 when Archibald Dingman found naphtha, thought at first to be oil, in the Turner Valley, south of Calgary, in 1914. Oil was later extracted in moderate quantities. The modern Canadian oil industry dates from 1947, when oil was found in hugely commercial quantities at Leduc, near Edmonton (see page 245).

Above.
An oil well at Petrolia, Ontario, about 1902.

Below.
The Atlantic Petroleum Works in east London, Ontario, about 1875. Despite the building of a pipeline between Petrolia and Sarnia in 1864, much oil was stored and transported in barrels—many, many barrels. Oil production today is still measured in barrels, just as it was in the beginning.

Escape to Canada

Upper Canada was the first British territory to legislate against slavery. In 1793 importation of slaves was forbidden, and children of slaves were to be free at twenty-five, thus ensuring that the practice would eventually die out. Britain abolished slavery in all its territories in 1834.

But slavery continued in the Southern states until ended by the American Civil War, which was fought essentially over this issue. Between about 1840 and 1860 a system of escape routes and safe houses was in operation known as the Underground Railroad. Some of these routes led to the Free States of the north, but the passing of the Fugitive Slave Act in 1850 meant that slaves could be pursued onto free soil; hence coming to Canada was safer. In the period 1840–50 perhaps as many as 40,000 slaves escaped to Canada.

Several safe havens for escaped slaves were established where, by banding together and enjoying the support of the white population, they were as safe as they could be anywhere, although there were attempts to abduct them from time to time. The earliest colony for escaped slaves, near Dresden, in western Ontario, was called the Dawn Settlement. It was here that Josiah Henson settled in 1841.

Another settlement created for runaway slaves was the Elgin Settlement, now North Buxton, just south of Chatham, Ontario. In 1849 the Reverend William King purchased 3 600 ha and made 20-hectare lots available for ex-slaves. As might be expected, each settler had to clear his own land, build a house, and help with road construction.

Half of the population of nearby Chatham was black in the 1850s. One of the residents of that town was Mary Ann Shadd Cary, a teacher, feminist, civil rights advocate, and the first black woman editor of a newspaper in North America. She moved back to the United States after the Civil War and in 1869 became the first black person in North America to enroll in a university law school. Her father, Abraham Doras Shadd, became the first black person to hold political office in Canada when he was elected to the Raleigh township council.

Left.
Josiah Henson was a slave born in Maryland in 1789. He was sold three times before he was eighteen. He escaped in 1830 after being cheated of the money he had saved to purchase his freedom and made his way to Canada via the Underground Railroad. In 1841 he moved with his family to Dresden, Ontario, where he helped establish the Dawn Settlement, a village for escaped slaves. Henson was the inspiration for Uncle Tom in Harriet Beecher Stowe's famous abolitionist novel *Uncle Tom's Cabin*, published in 1852, a book credited by Abraham Lincoln as being a catalyst for the American Civil War.

Below.
Part of a map of the Elgin Settlement, now North Buxton, Ontario, a refugee settlement for slaves established in 1849.

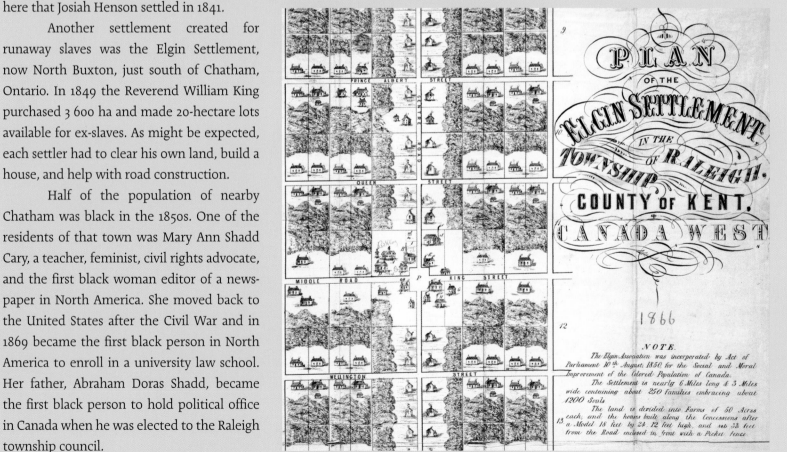

Farewell to Caledonia

When the forty-ninth parallel had been agreed upon as the international boundary with the United States in 1818, the region from the crest of the Rocky Mountains westwards had been defined as an area of "joint occupancy." This Oregon Country extended from 42° N north to the Russian territory of the Alaska Panhandle. It was this region that the Hudson's Bay Company had claimed as their own after the merger of that company with the North West Company in 1821. To the company, this was their Columbia Department, with its headquarters at Fort Vancouver, across the Columbia from what is now Portland, Oregon. The northern part of this country was what Simon Fraser had named New Caledonia. On the lower Fraser River was Fort Langley, a fur-trading post established in 1827.

By the 1840s it had become obvious to governor George Simpson that the post at Fort Vancouver would soon become untenable; settlers were flooding into the Willamette Valley just south of the fort and American sentiment for annexation of the territory was running high. In 1843 he sent James Douglas north to establish a new fort on Victoria Harbour.

In 1846 Simpson's fears were realized. The British government agreed to the extension of the forty-ninth parallel boundary to the sea, but excluding Vancouver Island. In 1849 the Hudson's Bay Company abandoned Fort Vancouver and moved its headquarters to Fort Victoria. The same year the Colony of Vancouver Island was created and ceded to the company for a rent of seven shillings a year, on the condition that settlement was forthcoming. Some colonists were settled, but in general the company did not want them, for it saw them as destroying the fur trade. James Douglas became the colony's governor in 1851, after the first governor, Richard Blanshard, clashed with him in his capacity as company factor and resigned.

In 1858 gold was discovered in the sandbars and canyons of the Fraser and Thompson Rivers on the mainland, setting off a gold rush. Before the end of the year perhaps 25,000 miners poured into New Caledonia, mainly from the United States. This territory was not formally a British colony and Douglas, having experienced the problems that an influx of Americans could bring, took it upon himself to impose British law and order on the mainland, technically not under his jurisdiction.

In Britain, the catalyst for the idea of creating a new colony was the colonial secretary, Edward Bulwer Lytton (whose other claim to fame is as the author of the novel that begins with the legendary words "It was

Above.
Fort Victoria in 1845, two years after it was built, in a painting by British military engineer Henry Warre.

Below.
Fort Yale, at the southern entrance to the Fraser Canyon, surrounded by the tents of gold miners during the 1858 gold rush.

Opposite, top. James Douglas.

a dark and stormy night . . ."). A bill to create a new colony, to be called New Caledonia, was introduced into the British Parliament on 1 July 1858. It was passed on 2 August, but not before Queen Victoria herself had suggested a new name—British Columbia. The colony could be confused with French Caledonia in the South Pacific, it was thought; instead it would now be confused with a South American country. At the same time that Britain was trying to divest herself of colonies on the east coast it had created a new one on the west.

James Douglas, whom the British government had belatedly recognized as having done the right thing in imposing British law earlier in the year, was appointed governor of British Columbia, in addition to Vancouver Island, and he was sworn in at Fort Langley on 19 November. The next year a site for a capital was chosen by Richard Clement Moodie, a Royal Engineer sent with his men to improve the infrastructure of the new colony. On the north side of the Fraser River, Albert City was laid out. But Queen Victoria again got into the act and renamed it New Westminster.

In 1862 another gold rush occurred after William (Billy) Barker found gold in the Cariboo. To service the goldfields, the Royal Engineers built a road through the Fraser Canyon. The Cariboo Road was an amazing engineering feat along the route Simon Fraser thought "no human being should venture" (see page 108).

British Columbia and Vancouver Island remained separate colonies for eight years. In 1866, as an economy measure, the two were combined into one, which took the mainland colony's name, British Columbia, becoming a province when it joined Confederation in 1871 (see page 154).

Below.
Barkerville, a gold rush town on the edge of the Cariboo Mountains, named after prospector Billy Barker. At its peak the town was home to 10,000 people and was the largest settlement in western Canada. Today it has been rebuilt as a tourist attraction.

Fortunes of Which They Little Dreamed

The coming of the railway had a profound effect on the economic development of Canada, for here was a relatively fast, almost year-round communication system that suddenly put every rural village within hours of a big city market. Yet it would prove difficult for a private company to make a profit from a railway in such a vast country so sparsely populated.

The very first Canadian railways were portage railways, designed to carry passengers and goods from one watershed to another. The first was built to create a shortcut from the Rivière Richelieu at Saint-Jean to La Prairie, opposite Montré-al. This was the Champlain and St. Lawrence Railroad, which opened on 21 July 1836 with the steam engine *Dorchester,* burning wood and running on iron rails.

The second railway was an industrial one, built to carry coal from Albion Mines, now Stellarton, to Pictou Harbour, in Nova Scotia. Its locomotive, the *Samson,* is now the oldest surviving original Canadian locomotive. It was the first on the continent to burn coal and run on all-steel rails.

Almost ten years passed before Canada's third railway was built. This was another portage railway, between Montréal and Lachine. It opened on 19 November 1847 and then promptly shut down again for the winter. Although the railway itself could run during most of the winter, since it was serving steamers, as a portage, the traffic stopped when the rivers iced up.

There were other short portage railways, but by the 1850s attention was being turned to longer-distance lines. In 1849 the Great Western Railway began construction of a line to connect the Niagara River with the Detroit River, from Niagara Falls to Windsor via Hamilton. The line was completed in 1854. Due to the line's connections at Niagara Falls and Detroit, this marked the first achievement of a rail line from the Atlantic to the Mississippi. Other local lines were built, so that by 1882 the Great Western had 1 280 km of lines in southwestern Ontario and another 280 km in Michigan.

In July 1853 a rail line connecting Longueuil, opposite Montréal, with Portland, Maine, was opened. This was the world's first international railway. It was at first two separate companies, the St. Lawrence and Atlantic (which ran the Canadian part) and the Atlantic and St. Lawrence (which ran the American part). For the first time Montréal could be reached even when the river was frozen. A year later Lévis, across the river from Québec, was also connected. The economic benefits were extolled by all. A Portland newspaper remarked that "the railway to Montreal has turned the forests along its line into gold [and] the whole region has been touched with new life, realizing [for landowners] fortunes of which they little dreamed."

Above, top.
Replica of the *Dorchester,* the first Canadian locomotive, which ran on the Champlain and St. Lawrence Railroad in 1836. This locomotive is in the National Railway Museum in Montréal.

Above.
The Victoria Tubular Bridge, built by the Grand Trunk Railway and completed in 1859. The trains ran through a rectangular tunnel-like tube. The already operating bridge was officially opened by the visiting Prince of Wales (later Edward VII) in 1860.

The international line was incorporated into the Grand Trunk Railway in 1853 (the American part) and 1854 (the Canadian part), and the railway grew significantly by amalgamation with shorter lines. The Grand Trunk had been chartered in 1853 to build a rail line from the Atlantic to Sarnia and thence to the American Midwest. Railway building went on apace, helped by thousands of navvies from England, who earned five shillings a day. In 1854 work had begun on a link across the St. Lawrence at Montréal, to connect the original international line with the rest of the emerging network. The Victoria Bridge, considered an engineering wonder in its day, was a tubular structure 2 km long on special abutments and twenty-four piers designed to repel ice in the winter. Along the top of the tube was an opening designed to let out the steam. The bridge was completed in 1859 and opened on 17 December after a test train successfully passed over—or rather, through—the bridge loaded with stone to twice the weight of a regular train.

The Grand Trunk Railway was by Confederation the largest railway system in the world, with over 2 000 km of track, a system that became even larger in 1883, when the Grand Trunk merged with the Great Western. In 1873 the International Bridge was opened across the Niagara River, replacing a ferry and providing a direct connection with railways in New York state, and in 1891 the St. Clair Tunnel was opened across the St. Clair River at Sarnia.

The other major railway project of the nineteenth century was the Intercolonial Railway, required as a condition of Confederation (see page 147), though planned before. It ran from Rivière-du-Loup through northern New Brunswick to Truro and Halifax, this route having been chosen because it was as far from the American border as possible. Under the expert guidance of its chief engineer, Sandford Fleming, the rail line was completed in July 1876. This provided the link between the new provinces and an all-British connection with an ice-free port on the Atlantic seaboard. The far-sighted Fleming insisted that all significant bridges be made of iron, not the much cheaper wood, and that the railway use only steel rails. Despite these qualities, which yielded operational savings, the Intercolonial was never a financial success, for it had been built for political rather than commercial reasons. Fortunes, for this railway, remained a dream.

Above.
The *Samson*, the oldest surviving Canadian locomotive, now in the Museum of Industry in Stellarton, Nova Scotia. The firebox, seen at the *front* of the engine, was dangerous to stoke when the engine was on the move.

Below.
The locomotive *Toronto*, the first to be manufactured in Ontario, was completed on 16 April 1853 for the Ontario, Simcoe and Huron Railway. A month later it became the first locomotive to haul a regular steam train in Ontario, from Toronto to Machell's Corners (now Aurora), taking two hours to travel 40 km. The railway reached Georgian Bay in 1855.

Confederation

The bold new design, of course, was a confederation. And the man who got it going was none other than George Brown. In 1864, seeing the deadlocked condition of the united Province of Canada, he offered to put aside party politics and back a government willing to remake the union entirely. In an extraordinary display of co-operation, the legislature approved a resolution by Brown to create an all-party committee to study the options and even appointed him its chairman, and it was out of this co-operation that a coalition was formed with Brown's reformers. It was this coalition that finally negotiated Confederation.

The choice came down to federation of Canada East and Canada West or a confederation that brought in the Maritime colonies as well. The Macdonald-Cartier-Brown coalition lost no time in exploring the wider option. As it happened, the Maritime colonies were at this time almost bankrupt because of their investment in railway schemes, and were considering a conference to discuss a Maritime union as a way out of their troubles. In July, a formal request was sent to the Maritime colonies requesting that they receive a delegation from Canada. They could hardly refuse.

But agreeing to a conference was a long way from agreeing to a confederation. When the eight delegates from Canada arrived at Charlottetown on the steamer *Queen Victoria* on 1 September they began a carefully prepared sales job, supported by parties, balls,

Below.
One of the most famous Canadian photographs, showing the participants in the Charlottetown Conference in September 1864. It was taken by photographer G. P. Roberts. At centre, sitting on the step, is John A. Macdonald, and standing to his right, top hat in hand, is George-Étienne Cartier. Between them, in front of a column, is Thomas D'Arcy McGee.

and feasts on board their steamer. In this at times almost carnival-like atmosphere, the Maritime delegates were quickly persuaded of the virtues of Confederation. Possibly the world's first mobile conference, they all set off in the *Queen Victoria* first for Halifax and then to Saint John and Fredericton, to continue the process of gaining support for the Confederation proposals, finally agreeing to meet again in Québec in October. The whole process had taken the Canadian delegates three weeks.

Many in the Maritimes were outraged at what one writer succinctly called the Canadian *coup de théâtre:* they had sent their delegates off to discuss a possible Maritime union and they had come back with a Canadian one. "Such prostitution of intellect has seldom been equalled," sniffed the Saint John *Morning Telegraph.*

The Québec Conference met over an eighteen-day period beginning on 10 October. Most of the Charlottetown delegates were present, and in addition Newfoundland sent two delegates. It was at Québec that the details of Confederation were hammered out. The most contentious issue was that of representation in a federal parliament. Prince Edward Island, not unsurprisingly, did not like the idea of the allocation of seats by population. The result of the Québec deliberations was seventy-two resolutions, which would form the basis for

Above.
The new Parliament Buildings under construction in Ottawa in 1863. Begun in 1859 for the united Province of Canada, they were completed in 1866, in time to become the Parliament Buildings of the Dominion.

Above.
The delegates to the Québec Conference, October 1864.

Right.
Proclamation of the Dominion of Canada by Queen Victoria.

Far right.
The editorial, written by George Brown, that appeared in his *Globe* on 1 July 1867.

Below.
In this caricature model from the George-Étienne Cartier house in Montréal, now a National Historic Site, (*left to right*) Macdonald, Cartier, and Brown get into the Canadian bed while Canada East Rouge leader Antoine-Aimé Dorion is left out in the cold.

the British North America Act, creating the Dominion of Canada. The delegates took them back to their legislatures for debate. Prince Edward Island and Newfoundland decided that they did not want to be part of the proposed confederation; their joining would wait until 1873 and 1949, respectively.

John A. Macdonald would have preferred a simple legislative union, with a single parliament and apparatus of government. He thought that would be the cheapest, most vigorous, and strongest system. But the pragmatic Macdonald knew that since there were considerable differences between the provinces, "there was a great disinclination on the part of the various Maritime Provinces to lose their individuality, as separate political organizations." Macdonald pointed to the United States' difficulties with "states rights," a war over which was raging in that country. The system devised and agreed to was one that learned from the American experience; instead of starting with the idea of a state as sovereign and then allocating specific responsibilities to a federal government, the Canadian system would do the reverse. All powers not specifically given to a province would remain with the federal government.

The debate in New Brunswick was rancorous, and the whole scheme for Confederation nearly foundered when the premier, Leonard Tilley, was thrown out on the issue in an election he had to call in 1865. The new government, however, lasted barely a year. London-ordered pressure to support Confederation was brought to bear on the new premier, Albert Smith, who resigned. He was replaced by a pro-Confederation premier, Robert Wilmot, who was then promptly defeated, causing a new election. This election, famously corrupt, saw Tilley writing to Macdonald for "forty or fifty thousand of the needful." Money poured in to support the confederative cause. And it worked; Tilley was re-elected in June 1866 and his new government ratified Confederation.

One more hurdle remained, the agreement of Britain. Delegates travelled to London, where, on 4 December 1866, a new conference was convened, intended to supervise the translation of the Québec Resolutions into the formal language of an Act of Parliament. But the provinces, which had now had time to consider and debate the matter, wanted changes. The Canadian delegates now wanted protection for minority schools,

BY THE QUEEN.
A PROCLAMATION
For Uniting the Provinces of Canada, Nova Scotia, and New Brunswick into One Dominion under the Name of CANADA.

VICTORIA R.

WHEREAS by an Act of Parliament passed on the Twenty-ninth Day of March One thousand eight hundred and sixty-seven, in the Thirtieth Year of Our Reign, intituled " An Act for the Union of Canada, Nova Scotia, and New Brunswick, and the " Government thereof, and for Purposes connected therewith," after divers Recitals, it is enacted, that " it shall be lawful for the Queen, by and with the Advice of Her Majesty's most Honorable " Privy Council, to declare by Proclamation that on and after a Day therein appointed, not being " more than Six Months after the passing of this Act, the Provinces of Canada, Nova Scotia, and " New Brunswick shall form and be One Dominion under the Name of Canada, and on and after " that Day those Three Provinces shall form and be One Dominion under that Name accordingly:" And it is thereby further enacted, that " such Persons shall be first summoned to the Senate as " the Queen, by Warrant under Her Majesty's Royal Sign Manual, thinks fit to approve, and " their Names shall be inserted in the Queen's Proclamation of Union:" We therefore, by and with the Advice of Our Privy Council, have thought fit to issue this Our Royal Proclamation, and We do Ordain, Declare, and Command, that on and after the First Day of July One thousand eight hundred and sixty-seven the Provinces of Canada, Nova Scotia, and New Brunswick shall form and be One Dominion under the Name of Canada. And We do further Ordain and Declare, that the Persons whose Names are herein inserted and set forth are the Persons of whom We have, by Warrant under Our Royal Sign Manual, thought fit to approve as the Persons who shall be first summoned to the Senate of Canada.

FOR THE PROVINCE OF ONTARIO.

JOHN HAMILTON,
RODERICK MATHESON,
JOHN ROSS,
SAMUEL MILLS,
BENJAMIN SEYMOUR,
WALTER HAMILTON DICKSON,
JAMES SHAW,
ADAM JOHNSTON FERGUSON BLAIR,
ALEXANDER CAMPBELL,
DAVID CHRISTIE,
JAMES COX AIKINS,
DAVID REESOR,
ELIJAH LEONARD,
WILLIAM MACMASTER,
ASA ALLWORTH BURNHAM,
JOHN SIMPSON,
JAMES SKEAD,
DAVID LEWIS MACPHERSON,
GEORGE CRAWFORD,
DONALD MACDONALD,
OLIVER BLAKE,
BILLA FLINT,
WALTER M'CREA,
GEORGE WILLIAM ALLAN.

FOR THE PROVINCE OF QUEBEC.

JAMES LESLIE,
ASA BELKNAP FOSTER,
JOSEPH NOËL BOSSÉ,
LOUIS A. OLIVIER,
JACQUE OLIVIER BUREAU,
CHARLES MALHIOT,
LOUIS RENAUD,
LUC LETELLIER DE ST. JUST,
ULRIC JOSEPH TESSIER,
JOHN HAMILTON,
CHARLES CORMIER,
ANTOINE JUCHEREAU DUCHESNAY,
DAVID EDWARD PRICE,
ELZEAR H. J. DUCHESNAY,
LEANDRE DUMOUCHEL,
LOUIS LACOSTE,
JOSEPH F. ARMAND,
CHARLES WILSON,
WILLIAM HENRY CHAFFERS,
JEAN BAPTISTE GUÉVREMONT,
JAMES FERRIER,
Sir NARCISSE FORTUNAT BELLEAU, Knight,
THOMAS RYAN,
JOHN SEWELL SANBORN.

FOR THE PROVINCE OF NOVA SCOTIA.

EDWARD KENNY,
JONATHAN M'CULLY,
THOMAS D. ARCHIBALD,
ROBERT B. DICKEY,
JOHN H. ANDERSON,
JOHN HOLMES,
JOHN W. RITCHIE,
BENJAMIN WIER,
JOHN LOCKE,
CALEB R. BILL,
JOHN BOURINOT,
WILLIAM MILLER.

FOR THE PROVINCE OF NEW BRUNSWICK.

AMOS EDWIN BOTSFORD,
EDWARD BARRON CHANDLER,
JOHN ROBERTSON,
ROBERT LEONARD HAZEN,
WILLIAM HUNTER ODELL,
DAVID WARK,
WILLIAM HENRY STEEVES,
WILLIAM TODD,
JOHN FERGUSON,
ROBERT DUNCAN WILMOT,
ABNER REID M'CLELAN,
PETER MITCHELL.

Given at Our Court at Windsor Castle, this Twenty-second Day of May, in the Year of our Lord One thousand eight hundred and sixty-seven, and in the Thirtieth Year of Our Reign.

God save the Queen.

LONDON: Printed by GEORGE EDWARD EYRE and WILLIAM SPOTTISWOODE, Printers to the Queen's most Excellent Majesty. 1867.

CONFEDERATION DAY.

The Dominion of Canada.

HISTORICAL NOTES

HOW CONFEDERATION HAS BEEN BROUGHT ABOUT.

STATISTICS OF THE UNITED PROVINCES.

Extent, Population, Trade and Resources of the Dominion.

With the first dawn of this gladsome midsummer morn, we hail the birthday of a new nationality. A united British America, with its four millions of people, takes its place this day among the nations of the world. Stamped with a familiar name, which in the past has borne a record sufficiently honourable to entitle it to be perpetuated with a more comprehensive import, the DOMINION OF CANADA, on this First day of July, in the year of grace, eighteen hundred and sixty-seven, enters on a new career of national existence. Old things have passed away. The history of old Canada, with its contracted bounds, and limited divisions of Upper and Lower, East and West, has been completed, and this day a new volume is opened, New Brunswick and Nova Scotia uniting with Ontario and Quebec to make the history of a greater Canada, already extending from the ocean to the head waters of the great lakes, and destined ere long to embrace the larger half of this North American continent from the Atlantic to the Pacific.

Let us gratefully acknowledge the hand of the Almighty Disposer of Events in bringing about this result, pregnant with so important an influence on the condition and destinies of the inhabitants of these Provinces, and of the teeming millions who in ages to come will people the Dominion of Canada from ocean to ocean, and give it its character in the annals of time. Let us acknowledge, too, the sagacity, the patriotism, the forgetfulness of selfish and partisan considerations, on the part of our statesmen, to which under Providence are due the inception of the project of a British American Confederation and the carrying it to a successful issue. Without much patient labour, a disposition to make mutual concessions, and an earnest large-minded willingness to subordinate all party interests to the attainment of what would be for the lasting weal of the whole people of British America, the result we celebrate this day would never have been achieved. It has taken just three years to accomplish — not certainly an unreasonable space of time for a work of such magnitude. Three years ago, Mr. Brown, Mr. Mowat, and Mr. McDougall, as representing the Reformers of Upper Canada, joined Mr. John A. Macdonald, Mr. Cartier, and their political associates, in forming a Government whose single and sole mission it should be to aim at the establishment for these Provinces of a new state of political existence, in which we should be rid of the peculiar evils and grievances which had hitherto obstructed our progress, and enter on a happier and brighter era. That Government was formed on the 30th June, 1864. On the 1st July, 1867, we witness the fruition of what was then undertaken. The public men of the Maritime Provinces joined in the good work, the sympathy and support of the great mass of the people were soon found to be heartily enlisted in the movement, the cordial and generous co-operation of the mother country was given to it, and this day the Dominion of Canada is proclaimed; and, as Canadians, no longer confined within petty Provincial limits, but members of a larger nationality, New Brunswick and Nova Scotia, Quebec and Ontario, join hands, and a shout of rejoicing goes up from the four millions of people who are now linked together for weal or for woe, to work out in common the destinies of a united British America.

Above.
The Battle of Ridgeway, 2 June 1866, in which a Fenian army of about eight hundred defeated a Canadian militia force of about nine hundred.

Opposite, top.
Thomas D'Arcy McGee, one of the most prominent Fathers of Canadian Confederation.

Opposite, bottom.
Part of the procession for McGee's funeral in Montréal in 1868, on what would have been his forty-third birthday.

for example. And so the delegates first debated amongst themselves. It was Macdonald who skilfully steered them to a conclusion everyone could live with, despite suffering from burns incurred when he set his hotel room on fire after falling asleep reading with a lit candle. The deputy minister at the Colonial Office wrote of Macdonald that he "was the ruling genius and spokesman, and I was very much struck by his powers of management and adroitness." On Christmas Day 1866, the delegates' final resolutions were delivered to the British government (something that would be difficult to do nowadays at any time over Christmas).

During January and February 1867 the resolutions were drafted into a bill by the British government. Few changes were made to the delegates' final resolutions. One change that was made was the ability of the government to create extra seats in the Senate if the Commons and upper house were deadlocked, a power never used until 1990, when it was employed by the Conservative government of Brian Mulroney to pass the Goods and Services Tax (GST) bill.

The British North America Act, establishing the Dominion of Canada as a federation of Canada West, now to be called Ontario; Canada East, now to be called Québec; New Brunswick; and Nova Scotia was signed on 29 April 1867 and proclaimed by Queen Victoria to come into force on 1 July.

Canada was designated a "dominion" as a result of Tilley, the New Brunswick premier. Most of the Fathers of Confederation (as the delegates are now generally referred to) wanted to call their creation the Kingdom of Canada. But the British government, sensitive to the possibility of offending the Americans, insisted on a different title. The religious Tilley consulted his bible and found Psalm 72:8—"He shall have dominion also from sea to sea." And so "Dominion" it was. Legally, it is the Dominion of Canada to this day.

One of the essential clauses of the British North America Act provided for connecting glue for the federation in the form of a railway, the Intercolonial Railway, "connecting the River St. Lawrence with the City of Halifax in Nova Scotia, and for the Construction thereof without Intermission, and the Completion thereof with all practical speed." Originally proposed by Lord Durham in 1839, the railway had been much talked about but little acted upon. Guaranteed now by the federation, the railway was finally completed under the direction of Sandford Fleming in 1876.

The drive for Confederation was aided, strangely enough, by an outside force. The Fenians were an organization of American Irish who wanted Irish independence from Britain. Although founded in 1857, they did not become a danger until towards the end of the Civil War, when thousands of their supporters were suddenly war veterans with time on their hands. Invasions of Canada, seen as the back door to Britain, were planned. New Brunswick was attacked in April 1866 in an abortive raid that was easily repelled. But it did have the effect of swinging public opinion in favour of Confederation.

About eight hundred Fenians crossed into the Niagara Peninsula on the night of 31 May 1866 and on 2 June were engaged by a slightly larger Canadian militia force at Ridgeway, just west of Fort Erie. The militia commander became confused and the Canadians were driven from the field; about ten men were killed. The Fenians, however, did not press their advantage and withdrew back across the Niagara River. Another Fenian attack took place in Québec a week later, again to no advantage. When an Irish uprising failed in 1867 the Fenian military movement disintegrated. But there is no doubt that the Fenian threat, coming at such a crucial time for Canada, rallied support for Confederation.

In 1868 one of the Fathers of Confederation, Canada's Thomas D'Arcy McGee, a journalist and poet as well as a politician, was assassinated, it is assumed, by a Fenian supporter. McGee was an Irish immigrant who had, in Fenian eyes, "gone over" to the British cause. He was in fact an ardent supporter of Irish nationalism, but was vehemently against the violence advocated by the Fenians. McGee was shot from the shadows as he entered his residence in Ottawa late on 7 April after making a speech in the House of Commons. The perpetrator, Patrick James Whelan, was caught and hanged in what was the last public hanging in Canada. But it was never actually proved that Whelan was a Fenian, or even that it was he who committed the foul deed; there have been recent moves to win Whelan a posthumous pardon.

McGee was well liked, and his funeral, in his hometown Montréal, was a massive affair that reflected the new nation's shock at losing one of its founding fathers so soon.

To Commune with Their Corrupt Hearts

Until quite recently, the best deterrent to crime was considered to be brutal punishment carried out in public for any other would-be offenders to see. This was the case in Europe, and the colonial administrators saw things no differently. The idea of rehabilitation rather than retribution is a relatively modern idea. Flogging with the cat-o'-nine-tails was only removed from the Canadian Criminal Code in 1968, as were other forms of corporal punishment. The last execution in Canada took place in 1962, and capital punishment has been abolished, although theoretically it is still applicable under the National Defence Act for cowardice, desertion, unlawful surrender, and spying.

The first recorded execution in Canada seems to have been the hanging of a colonist by the Sieur de Roberval for theft of food in September 1542; others were put in irons or whipped. In New France the same law as that in Paris applied. Penalties could be exacted for the most trifling of crimes and included hanging, serving on France's galleys, horrific tortures such as breaking on the wheel, flogging, branding (on hands, backs, and tongues) and various other mutilations, pillorying, confiscation of property, fines, and imprisonment.

British Canada was by no means a better place for a criminal to be. The range of punishable crimes and the severity of the penalty was similar. Death was the prescribed punishment for a range of petty crimes, including stealing just about anything. One did not have to be a murderer or a rebel to suffer this consequence. And hanging did not necessarily mean a quick death; when Samuel Lount and Peter Matthews were hanged in Toronto for their part in the rebellion of 1837 they were simply roped up and left to die by strangulation. The rebels of Lower Canada, by comparison, suffered the usually quick form of hanging where the neck is broken on release of a trap door beneath the feet. But all executions were public, and one's patriotism could be questioned if you did not watch.

In general, punishments were becoming less harsh by the 1830s, although by modern standards one would hardly know it. Public outrage over the hanging of three men in Montréal in 1829 for stealing cattle brought an end to capital punishment for that offence. Fines became more common, and the idea that convicts should be

Above.
Five of the Patriote rebels are hanged in Montréal on 15 February 1839.

Right.
The water bath punishment used at Kingston Penitentiary on 358 occasions between June 1855 and July 1859. The unfortunate's head was placed in the small barrel and water poured into it from the larger barrel above. This was supposed to be a more humane punishment than flogging. The contraption is preserved at Canada's Penitentiary Museum at Kingston Penitentiary.

put to useful work gained acceptance, if only to reduce the public costs of their upkeep.

In 1835 a new kind of prison was opened at Kingston. The prison was now to give inmates "pure air, wholesome food, comfortable clothing, and medical aid when necessary," *but* the prison was to be so unpleasant that fear of returning there would prevent future crimes. The cells were 30 inches (76 cm) wide. A highly disciplined regime with punishment for those that strayed from it was ordered. Prison rules forbade imates to communicate with each other. They could not "exchange looks, winks, laugh, nod, gesticulate to each other." Guards were told to strictly enforce the regime and flogged any who transgressed the rules. "Let them walk their gloomy abodes," the policy ran, "and commune with their corrupt hearts and guilty consciences in silence." The mere prison now became a penitentiary.

There was a stone pile at Kingston, as in most prisons, for prisoners hard at work were less likely to turn their minds to mischief. Hard labour was thought to be the "penance that would cleanse the soul." But there was a slow movement towards less brutality—at least as far as inured minds of the nineteenth century thought of it. At Kingston in the 1850s the "water bath punishment" was introduced as a way—believe it or not—to reduce the use of corporal punishment, a somehow gentler way of inflicting pain. The unfortunate victim was stripped and placed in stocks. His head was placed in a small barrel, into which water was poured in torrents, half drowning the convict. Water leaked out at an indetermi-

Above.
Convicts at work at the stone pile in Kingston Penitentiary in 1873.

Below.
An extract from the punishment book at Kingston Penitentiary for August 1866. An unfortunate Alphonse Sobourin is condemned to sixty lashes with the cat-o'-nine-tails for being drunk in his cell; the names of the guards who administered the lashes are noted at right. Charles Fitzpatrick is given three meals of bread and water for idling in the tailor's workshop.

nate rate, and water was poured in at the operator's whim, so some victims likely suffered more than others. This punishment was used at Kingston between 1855 and 1859.

By 1865 only murder, rape, and treason were capital offences. A slow move towards reform of the penal system was taking place. Lip service, if nothing else, was paid to the idea that the penal system should reform an offender, but the necessity for punishment and deterrence still overrode the desire for reform. Not until after World War II did the emphasis truly begin to change from punishment to rehabilitation.

9 Building a Nation

When the British lost the Indian Territory of Michigan and the Ohio Valley after the American War of Independence and a boundary line was later drawn on the forty-ninth parallel, it became inevitable, once central Canada was settled, that colonists would find land for expansion in the West. Confederation had specifically allowed for the inclusion of the Northwest and growth by the addition of new provinces, and the government of John A. Macdonald and George-Étienne Cartier realized from the start that in order for Canada to counteract the power of the much more populated United States, the country would have to grow. If Canada did not take on the Northwest, the Americans would, and encirclement would likely be the death knell of the nascent confederation.

This situation was exacerbated by the American purchase of Alaska in 1867. It seemed that the besieging of Canada had already begun; only the sparsely populated British colony of British Columbia stood between American geographical contiguity, and murmurings of annexation had already been heard in that colony.

Yet one of the four original signatories of the Confederation scheme, Nova Scotia, was now having second thoughts. Even before the passage of the British North America Act a delegation from the province, headed by Joseph Howe, had travelled to London to attempt to prevent its passage. In September 1867 a thoroughly anti-Confederation legislature had been elected, and in 1868 Howe once again led a delegation to London, this time to persuade the British government to allow Nova Scotia's secession. A new British government under William Gladstone finally rejected the Maritimers' arguments in December 1868. The political adept John A. Macdonald then allowed Nova Scotia to renegotiate some of the financial terms of Confederation and finally took an at first reluctant Howe, now a federal member of Parliament, into his cabinet.

Meanwhile, in December 1867 the Macdonald-Cartier government had introduced a bill requesting the transfer of Rupert's Land to Canada. It passed, for this was an extension of Canada, not Ontario. As Cartier said, "The acquisition ought to excite no internal jealousy [for] it would increase the importance of the whole Dominion." From October 1868 until April 1869 Cartier was in London, negotiating the terms under which the Hudson's Bay

Left.
Cree chief Pi-tikwahanapiwi-yin—Poundmaker—in 1885. Although he had largely tried to restrain his followers from rebellious acts, he was held responsible for them and was imprisoned after the Northwest Rebellion.

Above.
The Great Seal of the new Dominion of Canada, 1869.

Company territory would be transferred. Canada was to pay £300,000 but allow the company to retain a twentieth of the fertile land and keep lands around existing trading posts. The company signed and sealed the deed of transfer on 19 November 1869 and the transfer date was set for 1 December. But events intervened, and the transfer did not actually take place until 15 July 1870.

A Rebellion on the Red River

For Macdonald was in too much of a hurry. He authorized the land in the Red River Settlement to be surveyed so as to provide lots for the expected influx of new settlers, but with a disregard that was all too typical up until relatively recently, he had overlooked the fact that the land he was about to obtain for Canada was already occupied. He also overlooked the fact that Canada had no legal authority in Rupert's Land until the transfer was finalized. The Métis of Red River, the descendants of French fur traders and their native wives, occupied long plots of land back from the river frontage. When Canadian surveyors appeared on their land with their survey equipment, apparently in disregard for any existing boundaries, this caused an uproar. On 12 October 1869 a group of Métis led by Louis Riel intercepted the surveyors under Major A. C. Webb and stood on their surveying chains. Webb saw that it was hopeless to continue surveying and withdrew.

Macdonald had appointed a lieutenant-governor for the new North-West Territories again prematurely. At the end of October Riel's men blocked the trail from Pembina and prevented William McDougall from entering the territory. Two days later Riel seized the Hudson's Bay Company's Upper Fort Garry without a fight. Thus began the incident that has come to be known as the Red River Rebellion.

Louis Riel was the natural man to whom the Métis had turned when their rights were threatened. Riel's father, also named Louis, had led a minor Métis revolt against perceived injustices by the Hudson's Bay Company in 1849. The younger Riel was educated, and fired with a religious zeal that gave him a sense of mission, to an extent that would later prove to be his undoing.

Riel declared a provisional government for Red River on 23 December and prepared a "List of Rights" and a "Declaration of the People of Rupert's Land and the Northwest." The Canadian government then sent commissioners, including Donald Smith of the

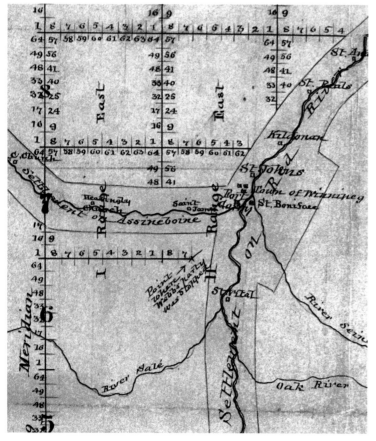

Left, top.
Louis Riel, from a photograph taken when he went to Ottawa in 1873 to register as a member of Parliament.

Left.
This map of the survey that was being carried out by Major A. C. Webb shows the *Point where Webb's party was stopped,* just to the southwest of the confluence of the Red and Assiniboine Rivers. Here Riel and his men stood on the surveyors' chains.

Right.
Upper Fort Garry is shown in 1879 in this painting by Lionel Stephenson.

Hudson's Bay Company, to negotiate with Riel. Smith succeeded in getting Riel to agree to a meeting in which delegates were elected to discuss the terms of union with Canada. But Riel used the same meeting to elect officers for his provisional government, which in turn drew up a "Bill of Rights." This document, somewhat further modified on the advice of the spiritual leader of the Catholic Métis, the bishop of St. Boniface, Alexandre-Antonin Taché, would be used the following year to negotiate the terms on which the new province of Manitoba would enter Confederation.

Macdonald was concerned that the longer the takeover of the North-West Territories was held up, the more likely was American intervention. The Canadian government agreed to recognize Riel's provisional government, provided only that some captives he held were set free. But before Riel could release them, Fort Garry was attacked by a group of men from Portage la Prairie attempting to free the original captives. The venture failed, and Riel thus released one group and held another. This new group of captives included an abrasive Irish Orangeman named Thomas Scott, who by all accounts was a particularly difficult prisoner. When Scott struck some of his guards, Riel snapped. Scott was summarily tried, found guilty, and executed.

Riel could not have picked a worse subject for his wrath. The Protestant Orangemen of Ontario demanded Macdonald act to

Above.
This well-known depiction of the execution of Orangeman Thomas Scott at Upper Fort Garry on 4 March 1870 appeared on the front cover of the *Canadian Illustrated News* and inflamed public opinion in Ontario.

Fort Garry

With the extension of Canada to the Northwest and the creation of the new province of Manitoba, many in Ontario wanted to move west. But before the advent of the railway, moving was not such a simple task, as this 1872 advertising broadsheet attests.

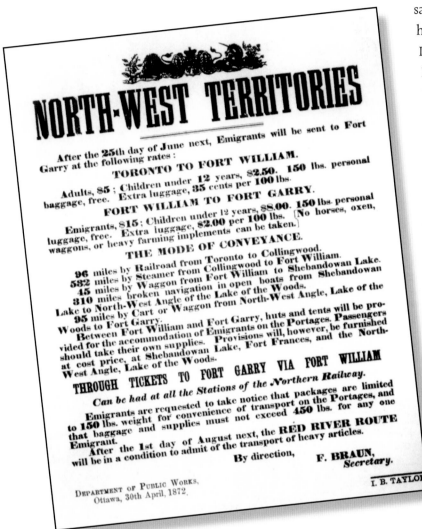

NORTH-WEST TERRITORIES

After the 25th day of June next, Emigrants will be sent to Fort Garry at the following rates:

TORONTO TO FORT WILLIAM.

Adults, $5; Children under 12 years, $2.50. 150 lbs. personal baggage, free. Extra luggage, 35 cents per 100 lbs.

FORT WILLIAM TO FORT GARRY.

Emigrants, $15; Children under 12 years, $8.00. 150 lbs. personal luggage, free. Extra luggage, $2.00 per 100 lbs. [No horses, oxen, waggons, or heavy farming implements can be taken.]

THE MODE OF CONVEYANCE.

96 miles by Railroad from Toronto to Collingwood.
582 miles by Steamer from Collingwood to Fort William.
45 miles by Waggon from Fort William to Shebandowan Lake.
310 miles broken navigation in open boats from Shebandowan Lake to North-West Angle of the Lake of the Woods.
95 miles by Cart or Waggon from North-West Angle, Lake of the Woods to Fort Garry.

Between Fort William and Fort Garry, huts and tents will be provided for the accommodation of Emigrants on the Portages. Passengers should take their own supplies. Provisions will, however, be furnished at cost price, at Shebandowan Lake, Fort Frances, and the North-West Angle, Lake of the Woods.

THROUGH TICKETS TO FORT GARRY VIA FORT WILLIAM

Can be had at all the Stations of the *Northern Railway*.

Emigrants are requested to take notice that packages are limited to **150** lbs. weight for convenience of transport on the Portages, and that baggage and supplies must not exceed **450** lbs. for any one Emigrant.

After the 1st day of August next, the **RED RIVER ROUTE** will be in a condition to admit of the transport of heavy articles.

By direction,

F. BRAUN,
Secretary.

DEPARTMENT OF PUBLIC WORKS,
Ottawa, 30th April, 1872.

I. B. TAYLOR

Canada Worth a Billion?

After the American Civil War, an arbitration tribunal was set up to consider claims against Britain and other countries for alleged violation of neutrality during the war. Massachusetts Senator Charles Sumner in 1872 demanded damages from Britain totalling $1 billion, and he had figured out how such a staggering sum could be paid—he demanded the cession of Canada. Luckily for us, the tribunal didn't agree.

punish Riel. A military expedition that had been planned for some time now set off. Seven hundred militia were joined, to Macdonald's delight—for he wanted to demonstrate to the Americans that the British still cared about their territory—by about four hundred British regulars. The army was led by Colonel Garnet Wolseley. It had to follow the old Canadian canoe route, since as a military expedition it could not traverse American soil. Wolseley finally arrived at the Red River on 24 August—just in time, it is said, to drive Louis Riel from his breakfast. Riel fled as soon as he heard that Wolseley's soldiers were at hand; no one came to fight. It was a long toiling road for next to nothing. A young lieutenant, Redvers Buller (who would later become famous for his relief of Ladysmith during the Boer War), wrote in his diary that it had been "a long way to come to have the band play *God Save the Queen.*"

By this time the Manitoba Act had been passed; it came into effect on 15 July, admitting the fifth province into Confederation. Wolseley was able to oversee the installation of the first lieutenant-governor, Adams Archibald, a Nova Scotian who had at one point been the sole supporter of Confederation in that colony's legislature.

In an election in 1872, George-Étienne Cartier, a long-time defender of French rights and later a staunch supporter of French rights in Manitoba, was defeated in his Montréal riding. Riel, who had been persuaded to stand for election in the riding of Provencher, withdrew his candidacy, as did his opponent, so that Cartier could take the seat by acclamation. The folllowing year, however, Cartier died, leaving the Provencher seat vacant. This time Riel was elected, but although he showed up in Ottawa long enough to have his photograph taken (page 152), he never felt safe enough to take his seat, for there was a price on his head in Ontario. Riel exiled himself to the United States—until the next time (see page 165).

The Americans had decided not to intervene in the Northwest, for what they desired more than anything was the withdrawal of the British military presence. This they achieved with the retreat of Wolseley. Britain, in turn, got what it wanted: to be able to finally to pull its troops out of North America (except for a base at Halifax). The Canadians could now look after themselves.

Dominion from Sea to Sea

In 1871, the confederation gained its sixth recruit: British Columbia. In 1869 Anthony Musgrave had arrived as governor, having requested a transfer from the same position in Newfoundland, where he thought his work done. On the west coast his mission was the same as it had been on the east: ensure the colony's admission to Confederation. British Columbia was to prove much more malleable than Newfoundland.

A delegation from British Columbia, including Musgrave, arrived in Ottawa on 3 June 1870, after a three-week journey via San Francisco, the only practicable way to travel east at that time. They were received by Cartier as Macdonald was ill, or perhaps just drunk. Macdonald had a well-known penchant for imbibing and often overdid it. The demands of the British Columbians were simple—assumption of a debt of over a million dollars (British colonies always seemed to be in debt), a program of public works, and a wagon road connecting the coast with Red River. Cartier offered a railway instead. The British Columbians were delighted, the Canadian Parliament less so, but Cartier managed to get the bill passed. A railway was to be begun within two years and completed within ten. "Sir George Cartier says they will do that or burst," wrote Musgrave. British Columbia became Canada's sixth province on 20 July 1871. "Today British Columbia and Canada join hands and hearts across the Rocky Mountains," Victoria's *British Colonist* newspaper waxed lyrically, "and John Bull the younger stands with one foot on the Atlantic and the other on the Pacific."

Above. Government House, Battleford, Saskatchewan. In 1876 Battleford was selected as the capital of the North-West Territories, from that date governed separately from Manitoba. The Canadian Pacific Railway was later constructed to the south, and the capital was moved to Regina in 1883.

Below. The Cariboo Road in British Columbia, with a prairie schooner pulled by oxen, was superbly painted by Edward Roper in 1883.

For now, Newfoundland having decided to stay out of the confederation, only Prince Edward Island remained. In 1871 the colony had begun work on a narrow gauge railway planned to run the length of the island, agreeing to pay a fixed price per mile, with the result that the contractor made the line as curvaceous as possible. This, plus shoddy workmanship on the line, increased the cost until the government was deeply in debt. Renewed overtures from the Canadian government, which promised to assume this debt, and continued pressure from the British combined to persuade Prince Edward Island to join Confederation in 1873. Canada also agreed to fund a compulsory buyout of the colony's absentee landlords, thus finally solving a long-term Island problem. Money, and promises, had once again added a province to Confederation.

Speaking by Wire

Above.
Alexander Graham Bell, inventor extraordinaire.

Below.
Until about 1878, telephone switchboard operators were male, but it soon became an exclusively female occupation. Here a closely supervised group of operators work the British Columbia Telephone Company's "B" switchboard in Vancouver in 1915.

Arguments still rage about who invented the telephone, and even some who agree that it was Alexander Graham Bell maintain that he invented it while in Boston, while working at a school for the deaf. As recently as 2001 the U.S. Congress passed a resolution recognizing not Bell but Italian Antonio Meucci as the telephone's inventor; the Canadian House of Commons retaliated by passing a motion enshrining Bell as its inventor. The "official" date was 26 July 1874, at Bell's house in Brantford, Ontario. The first long-distance call was made from Brantford to nearby Paris, Ontario, on 10 August 1876, but the first two-way phone conversation was in the United States: a call in Boston to his assistant, Thomas Watson, in October that year.

Regardless of which nation claims Bell as its own, he was neither a Canadian nor an American to start with; like so many others he emigrated from his native Scotland, in his case when he was twenty-three. Bell arrived in Brantford in 1870. His father was a noted teacher of deaf people and had invented a new teaching system. So the younger Bell started off in life with a keen appreciation of the value of sound. Bell was a consummate businessman as well as a brilliant inventor, and moved to the United States soon after coming up with his invention. He set about securing patents for his telephone system, founded the Bell Telephone Company (and its Canadian arm in 1880), and was so successful that he was a rich man by thirty-five. His invention was so revolutionary that it was one of those rare technological advances that by itself induced social change.

With his wealth growing daily, Bell was free to indulge his inventive mind. In 1890 he purchased land at Baddeck, overlooking Bras d'Or Lake on Cape Breton Island. It is typical of the man to note that before he built a house, he and he wife rode around the property in two chairs tied to the top of a hay wagon so as to locate the best view. One of his fields of interest was aviation, and he gathered a small group of like-minded engineers about him and tested all manner of kites, and then airplanes, with the result that the first heavier-than-air manned flight in Canada took place at his Cape Breton estate in 1909 (see page 214).

Bell died at his Cape Breton estate in 1922, but not before he had selected his own gravesite by lying down in various locations—again to see which had the best view!

A Standard of Time

The Canadian responsible for the invention of standard time throughout the world was also a Scottish immigrant to Canada. Sandford Fleming was a surveyor and lithographer whose skills were such that he had drawn and published a map of Toronto in 1851 and designed Canada's first postage stamp—the threepenny beaver—in 1854, the latter becoming the first promotion of the beaver as a Canadian national emblem. After Confederation Fleming surveyed the route for the Intercolonial Railway from the St. Lawrence to Halifax and was the chief engineer for that railway until its completion in 1876. In the 1870s he was responsible for the first surveys for the Canadian Pacific Railway to find a route through the Rockies, although his recommendation of the northern route through what is now Jasper was not followed. He was on the board of the Canadian Pacific Railway when the line to the Pacific was finally completed in 1885; he is the prominent figure standing behind Donald Smith as he drives the last spike in the famous photograph (see page 161).

Fleming was also a promoter for a telegraph cable across the Pacific Ocean to Australia and New Zealand, the "final communication link in the Empire," and in 1902 saw his dream realized with the Pacific cable from Vancouver Island.

But Sandford Fleming is most remembered for his conception of standard time. Until the coming of the railway, time had always been local time, the time by the sun, and had varied from one town or village to the next. Railways ended up running on the time of their main terminus, meaning that others had to adjust their clocks to some often distant city. Where several railways crossed, confusion reigned. Fleming was in Ireland in 1876 when, so the story goes, he missed a train due to a timetable that said just 5:35 but meant in the morning, not in the afternoon. Fleming soon hatched the idea of the twenty-four-hour clock. He then developed the idea of time zones for the whole world, where twenty-four zones each representing fifteen degrees of longitude would standardize their time to the midpoint of that zone. Trains would now all run on the same time in the same zone, and confusion would disappear.

It remained to select a starting point for this system. At the International Prime Meridian Conference in Washington, D.C., in 1884, which Fleming was instrumental in convening, agreement was finally reached that Greenwich, site of the Royal Observatory in England, would become the 0° and 360° meridian, with a time zone boundary 7° 30′ either side of it, and adjoining zones 15° apart would encircle the globe. It was an elegantly simple system, useful for trains but essential for modern air transportation and instantaneous communication. Canada adopted standard time on 1 January 1885, as did most of the United States, although it did not become law there until 1918. By the end of the nineteenth century most countries subscribed to the system, though the last holdout, Liberia, did not join until 1972.

Sandford Fleming, railway surveyor, engineer, and inventor of time zones for the world.

British Columbia had been promised a railway. Macdonald thought he knew how to get it built. One of his supporters was Sir Hugh Allan, shipping magnate and railway builder. For an election that was held in 1872, the chronically in debt Macdonald had been in trouble and had called on Allan to contribute large sums of money to the election campaign. Allan was all too ready to oblige, for he hoped to acquire the contract to build the Pacific railway, and he gave the Conservatives about $350,000. With this, Macdonald's government was re-elected, although with a reduced majority.

Allan's Canadian Pacific Railway Company was granted a charter to build the line, but the following year the opposition Liberals found out about the contributions and exposed them. Political corruption was not new to Canadian politics, but this huge amount of money had, it seemed, been a direct payment for the grant of the charter. Macdonald tried to fend off his critics in the House, but in the end it became apparent he could not survive, and he resigned on 5 November 1873. The governor general, Lord Dufferin, called on the leader of the Opposition to form a government. His name (as if to confuse history) was Alexander Mackenzie.

Taming a Prairie

Before the government could sell land to the settlers it was hoping would flood in to the Northwest, or grant it to any railway company, it had first to do two things. Under the Royal Proclamation of 1763 (see page 80) the land belonged to the native peoples. Thus the first thing the government had to do was buy the land from them. Between 1871 and 1877 seven treaties were concluded with various tribes. These provided for a formal cession of the land to the government, save for reserves and the retained right to hunt over lands not already occupied. For this land payments were made on a per capita basis, sometimes adding agricultural implements or grain. The idea was that the native peoples be encouraged—some would say forced—to settle in one place and become farmers in the same mould as the colonists who would soon appear to join them. In this fashion the way was cleared for European settlement in Manitoba and what is today central and southern Saskatchewan and Alberta. Later treaties would deal with the more northerly regions.

The rapid disappearance of the buffalo herds that once roamed so thick across the land was a matter of great concern to the native peoples, to whom the herds were essential for their food and culture, but to Europeans the absence of buffalo was a benefit, allowing fencing of fields and the turning loose of cattle on an open range.

The second thing that had to be done by the government was subdivision; land could not be sold unless it was in some way

Above.
Hunting buffalo on the prairie in 1870, a painting by George Caitlin. Between 1870 and 1885 buffalo were hunted virtually to extinction by Europeans who saw them as a nuisance rather than a way of life. Some foresaw the result. MP John Schulz told the House of Commons in 1876 that the government would soon have to deal with "a race of paupers rendered dangerous from want of food."

Below.
The notorious post of the American whiskey traders, Fort Whoop-Up, near present-day Lethbridge, Alberta. Note the American flag.

defined. And so in 1872 the Dominion Lands Survey was established, allowing for the wholesale carving up of the prairie into townships, sections, and quarter sections, the last being the unit of land that would become the standard settler's land grant or purchase. Thus in a few short years a prairie once blanketed with buffalo was instead covered with the checkerboard squares of the Dominion Lands Survey.

There remained the task of chasing out the American whiskey traders who were reported to be debauching the native peoples, and providing for law and order in the West. It was hoped to avoid the warfare that had overtaken the lands south of the border, culminating in Custer's Last Stand, the famous Battle of the Little Bighorn, which was fought in June 1876 in Montana Territory. The Canadian answer was the North-West Mounted Police, the forerunner of today's Royal Canadian Mounted Police. Formed in 1873, the NWMP with its distinctive scarlet jackets was deliberately made a civilian force, all the better not to provoke violence. Fort Macleod was built in October 1874 on the Old Man River. The mere presence of the police in the region was in most cases sufficient to stop the flow of whiskey. The most notorious whiskey trading post was Fort Whoop-Up, which had been built in 1869 (and rebuilt in 1870 after being burned down by the Blackfoot) near present-day Lethbridge, Alberta. But by the time the NWMP reached it, the American traders had emptied it of evidence; not a drop of whiskey was to be found.

In the fall of 1875 a new NWMP fort was built at the confluence of the Bow and Elbow Rivers, called Fort Brisebois after the commanding officer. The following year the name was changed to Calgary.

A Railway to the Pacific

Macdonald's successor, Alexander Mackenzie, was not at all like him, or, for that matter, his explorer namesake either. A Liberal in name he was conservative by nature, and his plodding ways did not excite a loyal following the way Macdonald's excesses did. Under Mackenzie the promised Pacific railway project was considered likely to produce unacceptable costs and was put on the back burner, although some essentially portage sections of track were laid to link Thunder Bay with Winnipeg. The economy was not in good shape at this point anyway. But in an election in 1878, using a set of protectionist tariffs he cleverly promoted as his "National Policy" to assure Canadians of coming prosperity, Macdonald swept back into power. This

Above.
Fort Calgary in 1878, with NWMP officers and men and a group of Blood native people. This is one of several early photographs taken by pioneer Calgary photographer Ernest Brown (see pages 170–71).

Below.
NWMP "F" Troop parade at Fort Calgary in 1878.

National Policy, with its patriotic undertones, was to grow to include the Canadian Pacific Railway, western development, and a host of other Conservative policies. And it would be long-lasting; as late as the 1930s R. B. Bennett was using it to get rid of Mackenzie King.

Macdonald was keen to get going with the building of a Pacific railway, but the immense cost worried him. Attempts were made to find a private company to do the work, and Macdonald visited England in 1879 for the purpose, but to no avail. As a beginning, and to placate a by now concerned British Columbia, a government contract was tendered to build about 175 km of line through the Fraser Canyon to Savona, at the western end of Kamloops Lake, perhaps the most difficult part of the entire line. Andrew Onderdonk began work on this section in May 1880, fixing the selection of the Fraser Valley as the route to the coast. Railway surveyor Sandford Fleming did not think the Fraser route the right one, and he resigned.

Macdonald finally found his private investors to build the railway in the shape of a group led by George Stephen, president of the Bank of Montreal, and Donald Smith, chief commissioner of the Hudson's Bay Company. With them were James J. Hill, a successful American railroad builder and operator (who would in 1893 complete his Northern Pacific Railroad to Seattle), and Norman Kittson, operator of steamboats and barges on the Red River.

On the initiative of Charles Tupper, Macdonald's minister responsible for the railway, the government offered the investors a cash subsidy of $20 million and 30 million acres (12 million ha). Stephen countered with an offer to build the railway requiring a cash subsidy of $25 million and a land grant of 25 million acres (10 million ha). This was accepted by the government and Stephen's syndicate signed a contract to build the Pacific railway on 21 October 1880. The bill confirming the contract was passed on 15 February 1881, and the Canadian Pacific Railway was incorporated the following day.

Stephen was the driving force behind the railway, and he was well positioned to attract the financing that would be needed to keep the work going. His skills as a financier would be tested many times. Hill thought it unlikely that the line to the north of Lake Superior would be built, and thus his own lines to the south would be used; he later dropped out of the syndicate when he found an all-Canadian line was indeed to be built, despite the difficulties put in its way by the unforgiving Canadian Shield.

The Canadian Pacific Railway's hotel at Field, B.C., about 1890, painted by Edward Roper. The railway not only opened the West to settlement but opened the Rockies to tourism, and the CPR built luxury hotels to accommodate visitors.

During the first season of mainline construction, 1881, only about 165 km of line was laid. At this rate the company would long be bankrupt before the line could generate any traffic. In a move that would prove to be the salvation of the railway, in October 1881 James Hill recruited William Cornelius Van Horne, an experienced railway builder from the United States, to oversee the construction. Van Horne took over on 2 January 1882, hired an experienced man he knew he could trust, Thomas Shaughnessy, as his purchasing agent, and awarded the contract for the line as far as Calgary to a company he knew could perform, Langdon and Shepard.

Despite a slow start due to flooding, once the Van Horne–Shaughnessy team took over, the work went much faster. Some 675 km of track was laid during the 1882 season and in October trains were operating as far west as the newly created city of Regina. The company, however, was now burning through its cash reserves, and when the contractor asked for an increase in its rates to cover expenditure in the undulating countryside of what is now southern Alberta, Van Horne found another contractor able to take payment partly in CPR shares. Improving finances in 1883 in fact led the CPR to complete the line itself. A feeling amongst investors that the line would actually be completed allowed Stephen to raise more money in New York by selling shares.

In May 1883 the government-built line from Winnipeg to Thunder Bay was handed over to the CPR, and the first train from Winnipeg arrived at Port Arthur on 8 July.

The track westward reached Medicine Hat on 1 June 1883 and the NWMP fort at Calgary by mid-August. At one point a record 6 miles (9.7 km) of track was laid in a single day. Twenty-ninth siding—later renamed Banff—was reached on 27 October, and by the end of the 1883 season the rails were almost at the Continental Divide.

Right, top.
In what is perhaps the single most famous Canadian image, Donald Smith drives the last spike to complete the line across Canada on 7 November 1885, at Craigellachie, in Eagle Pass. Behind him are William Van Horne (with waistcoat visible) and Sandford Fleming (in a top hat).

Right, centre.
The Mountain Creek trestle, the scale of which is indicated by the train and the men on the bridge deck. It was probably the most spectacular of the engineering works of the railway builders, but there were many others.

Right, bottom.
Engine 374 and its crew and admirers after arriving in Vancouver, the first train to do so, on 23 May 1887, a year after the first transcontinental train had arrived at Pacific tidewater at Port Moody. The engine is decorated to also celebrate Queen Victoria's jubilee, commemorating fifty years on the throne, 1837–87.

From here on the going would be much slower, for the line now ran down the steep western slope of the Rockies and across the Selkirk Mountains. During the entire 1884 season only 120 km of track was laid. A temporary grade of 4.4 percent, twice the normal maximum, was allowed above today's Field, B.C. It necessitated the provision of an array of "helper locomotives" to push trains up the hill and a number of runaway sidings for trains coming down, whose brakes might well overheat and fail. This was the famous "Big Hill," and it was not so temporary, lasting until 1909, when spiral tunnels were completed.

George Stephen, meanwhile, was trying to deal with a decline in CPR stock—serious for a company selling stock to raise money—and a partial collapse of the Prairie land boom. By March 1885 Stephen felt the end was near, but was saved by a promise of assistance from Macdonald, who could not let the railway founder at this late stage. He was aided by a change in public sentiment caused by the railway's ability to move troops quickly to deal with the North-West Rebellion (see page 165). The line north of the Great Lakes was almost complete and only a few difficult sections remained, which the troops could "portage" over. When it was connected, the honour of driving the last spike in the line between Montréal and Winnipeg was given to a military commander, Lieutenant Colonel W. R. Oswald. He drove the spike at Jack Fish Bay on 18 May 1885.

By the end of 1884 the tracks were on the Columbia River. Andrew Onderdonk had been given another contract to continue eastwards from Savona, and he would finally run out of rails on 26 September 1885 in Eagle Pass in the Monashee Mountains. Thus it only remained for the track to be laid across the Selkirks. But what a challenge they were.

From the Columbia the route lay up the Beaver River valley, found by surveyor Major Albert Rogers in 1882 but only surveyed in 1884. The summit of the Selkirks was reached on 17 August 1885, and a way down the difficult gorge of the Illecillewaet River was only found by building a dizzying series of loops involving seven complete rotations.

Finally, with the season running out, they met the Onderdonk track at a place they named Craigellachie, where, on 7 November 1885, Donald Smith drove the last spike. Canada's trancontinental railway was a reality. Many, many improvements would still be needed—ballasting, repairs from avalanches, bridge replacements—but these were a minor consideration compared with the completion of the line itself. A demonstration shipment of forty drums of oil, consigned from Halifax to Victoria, passed a few days later, the first freight train to the Pacific, but then the line was closed until the following year. On 4 July 1886 the first transcontinental passenger train arrived at Port Moody and Pacific tidewater.

A year later, on 23 May 1887, the first train steamed into Vancouver. Van Horne had seen that the magnificent harbour that ends at Port Moody had a great deal of potential and had persuaded the Province of British Columbia to grant the CPR much of what is now downtown Vancouver for a new railway terminal and associated marshalling yards. Van horne was also responsible for the company acquiring another 2 350 ha south of English Bay and False Creek for residential use, including the upscale Shaughnessey district, named after Van Horne's purchasing agent, who went on to become president of the company.

It was Van Horne who suggested the name "Vancouver" for the place he felt sure was destined to become a great city, and the settlement was incorporated under this name on 6 April 1886. Two months later, on 13 June, the city was almost completely destroyed by a fire. But the railway was coming, and everything was quickly rebuilt. And so the scene was set for the growth of Canada's third city, the staging point between the new and finally real Northwest Passage and the route across the Pacific to the East.

The settlement of Granville, as Vancouver was named before its incorporation as a city in 1886. This photograph was taken in 1884 or in 1885 before August. This idyllic scene at the edge of a virgin forest was soon to be intruded upon by the industry made possible by the arrival of the railway, and the forest would soon disappear.

THE NEW NORTH-WEST PASSAGE.

Above.

When the railway was finally complete, there came the problem of ensuring its economic viability. The truth is that most early revenues would come from points along the line, not by traffic from one end to the other. The line had cost too much to chance a "build it, and they will come" philosophy. To attract the settlers who would create the farms, the towns, and the freight for the railway— and buy its land—the Canadian Pacific Railway needed to begin a big marketing job. This poster extolling the fertile virtues of the West was published between 1883 and 1885.

Left.

The new Canadian Pacific Railway at last achieved the goal that had been sought for centuries, a practical route to the East around, or through, the continent that had so rudely got in the way of the early explorers—indeed, a Northwest Passage. This cartoon, published in the British magazine *Punch* in October 1887, shows Britannia pointing to a train named Canada, an all-British route to the Pacific.

A Rebellion in the Northwest

The North-West Rebellion of 1885 was a revolt of both Métis and native peoples against what they perceived as an unresponsive central government. By the 1880s the native people, after signing the treaties that confined them to small reserves, found themselves starving. Food promised under the treaties often did not materialize, and with the numbers of buffalo dwindling, many were becoming desperate. The insurrection of the Métis provided a catalyst for a larger native uprising.

The Métis were in a similar situation to that of 1869 in Red River. European settlement, over which they had no control, was overtaking them. Their protests were heard but went unanswered. Suggestions from government land agents went unheeded, such as one that recommended river lot subdivision of land instead of the township divisions of the Dominion Lands Survey. Why not, thought the Métis leader Gabriel Dumont, try what was done in Red River: cause a bit of a stir—and get results. And what better person to get these results than Louis Riel? In June 1884, Dumont sought out Riel, then teaching at a mission school in Montana Territory. Dumont brought letters from European settlers urging him to come; they hoped to see a repeat of what happened in Manitoba. Riel agreed to return, and arrived at Batoche, on the South Saskatchewan River south of Prince Albert, in July. But the settlers got more than they bargained for.

Above.
A nine-pounder field gun used by Middleton's men against the Métis at Batoche. The gun is now in the museum at Fort Battleford.

Below.
"Action and retirement" at Cut Knife Hill, 2 May 1885, painted by Lieutenant Robinson Lyndhurst Wadmore, one of Otter's officers.

A coloured lithograph of the action at Batoche on 12 May 1885, as the Canadian militia storm the Métis rifle pits.

Opposite, bottom.
Poundmaker surrenders to Middleton at Battleford on 26 May 1885.

Riel saw himself as a heaven-sent saviour of the Métis. In his exile after the Red River Rebellion, Riel's stories of visits by spirits in burning clouds telling him he was God's instrument for the elevation of the Métis to their rightful place in the world only got him committed to a lunatic asylum, diagnosed with "psychotic disintegration." Nevertheless, to the Métis, and even to the European settlers, he was the leader who would get their demands heard. When Riel arrived at Batoche he promised that there would be no violence; when this promise was broken he quickly lost the support of the European settlers.

In December 1884 a large petition was prepared, in both French and English, outlining the grievances and asking for their resolution. It was sent to Joseph-Adolphe Chapleau, the secretary of state. Since Chapleau was a French-speaking former premier of Québec, Riel no doubt hoped for sympathetic consideration. But the petition was acknowledged and then—nothing. The hand of Macdonald was at work.

Unfortunately for Riel, his second rebellion was not going to work the way the first one had. Macdonald was not this time going to be intimidated, for now he had the North-West Mounted Police on the spot, and he had a a militia force of eight thousand men that could be speedily tranported to the conflict by the newly constructed Canadian Pacific Railway. The world had changed and Riel had not allowed for this. On 23 March Major General Frederick Middleton was ordered west with the militia, and within two weeks he was at Qu'Appelle ready to move north.

North-West Mounted Police reinforcements had been ordered north to Fort Carlton on 15 March. Riel was angry when he heard this, for he wanted negotiation, not confrontation. He seized an Indian agent and a few other government officials who happened to be at hand, cut the telegraph wires from Prince Albert to Regina, and, on 19 March, declared a provisional government which he called the "exovedate."

On 21 March Riel demanded the surrender of Fort Carlton. The NWMP superintendent in charge of the fort, L. F. N. Crozier, refused, but a few days later unwisely ventured out to obtain supplies from a store at Duck Lake. The small party was simply turned back by Dumont, whereupon Crozier decided to act. Despite the imminent arrival of the reinforcements, a force of about a hundred police and volunteers set out for Duck Lake. They were ambushed by Dumont; twelve men were killed and eleven wounded. As the survivors returned to Fort Carlton, the reinforcements arrived. The following night, the police evacuated the fort, retreating to Prince Albert.

The news of Duck Lake spread like wildfire throughout the Saskatchewan Valley, and at this the Cree went on a rampage of frustration in Battleford, and the residents of that settlement fled to a refuge in Fort Battleford. At Fort Pitt, farther northwest up the North Saskatchewan, Inspector Francis Dickens (son of author Charles Dickens) prepared for a siege, but because of civilians decided to evacuate his fort when he received an offer of safe passage from the natives. A little to the west, Plains Cree from the tribe of Mistahhimaskwa (Big Bear) attacked settlers at Frog Lake, killing nine people. The settlers had previously turned down the opportunity to seek shelter at Fort Pitt.

The militia now moved northwards from several points on the rail line. Middleton marched from Qu'Appelle towards Batoche, the Métis stronghold, while another force, under Lieutenant Colonel William Otter, marched to relieve Battleford from Swift Current; another force went to Calgary and then north to Edmonton and east to Fort Pitt to engage Big Bear's Cree. Middleton, with eight hundred men, half on each side of the river, was approaching Batoche when he was ambushed by Dumont at Fish Creek, and ten militia were killed. Middleton, however, was unsure of the Métis strength and so camped at Fish Creek for two weeks, waiting for reinforcements to arrive.

Meanwhile Otter moved north from Swift Current with 550 police and militia and relieved Battleford on 24 April, the same day Middleton was being attacked at Fish Creek. But when Otter tried a surprise move against the warriors of Pi-tikwahanapiwi-yin (Poundmaker), another Cree chief, to prevent them joining up with Riel, he was defeated at Cut Knife Hill, west of Battleford. Poundmaker, however, was

Above.
Two photographs taken in the field at Batoche by one of Middleton's officers, James Peters. The top image shows field guns firing into Batoche while the other shows dead Métis fighters after the battle.

not directly involved; he had always tried to resolve issues peacefully, but his younger and more impetuous braves were hard to control.

Middleton renewed his march towards Batoche on 7 May and arrived before the village two days later. By this time, Dumont's Métis were well entrenched, having built numerous rifle pits on the gentle slope down towards the village in positions where they could open fire on Middleton's men as they showed up on the horizon. On the first day of battle the steamer *Northcote,* suitably boarded up, was sent down the river full of militia firing at the Métis, mainly as a diversion for a land attack, which failed. The steamer's funnels were lost to a ferry cable the Métis pulled out of the water, but the steamer itself got away. For three days the Métis held the militia at bay, despite the fact that Middleton had the new Gatling gun, that early machine gun that saw its first use in action at Batoche.

But the Métis were not resupplied, and their ammunition soon ran low. Many of them resorted to firing nails. Finally, a group of militia, impatient with three days of getting nowhere, made an impetuous frontal attack on the rifle pits. Middleton was having his lunch at the time and was interrupted by the shouting. As soon as he realized what had happened Middleton sent in reinforcements and it was soon all over.

Dumont and Riel escaped. Dumont fled to Montana but Riel decided to give himself up, clearly not anticipating the consequences. For the Cree, the situation was now hopeless; they could not hope to fight an expanding militia force forever. Poundmaker gave himself up to Middleton at Fort Battleford on 26 May, and with the surrender of Big Bear on 2 July, the rebellion was over.

Many of the native chiefs were tried and imprisoned, including Poundmaker, who had always tried to remain peaceful but whose patience had been tested so often. Many of the chiefs were convicted because of crimes by their followers. Poundmaker and Big Bear died, broken men, soon after. It was a sorry chapter in the annals of Canadian justice.

Riel's trial has been debated time and time again. The truth is that Macdonald was not about to see Riel get away once more. He made sure that the trial was held in Regina rather than in Winnipeg, where Riel could have demanded that half the jury be French-speaking. Macdonald also had Riel charged with treason under an ancient 1352 English law because he thought a conviction more likely. Riel's lawyer claimed that Riel was insane, but Riel insisted that he was not, and by so doing sealed his fate. On 16 November, Riel was hanged, causing outrage in French Canada. The legitimacy of Riel's trial continues to be debated to this day.

The rebellion in the Northwest did achieve something: parliamentary representation. In 1886 four members of Parliament were sent to Ottawa from the North-West Territories.

Sir William Dillon Otter, whose medals and tunic are displayed here, was Colonel Middleton's second-in-command during the North-West Rebellion and suffered defeat at the hands of Poundmaker's Cree at Cut Knife Hill. A veteran of the Battle of Ridgeway, fought against Fenian invaders in 1866 (see page 147), Otter went on to become the first Canadian-born chief of the general staff in 1908, a position which until then had been filled by British officers. Otter ended his long career, traced by his medals, as a general in 1922.

Opposite, top.
Edgar Dewdney, the lieutenant-governor of the North-West Territories (with white beard, at front left), with Plains Cree chief Payipwat (Piapot) and other chiefs . Piapot had been a thorn in the side of government policy for years, and in 1885 a military base was established beside his reserve and some of his more troublesome associates were arrested as rebels. Behind the chiefs are the men of the Montreal Artillery Garrison. This unusual photograph is a hand-coloured lantern slide.

Opposite, bottom.
The trial of Louis Riel in Regina in July 1885. Riel is at centre, addressing the jury.

To Wait on All Who Call for Likenesses

Below.
Photographers (*left to right*) William Manson Boone, Ernest G. May, and Charles W. Mathers take photographs of a pageant, "The Crucifixion, as played by the Indians," at Mission, B.C., in 1892. There was a fourth photographer present, Ernest Brown (see photo, right), who took this photograph of his colleagues in the profession at work.

Photography came to Canada in 1840. In that year a Mr. Halsey and Mr. Sadd set up a studio "over Mr. Grace's confectionery store" in Québec and advertised portraits for the princely sum of five dollars, to be taken in four minutes "on sunshiny days only." The year before, on 15 April 1839, the *Quebec Gazette* had published a report on "The New Art of Sun Painting" with little detail, for the process was then still secret. This was the first mention of photography in Canada, a new art that was to change forever the accuracy and immediacy of recording images.

By the middle of the century "daguerrotypists" had set up in all the major cities, offering portraits by this new process. The public flocked to their studios. Improvements were soon made. In the 1850s the collodion process superseded daguerrotypes. Collodion was gun cotton dissolved in ether and alcohol which, after a quick dip into a bath of silver nitrate, was exposed while still moist. This was the "wet-plate" process, and it required a dextrous hand to complete the procedure before the plate dried. An excellent example of a photograph taken with this process is the William Notman photograph of Fort Chambly on pages 40–41, taken in 1863. A later variation where the collodion was coated onto thin, black-japanned metal plates produced photographs popularly called tintypes, such

as the example of the family bicycling group on page 175. A similarly sensitized mixture on paper produced an albumen process print, such as the 1878 view of Montréal by the Notman studio on the title pages or the superb view of Parliament taken by the official government "photographist" Samuel McLaughlin in 1865, shown on page 132. These were all incredibly inconvenient processes requiring photographers to have light-tight tents containing virtual chemical factories on the spot for coating and developing their work.

Studio portraiture was the source of most photographers' business. Long exposures required often elaborate supports—"photographic rest and posing machines"—carefully hidden from the camera's view, which accounted for the typically sour expressions of those having their photographs taken.

About 1882 the dry gelatine plate superseded the wet process. For photographers this was revolutionary, as it cut down the paraphernalia with which they had to travel. Just as importantly, the speed of the dry plate was ten times as fast as the wet plate, allowing instantaneous picture-taking. Explorer-photographers, not surprisingly, embraced the new process at once. Collodion-bromide dry plates were used by the Nares Arctic expedition in 1875–76 (page 112) and by George Dawson of the Geological Survey in 1879 (page 12, bottom). And amateurs adopted photography in a big way, leading to an explosion in the number of photographs which today have become historical records.

The revolution was completed in 1888 when George Eastman marketed the first Kodak, a small box-like camera with a roll of gelatine-bromide-coated paper that was returned to the factory after a hundred exposures. The following year Eastman substituted transparent roll film, changeable by the user, and modern photographic film was born. This, in turn, now seems destined for history with the advent of the digital camera.

Above.
Calgary photographer Ernest Brown stands with a collection of his cameras and photographic equipment in this 1905 photograph. Cameras at the time tended to be more single-purpose than they are today, hence the need for cameras of many shapes and sizes. Brown may well have used the photograph for advertising purposes, to impress his potential clients with technology.

The title of this section comes from a much earlier advertising card for the Red River Portrait Gallery, set up in Winnipeg in 1860. "A. Barnard begs to announce," it read, "that he has fitted up a room in the house formerly occupied by Mr. Henry Hallett, where he will be prepared to wait on all who call for likenesses."

Arguably the world's most famous photographer, Yousuf Karsh, was a Canadian, an immigrant from Armenia in 1924. In 1932 he opened a studio in Ottawa for the stated purpose of photographing what he called "people of consequence." For the next sixty years, a long line of the rich and famous sat for "Karsh of Ottawa." Photographs by Karsh can be found on pages 230 and 273.

Putting Out the Fire

North American cities were often constructed principally of wood, had no system of water delivery, and little in the way of fire codes governing, for example, how close together houses might be built. Not surprisingly, then, fire was a major concern of all cities. Most Canadian cities have had major fires at some point in their history: Québec in 1682, 1768, and two in 1845; Montréal in 1721, 1734, and 1765; Vancouver in 1886; St. John's in 1892; Saint John in 1837 and 1845; and Toronto in 1904. And these are just some of the big ones.

The 1734 Montréal fire, which was an act of arson by a slave, resulted in the creation of the first firefighting organization in Canada. Firefighting equipment such as leather and wooden buckets, axes, hooks, shovels, and ladders were distributed throughout the city, and an ordinance was passed to enforce already-existing chimney-cleaning rules. In 1726 a law had been passed that commanded every citizen to clean their chimneys every two months, but it had not been enforced, and there was a natural reluctance to put out one's fire in the middle of a Canadian winter. Creosote buildup in chimneys kept constantly burning to repel the cold was one of the principal causes of fires; the creosote would ignite and rapidly spark fires on neighbouring wood-shingle roofs, even if snow-covered. Indeed, some chimneys were themselves made of wood simply covered with a layer of clay.

Although a "fire engine"—a device capable of directing water onto a fire—had been ordered for Québec in 1691, there is no record of it ever having arrived. It is known that two arrived in Montréal from England following the 1765 fire, hand-pumped machines that forced water into a hose and had to have their reservoirs constantly refilled by a bucket brigade. Two engines were in Québec in time for a fire in 1768 that still managed to destroy ninety houses.

In Britain, fire protection had since the Great Fire of London in 1666 been aided by the formation of fire insurance companies that, with their money at risk, were encouraged to

A view from the foot of Bay Street, Toronto, after a devastating fire in 1904. The fire almost wiped out the area that today is the financial centre of Canada, although at the time it was mainly a warehouse district.

Below. The New Westminster, British Columbia, fire of 10 September 1898, as seen from across the Fraser River.

Right. In 1887 the Calgary Fire Brigade demonstrated their new equipment outside their newly completed fire hall. The smoke coming from the steam pumping engine could easily be mistaken for the fire itself!

provide for fire protection and control. The first fire insurance risks in Canada were taken by the aptly named Phoenix Fire Office, which first insured buildings in St. John's in 1782, and by 1825 there were many companies offering coverage. Insurance companies assessed and classified their risks, surveying the type of construction and use of buildings, producing fire insurance maps that today provide historians with a valuable record of yesterday's cities.

Steam power was harnessed to the fire pump in the 1850s, and with it emerged the paid firefighter. The steam engine could pump as much water as a hundred volunteers, who were sometimes unreliable, and so the new technology allowed cities to fight fires more effectively with a paid trained and on-call workforce that could be deployed in a rational and preplanned way.

Today firefighting in cities is made easier by the ability to get firefighting equipment swiftly to a fire. Today's most devastating fires are not in cities at all, but in the 40 percent of Canada covered by forests. Each year there are about 9,500 separate forest fires in Canada and about 2 000 km² burns. Considering the economic importance of the forest to the country, this represents a huge and ongoing loss.

The New Freedom

MASSEY-HARRIS WHEELS
RUN SO NICELY

They all learnt to ride at our **Riding Academy, Victoria Rink, Huron Street,** north of College Street.

MASSEY-HARRIS CO., Ltd., TORONTO

Above.
An 1896 advertisement for Massey-Harris bicycles from *Saturday Night*. Bicycle riding was so new that instruction was thought necessary, and riding schools sprang up everywhere.

A near social revolution was wrought in Canada in the closing decade of the nineteenth century by the lowly bicycle. Suddenly, it permitted individual mobility in a way not possible before, and a way which was not to be transcended until the rise of the mass-produced (and thus cheaper than hand-made) automobile (see page 217).

Bicycles had had a brief popularity in the late 1860s but the comfort level was so low that the fad did not last, although plenty of enthusiasts kept their wheels turning. Not only were bicycles ungeared, iron contraptions with unsprung seats, the roads were so bad as to test even a modern bicycle. Then, about 1890, the basic modern form of the bicycle was introduced, with gears and, most importantly, pneumatic tires, and the cycling craze took off once more. And roads, while still typically seas of mud for three seasons, were hardened in summer. Freedom in comfort had arrived, at least for the summer.

Bicycles could be mass-produced relatively simply in small factories. Many sprang up to satisfy the demand, with the result that by 1898 there were at least twenty-five bicycle manufacturers in Canada. And to sell and service the new beast, retail establishments opened; Toronto alone had over ninety bicycle shops by the end of the century.

The bicycle was a great equalizer, both between social classes and between the sexes. On a bicycle, differences disappeared. And to cycle at all, women's fashions had to change. Ankles were shown and bloomers, the predecessor to women's pants, appeared. This was a manifestation of societal change, for sure, but the bicycle was its most obvious display. With a bicycle, the individual was king; "simply being able to separate themselves from the mass and go by [themselves]," trumpeted *Saturday Night* in May 1896, makes the bicycle "the most startling development of the century." Now, it continued, "the citizen is much more of a personage and less of a fraction of a mass than ever before."

The churches did not take to the bicycle craze, for Sunday turned out to be a convenient day for the family bicycle outing, instead of going to church. To the churches' chagrin, the godless bicycle wrested the Sabbath from the pulpit.

As was the century, the bicycle boom was almost over—but the automobile was about to ascend—when no less than five companies, including the agricultural-machinery giant Massey-Harris, merged their cycle manufacturing divisions to form the Canada Cycle and Motor Company in September 1899. The company—CCM—churned out about forty thousand bicycles a year, selling them for as little as $25. This pace could not last, and bicycle sales declined after that, but while the craze lasted, bicycles were responsible for a migration of city-dwellers to the great outdoors the likes of which would not be repeated. And it had brought with it a demand for better roads, a demand that was about to become much more strident with growth in automobile ownership.

Above, right.
A typical bicycling family, thought to be the Bastia family from London, Ontario, pose with two of their prized bicycles in this tintype (see page 170) taken in the 1890s. Father obviously was the one taking the picture.

Below.
A balancing act for twenty-three. This group was photographed in Aylmer, Ontario, in the 1890s.

The Passing of the Old Chieftain

John A. Macdonald called an election in early 1891 with a rallying cry against the forces calling for annexation to the United States. Many Americans at this time saw it as the "manifest destiny" of their country to inherit the entire continent, and some Canadians agreed with them. Macdonald saw it as a good election issue. Wrapping himself in the flag, Macdonald and his Conservatives won the election. He seemed set to remain in power for at least another five years when in May he had several strokes; the last on these, on 6 June 1891, killed him. He was seventy-six. He had died, as he had once vowed he would, a British subject, but the ultimate Canadian nationalist.

Macdonald's death produced an outpouring of grief from the public, so much that he seemed more popular in death than in life. A black-draped funeral train took his body back to Kingston for burial. Mourners lined the tracks, much as they would do for Pierre Trudeau, another prime minister who was perhaps respected in death more than in life, over a hundred years later.

Macdonald's shoes were hard to fill. In the space of five years Canada had four prime ministers: John Abbott, John Thompson, Mackenzie Bowell, and Charles Tupper. Of these, Thompson remained in office for two years and notably introduced the first Criminal Code, dying in office in 1894. The others, unable to control their party effectively, resigned, except for Tupper, who was thrown out

of office in 1896 after calling the required general election that year. The country had had enough of the Conservatives; now a new and dynamic Liberal took over the reins of office. He was Wilfrid Laurier, Canada's first francophone prime minister.

The First French-Canadian Prime Minister

Laurier had first achieved national recognition when he was brought into the government of Alexander Mackenzie. The French-speaking Laurier was nevertheless intensely loyal to Britain, for he saw no reason why the language one spoke should make any difference to one's loyalty. He espoused Liberal reforms in England as a model for Canada, believing them to have made Britain "the freest of nations." He believed in the British governmental model and a duality of language. After the North-West Rebellion he again achieved prominence as he attacked Macdonald over the fate of Louis Riel, calling the latter's execution judicial murder. In the House in 1886 he took Macdonald to task over Riel. "We cannot make a nation of this new country by shedding blood," he said, "but by extending mercy and charity for all political offences." The next year Laurier became leader of the Liberal party.

Laurier set out to revitalize the country, which had been suffering an economic downturn for much of the decade. He put together a team of talented ministers that included Clifford Sifton as minister of the interior, a post in which he would reinvigorate the peopling of the West (see page 183).

(see page 183)

In October 1899 the British declared war on the Boers in South Africa. Laurier had to decide how to react; Britain naturally expected full support, but the sentiment in French Canada was against any involvement. English Canada, on the other hand, demanded immediate action. Laurier, without the agreement of Parliament, agreed to arm and dispatch Canadian volunteers to South Africa, seven thousand of whom answered the call. It was a clever political compromise in what would become a typical Canadian balancing act between French and English sentiments.

By 1904 Laurier was so popular that his government was returned with an increased majority. The same year Laurier began planning a second transcontinental railway (see page 198). In 1905 he masterminded the creation of two new provinces (see page 185).

(see page 198)

(see page 185)

Laurier's government lasted until 1911, when he was defeated by a more imperialistic Robert Borden, just in time for the First World War.

Left, top.
A poster from the 1891 election. Macdonald is depicted as the champion of the working man through his protectionist "National Policy." The voters are urged to stay with what they have.

Left, bottom.
Macdonald leaves Parliament Hill for the last time. "The life of Sir John A. is the history of Canada," said Wilfrid Laurier. This photograph was published in the *Dominion Illustrated* on 20 June 1891.

Above, top.
Sir Wilfrid Laurier, prime minister of Canada from 1896 to 1911.

Above.
Soldiers from Prince Edward Island photographed in 1899 before leaving for the Transvaal to fight for Britain and the Empire in the Boer War.

Bonanza on Rabbit Creek

Robert Henderson, a gold prospector from Nova Scotia, had been living in the North for three years when in August 1896 he found what seemed to be a promising gold stream on a tributary of the Klondike River in today's Yukon. He named his find Gold Bottom Creek. A generous man, he invited his prospector friends over to try their luck, and George Washington Carmack, an American, with two native partners, Skookum Jim and Tagish Charlie, were on their way, fishing en route, when they found dense gold in their pans at Rabbit Creek nearby. The trio, realizing they had struck it rich, staked claims and hurried to register them at Forty Mile, a prospectors' camp. When they reached Forty Mile the news of the find soon spread and the camp immediately emptied, with the prospectors rushing to secure their own claims. Rabbit Creek became Bonanza Creek. By the time poor Robert Henderson found out about it, there was no good claim left. Later there was a public outcry about this apparent duping of a Canadian by an American, and the government awarded Henderson a pension of $200 a month in recognition of his role in the discovery of gold.

This was to be the story of the Klondike gold rush; those first on the scene became rich; virtually everyone else was out of luck. The ones who made money from the rush were those who supplied the goldbugs with food and equipment, transported them, or entertained them. For it was not until those first lucky men arrived in San Francisco and Seattle in July the next year that an exodus of would-be gold miners was sparked. In the next few years perhaps 100,000 hopefuls set out for the Klondike; of these, only 40,000 actually arrived at their destination.

Above.
Most of those who made money from the Klondike gold rush were equippers and suppliers, not those who searched for gold. Vancouver and Victoria competed with each other, and with Seattle and San Francisco, to convince miners that their city was the place to start out from. This was an advertisement promoting Vancouver.

Quick action was needed by the Canadian government to control the flood of Americans. The North-West Mounted Police were dispatched to regulate the influx. They set up a control point at the top of the Chilkoot Pass, the point of entry into Canada for many of the miners, and insisted that they take with them 520 kg of solid food per person. This regulation doubtless saved many lives, although it necessitated numerous gruelling round trips up the trail to bring up all the supplies.

Officials of the North-West Territories government began to collect fees for the importation of alcohol. This was a federal responsibility, and as a direct result of this the federal government of Wilfrid Laurier created the Yukon District as a distinct entity apart from the North-West Territories, effective 13 July 1898. A year later the White Pass and Yukon Railway was completed from Skagway to Lake Bennett after a terrible—and expensive—struggle, and in 1900 the line was extended to Whitehorse, a town that had sprung up at the head of navigation on the Yukon River. But by this time the gold rush was all but over, for the gold-yielding area was limited to a few creeks around the original find.

It has been estimated that only four thousand people found any gold and that only three hundred of them found enough to be considered rich. Even more telling, only fifty managed to retain their new-found wealth. The Klondike gold rush opened up the North but emptied many pockets.

Gold rush hopefuls labour up Chilkoot Pass laden with their supplies and equipment in this classic photograph. At the top, the boundary with Canada, a North-West Mounted Police checkpoint awaited them, to ensure that they had 520 kg of solid food per person before they were allowed to proceed.

Mr. Knapp's Revolutionary Boat

Of all the inventions of the age, none was more beguiling than Knapp's Roller Boat. It seemed so reasonable. Why plough through water when you could simply roll along the top of it? Normal boat motion would be all but eliminated. So went the reasoning of one F. A. Knapp of Prescott, Ontario. He convinced investors to finance his invention, and the prototype was demonstrated in Toronto Harbour on 27 October 1897. It worked, as can be seen from this photograph. The inside of the boat, which was 33 m wide and 7 m in diameter, remained level—as least in theory—while the exterior turned. It worked so well that "all that remains to be solved are in the nature of details," claimed the inventor's promotional literature. Knapp intended to establish "Knapp's Ocean Navigation Company" and build roller boats "of the largest dimensions" to cross the Atlantic. But Knapp's boat proved to work only on calm waters; as soon as it encountered large waves the roller boat got stuck in the wave trough, like a wheel in a rut, and forward progress stopped.

Claiming the North

Towards the end of the nineteenth century, Norwegian explorer Otto Sverdrup came to believe that land might exist in the extreme north of the North American continent, beyond the boundaries of exploration to that time. In 1898 he set out to find it, to fill some of the "white spaces on the map" with "Norwegian colours," as he put it. In a wide-ranging exploration over the next four years he found the land he sought in the form of large islands, which he named, after his Norwegian sponsors, Axel Heiberg, Amund Ringnes, and Ellef Ringnes Islands, together some 60 000 km² of land. Naturally enough, Sverdrup claimed the islands for Norway.

In 1903 he published an account of his travels, causing an uproar in Britain and Canada, for it had long been assumed that this part of the world was British, or, after 1880 (when the British handed off responsibility to Canada), Canadian.

So concerned was the Canadian government that it dispatched a number of expeditions to physically claim the remotest islands of the Arctic Archipelago for Canada. First geologist A. Peter Low was sent north in 1903, then Joseph-Elzéar Bernier sailed around the Arctic between 1906 and 1910 erecting cairns and performing "official" ceremonies of possession. From 1913 to 1918 a Canadian Arctic Expedition under Viljhalmur Stefansson further explored the Arctic and did find a new island, Meighen Island, in 1916. In the twenties, sovereignty patrols were continued by the RCMP.

Over the years Sverdrup continued to urge his government to press the Norwegian claim to the North, but nothing was done. Nevertheless the Canadian government was conscious of the possibility of a challenge to its sovereignty if ever the Norwegians changed their minds. In 1930, a deal was struck whereby Norway dropped its possible claim to the Arctic in return for the purchase by the Canadian government of Sverdrup's diaries and maps, for which $67,000 was paid, a fortune in 1930. The diaries were later returned to his family, but the maps, the overt claim of discovery, have, amazingly enough, been lost.

Between 1903 and 1906 another Norwegian, Roald Amundsen, guided a small converted herring boat named *Gjøa* through the maze of the southern Arctic islands, becoming the first to sail through the Northwest Passage. It was the final achievement of a goal sought for centuries. Amundsen kept close to shore, where a small boat could thread its way through the ice-choked channels.

Amundsen went on to become perhaps the most famous polar explorer of all time; he was the first to the South Pole, famously beating Robert Scott in 1911, and was the first to fly across the North Pole, in an airship in 1926.

Above.
A Norwegian goddess, perhaps, captures the Canadian North in this metaphorical illustration from the front cover of Sverdrup's 1903 book *Nyt Land*, "New Land."

Left.
Otto Sverdrup, explorer of Canada's Far North.

Right.
Roald Amundsen, arguably the most accomplished polar explorer.

Below.
Amundsen encountered Kunak and his family at King Point, just west of the Mackenzie Delta, on the last leg of his voyage through the Northwest Passage.

A Society of Artists

Members of the Ontario Society of Artists in 1904 at their annual spring exhibition in Toronto.
The society, an association of professional artists, was founded in 1872. Most of Ontario's well-known
visual artists have been members, including some of the Group of Seven (see page 220). In 1904
the society had thirty-five members. Some of the artworks in this book are paintings by artists in
this photograph; numbers in parentheses are the page numbers on which works by the artist are
reproduced.

Back row, from left: A. P. Coleman, F. McGillivray Knowles, F. M. Bell-Smith, C. M. Manly, R. F. Gagen,
W. E. Atkinson, George Agnew Reid (*bending over*) (18), Charles W. Jefferys (27, 61, 64, 67).
Middle row, from left: Harry Spiers, W. Cutts, Joseph T. Rolph, Emma May Martin, Gertrude Spurr,
James Smith, W. Cruikshank, Owen P. Staples (92).
Front row, from left: J. D. Kelly, F. S. Challener, J. W. Beatty.

The Transformation of Canada

The diversity that is modern Canada really began with the policies of Wilfrid Laurier's government between 1896 and 1911. In an effort to people the Prairies, immigration was promoted in many European countries, although immigration from Asian countries was still discouraged, a situation that would not be remedied until the 1970s.

The chief architect of this new policy was an energetic thirty-five-year-old lawyer from Brandon, Clifford Sifton, who became Laurier's minister of the Interior. Sifton was helped by world economic conditions; European industrialization produced a growing demand for Canadian foodstuffs, especially wheat, thus providing a solid market for the produce of the Prairies. The Canadian Pacific Railway was in place, and branch lines proliferated; at the beginning of the new century other lines were planned and constructed (see page 198). Although the explosive population increase was concentrated in the West, all of Canada saw a substantial growth. With the building of the railway immigration had peaked in 1883 at 134,000 persons, but had since that time fallen off; in 1896, when Laurier came to power, immigration stood at only 17,000 persons for the year. By 1905 it exceeded that of the 1880s peak, and in the years 1910 to 1913 Canada had more immigrants than she ever did again. At its apex, in 1913, immigration was over 400,000 persons.

One of the first things Clifford Sifton did was to strip away many of the regulations that made it harder for settlers to obtain their homesteading land. Under the Dominion Lands Act of 1872 a colonist could obtain a quarter section (160 acres / 65 ha) after building a house on it and cultivating the land for three years, although he had to swear allegiance

Right, top.
Clifford Sifton, until 1905 minister of the Interior in Laurier's government.

Right, centre.
A government poster advertising the free 160-acre homestead available in western Canada.

Below.
A typical Ukrainian homestead made of logs plastered on both sides with a mud and straw mixture, and a distinctive little Ukrainian church, the likes of which popped up all over the Prairies. These are reconstructions at the Western Development Museum in North Battleford, Saskatchewan.

Above.
Fruits of Canadian Enterprise, an advertising card celebrating the Canadian immigrant settling on the Prairies—and becoming a customer of Massey Harris Co., a manufacturer of farm implements and equipment.

to the British Crown in order to obtain his title. A three-year pre-emption to purchase an adjacent quarter section was also allowed. The simplifying of regulation not only speeded up the process but permitted easier access by those who did not speak much English.

Sifton preferred to get his immigrants from Britain and the United States but recognized that these countries alone were not going to be able to supply enough immigrants to populate the empty spaces he wished to fill. And so he turned to southern and eastern Europe, to countries never before considered as a source of immigrants. He famously spoke of the "stalwart peasant in a sheep-skin coat," considering them "good quality" immigrants. He was referring to immigrants from Poland, Russia, and the Ukraine, then part of the Austro-Hungarian Empire. As these people came from hard lives as landless labourers in a harsh climate and families that had lived that way for generations, there is little doubt that they were better suited for the rigours of the Canadian Prairies than many others. But there was one important difference: in Canada they could own the land they laboured on. This was why they came to Canada: *vilni zemli*—free land. The Ruthenians, the Galicians, and the Bukovinians—later known collectively as Ukrainians—settled in some of the most isolated and arid, yet often the most fertile lands in the West. About 200,000 arrived in Canada between 1896 and 1914. Ray Hnatyshyn, Canada's twenty-fourth governor general (1990–95), was always proud of the fact that his grandparents were illiterate immigrants from the Ukraine, and there is no better example of the ultimate contribution of Ukrainians and other diverse ethnic groups to the Canadian population mosaic.

In 1903 a group of almost two thousand settlers arrived together from Britain. These were the Barr colonists, led by Isaac Barr, an Anglican church minister who wanted to "save Canada for the British Empire." He had conceived of the idea of sending out to Canada a large group of like-minded emigrants together, reasoning that they would give each other moral as well as physical support. He planned to ensure that colonists from the same English county became neighbours. Although somewhat of a visionary, Barr proved not to possess the organizational skills required for such a massive undertaking. In addition, his carefully recruited colonists included some unsuited to the rigours of starting a new life on the Canadian Prairies. By his own account, Barr had no less than five "earl's nephews," unlikely to want to sully their hands with manual labour. But at the last minute the colonists were joined by another clergyman, George Exton Lloyd, who would soon look after their salvation in more ways than one.

The settlers arrived in Saskatoon after a cramped voyage and train journey only to find that city to be yet still a prairie, but here Barr had at least arranged for hundreds of tents to be available. Normally colonists took land near the railway, as a lifeline to their markets. But Barr, in anticipation of a railway to come, had claimed land up the North Saskatchewan Valley for his colony, well away from any existing line. And so it was a long walk to the northwest for most, alongside wagons so laden they could not accommodate people. When they arrived, Barr was accused of incompetence and even profiteering and was booted from his position as colony organizer. His place was taken by Lloyd, who proved to be a wise leader, and the settlement, now renamed the Britannia Colony, soon thrived, aided by the arrival of a railway in 1910. Whether any of the earl's nephews stayed the course is not recorded. Today the colony's central settlement is the city of Lloydminster, straddling the Alberta-Saskatchewan boundary, the only Canadian city in two provinces.

With the arrival of settlers, there were demands for self-government, for the whole of the prairie west of Manitoba was still federally controlled. Wilfrid Laurier decided to create additional provinces. But how many? Frederick Haultain, president of the executive council of the North-West Territories, was in favour of a single province. He even had a name for it—Buffalo. Others wanted two provinces, with the boundary line drawn west to east. Calgarians, desperate for provincial capital status, supported that idea. Still others wanted

Above.
Lieutenant-Governor George Bulyea addresses the crowd at the inauguration of the new Province of Alberta, 1 September 1905.

Below.
The tents of Isaac Barr and George Lloyd's colonists fill the trackside at Saskatoon in 1903. They would soon trek up the North Saskatchewan River to found their colony at what would become Lloydminster, a little bit of Britain on a bare prairie.

four provinces; there were after all already four administrative districts of the North-West Territories: Athabasca, Alberta, Saskatchewan, and Assiniboia. Late in 1904 Laurier made the decision. There would be two, Alberta and Saskatchewan; Athabasca and Assiniboia went the way of Caledonia. Their northern boundary would be 60° N, considered the farthest north for any possible agriculture; beyond that would be the Northwest Territories.

The federal government retained public lands within the new provinces because Sifton thought that any change might cost "tens of thousands of settlers in the next two years"; settlement of the West was not to be slowed. But Laurier, the French Canadian, insisted on separate schools, which he thought necessary for the French Catholic minority. Laurier thought religious instruction, the teaching of Christian morals and Christian dogmas, was what distinguished Canada from the lawless West of the United States. Sifton could not agree with him and resigned. The West lost its champion. Nevertheless, his hand could be seen in the growth of the Prairies for another eight years. For immigrants streamed still into Canada.

Immigration continued despite the fact that Sifton's successor, Frank Oliver, introduced a more restrictive immigration policy right away. More of the less fortunate arriving in the country could be rejected and deported, and many were. Oliver, who had started Alberta's first newspaper, the Edmonton *Bulletin,* in 1883, wanted the West populated by what he called "our own people." By this, in order of his preference, he meant eastern Canadians, British, or Americans. Gone were the days when American immigration was viewed as a threat to Canadian security. From henceforth it would be encouraged.

And indeed, it made sense. The majority of Americans coming to Canada were European immigrants to the United States who had taken up farming on the western frontier and, because of rising farmland prices, were now receptive to the offer of more fertile land, free for the taking, in the Canadian West. Because of their twenty years or more of interior farming experience, they knew what to expect and felt quickly at home in their new surroundings. Oliver's department, through its network of land agents in the United States, boosted Canada, and more than one whole trainload of settlers came to Alberta, carefully advertised to encourage others to follow to what was cleverly promoted as "the Last, Best West."

Oliver chaperoned a new Immigration Act through the Commons in 1906. The debate brought out all sides. "In building up our nation we should aim to have the best kind of men, men who would be prepared to maintain here the institutions of a free people," said one. "They may not in all cases be desirable but we will endeavour to lead them in the proper paths and make them desirable when we get them here," said another. Industrialists such as William Van Horne, recently resigned president of the Canadian Pacific Railway, were even more outspoken. "The governments of other lands," he said, "are not such idiots as we are in the matter of restricting immigration. Let them all come in. Every two or three men that come into Canada and do a day's work create new work for someone else to do."

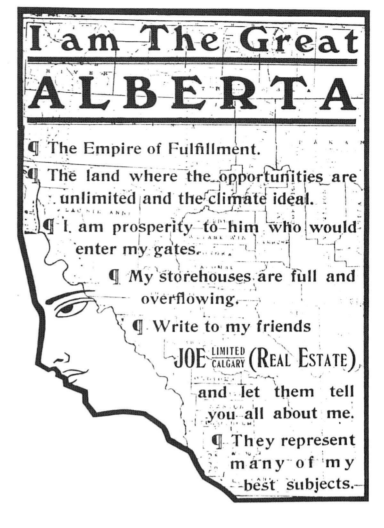

Above.
This innovative advertisement by a real estate company appeared in the *Calgary Herald* in June 1910.

Left, top.
A poster created by the Department of the Interior in 1911 in conjunction with a railway company in the United States to encourage men to come to the Canadian West to help with the harvest. Temporary workers, of course, could turn into permanent ones.

Left.
As part of an advertising effort, this trainload of settlers from Colorado were photographed on their arrival at Bassano, Alberta, after a massive banner had been attached to the train as a backdrop. After 1906 much promotion was done by land agents in the United States to encourage immigration of these preferred settlers.

Right.
Poster advertising the Alberta Provincial Exhibition—now the Calgary Stampede—in 1910. Agricultural shows of one sort or another were an excellent way to promote better farming. This one has a futuristic touch. The bottom illustration shows ploughing being done by airship!

Wheat drove the growth of the Prairies, and farmers' wealth was increased after about 1911 by the introduction of a new improved wheat variety called Marquis. It matured eight days earlier than Red Fife, the variety most commonly planted up to that date, and had a higher yield. This was very significant in the short-season parts of the prairie.

In 1910 the government introduced another immigration act, which gave the federal cabinet the authority to exclude "immigrants belonging to any race deemed unsuited to the climate or requirements of Canada." In 1910 you were "unsuited" if you were of Asiatic origin— Chinese, Japanese, or East Indian. And the means of exclusion was the hated "head tax." There had been such a charge on Chinese immigrants since the 1880s but in 1910 the tax was increased to $500, an amount so high—higher than the annual wages of an industrial worker—that it had the effect of cutting immigration drastically. The same year a tax was imposed on all immigrants, but for those from Britain it was only $25. The head taxes mainly affected immigration to British Columbia, for the Prairies had not been attractive to Chinese immigrants, who were not allowed to obtain the free land available to just about everybody else.

Above.
Lost without his top hat and trouser stretchers, the stereotypical well-to-do Englishman of Empire comes ashore in "Cawnada." This was one of a series of cartoons run by the Montreal *Daily Star* in 1901 lampooning English immigration. Laurier's government at first deliberately avoided encouraging the southern English from emigrating to Canada, feeling that they somehow expected special status in a "colony" of the Empire. Many, including the Barr colonists in 1903, proved the stereotype wrong.

Right.
The *Komagata Maru* was in Vancouver Harbour from May to July 1914.

Far right.
In 1911 the government assigned official photographers to take pictures of immigrants as they landed in Canada. The result was a historically valuable series of documentary images. One of the photographers was William James Topley, who took this image of a Galician (Ukrainian) family at the Québec immigration shed.

Another proscribed group were Indians. In 1914 a shipload of "hindus," as they were derisively called, arrived in Vancouver Harbour, but were not allowed to leave their ship, the *Komagata Maru,* despite the fact that every one of them carried a British passport. At the end of this sorry episode HMCS *Rainbow,* one of two ships in the newly formed Canadian navy, escorted the *Komagata Maru* back out to sea.

In the period from 1896 to the outbreak of the First World War in 1914, a total of 1,417,000 persons came to Canada, of which 752,000 were from Britain, 388,000 from the rest of Europe, 243,000 from the United States, and only 34,000 from Asia. The population, helped by this influx, grew from 5,074,000 in 1896 to 7,879,000 in 1914, an addition of nearly three million people—a 55 percent increase—in eighteen years. Canada's days as a small colony had passed.

Right.
For more than fifty years the British organization for homeless children, Dr. Barnado's, sent some of its charges to Canada to find a better life than that which likely awaited them in Britain. Between 1882 and 1939 the organization sent about 30,000 children to Canada. Most of these children were sent to help out on farms and as domestic servants, and only a few were adopted. This group has just arrived on the dock at Saint John, New Brunswick. This is part of a larger photograph reproduced on the half-title page.

A Catalogue of Canada

As Canada's population grew, the demand for consumer goods increased dramatically. But much of the new population was scatttered all over the Prairies, and even Ontario and Québec were still primarily rural in nature. How then to effectively provide these widely dispersed peoples with the huge variety of goods they now demanded? At one time self-sufficiency had been almost mandatory, but with increasing industrialization the expectation of being able to buy fashionable factory-made clothes or that "essential" kitchen gadget also increased. It was not so much need as want. And, of course, merchants drove the creation of desire for what they sold through advertising. The king of Canadian advertising was Timothy Eaton, who had opened the first Canadian department store, in Toronto, in 1869. In 1884 he realized that there was a vast untapped market waiting for him if he went to the market, instead of waiting for the market to come to him.

Timothy Eaton was an Irish immigrant. When he opened his first store he sold his wares for cash and for a fixed price. This was a novel concept in an age when well-heeled customers offered a sum and then paid their accounts—you hoped—at the end of the month, but often after a far longer time. Although Eaton was not the originator of the idea, it was he who popularized it, and with it came the "democratization" of the retail store. Now anyone could buy, as long as they had the money. Eaton also introduced his famous "goods satisfactory or money refunded" policy, which put him ahead of most other merchants, who were reluctant to stand behind goods for which they were only the middleman.

In 1884, as the West was being opened up by the Canadian Pacific Railway, Eaton began his catalogue operation, using the same cash and refund policy used in his store. The railway allowed the remotest settler to obtain the goods he wanted relatively speedily and, more importantly perhaps, the catalogue gave him the feeling of being part of the metropolitan mainstream, effectively reducing his isolation. Local merchants, of course, hated the catalogue, but the reality was that they could not compete with the scope or variety of the products offered.

For over a hundred years, the Eaton's catalogue became an essential part of the Canadian landscape. The arrival of the new catalogue marked the changing of the seasons and a chance to really shop, twice a year. At the end of its life, and after the new catalogue had arrived, the old one found a new utility out back in the outhouse.

Almost everything, it seemed, could be found in an Eaton's catalogue. A wedding dress, a washing tub, a wireless—or a wife? The last was one of the few items *not* offered in the catalogue, but that didn't stop more than one lonely settler writing to Eaton's to ask

Far left, top.
Timothy Eaton about 1875.

Far left, centre.
The cover of an Eaton's road map from the 1930s, when the company advertised itself as "the Greatest Store within the British Empire."

Far left, bottom.
The catalogue department at Eaton's in 1943. A vast army of clerks was needed to deal with the daily flood of orders, even in wartime.

Left.
Eaton's summer catalogue, 1905.

Below.
Eaton's fall and winter catalogue, 1926–27. Old catalogues provide a fascinating glimpse into the social mores of the past.

for one. After all, there it was on the front of the catalogue: "Write us for any thing you require not listed here."

A generation of immigrants who spoke no English when they arrived in Canada learned what has been termed "Eaton English" from the catalogue, likely the only English-language book they had. But it was a good textbook, with its huge variety of items and complete set of illustrations. If you knew all the words in an Eaton's catalogue you were well on the way to fluency.

The Eaton's catalogue had rivals from time to time. but none entered the Canadian pysche the way the Eaton's one did. Coupled with the expansion of the retail store chain, Eaton's progressed into printing their own catalogue and manufacturing or sourcing much of what they sold.

The Eaton's catalogue finally ended in 1976, the victim of urbanization and easier access to regular retail stores. A vast reorganization of the company then took place, but the Canadian icon still could not keep pace with modern merchandising requirements, and the company went bankrupt in August 1999.

Carrying the Mail

The modern postal system dates from May 1840, when Rowland Hill introduced the penny post to Britain. For a universal penny, paid by the sender, a letter would be carried anywhere in the country. To show that the fee had been prepaid, the adhesive postage stamp was born. This system was soon adopted in the British North American colonies, and the first stamps were issued by Canada, Nova Scotia, and New Brunswick in 1851, Newfoundland in 1857, British Columbia and Vancouver Island in 1860, and Prince Edward Island in 1861.

Canada's first postage stamp was designed by the multi-talented Sandford Fleming, who introduced the beaver as a specifically Canadian icon on his design.

When the Canadian Pacific Railway was under construction, a letter could be addressed to the "end of the line," where a moving office was set up to supply construction workers and settlers. With the line's completion, mail service to the Pacific began in June 1886. Prevously mail to or from British Columbia had had to go through the United States.

At first, mail was collected from post offices by the recipient. Free delivery of mail was introduced slowly, in Montréal in 1874; Toronto, Ottawa, Québec, Hamilton, and Saint John in 1875; Winnipeg in 1882; Vancouver in 1895; and Calgary and Edmonton in 1907. Free rural delivery took longer, beginning in 1908 between Hamilton and Ancaster.

In 1898 postmaster general William Mulock proposed the "Imperial Post," whereby a letter could be sent anywhere in the British Empire for two cents. This was accepted by Britain and a special stamp was issued with a map of the world showing the British Empire in red (see right).

The first Canadian airmail was flown by Captain Brian Peck between Toronto and Montréal on 24 June 1918, and in 1927 contract airmail was introduced, keeping many new airline companies financially as well as physically aloft. Planes began meeting ocean liners at Rimouski, speeding the arrival in eastern cities of mail from Europe. Airmail was clearly very important in a vast country like Canada. On 1 July 1948 Canada became the first country in the world to introduce "all-up" air service, whereby all domestic letters were carried by air.

The post office department became a Crown corporation, Canada Post, in 1981, and with its courier affiliate now carries an astonishing ten billion letters and parcels each year, well over three hundred pieces for each Canadian.

Stamps: Far left: 3 cent, 1888–97, cancelled in Vancouver in 1897. *Right, from top:* British Columbia and Vancouver Island 2½ pence, 1860; 3 cent "beaver," 1859; 2 cent "Imperial Post," 1898, also the world's first Christmas stamp; Western Canada Airways (10 cent) private air surcharge stamp, 1927.

Left. A horse-drawn postal delivery van and crew in Edmonton, 1908.

Below. Pilots and a crowd of worthies pose before the inaugural airmail flight from Rimouski to Montréal, 5 May 1928.

Below, bottom. This Bombardier snowmobile was used to transport mail between L'Anse-Sainte-Jean and Port Alfred, Québec, in the 1940s.

Below, right. New post office "mailmobiles" head out from Vancouver's main mail depot in 1960.

Linking Canada to the World

A company had been formed as early as 1854 to lay a submarine telegraph cable across the Atlantic. This was New York financier Cyrus Field's New York, Newfoundland and London Telegraph Company. Two years later he helped organize a British company with the same aim, the Atlantic Telegraph Company. Plans were made to lay a cable from Newfoundland to Ireland, the shortest possible distance across the ocean.

A number of unsuccessful attempts were made to lay the cable, beginning in 1857, and one of the cables even operated for a short time before its insulation broke down. In 1866 the cable was successfully laid, using the largest ship then existing, the *Great Eastern*, which could carry the enormous length of somewhat thicker wire.

While the unsuccessful attempts were being made to lay a transatlantic cable, another cable was being laid on the west coast of Canada. This was intended to traverse Alaska, cross Bering Strait, and continue to Europe overland. Its initiator, Perry McDonough Collins, interested the Western Union Telegraph Company, which had completed a transcontinental line in 1861, and work began in 1864, just after the fourth attempt to lay a transatlantic cable had failed. The line was strung north from San Francisco and reached New Westminster in April 1865 just in time to bring the news of President Lincoln's assassination. It was then extended north to meet up with a section being built in Alaska. The cable had reached only as far at Fort Stager, at the confluence of the Skeena and Kispiox Rivers near today's New Hazelton, when news arrived—on the telegraph—of the completion of the transatlantic cable. The overland telegraph project was abandoned after $3 million had been spent, a staggering sum at the time.

In 1879 Sandford Fleming started to lobby for laying of a Pacific telegraph line to connect Australia and New Zealand to Canada's west coast and thus link these remotest countries of the British Empire with London via an all-British route. The cable was successfully completed in October 1902 with a station at Bamfield, Vancouver Island, connecting to Fanning Island, in the South Pacific south of Hawaii, via a 6 000-km link, part of a total 13 555-km continuous cable. That year the first telegraphs ever to encircle the globe were sent out, one east, one west, by Sandford Fleming and Lord Minto, the governor general. The messages arrived back in Ottawa, one after ten hours and the other after thirteen and a half hours.

But the seeds of supersession had already been sown for cables. The Italian inventor Guglielmo Marconi had for several years been demonstrating wireless radio wave transmission and reception at increasing distances. In December 1901, on high ground at the entrance to the harbour of St. John's, Newfoundland—later named Signal Hill—he received radio signals transmitted across the Atlantic from Poldhu, in Cornwall, England. This proved for the first time that such signals would follow the curvature of the earth,

Below.
The Atlantic telegraph cable comes ashore at Heart's Content, on Trinity Bay, Newfoundland, in 1866.

Below, bottom.
Prime Minister Mackenzie King, surrounded by his cabinet, makes the first transatlantic telephone call from Canada in 1927. The call was to the British prime minister, Stanley Baldwin, in London, by radio telephone.

a fact uncertain to physicists up to that time. Suddenly long-distance wireless telegraphy was a reality. The news caused a sensation.

The following year Marconi set up an elaborate transmitting and receiving station at Table Head at Glace Bay, on Cape Breton Island, and began commercial telegraphic operations.

The first achievement of voice transmission across the Atlantic occurred in 1915, but it was not until 1927 that commercial radio telephony became available. The cost, however, was prohibitive and the connection unreliable, fading in and out as atmospheric conditions dictated.

The first transatlantic telephone cable, from Scotland to Newfoundland, began operating in 1956, following the development of coaxial cable and submarine vacuum tube repeaters that could re-amplify the signal. The cable could carry thirty-six telephone circuits. Cables were in turn replaced by satellite retransmission beginning in 1962, but only in the 1990s was the characteristic echo-pause of such transatlantic telephone conversations eliminated.

Marconi's 64-metre-high wireless receiving and transmitting towers at Glace Bay, Cape Breton Island, in 1902. The location is now a National Historic Site.

Above and left.
The first Québec bridge after its collapse on
29 August 1907.

Right, top.
The middle span of the second Québec bridge
after its collapse on 11 September 1916.

Right.
A lone sentry guards one of the piers of the
Québec Bridge in 1916. Sabotage was considered
a possibility at the time, but the bridge was to fall
once more even without the help of saboteurs.

The Bridge That Collapsed Twice

The Québec Bridge, perhaps still Canada's most famous bridge, is certainly the one with the most checkered history. A few bridges have collapsed, but the Québec Bridge is the only one to have collapsed twice.

The bridge, patterned on the Forth Railway Bridge in Scotland, was intended to carry the National Transcontinental Railway across the St. Lawrence at a point 11 km upstream from the city of Québec. It was to be the longest steel cantilever bridge in the world. The bridge was to be constructed on what was termed a "best and cheapest" design; the company building it was not in the best financial health. The proper engineering studies were not done at the beginning but rushed through once governmental monies were guaranteed for the bridge's completion.

Work on the bridge began in 1900. By 1906 there were worrisome reports that more weight of steel had been put into the bridge than its design allowed for, but the engineer in charge, Theodore Cooper, decided that the extra stresses would be acceptable. He was wrong. Steel beams started bending, slowly and almost imperceptibly. Cooper became concerned and on 29 August 1907 sent a message to the on-site engineer, John Deans: "Add no more load to bridge till after due consideration of facts." But Deans did not stop the work, and neither did he take his men off the bridge. At about five in the afternoon, the southern cantilever span suddenly shed its built-up stresses, twisted, and fell into the river below. Seventy-five men lost their lives. The collapse was Canada's worst bridge disaster ever. An inquiry concluded that the cause of the collapse was faulty design coupled with improper supervision—human error—of the work in progress.

After redesign, and the appointment of a board of engineers to supervise the work, construction resumed, and on 11 September 1916 the bridge was nearing completion for the second time when tragedy struck once more. As a centre span was being hoisted into position some bearings failed and it fell into the river, taking workers with it. This time thirteen were killed.

The bridge was finally completed in 1917, and the first train was driven proudly—though one would suspect a little nervously—across the bridge.

This great engineering feat, twenty years in the making and marred by the deaths of so many, was "officially" opened after the First World War by the visiting Prince of Wales on 22 August 1919. To this day it remains the longest cantilever railway bridge in the world.

In 1970 the New Québec Bridge was completed beside the original. A road bridge and this time a suspension bridge, its name was changed to the Pierre Laporte Bridge in honour of the minister murdered during the October Crisis of that year (see page 265).

To Carry Elections

In the growth euphoria of the first decade of the nineteenth century, investors and government alike were alive to the possibilities of the West. The engine of this growth, it was felt, was the railway. Farmers, stung from time to time by a shortage of railcars to take their grain to market, clamoured for more railways. Laurier's government thought that competition was preferable to subsidies, and politically easier too. Politicians at every level loved railways. The provision of a branch to a community might well mean the difference between re-election and defeat. Laurier was a man of vision, and he saw his legacy in the accelerated growth of a more united country. "The flood tide is upon us that leads on to fortune," he said. "If we let it pass it may never recur again."

Two new transcontinental railways were proposed and built, leading, when economic activity declined, to a cutthroat oversupply, for despite the optimism, Canada was still a very large country with a very sparsely distributed population.

The government chose to support a proposal by the Grand Trunk Railway. Its subsidiary, the Grand Trunk Pacific Railway, would build west of Winnipeg while the government agreed to construct a line, dubbed the National Transcontinental, from Winnipeg to Moncton, through Québec (and over the Québec Bridge; see previous page). Not coincidentally the Grand Trunk would also gain access to the West. That the plan was popular at the time there can be no doubt; Laurier won the 1904 election essentially on its merits, despite derision from the Opposition that the line was designed "to carry elections rather than passengers."

The Grand Trunk Pacific was built between 1906 and 1914, with its western terminus at the railway-created town of Prince Rupert, on the north coast of British Columbia, shacks in the wilderness, to be sure, but a thousand kilometres nearer to the Orient than Vancouver. Its townsite was named after a competition in 1905 in which "Port Laurier" was a contender. The last spike was driven on 14 April 1914 at Fort Fraser, west of Prince George—just in time for the disruption of the First World War.

The other trancontinental railway was that of railway barons William Mackenzie and Donald Mann. Their Canadian Northern Railway had grown largely by the purchase and merging of existing smaller lines and the acquisition of railway charters that had lain unused since the days of John A. Macdonald and which often came with

Above.
In this delightful family photograph, little Jack and Jim Barford watch a Canadian Northern train in 1912 or 1913 on the grandiosely named Edmonton, Yukon and Pacific line, actually 7 km of track between Strathcona (South Edmonton) and Edmonton.

Below.
A Canadian Pacific train arrives at Strathcona in 1906, after a branch line from Calgary was completed. The CPR built many branch lines in the 1895–1910 period simply to protect its pre-eminent position from the incursions of new companies.

Rather Than Passengers

land grants attached. Mackenzie and Mann had made themselves very popular on the Prairies by offering what the Canadian Pacific did not—service and apparent concern for the farmer.

Mackenzie and Mann decided to extend their network to the West Coast in 1909. They chose Vancouver as their terminus and followed a route surveyed in the 1870s by Sandford Fleming. The line was an expensive one. The sides of the Fraser Canyon would not permit two lines, so every time the Canadian Pacific line crossed the river to the easier side, the Canadian Northern had to cross to the worst. In Vancouver all the suitable land had been pre-empted by their rivals and the line stopped well outside Vancouver at a place called Port Mann. Then Mackenzie and Mann came up with a brilliant idea; they drained the eastern end of False Creek, at that time a long arm of the sea, and thus *created* land for their terminal. The last spike of the Canadian Northern was driven at Basque, south of Ashcroft, B.C., on 23 January 1915, completing Canada's third transcontinental railway.

With the advent of the First World War the credit that had financed the railways was diverted into the war effort. Since, in reality, there was not enough traffic for three cross-country railways, two of them (but not the by now well-established Canadian Pacific) found themselves in deep financial trouble, as did other, non-continental lines. (In British Columbia, the Pacific Great Eastern ran out of money and, lacking federal backing, construction was halted with the line still incomplete.) The federal government had already invested vast sums in both the Canadian Northern and the Grand Trunk Pacific but was no longer prepared or able to keep them afloat. Mackenzie and Mann's railway was taken over by the government in 1918. A year later Canadian National Railways was created as the government's railway operation. The following year the entire Grand Trunk Pacific and the Grand Trunk itself followed into the government fold. With the inclusion of the still government-owned National Transcontinental, the system became the longest on the continent and a potent rival for the Canadian Pacific.

10 *For King and Country*

Canada had grown up fast during the first decade of the twentieth century. Wilfrid Laurier had predicted that the century would belong to Canada and for a while it looked like it would. But by 1910 the boom was winding down and by 1913 the country was in an economic slump. Robert Borden, a Conservative, had beaten Laurier at the polls in 1911 mainly on the latter's support for reciprocity of trade with the United States, but in a declining economy the voters would have none of it; they wanted protection. Even world wheat markets became more competitive with the entry of new producers such as Argentina and Russia. Exports dropped, yet the flood of immigrants continued, causing widespread unemployment.

Then, in the summer of 1914, European events intervened. On 28 June a Bosnian terrorist assassinated an Austrian grand duke in Sarajevo, Serbia, starting a chain of events that would precipitate a world war. A complex series of alliances pitted the Austro-Hungarian Empire and the German Empire against Russia, Serbia's ally, and France, Russia's ally. An 1831 treaty that had guaranteed the neutrality of the new country of Belgium had been subscribed to by Britain. When Germany tore up this "scrap of paper" and attacked Belgium on 1 August 1914, Britain issued a warning that, left unanswered, led Britain to declare war on Germany three days later. Britain's declaration was automatically also that of its empire, including Canada.

Canada was not ready for a war, but then neither was most of the Empire. Britain and Germany had been in an arms race for years, building dreadnought battleships. Canada had precisely two ships, almost out-of-date cruisers purchased from Britain when Laurier started to build a Canadian navy in 1911. But there was alarm on the West Coast, for German cruisers were known to be at large in the Pacific. The day before war was declared, a Seattle shipyard offered Premier Richard McBride of British Columbia two submarines they were building for the Chilean navy. McBride accepted without hesitation and delivery was taken at dawn two days later, in the Strait of Juan de Fuca, to circumvent American neutrality. Thus it was that British Columbia briefly had a navy of its own rivalling that of the Dominion government.

And there was excitement. Men rushed to joined the jingoed fray, to fight for king, country, and empire before it was "all over before Christmas." But it was not going to be over, this time, for four years. No one would miss it.

Thoroughly modern Leduc, Alberta, in 1921. A train passes the collection of elevators while a car waits at the crossing and, miraculously, a plane flies overhead at precisely the same instant. One feels the scene must have been staged for the photographer.

Above.
On 3 October 1914 thirty ships sailed for England carrying 32,000 men of the Canadian Expeditionary Force.

Opposite, top.
A recruiting poster aimed at French Canadians through a patriotic reminder of the defence of Montréal in 1813 by Salaberry and his Voltigeurs (see page 95).

Opposite, below.
One wonders whether any of the employees of the Edmonton City Dairy who had signed up had any idea what they were getting into when they posed for this photograph in 1915.

Borden's government quickly passed the War Measures Act, giving the federal government extraordinary powers to fight the war. One of these powers was that of "arrest, detention, exclusion and deportation," which led to the internment of "aliens." (This same act, still on the statute books in 1970, was invoked by Pierre Trudeau in the October Crisis of that year; see page 265.) Suddenly many of those who had been encouraged to emigrate to Canada were less than welcome. Many of those of German or Austro-Hungarian (including Ukrainian) origin found themselves in internment camps. Anti-German sentiment swept the country. German people, or even those with German-sounding names, and their properties were attacked, especially after the sinking of the British liner *Lusitania* in May 1915, which killed more than a thousand civilians, including Americans (and which would be one of the factors dragging the United States into the war in 1917). In Victoria a crowd rampaged through the Kaiserhof Hotel, one example of many such incidents across the country. By 1916 the town of Berlin, Ontario, was pressured into changing its name to a much more patriotic one—Kitchener, after the British general of the same name.

The Canadian war effort was intitially orchestrated by the minister of Militia, Sam Hughes, who was behind the times in his thinking. He insisted that the Ross rifle be used, a superb rifle in ideal conditions, but far too heavy and susceptible to jamming to be of much use in the ungentlemanly conditions of this war. Borden would fire the inept but controlling Hughes in November 1916.

A War of Attrition

Hughes asked for 25,000 volunteers to report to Valcartier, just north of Québec; 32,000 turned up. Many of them were British immigrants, but the high level of unemployment made recruiting easy at this stage. The first Canadian Expeditionary Force, as the Canadian contingent was known throughout the war, sailed for England in October 1914. It was sent to France the following April just in time for the second battle of Ypres, in which the Germans used poisonous gas as a weapon for the first time. The battle was a ghastly introduction to this appalling war. It was here that medical officer John McCrae, from Guelph, Ontario,

Above.
The maelstrom that is war is conveyed by Louis Weirter's painting of the battle for Courcelette, in which Canadians played a major role. Weirter was present at the battle. The French city was finally captured on 15 September 1916.

Below.
Richard Jack's painting of the taking of Vimy Ridge in 1917 almost ignores the human toll, concentrating instead on depicting the technology involved. Unlike Weirter, Jack was not present at the battle and relied on second-hand accounts for his painting.

wrote his famous poem that begins: "In Flanders fields the poppies blow / Between the crosses, row on row . . ." The Canadians lost more than 6,000 men at Ypres.

The Western Front had by this time reached near stalemate, where the opposing armies faced each other across a line from western Belgium south into Flanders. Men fought and died in the thousands gaining or losing a small patch of quagmired trenchland. It was a war such as no man had seen before.

A Canadian Corps was formed in September 1915. After a debacle at Messines in April 1916 due in part to casualties from "friendly fire" (as it has come to be well known after Canadian involvement in Afghanistan in 2002), the Corps was commanded by Julian Byng, a British lieutenant general who would later become a governor general of Canada.

On 1 July 1916 came the infamous Battle of the Somme. In the first day the British army lost 20,000 men, including the majority of the Royal Newfoundland Regiment, and another 40,000 were wounded. The battle lasted until November with casualties totalling a stunning and almost unbelievable 1,265,000 on both sides. For this, the Allies gained 8 km of wasteland. In September the Canadians took the village of Courcelette, just north of the Somme River, and held it against many counterattacks. In the process they gained a considerable fighting reputation, but at the cost of 24,000 casualties. This was the battle at which the Allies' new "secret weapon," the tank, first saw action.

On Easter Monday, 9 April 1917, came another trial by fire. The Canadians were ordered to take Vimy Ridge, which overlooks the little French town of Arras. Byng and his second-in-command, Arthur Currie, had meticulously planned the attack and carried out extensive training. Artillery gunners could now shell immediately in front of their own advancing troops. In four days of vicious fighting all four divisions of the Canadian Corps, working together for the first time, took and held the ridge. Nearly 3,600 died and 7,000 more were wounded. Today Canada's greatest war memorial stands on the crest of Vimy Ridge, a monument to the bravery of so many.

Byng was promoted and Currie took over command of the Canadian Corps. On 15 August they took a strategic hill north of Vimy called simply Hill 70, and held it against twenty-one German counterattacks.

Perhaps the worst battle of the war for the Canadian Corps was that of Passchendaele, near Ypres. Currie was ordered to take a ridge across reclaimed marshes that had been shelled so much that there was no drainage. The mud seemed bottomless. The British army had already lost 68,000 men in the mire trying to take the ridge. Currie protested that the attack would cost him 16,000 men, an uncannily accurate forecast. Despite very careful preparations that undoubtedly reduced losses, the Corps took the ridge at a cost of 15,654 dead and wounded. Total casualties of half a million men, more or less equally divided between the Germans and the Allies, resulted from the horror of Passchendaele.

By 1916, the rush of recruits signing up had slowed. The wartime economy was booming, wages had risen, and unemployment had fallen. An Imperial Munitions Board had been set up in November 1915 headed by a millionaire entrepreneur, Joseph Flavelle. His organization had made a big difference to the supply of munitions to the front and, in turn, industrial activity in Canada. The result was a serious shortage of men to replace the incredible carnage at the front. French Canadians had turned against the war, which was more and more perceived as a war for the British Empire. Prime Minister Robert Borden risked German submarines to go to England in February 1917 for the Imperial War Conference, at which the Dominion was for the first time consulted about the progress of the war; up to this point Borden knew little more than what he read in the newspapers. He also visited the trenches in France and was in Europe during the battle of Vimy Ridge. He returned with a deeper knowledge of the cost of war and a grim determination that Canada had no alternative but to supply more men. The only possible answer seemed to be conscription.

Borden was afraid that conscription would tear the country apart, and indeed the issue did by March 1918 lead to riots in Montréal. He asked Laurier to join him in a coalition government, but Laurier, cognizant of what this would do to his position as a champion of

Below.
Canadian artillery in action east of Arras, France, during an advance in September 1918.

French Canada, refused. On 11 June 1917, Borden introduced the Military Service Bill. Each citizen, he announced, had an "obligation to assist in defending the rights, the institutions and the liberties of his country." Henri Bourassa, the premier of Québec, opposed the bill, pointing out that Canada had already sent a greater proportion of its population to fight than had Britain and France. Borden managed to persuade a number of English-speaking Liberals to join a coalition government, and this Union government went to the polls for a mandate in December. Borden made sure he would be re-elected. He disenfranchised immigrants from enemy countries and conscientious objectors, set up voting for the troops in France, and gave the vote to female relatives of soldiers serving abroad, the first time women were allowed to vote. He got his mandate.

Call-ups began in January 1918. Over 400,000 men were registered but the process was slow; 380,000 appealed. When Borden again visited Britain in the spring he found recruitment was not keeping up with losses at the front, and when he returned he abolished farm labour exemptions, which had applied to that point. By war's end, 124,000 men had been added to the Canadian forces, but only 24,000 of them had reached France. Conscription may have been militarily justified, but it left the Conservatives with a huge political liability in Québec and in farming communities on the Prairies.

As it happened, the war came to an end unexpectedly quickly in 1918, when the Allies made breakthroughs which forced the Germans back deep into Belgium. This resulted in a German request for an armistice, granted on 11 November.

Above.
Planes in France, 1918, from Billy Bishop's first book, *Winged Warfare.*

Below.
Billy Bishop with his Nieuport 17C aircraft at Filescamps Farm, a landing ground near Arras, France, on 4 August 1917.

Aces in the Air

When Canadians fought in France they did so as an integral part of the British army. It was no different for those who took on a new form of warfare—that in the air.

The First World War was the first in which generals could not physically see what their armies were doing, so vast was the field of conflict. The airplane, as the eyes of the strategists, came into its own. The ability to determine from the air the location of the enemy's trenches was of enormous significance. And it was not long before the reconnaissance planes were shooting at each other—blinding the enemy being as significant as being able to see the course of a battle yourself—and dropping bombs onto enemy emplacements.

The Canadian government before the war, and to a large extent even once it had begun, was somewhat indifferent to aerial warfare and had no air force of its own. Canadians who wanted to fly, therefore, signed up with the British, either with the Royal Naval Air Service (RNAS) or the Royal Flying Corps (RFC). By war's end, well over a quarter of the British military air forces were made up of Canadians. And quite a few of them were very good at their job.

Without a doubt the most famous Canadian air ace was William Avery Bishop, Billy Bishop. Although maligned by some after his death, it has never been shown that Bishop's war record was anything but exemplary. He became the British Empire's highest scoring ace, with seventy-two aerial victories to his name. Early in the morning of 2 June 1917 Bishop made a daring solo raid on German planes on the ground, damaging seven and shooting down three more as they took off to engage him. For this Bishop was awarded the Victoria Cross. He became so famous that the commander of the Royal Air Force (the RNAS and RCF merged in April 1918) ordered him out of combat in May 1918 to avoid the possibility of a detrimental effect on national morale if he were shot down.

Above.
A Sopwith F7.1 Snipe, the type of airplane William Barker was flying when he attacked sixty German planes in October 1918.

Bishop went on to become an honorary air marshal and director of recruiting for the Royal Canadian Air Force in World War II. He wrote a book called *Winged Peace* outlining his vision for future aviation, much of which was embodied in the United Nations International Civil Aviation Organization (ICAO) in 1947.

Somewhat overshadowed by Bishop until quite recently, but certainly his equal as an air ace, was William George Barker, who shot down fifty-two enemy aircraft in the course of the war. He was awarded the Victoria Cross for single-handedly attacking, in a Sopwith Snipe, a formation of no less than sixty enemy aircraft, shooting down four of them before crash-landing, terribly wounded.

Above.
William Barker with the Sopwith Camel in which he shot down 37 aircraft and 6 balloons.

Left.
Billy Bishop in his plane, 1918.

Right.
Ray Collishaw, another Canadian air ace, in 1918. Collishaw was credited with 62 aerial victories.

A Rain of Chimney Bricks

Two views of the results of the Halifax Explosion. *Above* is a panoramic print from a roll of paper apparently taken with a special panoramic camera. The view is to the south and east towards the harbour, and the photograph shows graphically how widespread the damage was from the blast. *Below,* rescuers search through the remains of a collapsed building looking for survivors.

Halifax Harbour was packed with ships during the war. At 8:45 in the morning of 6 December 1917, in the narrowest part of the harbour, at the north end of Halifax, a Belgian Relief ship, the *Imo,* collided with a French munitions ship, the *Mont Blanc,* which was steaming to join a convoy in Bedford Basin. Sparks from the collision ignited flammable benzol stored on the deck of the *Mont Blanc.* The captain and crew, anticipating an explosion, abandoned the ship, leaving it to drift. The spectacle drew a large crowd of onlookers, unaware of the danger. Flaming liquid soon found its way into the hold, which was packed with the military explosives picric acid, TNT, and gun cotton. At 9:06 the *Mont Blanc* erupted and disappeared in the largest man-made explosion before the atomic age. A "rain of chimney bricks, bits of steel, and . . . flying glass" hit Halifax and Dartmouth. The collapse of chimneys and the overturning of wood stoves started thousands of fires all over the city. A huge tidal wave generated by the explosion surged into city streets, sweeping people up and drowning them.

The explosion killed about 1,600 people and injured 9,000 more, including 200 who were blinded by flying glass. Some 1,600 buildings were destroyed and 12,000 were damaged; 6,000 people were made homeless and 20,000 more had inadequate shelter. Every pane of glass in the city was shattered. Much of Halifax had to be evacuated for a time as fire threatened the main dockyard ammunition stores. And all this in below-zero blizzard weather. The explosion produced misery for thousands.

Squads of soldiers and sailors worked around the clock to rescue the trapped. They patrolled the windowless shopping streets, but the explosion had affected everyone and there was little looting. Special trains shipped off the wounded to Windsor and Truro.

Halifax, however, was not alone. Soon trainloads of everything from medical supplies to panes of glass and clothing were arriving every hour from central Canada and from New England. A veritable army of skilled workmen arrived to begin reconstruction; the Dominion government voted an immediate million dollars in aid for the city. Eventually some $30 million would flow into the city from public and private sources to aid those to whom the war had come so close. The Halifax Explosion brought the war home to Canada in a way never thought possible, and with a devastation even the might of the German navy could not have wrought. Fifty-nine years later, in 1976, when the Halifax Relief Commision finally terminated its work, it still had sixty-five people receiving pensions.

A Canadian Nation

About 654,000 Canadian men and women served during the First World War in the Expeditionary Force or in British units. Nearly 10 percent of them were killed and more than a quarter of them were wounded, many seriously maimed. It was a tremendous sacrifice. Many who survived the war did not survive the peace. Thousands of soldiers died in an influenza pandemic, the so-called Spanish Flu, in 1918 or 1919, and they brought the virus back to Canada, where it killed more than 50,000 people.

The war's baptism by fire had a significant effect; in many ways it gave birth to Canada as an independent nation, though the conscription crisis had also exposed the country's Achilles heel, the tension between French and English.

After much deliberation and cajoling Canada was given a seat at the peace conference and became a separate signatory to the Treaty of Versailles, signed on 28 June 1919. The Americans were concerned that the British Empire would have too much representation, but Borden angrily pointed out that Canada had lost more men than the United States, which had entered the war only in 1917. And Canada was no longer prepared to accept an inferior position to Britain in the international arena. The country became a fully-fledged independent member of the League of Nations, the flawed organization that was supposed to guarantee the integrity of all nations and prevent another war. Canada received no spoils of war, but it did gain international recognition as a nation unto itself.

Three social trends got a boost from the war: socialism and unionism, votes for women, and the temperance movement. In addition, income tax got its start. The latter was introduced in 1917 as a temporary measure, a conscription of wealth to accompany a conscription of manpower. Most wages were too low to be affected, but high incomes were taxed by 1919 at almost 50 percent.

Towards the end of the war wage increases rarely kept pace with a spiralling cost of living, and the feeling grew that business was somehow making unreasonable profits from the labour of workers. Union membership almost tripled between 1915 and 1919. Some of the more radical labour organizations were outlawed by the government, which was coming to fear a Bolshevist-type revolution similar

Below.
Returning troops cheer as they arrive in Halifax in 1919. They are on the *Olympic*, an ocean liner converted for use as a troop transport, and the "dazzle" camouflage is visible as the wide stripes in two directions at the top of the photograph.

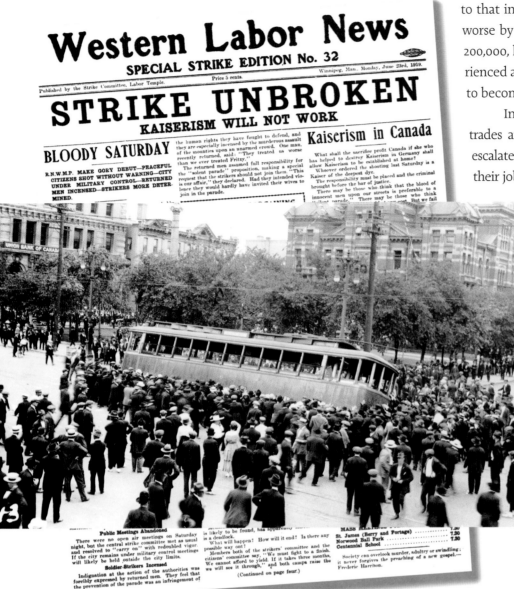

Western Labor News

SPECIAL STRIKE EDITION No. 32

Published by the Strike Committee, Labor Temple.   Price 5 cents.   Winnipeg, Man., Monday, June 23rd, 1919.

STRIKE UNBROKEN

KAISERISM WILL NOT WORK

BLOODY SATURDAY

R.N.W.M.P. MAKE GORY DEBUT—PEACEFUL
CITIZENS SHOT WITHOUT WARNING—CITY
UNDER MILITARY CONTROL—RETURNED
MEN INCENSED—STRIKERS MORE DETER-
MINED.

the human rights they have fought to defend, and
they are especially incensed by the murderous assault
of the mounties upon an unarmed crowd. One man,
recently returned, said: "They treated us worse
than we ever treated Fritzy."

The returned men assumed full responsibility for
the "solemn parade" proposition, making a special
request that the strikers should not join them. "This
is our affair," they declared. Had they intended violence they would hardly have invited their wives to
join in the parade.

Kaiserism in Canada

What shall the sacrifice profit Canada if she who
has helped to destroy Kaiserism in Germany shall
allow Kaiserism to be established at home?

Whoever ordered the shooting last Saturday is a
Kaiser of the deepest dye.

The responsibility must be placed and the criminal
brought before the bar of justice.

There may be those who think that the blood of
innocent men upon our streets is preferable to a
"silent parade." There may be those who think
... But we fail

Public Meetings Abandoned

There were no open air meetings on Saturday
night, but the central strike committee met as usual
and resolved to "carry on" with redoubled vigor.
If the city remains under military control meetings
will likely be held outside the city limits.

Soldier-Strikers Increased

Indignation at the action of the authorities was
forcibly expressed by returned men. They feel that
the prevention of the parade was an infringement of

is likely to be found, has apparently
is a deadlock.

What will happen? How will it end? Is there any
possible way out?

Members both of the strikers' committee and the
citizens' committee say, "We must fight to a finish.
We cannot afford to yield. If it takes three months,
we will see it through," and both camps raise the

(Continued on page four.)

MASS MEETINGS . . .   7.30
St. James (Berry and Portage) . . . 7.30
Norwood Ball Park 7.30
Centennial School 7.30

Society can overlook murder, adultry or swindling;
it never forgives the preaching of a new gospel.—
Frederic Harrison.

An incident in Winnipeg on "Bloody Saturday," as 21 June 1919 came to be known. Strikers overturn a tram. The newspaper is the strikers' *Western Labor News* for Monday, 23 June, reporting on the events of the weekend.

to that in Russia, a situation which, it was felt, might be made worse by returning soldiers. Winnipeg, a growing city of some 200,000, had become a hotbed of more radical labour and experienced a civic workers strike at the end of 1918 that threatened to become more general.

In May 1919, a dispute over wage claims in the building trades and collective bargaining in the metal trades suddenly escalated into a general strike. On 15 May 35,000 workers quit their jobs and went on strike. Business leaders and professionals and many others created a Citizens' Committee of One Thousand to oppose the strike and fill essential jobs that strikers had left. "No thoughtful citizen can any longer doubt that the so-called General Strike is in reality revolution," the committee's newspaper declared on 27 May. The federal government agreed and unanimously passed an amendment to the Immigration Act that permitted the deportation without trial of "advocates of the use of force in changing society." Ten strike leaders were arrested.

On 21 June returned soldiers called for a parade to protest the government's intransigence, the mayor read the Riot Act, and mounted police charged a crowd at Portage and Main, causing at least one death and many injuries. This effectively ended the strike, for the workers were in the main not the revolutionaries the government had mistaken them for, but the government had acted in what we would now regard as a distinctly unCanadian fashion. The strikers from that point took the political route, changing things from within the system. They got themselves elected to city council, the provincial legislature, and one, James Shaver Woodsworth, a Methodist minister, to Parliament. In 1933 Woodsworth would become a founding member and first leader of the Co-operative Commonwealth Federation (CCF), later the New Democratic Party (NDP) (see page 224).

Arthur Meighen succeeded Robert Borden in 1920, but was thrown out in 1921 with the first election of Canada's longest-serving prime minister, William Lyon Mackenzie King. By about 1924, prosperity had returned, led by new industries, pulp and paper making, mining, and hydroelectric power generation. It was the "roaring twenties" of popular mythology. And, as we all know, the common man started buying a piece of the prosperity. Social unrest almost disappeared for a while, buried in a flood of stock certificates. But economic boosterism was overdone. Paper production outstripped demand from the new American Sunday newspapers by 1927; demand for power was forecast to increase forever at the rate of the mid-twenties. The story was repeated over and over, but few saw the warning signs until in 1929 the facade came crashing down, along with the economies of most of the world's nations, ushering in the Great Depression of the thirties.

Respectable Men Shouldn't Have the Vote

"Or even want it," either. Activist Nellie McClung turned the tables on men in her satirical play *The Women's Parliament* in Winnipeg in 1914. Her play reversed roles; this was exactly what parliamentarians—male, of course—had been saying about *women*.

McClung was one of a number of pioneering women agitating for women's suffrage in Canada. Like many others she was a promoter of temperance, but had come to realize that little was going to be changed without women being able to vote. Women of property had at one time been allowed to vote, but even this limited right had long ago lapsed. Through the efforts of McClung and others, Manitoba in 1916 became the first province to allow women to vote; that year and the next all the western provinces and Ontario followed suit, and Robert Borden allowed female relatives of servicemen to vote in the federal election of 1917. The war changed everything; women were visibly involved in everyday life out of necessity and in a way never before thought possible. In 1920 women were finally given the vote federally, and in the election the following year farmers' representative Agnes Campbell Macphail became the first woman member of Parliament.

Women could not yet be appointed to the Senate, however, and in the 1920s this institution was more powerful than it is today, approving divorces, for example. The British North America Act said that only "persons" could be appointed to the Senate, and this had always been interpreted to mean men only. In 1927 a group of activist women (who came to be known as the "Famous Five") led by Emily Murphy asked the Supreme Court to define "persons." The court ruled against them in 1928, and so, since the law was a British statute, the group appealed to the British Privy Council, the highest appeal court for Canada at that time. The law lords of England had been influenced by the women's suffrage movement in that country, for in October 1929 they ruled that women were indeed persons, just as much as men. The exclusion of women from public office was, they wrote in their decision, "a relic of days more barbarous than ours."

This landmark decision, the so-called Persons Case, was a major step towards equality for women. In 1930, the first female senator, Carine Wilson, was appointed to that august body. Today statues of the Famous Five stand on the front lawn of Parliament.

Above.
Agnes Macphail, the first woman elected to Parliament, 1921.

Below.
The "Famous Five" (*left to right*), Emily Murphy, Irene Parlby, Louise McKinney, Henrietta Muir Edwards, Nellie McClung.

The Demon Drink

Rum, gin, and beer had long been seen as a barrier to economic success, but from the mid-nineteenth century on, societal evils associated with urban poverty were increasingly blamed on alcohol, and organizations arose whose goal was to ban alcohol altogether. A movement for temperance turned into one for Prohibition. Societies often had elaborate rules, ceremonies, and names. Leonard Tilley, one of the Fathers of Confederation who went on to become premier of Nova Scotia, was at one time "The Most Worthy Patriarch of the North American Sons of Temperance," a broadly based temperance organization originating in the United States.

The first major attempt at Prohibition was the Canada Temperance Act of 1878, which allowed local majorities to decide. But this law did not work very well. In Cornwall, Ontario, for example, the local member of Parliament noted that whereas before the town had twelve "respectable" hotels, it now had "from 100 to 150 unlicensed places dealing out poison morning, noon, and night, Sabbath day and week day." This was to be the ongoing problem with Prohibition; there were simply too many who wanted to drink, and one way or another, legally or illegally, they would find a means to do so.

Women, so often on the receiving end of the evils of drunkenness, were prime movers in bringing about more universal Prohibition. The Woman's Christian Temperance Union, founded in 1874 and still in existence, was one of the lobbyists, and demand for the female vote (see page 211) arose largely out of an inability to effect change without power.

It was the war that gave the prohibitionists the ammunition they needed, appealing to patriotism in a way no politician could ignore. Alcohol hindered the war effort, they said. Prince Edward Island had alone enacted Prohibition in 1900, but between 1915 and 1916 every province except Québec became dry. Then, after the election of 1917, the federal government banned manufacture of any beverage with more than 2½ percent alcohol, although this prohibition lasted only until the end of the war. With the war's end, the voices of moderation were again able to be heard, and most provinces repealed Prohibition during the 1920s in favour of controlled government sales. One, Prince Edward Island, continued Prohibition until 1948.

Four and twenty Yankees, feeling very dry
Sailed across to Canada to get a case of rye
*   When the case was opened, they all began to sing*
*   To hell with the President and God save the King*
*   — 1920s song, during American Prohibition*

Above.
This poor unfortunate was arrested and hauled off to jail by two police constables in Toronto in 1916 for merely having alcohol in his possession.

Left.
An illegal bar, or "blind pig," is raided by government agents in Elk Lake, Ontario, sometime in the early 1920s. A hundred and sixty barrels of illegal brew were tapped and poured into the lake.

Below.
The Reverend Peter Walker (standing at right) with a bedecked group from his Hillhurst Presbyterian Sunday School in Calgary about 1914. They were out to support the "dry" campaign.

HOPE

VOTE DRY

HELP US!
WE WOULD CLOSE THE SALOO

Canada Takes to the Skies

At the beginning of the twentieth century, scientists, engineers, and dreamers of a number of nations were trying to build a mechanical device that would fly. On 17 December 1903, flight was finally achieved by Orville and Wilbur Wright at Kitty Hawk, North Carolina.

The first flight in Canada of a heavier-than-air machine seems to be that of a glider piloted by Lawrence Jerome Lesh, who flew 10 km down the St. Lawrence near Montréal in 1907, but the first flight of a heavier-than-air machine powered by a motor is that of John McCurdy in 1909.

Above.

The Aerial Experimentation Association's plane *Baddeck No. 1* is shown being demonstrated to the military on 3 August 1909 at Petawawa, Ontario. Unfortunately it crashed, like *Silver Dart* the day before; the army officers were not impressed and passed on this early opportunity to take to the air.

Below.
Former World War I pilots John Alcock and Arthur Brown lift off from St. John's at the beginning of their record-breaking first transatlantic flight on 14 June 1919. The flight covered 3 040 km, lasted 16 hours 12 minutes, and ended in an Irish bog. Alcock and Brown won a prize of £10,000 that had been offered by a British newspaper for a successful flight acorss the Atlantic. Having survived the long flight, Alcock died a few months after this feat in a crash while delivering a plane from England to France, a comparatively short distance; Brown died in 1948.

A small group of engineer-inventors led by Alexander Graham Bell, inventor of the telephone (see page 156), and calling themselves the Aerial Experimentation Association (AEA), built a number of flying machines, each incorporating design changes in order to determine the best design for sustained flight. All had engines designed by Glenn Curtiss, one of the group. Several made short flights near Curtiss's workshop in Hammondsport, New York, but it was the group's fourth aircraft, christened *Silver Dart* from its covering of silver fabric, that became the first to fly in Canada. *Silver Dart,* piloted by John McCurdy, flew at 65 km per hour for 800 m at an elevation of about 18 m on 23 February 1909 near Bell's Canadian residence at Baddeck, Cape Breton Island. The following day McCurdy flew the plane on a 7-km circuit lasting six minutes. The AEA was sued by the Wright brothers for infringing their patent on "wing warping," their method of aircraft control, but the AEA was using a new French invention that moved part of the wing, the aileron, and the lawsuit came to nothing.

In Victoria, British Columbia, amateur engineer William Wallace Gibson independently designed and built several aircraft. His first flight was on 8 September 1910, when he flew 60 m at an altitude of 6 m. Another of his planes looked more like a set of venetian blinds—but it flew, regardless. Poor Gibson was the laughingstock of conservative Victoria society for some time, which failed to recognize his talent.

Little interest was shown and less progress made until the First World War, when the military advantages of aircraft became obvious (see page 206). By the time the war was over, the sophistication and reliability of aircraft as well as their numbers had increased dramatically. Such was the scale of the war that about twelve thousand Canadian pilots found themselves unemployed at its end. Not surprisingly, many created their own employment by utilizing some of the many surplus aircraft in a variety of tasks, from barnstorming to bush piloting. The period after World War I opened up the remoter regions of Canada, especially in the North. Suddenly it was possible to get to places in hours where before it had taken months. Bush planes generally carried freight and passengers from places reachable by rail to places that were not. In August 1919 Ernest Hoy became the first to fly across the Canadian Rockies. He flew from Vancouver to Calgary via Cranbrook and Lethbridge in a Curtiss JN4, a widely produced World War I plane. With the Rocky Mountains no longer an insurmountable barrier, there was nowhere in the country that could not be reached by air.

One popular plane, used by the U.S. Navy and made available as surplus in Canada after the war, was the Curtiss HS2L flying boat, also from Glenn Curtiss's factory. Able to make use of Canada's multitude of lakes, this versatile plane is usually credited as being Canada's first bush plane, and it has a string of other Canadian "firsts" to its credit (see next page). This plane flew from 1915 to 1918 as a military aircraft, then until 1932 as a civilian one.

Another common use for planes at this time was to carry mail (see page 192), but there were plenty of other uses. One of the saddest and most unusual was the bombing of whales. In 1926, after poor fish catches in the St.Lawrence around Île d'Anticosti, someone had the idea that beluga whales were responsible. A contract was given to an aircraft company to bomb them, and this was repeated again a few years later. This demonstrates how values have changed; one cannot imagine such a venture even being suggested today. A better use of aircraft was for emergencies; in December 1928 Wilfrid "Wop" May heroically flew diphtheria vaccine from Edmonton to Fort Vermilion under the most appalling conditions to stem a sudden outbreak of the disease.

By the end of the 1930s hundreds of small airlines occupied every region of the country. In 1939, the Canadian Pacific Railway, having turned down the opportunity to be a partner in the new Trans-Canada Airlines because of heavy government involvement, started on an airline buying spree that would in 1942 lead to the creation of Canadian Pacific Airlines, a first step towards an era of fewer but much larger airlines (see page 248).

The variable pitch propeller was invented by a Canadian, Wallace Rupert Turnbull. First modelled in 1918, it did not become a reality until 1928. It is as essential to propeller-driven planes as a gearbox is to cars. By allowing the pitch of the propeller blades to be changed in flight, Turnbull's invention allowed a plane to achieve maximum speed for takeoff as well as achieve optimal cruising efficiency. The first variable pitch mechanism was tested by Turnbull on an Avro 504K, a multipurpose World War I aircraft, as shown here.

Not exactly inflight service! The pilot and co-pilot of this Canadian Airways Curtiss HS2L flying boat have lunch after landing. The photograph was taken sometime in the late 1920s, probably in Québec. The HS2L was the world's first bush plane, the ideal plane for Canadian conditions, and the first plane many inhabitants of Canada's remoter areas ever saw. The plane was developed in 1916; many were bought from the U.S. Navy after 1918 and saw service in Canada right through the 1920s. The HS2L was affectionately dubbed the "flying forest" on account of the large number of wing struts required to keep it rigid, and sometimes called a "flying cigar box" because the body was made of wood, and had to be hauled out of the water frequently to avoid waterlogging. Pilots joked that the HS2L took off, cruised, and landed all at the same speed. Canadian Airways was eventually purchased by the airline that became Canadian Pacific Airlines, now part of Air Canada.

The Curtiss HS2L was used for the first bush flight in the world, by Stuart Graham in June 1919; for the first aerial forest survey and first forestry patrol, both in 1919; for the first mining claim staked with the use of an aircraft, 1920; for the initial leg of the first trans-Canada flight in 1920; for the first scheduled air service in Canada, by Laurentide Air Service in Québec, in 1924; and for the first regular airmail service, also in 1924.

The Horseless Carriage

The Canadian automobile is exactly the same age as Confederation. Henry Seth Taylor of Stanstead, Québec, became the first to build and own an automobile in 1867, a steam buggy that was merely a seat atop some wheels plus a big boiler. It was regarded as little more than a novelty, as were the first internal combustion engine automobiles brought into Canada from the United States around 1898. The main reason they were only a novelty was that there was nowhere to drive them; roads were in such appalling condition that only the hauling action of a horse would get you through, most of the year.

But the automobile, novelty or not, was here to stay, and as the number of owners increased so did the demand for better roads. More than one owner took instead to the rails; Charles Jasper Glidden's pioneering crossing of the Rocky Mountains in 1904 was done on the tracks of the Canadian Pacific, not on roads at all.

That same year the first Canadian automobile manufacturing began in Windsor, with the establishment of the Ford Motor Company of Canada, just a year after Henry Ford had begun making cars in Detroit. Parts were shipped across the river by the wagonload, the first act in what would one day evolve into a closely knit relationship between American and Canadian automakers.

Robert Samuel McLaughlin was a highly successful Oshawa carriage and sleigh maker who at the turn of the century was producing 25,000 carriages a year, yet he saw more clearly than most the writing on the wall and

converted his works to automobiles. In 1908 he arranged with William Durant, the founder of General Motors, to use Buick engines, and McLaughlin-Buicks became world-renowned. Then Durant offered him the Canadian rights to a car designed by Louis Chevrolet, and General Motors of Canada was founded in 1918 under McLaughlin.

The first service station appeared in 1908, in Vancouver, a mere garden hose connected to an Imperial oil tank, but it was a start. Gasoline was usually sold by filling your own can.

Although Canada later proved not to have a large enough market to support an automotive mass producer, the demand of the First World War led temporarily (from 1918 to 1923) to Canada being second only to the United States as a manufacturer of cars. This mass production brought the cost of cars within reach of many more people. In 1903, the first year vehicle registration was required, a grand total of 178 vehicles of all types were registered, and by the start of the First World War there were 74,000. Once again, the war changed everything; the new type of warfare required mechanization. In 1919 374,000 vehicles were registered. The building affluence of the twenties led to a million registrations being exceeded by 1928, and vehicle numbers peaked in 1930 at 1,232,000. Then the Depression hit, with the result that it was six more years before that level was reached again. During the Second World War numbers again fell, mainly due to wartime restrictions. Since that war vehicle numbers have only climbed, breaking the 2 million mark in 1948 and 3 million only four years later. Today there are more than 17 million registered vehicles in Canada, and the country has one of the highest per capita car ownership levels in the world.

Canada generally followed the American example by driving on the right. In British Columbia, still unconnected to the rest of Canada by road, residents drove on the left, as in Britain, until 1 January 1922, when the province changed to driving on the right. This was more to conform to adjacent (and connected) Washington state than to fall in line with the rest of Canada. Many drugstores and convenience stores carefully located at streetcar stops suddenly found their business had departed for the other side of the road. In Newfoundland, a separate British colony, motorists continued to drive on the left until it joined Confederation in 1949.

If the challenge of driving on the mud-bathed roads of an Ontario spring thaw were not enough, there was always the problem of simply starting a car's engine in the winter.

Above.
A car crossing the log bridge over the Seymour River, North Vancouver, in 1919. British Columbians still drove on the left at this time but you would not know it from this photograph; there is room for only one-way traffic anyway.

Below.
Reliability was the big problem for early autos. This Ford Model T broke down near Eastburg, Alberta, in the 1920s.

The approved method called for the pouring of boiling water into the radiator and jacking up one wheel to allow easier cranking. Then the general manager of the London, Ontario Public Utilities Commission invented the block heater, prompting a reporter to ask him why he had hitched his car to a tree. Despite its obvious utility, the block heater did not become universal in the colder parts of Canada until the 1950s.

Automobiles soon began to be capable of more than the low speed limits most provinces had set for the them. In 1912 Toronto inaugurated a police motorcycle squad to catch speeders. There were four of them, and they were not uniformed, making it easy for them to catch the unwary—by timing them over a measured distance, then presenting them with a fine that amounted to a week's wages. Initially the system was likely abused by some, because up until 1916 Ontario magistrates and police officers were entitled to pocket a portion of traffic fines.

To protect against lurking police the Ontario Motor League hired cyclists to watch and warn motorists—with a little "slow" sign. The league was formed in 1913 from an association of automobile clubs; in 1920 it became the Canadian Automobile Association (CAA). Its first president was Dr. Perry Doolittle, an unflagging advocate for the motorist who had with others founded the Toronto Motor Club as early as 1903. Doolittle used to roar around the country putting up road signs, which was not a government function in those days. He even wrote a magazine article called "The Pleasure of Erecting Road Signs."

Until his death in 1933 while still president of the CAA, Doolittle also went on longer trips, crossing the country three times to promote motoring and to rally for better roads, including a trans-Canada highway, for it was still not possible to cross Canada without either taking to railway tracks or diverting into the United States. Such a highway would come later (see page 258).

Above.
This superb view of market day in London, Ontario, was taken about 1925. Although some horse-drawn vehicles are still in evidence, they are overwhelmed by the popular automobile. Harness makers J. Darch & Sons must have looked out on the sea of motor vehicles with some trepidation. The view is of Market Square, looking west towards Talbot Street.

Right.
This official advisory for truck drivers was issued in 1933 and gives some insight into road conditions in Ontario at that time.

ONTARIO

Official Warning
To Truck Drivers and Owners

Loads Must be Reduced During March and April

Important clauses in The Ontario Highway Traffic Act are designed to protect roads, both paved and unpaved, during early spring. Because of moisture that lurks in road foundations, excessive weights and speeds do extensive damage to road surfaces at this time.

What the Law Says

The Highway Traffic Act declares that during March and April, on roads outside cities and towns:

Solid tired trucks and trailers shall be limited to half a load;

Pneumatic tired trucks and trailers, with a carrying capacity exceeding three tons, shall be limited to half a load;

Horse drawn vehicles with a carrying capacity exceeding one ton shall be limited to 250 lbs. per inch in width of tire.

Speed limits all the year round are: 15 miles an hour for solid tired vehicles and 20 miles an hour for pneumatic tired vehicles of more than 8 tons gross. During the spring months, drivers must be particularly careful not to exceed these speeds.

The Law Provides Penalties

The penalty for overloading during March and April is a fine, imprisonment or both. Licenses also may be suspended. Highway traffic officials have been directed to be especially vigilant in apprehending all who disobey.

The Department of Highways desires to impress upon truck and team owners and drivers the provisions of the law. It seeks their co-operation in seeing that the law is obeyed in all circumstances. Ontario's investment in good roads, now amounting to many millions of dollars, must be protected.

Ontario Department of Highways
The HON. GEORGE S. HENRY, Minister

A Canadian Art

In the first two decades of the twentieth century a style of art emerged that for the first time was recognized by the rest of the world as being distinctly Canadian. To this we owe the paintings of the Group of Seven and their contemporaries, especially Tom Thomson and Emily Carr.

The Group of Seven was formed in 1920 by, of course, seven artists, who realized that their painting style and their conception of art in general had something in common. Theirs was indeed a special Canadian impressionism, one that somehow seemed to fit the landscape of Canada. The Group rebelled against what they saw as the then current formalism of Canadian painting and set themselves up to be an alternative Canadian school of art. They found their art well received internationally, better, in fact, than by the Canadian establishment. Canadian painting, it seemed, had finally arrived.

This distinctively Canadian impressionism was particularly seen in the works of Tom Thomson. He was never actually a member of the Group of Seven because he died before it was formed. One summer afternoon in 1917 he set off to paint or fish and his up-turned canoe was found empty the next day. He was only forty. In the last two years of his life Thomson produced a considerable series of impressionist landscapes of the Canadian Shield in Algonquin Park that are today almost part of the Canadian psyche. He was friends with most of the Group of Seven and A. Y. Jackson was his particular mentor. Thomson was, in the eyes of Arthur Lismer, a particular genius who expressed moods "while the rest of us were painting pictures."

The original Group of Seven comprised Lawren S. Harris, A. Y. Jackson, Franklin Carmichael, Franz Johnston, Arthur Lismer, J. E. H. Macdonald, and F. H. Varley. In 1926 Johnston resigned and was replaced by A. J. Casson. As time went on the Group tended to become more stylized and abstract in their work; Harris, in particular, went this route and ended up doing pure abstracts as well as his stunning and powerful stylized landscapes, which were more often than not of the wild places of Canada: northern Ontario, the Rocky Mountains, and Baffin Island. But then Harris could afford to experiment; he was the only member of the Group who was independently wealthy.

The Group were trying to promote themselves as Canadian, and yet they all lived in Toronto. Recognizing that a wider membership was advisable if they were to claim a true national status, they admitted some other artists. Having largely achieved their aims, and indeed become perhaps the standard rather than the alternative, the Group disbanded in 1933.

The Victoria artist Emily Carr was developing her own distinctive West Coast painting style albeit along similar lines to the Group of Seven after she was inspired by a visit to France, perhaps the birthplace of Impressionism, in 1911. She visited Toronto in 1928 and was encouraged by Lawren Harris and others in the Group. The influence of Harris, in particular, is visible in her later paintings.

Harris was a theosophist—one who finds God in Nature. "To the artist," he wrote, "his art is adventure in which he seeks to regain unity with nature and the knowledge of his own immortal being." But all of the Group of Seven loved nature; they could not have painted the way they did otherwise. They and their contemporaries produced a corpus of distinctively Canadian paintings that have influenced artists for eighty years and continue to enrich us all today.

Now speaks the simple unutterable
So simply, directly, timelessly
A moment's egress into eternity
With a clarity
No man has voice for

From *Contrasts*, a book of poems by Lawren S. Harris, 1922

Perhaps one of the most brilliant Canadian
paintings ever, this stylized view of the north
shore of Lake Superior was painted by Group
of Seven member Lawren Harris in 1927, when
he accompanied fellow member Frederick
Varley on a painting trip.

11 *A Cauldron Once More*

In the fall of 1929, the twenties stopped roaring. The immediate manifestation of this was the stock market crash of 29 October, "Black Tuesday," when the Toronto Stock Exchange lost a million dollars for every minute it was open that day. But it was a sudden drop in demand for goods, especially from the United States, that caused the Canadian economy to collapse, domino-like, throwing thousands out of work and further reducing demand for goods and services. Few saw the gathering storm. Like American chairman of the Federal Reserve Board Alan Greenspan, who in 2000 warned of "irrational exuberance" before the tech stock bubble burst that year, Joseph Flavelle, as bright an entrepreneur as Canada ever saw, warned against the "almost irrational faith" investors showed in 1929. But despite the popular myth, most Canadians were not investors in 1929; most were workers, and the Depression started for them the day they lost their job.

The government, led by William Lyon Mackenzie King, grandson of the rebel reformer William Lyon Mackenzie (see page 126), did not see trouble coming either, and when it did, hardly knew what to do about it. They paid for their deaf ears and shortsightedness at the polls in August 1930, when Mackenzie King's Liberals were replaced by a Conservative government under R. B. Bennett, who, it turned out, knew no better than King what to do. In fact the Great Depression, as it came to be known, was a worldwide phenomenon, and mostly out of any Canadian government's control.

Richard Bedford Bennett, a wealthy lawyer who had made millions from his investments, *thought* he knew what to do. His government passed the Unemployment Relief Act. Monies were provided to provinces, which in turn provided financial aid to municipalities, but on the basis of population rather than need, with the result that some places had more than they needed while most had not enough. Make-work relief projects were financed with these funds. But these efforts did not work because they were not enough; the problem was much bigger than Bennett or most others realized. By 1933 unemployment was over 30 percent and may well have been more than this, for it was not measured very well at the time. Farm families, for example, were always considered employed, regardless of their real condition. Bennett never really came to grips with the magnitude of the problem he was dealing

A wartime appeal to valour. One would think that Canada once had an army of knights-in-armour, judging by this magnificent 1942 recruiting poster.

Above.
Any politician who offered a way back to prosperity was likely to be favoured by the electors. "Bible Bill" Aberhart's way was less usual than most, but it struck the right chord with the voters of Alberta in 1935.

Below.
The effects of wind erosion on the dry Prairie soil shown in a 1933 photograph.

with, and this resulted in a number of so-called temporary measures to provide first work and then, to avoid dependency—and perhaps revolution—just "relief," which was cheaper anyway. Unfortunately, government aid was often tied up in red tape, forcing municipalities to borrow money to feed their destitute, which cost them more money than they could afford or raise from their tax base.

The misery was compounded by the weather. Starting in the spring of 1931 the Canadian Prairies and American Midwest were hit with drought. Immigrants had been led into increasingly marginal farming areas in the 1920s; now they suffered from wind-driven erosion and in many cases the fertile topsoil was blown away. One of Bennett's ministers went to see for himself the extent of the problem. "The whole country for more than a hundred miles in extent," he wrote, "is a barren drifting desert." Men started "riding the rods" on the top of railway freight cars to escape to British Columbia. And agitation started for something to be done.

Many wrote personal letters to Bennett, and he was not unsympathetic to individual hardships, often replying himself and enclosing five or ten dollars. Bennett tried calling an Imperial Economic Conference in 1932, to urge the Empire to pull together to weather the storm. Expectations were high, but came to nought; Britain and the other dominions were far too busy trying to deal with the effects of the Depression themselves. Cars appeared pulled by horses; they were derisively called "Bennett buggies." Shacks of cardboard and corrugated iron became "Bennett boroughs," and newspapers, "Bennett blankets." The poor prime minister found himself lampooned at every turn.

The Depression years of the thirties saw the creation of a number of social or political movements designed to bring about change by some form of socialism. The feared Communists, who did not want to operate within the democratic process, were harassed constantly, with their leaders arrested in 1931. The Québec government of Maurice Duplessis passed the Padlock Act in 1937 to lock up all premises where Communism was being discussed, a law that was not declared illegal until 1957. In 1932 the Co-operative Commonwealth Federation (CCF) was formed and in 1935 returned seven members to Parliament. Conservative provincial governments were turfed out. In 1933 Thomas Dufferin ("Duff") Pattulo, a Liberal, came to power in British Columbia with a predictable promise—"work and wages." In Ontario, the Liberals of Mitch Hepburn were elected in 1934 and promptly auctioned off government limousines and closed the lieutenant-governor's residence, trying to get the province's finances back in shape. In 1937, to deal with a strike at General Motors, Hepburn infamously sent in a special force to deal with the strikers—Hepburn's Hussars, as they were known to his supporters, "Sons of Mitch" to his opponents.

Perhaps the most radical change of all came in Alberta, where a new Social Credit government led by William Aberhart swept to power in 1935. "Bible Bill," as he was known, was an evangelical preacher who essentially hijacked an existing economic philosophy for his own use. In July 1932 Aberhart stayed up all night reading a simplified social credit book and announced in the morning that he had "found a cure for the Great Depression." Each citizen was to be given a $25 per month "basic dividend" to spend on necessities. The government would take control of credit instead of leaving it to the private banking system. Swayed by Aberhart's evangelical style, the voters of Alberta thought this worth a try, and in 1935 Aberhart's Social Credit party was elected in a landslide victory.

The discontent of the average man surfaced time and time again during the Depression. A strike by coal miners in the Saskatchewan towns of Estevan and Bienfait in 1931 turned ugly when mine owners enlisted the police in their battle against "Communism." On 29 September 1931 the police drew their pistols and opened fire on a strikers' parade, killing three miners, a gross overreaction to an admittedly tense situation.

In 1932 the government had begun to set up a series of relief camps run by the army. They were located as far from cities as possible, the idea being to put men to work where they would not be able to promote revolutionary ideas. Inmates were disenfranchised and earned twenty cents a day for their work. It was no surprise that the camps bred discontent. In April 1935 seven thousand men struck and left the camps, and nearly two thousand converged on Vancouver, demanding "work and wages." They had public sympathy, for $22,000 was raised to assist them.

Vancouver mayor Gerry McGeer was convinced he was facing a Communist revolution and called out four hundred police to parade and be ready to take on the strikers. Instead, the strike leaders decided on a new course: they would go to Ottawa to make their case to the federal government. And so in June the "On-to-Ottawa" trek, as it became known, began. Men clambered aboard freight trains and headed east, picking up more men wherever the train stopped. Prime Minister Bennett, concerned about this apparent flood of possible revolutionaries heading for the seat of government, ordered the RCMP to stop the trek at Regina. The police blockaded the railways and the roads and the strikers were prevented from further movement east.

Strikers from relief camps board a freight train in Kamloops, B.C., in June 1935, joining the "On-to-Ottawa" trek.

A small delegation was allowed to meet with the government, but that meeting ended in disarray and a shouting match. The men in Regina faced starvation, and so, reluctantly, most decided to go back to British Columbia. A rally on 1 July to raise money for the trip turned into a riot when police tried to arrest trek leaders and the men fought back. Downtown Regina was left a "shambles," and many were injured. One plainclothes policeman was killed, by police who mistook him for a striker. The trek had been halted, but at the cost of tremendous ill-will.

Approaching the election he had to hold in 1935, Bennett, who was, we should remember, a Conservative millionaire, was coming to the conclusion as a result of all the turmoil that much more radical government intervention would be required, what he characterized as a "New Deal." But it was too late for him; his more socialist policies were seen as a deathbed conversion. The voters kicked him out and re-elected Mackenzie King and his Liberals, who had no real alternative policy and quite deliberately kept it that way. King was that familiar theme in politics, an alternative to what the voters already had, which clearly was not working. He was elected on the slogan "King or Chaos," and the average voter had been too near chaos under Bennett to chance it any more. King in fact won an

In the midst of the turmoil of the 1930s some fine and very innovative buildings were constructed in Canada. Most, but by no means all, were conceived in the latter years of the twenties when the economy was booming, but came to fruition just in time for the Depression.

The late twenties and thirties saw the manifestation in architecture of a decorative style known as Art Deco, named from the abbreviation for the Exposition des Arts Décoratifs et Industriels, an exhibition held in Paris in 1925. Since Art Deco is a decorative style, some prefer to reserve the term for the ornament of a building, classifying the structure itself as "Moderne" or "Modern Classical."

Vancouver City Hall is an excellent example of the style. Built in 1935–36, it is shown here in 1937, the year after its completion. It has Art Deco ornament on the friezes at the top of each of the blocks. This was one of the few buildings to be started during the Depression. The intention was to create a futuristic look in keeping with the newly expanded city. Vancouver, Point Grey, and South Vancouver had amalgamated in 1929.

overwhelming majority, 173 of 245 seats in the Commons. Economic conditions were gradually improving, in Canada and worldwide, and many resigned themselves to an extended period of slow growth and high unemployment. But much resentment remained.

In May 1938 several hundred unemployed men, this time with Communist leaders though they were not themselves Communists, occupied three public buildings in Vancouver, hoping to draw attention to their plight. Instead they got a violent reaction. Early on a Sunday, 18 June, the men were tear-gassed and then, as they poured out onto the streets to escape the gas, they were brutally clubbed by police. The police action provoked a riot. As the *Vancouver News-Herald* reported on 20 June: "Fleeing before a barrage of tear gas bombs and the swinging batons of city police officers, a swarm of shouting, blood-spattered men smashed hundreds of plate glass windows, looted stores, and for more than an hour created a reign of terror in the city."

But war was coming, and a different type of violence abroad would restore peace at home. Everyone could read of the failure of European appeasement, a policy which was, incidentally, fully supported at the time by Prime Minister Mackenzie King.

In large part to prepare the Canadian public for the coming support that would be needed for the Empire, the British king George VI and Queen Elizabeth arrived for a royal visit in May and June 1939. Mackenzie King tried to ensure that he was in all the press photos—King with king—cementing the idea in the public mind that the British king was Canada's king too. The visit was a public relations masterpiece, even in French Canada, where Québécois were astonished but delighted to hear the King address them in French. Queen Elizabeth, they discovered, was fluent in their language.

More than brilliant public relations would be needed, however, in the coming storm. The German steamroller was flattening all resistance to its expansion, encouraged by a weak-kneed response from those countries that had some chance to oppose it. But when the German military machine reached out for Poland, there was a difference. Britain and France had guaranteed the territorial integrity of the country. And so, on 1 September 1939, when the German blitzkreig on Poland began, Britain issued an ultimatum demanding withdrawal. When, on 3 September, it expired unanswered, Britain declared war.

When this had happened in 1914, Canada was automatically at war also. Not so in 1939. In 1931 Britain had passed the Statute of Westminster, which in establishing the de facto passing of the British Empire and the beginning of the British Commonwealth, had made Canada independent of Britain except for powers Canada chose not to assume. (The unassumed powers in 1931 were the amendment of the Constitution, assumed in 1982, and the use of the British Privy Council as the final court of judicial appeal, until 1949.) Mackenzie King duly put the matter to the House of Commons, where a debate was held on 9 September, and the following day King George VI declared war on Germany on behalf of Canada.

Above.
The Dionne Quintuplets in 1939. Born in 1934 in Ontario, they were taken away from their poor parents and placed under provincial government supervision, becoming a major tourist attraction. Three million people viewed them from behind one-way glass. The Ontario government later admitted it was wrong to do this and compensated the famous five.

Below.
King George VI and Queen Elizabeth during their visit to Canada in 1939.

Canada and the Second World War

Memories of the First World War had a great influence on the way the Second was conducted, as far as Canada and Mackenzie King were concerned. Firstly, there was the perfectly reasonable desire to prevent the kind of carnage that had occurred in 1914–18, and secondly, there was a perhaps even more fervent desire to avoid the divisive issue of conscription.

After the declaration of war in September 1939 came the period known as the "phony war," when German aggression had temporarily abated. It lasted until 9 April 1940, when the German invasion of Norway began, signalling the beginning of an almighty explosion of German military power that would sweep the Allies into the sea at Dunkirk, overrun Paris, and see France sue for peace. The phony war had created the illusion in Canada that the organization of a relatively small all-volunteer force to augment the existing army of ten thousand men would perhaps be enough of a war effort. With the idea in his head that an air war could never lead to an outrageous number of casualties, King agreed to the setting up of the British Commonwealth Air Training Plan, forcing Britain to agree in writing that this was to be considered the major Canadian contribution to the war. King was trying to tread that fine Canadian line between the aspirations of French and English Canada. He must have been doing this about right, for, as might be expected, to some his efforts were still too much and to others not enough.

In Québec the provincial nationaliste government of Maurice Duplessis had called an election in October on the pretext that provincial rights had been trampled on by the War Measures Act. King quickly organized a concerted effort to support the Liberal opposition in Québec, led by Adélard Godbout, and succeeded in routing Duplessis. In Ontario, Premier Mitch Hepburn, who hated King, did almost the opposite, attacking King for the "scandalous apathy" of the war effort. In January 1940 the Ontario legislature passed a vote of censure of King's government, which King promptly used as an excuse to dissolve the federal House and call an election in support of his "moderate" policies, a mandate he overwhelmingly received on 26 March.

The British flag is shown in all its forms in this patriotic design from a 1941 Eaton's road map of Ontario. The reality of the war was to be far different than these smiling faces would suggest.

Left.
When the British Columbia Regiment of the Duke of Connaught's Own Rifles marched down Eighth Street in New Westminster on 1 October 1940 en route to the railway station and overseas, wives, girlfriends, and children tagged along for a last goodbye. Warren (Whitey) Bernard ran after his dad, Jack Bernard, and Vancouver *Province* newspaper photographer Claude Dettloff captured the moment for posterity. Whitey's dad survived the war; he died in 1981 at the age of seventy-four. A close look at this photo reveals a variety of emotions on the faces of those about to be left behind, ranging from tearful to brave.

Right.
An almost festive crowd gathers at a Montréal newsstand on 3 September 1939 to read of Britain and France's declaration of war on Germany as reported in a special edition of the Montréal *Gazette.*

King's timing was impeccable, for only two weeks later the German war machine sprang again into high gear, making his "moderate" policy immediately untenable. By June 1940, Britain was all that stood against Hitler in Europe and it braced for an expected invasion. Suddenly, the "mother country" was in mortal danger and needed any help it could get. King split the ministry of Defence into three and appointed C. D. Howe as his minister of Munitions and Supply, a key portfolio in which the dynamic Howe was to make a crucial difference. In June a National Resources Mobilization Act introduced a limited conscription—for home service only. Four destroyers sailed for England; they were all that was then available. Two squadrons of the Royal Canadian Air Force (RCAF) flew across the Atlantic in time to take part in the coming Battle of Britain, the desperate fight for the skies over Britain; the Luftwaffe was attempting to wrest control from the RAF in preparation for an invasion.

On 17 August, American president Franklin D. Roosevelt met with King at Ogdensburg, on the American side of the St. Lawrence. The result of this meeting was the establishment of the Canada–United States Permanent Joint Board on Defence. This was the first such agreement with the Americans for mutual continental defence, and it is significant as the point at which Canada relinquished her dependence on Britain for defence, turning instead to the neighbour that had once been an enemy and later a threat.

Many German and later Italian prisoners were sent to Canada, thirty thousand over the course of the war. Here, surely, it would be harder for them to escape. But one—and only one—did. This was so unusual that the solitary feat was later made into one of the many war movies produced in the fifties and sixties: *The One That Got Away.* It was January 1941, and the escape was only possible because the prisoner, Luftwaffe officer Franz von Werra, was able to make it to a then neutral United States. He escaped from a train near Prescott, Ontario, which, of course, is right across the St. Lawrence from the United States. Others did escape from where they were held, but none made it, as Von Werra did, back to Germany.

In August 1941 a meeting was arranged between British prime minister Winston Churchill and American president Franklin D. Roosevelt. It took place in Placentia Bay, Newfoundland, on board the British battleship *Prince of Wales.* The event, which produced the well-known and stirring spectacle of the entire ship's company singing "Onward, Christian Soldiers," more significantly for posterity created the document known as the Atlantic Charter, which guaranteed "the right of all peoples to choose the form of government under which they will live." It was the final nail in the coffin of the British Empire.

A footnote is appropriate here: in December 1941 the *Prince of Wales* was sunk, along with its sister ship the *Repulse,* by Japanese planes off the coast of Malaya.

Above, left.
William Lyon Mackenzie King, photographed by Yousuf Karsh in 1941.

Left.
A recruiting poster designed by Henry Eveleigh, 1941.

Canada was Britain's biggest ally up until Russia entered the war on the Allied side in April 1941. By mid-1941 the war economy had completely erased the effects of the Depression and there was full employment; indeed, there was a shortage of labour that began what would prove to be a revolutionary change—women in the workforce, not just as secretaries and nurses and the like but in every field. Suddenly women were able to do anything a man could. And women were accepted in the armed forces in every role except that of actual combat. The War Measures Act controlled movement, and in October wage and price controls were brought in, establishing a general ceiling for wages, prices of foodstuffs, and rents. Actual rationing appeared the following year. It was all monitored and controlled by a Wartime Prices and Trade Board.

Beginning in June 1941, the incredible financial cost of the war—$18 billion by its end—was underwritten through government-backed Victory Bonds. "If they [swastika- and rising sun–marked rats] overrun Canada your money'll be useless," screamed the ads. Fully two-thirds of the cost of the war was financed by this means.

During 1941 a new threat was emerging on the West Coast, that from an ever-more-belligerent Japan, which culminated in the attack on the American Pacific fleet in Honolulu Harbor on that "day of infamy," 7 December 1941. The attack brought the United States into the war, an event that would prove ultimately decisive. Canada declared war on Japan the same day. The declaration was followed very soon after by the loss of the first Canadian battalions in action: 2,000 men had been sent to Hong Kong in October 1941; now nearly 300 were killed and the rest captured defending the island city from

Above.
Boats of the Japanese fishing fleet impounded and awaiting disposal near Steveston, B.C. The Fraser River is to the right of the jetty.

Below.
Deported people of Japanese descent unloading their worldly goods from a truck somewhere in the British Columbia interior in 1942.

Above.
The tragedy in Hong Kong was used for recruiting in this 1942 poster.

Below.
Dead soldiers and wrecked tanks and landing craft litter the beach at Dieppe after the disastrous failed raid of 19 August 1942.

an assault by a vastly numerically superior Japanese force, an attack that had begun the same day as Pearl Harbor and ended on Christmas Day. Many more Canadians taken prisoner did not survive the barbarous conditions in Japanese prison camps. The defence of Hong Kong was the only wartime involvement in Asia by Canadian troops.

Fear of an invasion by Japan swept British Columbia. Almost immediately Japanese fishboats were rounded up and in a continuing climate of fear the government decided to deport and intern those of Japanese origin; they were sent to camps hastily set up in the interior, well away from the coast. In addition, their property was to be confiscated. The deportation was carried out under the War Measures Act and has been roundly criticized in modern times for its overriding of the rights of many who had lived in Canada all their lives, including many who had been born in the country, whose only sin was to be of Japanese descent. Between February and October 1942 some twenty-two thousand were sent to the interior. At the end of the war the government offered internees a choice: permanent relocation east of the Rockies or deportation to Japan. Later cancelled due to public protest, this repeated deportation meant that by 1947 Ontario had as large a Japanese-Canadian population as British Columbia. But nearly four thousand were sent to Japan. In 1947 some compensation was paid to those whose property had been sold, and in 1984, after continued agitation from the Japanese-Canadian community, a formal apology and more compensation were offered, closing a sorry episode in the story of human rights in Canada.

Another result of the declaration of war on Japan was the building of the Alaska Highway. There was particular fear of a Japanese invasion of the Aleutians, as a stepping stone to North America—two islands were captured in June 1942—but the region was so remote that the army had no easy way of moving in men, heavy equipment, and artillery. The

highway, from Dawson Creek to Fairbanks, was built by the American army in eight months, being completed—for hardy military traffic, at any rate—in November 1942. The following year the road was considerably improved by civilian contractors, replacing some of the jerry-built bridges, regrading some of the worst grades, which went up to an amazing 25 percent, ironing out some ninety-degree bends, and making the road surface more durable. The highway, originally called the Alcan (that is, Alaska-Canada) Military Highway, was built at the same time as the Canol pipeline, from an oil refinery at Norman Wells, on the Mackenzie River, to Whitehorse. Some 1 954 km of the road is in Canada, and the Canadian government paid $120 million in 1946 for formal ownership of this part of the road.

A real Japanese attack did occur, though some have doubts about it (there are some discrepancies in witnesses' stories), on 20 June 1942, when a Japanese submarine shelled the lighthouse at Estevan Point, a remote peninsula on the northwest coast of Vancouver Island. As it turned out, this was the only attack on Canadian soil during the entire war.

But 1942 saw some more serious action in Europe. On 19 August 1942, some five thousand Canadian troops stormed the beaches of Dieppe. Planned as an improbable test of the German defences and a rehearsal for invasions to come, the raid was an utter disaster. Bombardment of the defences was inadequate, tanks that were to have given covering fire got stuck in small pebbles on the beach, and the commander who was supposed to be directing the operation was offshore on a ship, unable to see the action. In nine hours, 900 Canadian soldiers lost their lives and another 1,874 were taken prisoner. In the air over Dieppe, nine Canadian squadrons were involved, and total Allied losses amounted to a staggering 106 aircraft and 81 aircrew. The action was indeed a valuable lesson for the Allies, but one hardly worth the high cost in lives. It did cause Hitler to tie up thirty-two divisions along the Channel coast in case Dieppe was a prelude to a larger invasion. And some valuable information on a new radar system was captured that later allowed the Allies to devise countermeasures such as dropping tinfoil from bombers, which doubtless did save lives.

At home, Canadians were being warned to be careful of speaking about anything military, and some posters, such as the one presenting an improbable scenario shown here, emphasized

Above, right.
By 1943, when this photograph was taken, Canadian factories were turning out war *matériel* at a high rate. Here tanks are readied for shipment.

Right.
Poster warning of the amazing perils of loose talk, 1942.

Germans Land in Canada!

It is symptomatic of the remoteness of much of Canada that in October 1943 a German submarine was able to land and set up an automatic weather station at Martin Bay, on the north coast of Labrador. With so many submarines operating in the North Atlantic, weather information, hard to come by, was very important for the German fleet. The station transmitted information to the submarines every three hours and worked at least until January 1944. Its existence was unknown until 1981, when a German researcher found records relating to it. He contacted Canadian historians and the weather station was located. It is now, as photographed here, in the Canadian War Museum in Ottawa. Perhaps the most significant point in this story is the fact that Germans actually landed in Canada (still then the colony of Newfoundland and Labrador) in 1943.

The Newfoundland Railway ferry ss *Caribou*.

the point. But it was not altogether unlikely, for there were spies in Canada. On 9 November 1942 a German naval officer named Werner Janowski was arrested in New Carlisle, a village on the Baie des Chaleurs in the Gaspé. He had been dropped off by a submarine and was to report on ship movements. He was discovered when he tried to pass off out-of-date bills and told a hotel keeper he had arrived on a bus that no longer ran.

Knowledge of ship movements was at this time of vital importance to the Germans, who were mounting an increasingly ferocious submarine attack on the Atlantic supply line to Britain. One of the principal contributions of Canada to the war was the shepherding of convoys from Halifax, Sydney, Saint John, and other ports to Britain, and from New York after 1941; Churchill termed it the Battle of the Atlantic. At the beginning of the war the Royal Canadian Navy had only six ocean-going warships and 3,500 personnel, both regular and reserve. By war's end, this force had grown to some 270 ocean escort warships and 106,000 personnel, including 6,000 women. By 1945 Canada had the third largest navy in the world. Even this did not represent the output of Canadian shipyards, for another 403 merchant ships were built, 220 for Britain and 183 for Canada. Canada's merchant navy grew to 12,000 personnel and about 210 ships. The war claimed the lives of 2,000 of those on naval ships and 1,700 on merchant ships.

By 1941 German submarines developed techniques for attacking convoys in mid-ocean, where they were at their most vulnerable, being unsupported by air. The wolf packs would typically attack at night and on the surface, where their low profiles were difficult to spot. On the surface they could move much faster than underwater and could make multiple attacks, concentrating on the precious cargo ships, each submarine often sinking three or four. And in the icy waters of the North Atlantic there was a poor chance of survival for any sailor in the water. It was a vicious and nerve-wracking business which many times threatened to overwhelm the rapidly expanding but very basically trained resources of the Canadian navy. But it did not. By the end of the war, 25,421 merchant ships had been sucessfully convoyed across the Atlantic under Canadian escort.

After the United States entered the war at the end of 1941, the German navy began a major submarine offensive against the North American coast and many ships were torpedoed within a kilometre or two of the coast. This required the organization of local shipping into convoys. Submarines lurked along the coast for much of 1942, looking for targets of opportunity. One of these was the Newfoundland Railway ferry ss *Caribou*.

The ferry sailed on its regular run across Cabot Strait from North Sydney on Cape Breton Island bound for Port au Basque, at the southwestern tip of Newfoundland, 160 km away, on the evening of

13 October 1942. The *Caribou* carried 237 passengers, military and civilian, and a crew of 45. No one thought it likely that a local civilian ferry would be in any danger, but as a precaution the corvette HMCS *Grandmere* was assigned to look after her. Unfortunately, a German submarine was in Cabot Strait, looking for targets. It is still unclear whether the submarine commander thought the *Caribou* was a freighter (as in his record) or whether this was a deliberate attack on a civilian ferry.

At 3:30 in the morning the *Caribou* was hit by a torpedo fired from the German U-boat *U-69*. A gaping hole was blown in the side of the ship, sending her to the bottom five minutes later. The *Grandmere* was immediately on the scene but was unable to locate the submarine. German records revealed much later that the submarine had positioned itself right below the area in which survivors were in the water, knowing the corvette would be reluctant to release depth charges there. *Grandmere* picked up the survivors after a fruitless search for the submarine. In all, 136 men, women, and children perished that night. Some 31 of the crew of the *Caribou* died, and 48 of the dead were civilians, including 10 of the 11 children under ten years old. It was the worst attack on civilians in Canada of the entire war.

Submarines continued to operate in the St. Lawrence for much of the rest of the war. On 14 October 1944, two years to the day after the *Caribou* disaster, a torpedo fired by *U-1223* blew 18 m off the stern of HMCS *Magog* off Pointe de Monts, near Québec. This was the deepest attack into Canadian territory during the war.

Bedford Basin, at the western end of Halifax Harbour, was the ideal place to assemble convoys. Here, on 1 April 1942, a convoy is ready to go.

If the transformation of the Canadian navy during the war was striking, then that of the Royal Canadian Air Force was spectacular. The British Commonwealth Air Training Plan made it relatively easy for volunteers to sign up, and sign up they did, in droves. The RCAF was always an all-volunteer force, and went from 3,100 personnel at the beginning of the war to 215,000 (including 15,000 women) in 1944. Some 17,000 of them died. Many more Canadian pilots served with the British RAF. The training plan was very successful, turning out 131,000 aircrew, and it made a vital difference to the fortunes of war. And in the war's six years Canada built 16,409 new planes.

The largest operational group of the RCAF was No. 6 Bomber Group of the RAF Bomber Command. Their job was the sometimes controversial one of the night bombing of German cities in the Ruhr and elsewhere, which had as its goal the elimination of the German ability to manufacture weapons. It was a brutally hazardous job: nearly 10,000 Canadians lost their lives in countless untold heroic episodes.

In July 1943 the Canadian army, with the British and Americans, invaded Sicily and pushed north into the Italian mainland, where fierce German resistance was encountered. One major objective was the town of Ortona, on the Adriatic coast halfway up the peninsula. A strategic hamlet, Casa Berardi, was taken by eighty-one men and seven tanks led by Captain Paul Triquet, but at a cost. Finding themselves surrounded Triquet urged his men on and they took the hamlet, and held it for two days against repeated counter-attacks. By the time it was all over there were only nine men left.

Franklin D. Roosevelt, Mackenzie King, and Winston Churchill on the ramparts of the Québec Citadel in August 1943, during the first Québec Conference, called Quadrant. Thirteen months later they would meet again at a second conference in Québec, called Octagon. The two Québec conferences were part of a string of such meetings between Churchill and Roosevelt (and later, Truman) and sometimes Stalin, at which the conduct of the war and the post-war division of Europe were discussed. Mackenzie King, always the consummate politician, was in the photograph as the leader of the host country, not because he was involved in the conference as such. But King deliberately got himself in most of the official photographs, knowing that most Canadians would assume he was important enough to be hobnobbing with Roosevelt and Churchill. One onlooker reportedly said King "looked like a man who has lent his house for a party."

At Ortona, held by crack German paratroops, the town was only won after heavy house-to-house fighting. During this battle, on Christmas Day, the men still fitted in a quick Christmas dinner. In all, nearly 93,000 Canadians served in Italy, and 5,764 lost their lives.

On 6 June 1944—the long-awaited D-Day—the invasion of Normandy began. The Canadian army played its part, integrated into the British forces and under the overall direction of the British general Bernard "Monty" Montgomery. Early in the morning after an all-night crossing of the Channel, Canadian forces stormed onto the beaches at Courseulles-sur Mer, Bernières-sur-Mer, and St. Aubin-sur-Mer—part of the stretch of coastline dubbed Juno Beach—and pushed inland towards an airport near Caen. They encountered fanatical troops of the Hitler Youth, and it took thirty-three days to take Caen. In one infamous incident the Germans shot more than a hundred Canadian prisoners. By late August the battle for the European foothold was won, but at high cost once again; more than five thousand Canadians died in the fields of Normandy.

Opposite, top.
Bombers and transports amass at a Canadian airfield awaiting ferrying to England.

Below.
Official war artist Orville Fisher painted this rendering of Canadian troops coming ashore in Normandy on D-Day. Fisher went ashore with the troops, making fast sketches with glycerin and watercolours on waterproof paper as he went. Shortly thereafter he transformed his field sketches into this large oil painting.

The next Canadian objectives were the Channel ports of France and then Belgium, including Antwerp. It took five weeks of heavy fighting to capture that city.

But the losses were mounting, and with them pressure to introduce conscription for service abroad. In his handling of the conscription issue, so divisive for a Canada fighting what to many seemed an imperial war, Mackenzie King proved himself a master politician. In 1939 King had been able to declare war without much domestic opposition because he had pledged that there would be no conscription. Limited conscription but for a much more acceptable home defence only had been introduced in June 1940. In April 1942, soon after the entry of Japan and the United States had made the war truly a world war, King realized that the no conscription pledge might not be sustainable and so he arranged for a plebiscite to release the government from its pledge. This he won, although without many votes from French Canada. In July 1942, aided by public alarm from the supposed Japanese shelling of Estevan Point lighthouse on Vancouver Island on 20 June, a law was passed allowing conscription by cabinet order, "if necessary." Although not imposed at the time, the mechanism was now in place for general overseas conscription. In August the National Resources Mobilization Act was amended to permit the sending of conscripts overseas, and in September the age limit was dropped from twenty-one to nineteen.

King continued to hope that conscription would prove unnecessary, and indeed there is evidence in his diaries that King thought it possible a civil war might erupt in Canada if conscription were generally imposed. To King, limited conscription meant taking no chances with human lives. After D-Day, King began to think that he might get through the war without general conscription. But by October 1944, with the more massive participation of Canadian forces in the land war

Above, top.
Canadian troops in landing craft approach the French coast on D-Day, 6 June 1944.

Above.
Canadian troops landing on Juno Beach. Ropes guide them through the deeper water; many are carrying bicycles, to facilitate, it was hoped, speedy movement inland.

Right.
A cartoon depicting Mackenzie King's navigation of the conscription crisis of November 1944. The skilled politician makes it through.

in Europe and mounting losses fighting the retreating German army, it became evident that something had to be done. Still hoping for a miracle, on 1 November King fired his defence minister, James Layton Ralston, who wanted conscription, and appointed Andrew McNaughton, a general who believed in a volunteer army and thought more volunteers could be found—somewhere. For three weeks McNaughton tried desperately to corral more volunteers, to no avail. But men had to be found, and so, on 22 November 1944, King passed an Order-in-Council introducing general conscription, putting it to a vote of confidence in the House the next day. By delaying

and delaying, King was able to show French Canada that conscription was a measure of absolutely last resort and thus the issue ultimately did not split the country the way he had feared it might.

As it happened, King might almost have gotten away with only limited conscription after all, for from November 1944 to February 1945 there was less fighting by Canadians and the strengths of the various battalions grew once more. In the end slightly fewer than thirteen thousand conscripts actually made it to the war in Europe.

In late February 1945, troops were transferred from Italy, and for the first time Canada's army was fighting together, under General Harry Crerar. Canadian troops played a major role in the liberation of the Netherlands, relieving a hunger-stricken and grateful Dutch population. More than five thousand men died in this effort.

Late in 1944, the Japanese launched a series of so-called fire balloons against the west coast of North America. Having established that the prevailing high-level winds blew eastwards, they released balloons with explosives attached. When the balloon had been in the air for the length of time calculated to reach Canada, four incendiary bombs were dropped, one at a time. These were supposed to set fire to the forests of western Canada. It is thought that about nine thousand of these balloons were sent towards North America, and many dropped on western Canada. Three hundred were actually recovered. The public was not told of these attacks at the time, as it was thought the news might cause panic. It seems that they were intended to demoralize the civilian population in a similar way to the German rockets raining down on London towards the end of the war. But little damage was done to wet or snow-covered Canadian forests.

On 30 April 1945 Hitler committed suicide, and a week later the German armies surrendered. The European war was over. On 6 May Halifax was wrecked by frenzied celebrating servicemen.

The Japanese military machine, however, continued to fight the American forces as they advanced towards Japan. Few Canadians were involved in this war; those who were fought with the British. In an attack on Japanese warships at Onagawa, Honshu, on 9 August pilot Robert Hampton Gray earned the last Victoria Cross of the war, and in another wave of attacks G. A. Anderson became the last Canadian to be killed in action. Japanese resistance collapsed after the atomic bombing of Hiroshima on 6 August and Nagasaki on 9 August, and Japan surrendered on 15 August.

In all, 42,042 Canadians lost their lives during the Second World War, a war in which well over a million men and women served their country in the armed forces.

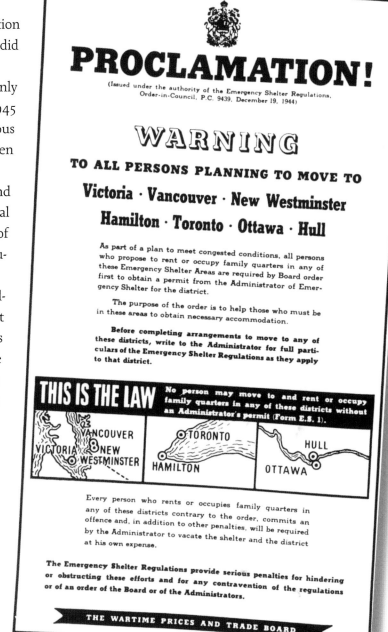

Above, right.
This advisory issued by the Wartime Prices and Trade Board shows the restrictions on movement in some of Canada's largest cities towards the end of the war. This was released in December 1944.

Right.
A Japanese fire balloon that landed at Point Roberts, just south of Vancouver, in 1945.

A Different Canada

Troops returning from the war half expected to come back to the Depression many of them had left. But Mackenzie King was not about to let that happen. As early as 1940 he had initiated an unemployment insurance scheme, deliberately bringing it in when there was nearly full employment so as to create a positive account for later. In 1944 he brought in a family allowance system, to start the following year. There were proposals for health insurance. And there were benefits for veterans, too, to help returning troops get re-established, educated, or start a business or a farm.

King won re-election—though narrowly—once more on 11 June 1945, promising full employment and social security. His slogan was "Vote Liberal and Keep Building a New Social Order in Canada." In Britain, a month later, the great war leader Winston Churchill was thrown out of office by the voters in order to obtain such social welfare measures through a Labour government; in Canada, the far-sighted King had adeptly moved to give the voters what they wanted beforehand. As a result, he stayed in power.

For Canadian politics had moved subtly to the left during the war. There had been strikes in 1943, resulting in new, more liberal labour legislation. Saskatchewan's provincial government fell to the CCF in 1944, and Tommy Douglas had become Canada's first socialist premier. Even the Conservatives had become the *Progressive* Conservatives in 1942, not that the change did them much good. Indeed, in 1943, the CCF was leading in federal polls. But times had changed and King had outmanoeuvred all his opponents.

Immigration, which had fallen to almost nothing during the war, again picked up. Most of the initial immigrants were war brides and children. British women, it seems, liked Canadians and their relatively classless system and married them in droves. By the end of 1946, over 47,000 women had come to Canada, with over 21,000 children, to join their husbands and fathers. Ninety-three percent of them were from Britain. And although they found conditions different from home, almost all stayed and adapted.

Although Canada was to find a new role in the world as the first of the so-called middle powers, the reality of the new world was that it was dominated by two superpowers, the Soviet Union and the United States. And Canada lay between them. Canada had also joined the *Permanent* Joint Board on Defence with the Americans in 1940. But Britain was no longer able to guard Canada anyway. In February 1947 a new bilateral agreement was signed with the United States, and Canada's military was integrated into the defence of the continent. It was one more step away from the British fold and into the hands of the new empire, that of America.

Left.
Vancouver on VJ day, 15 August 1945. This photograph was taken by newspaper photographer Jack Lindsay.

Some determined, most unsure: the first of some 47,783 women and 21,950 children of Canadian forces personnel married in Europe wait at London's Euston station for the train to Liverpool, where the ship to Canada awaited. The Canadian government provided free passage to Canada for the war brides, as they were known.

MINING OIL F...
Western Examiner
Vol. XXI. No. 41
THE WESTERN EXAMINER, CALGARY, SATURDAY, FEB. 15, 1947

LEDUC No. 1 BLOW...

THREE RESERVES DUE FO...

Crowds Thrilled By ... Display At Imperial W...

(By FRANK GIBBONS)

Giving a spectacular display of power whi... spectators to recall memories of the early days o... the Imperial Oil's Leduc #1 well blew into oil p... day afternoon in a perfectly staged setting and ... which would have done credit to a popular spor...

The well's be... appear a real d... big, rich oilfield... company offici... their usual cautio... difficulties and ha... be faced, it was n... sense their satis... the Leduc promise...

After blowing ou... low of black smoke... flame complete with... best smoke rings... Brown wells in the ... well slugged off after... minutes to burst out a... in a more impressive... after the completely... public had deserted... tion.

Latest word was to th... that the well was runni... storage tanks on pro... with future plans for c... tion to be arranged by... pany. In all probability... will be acidized later.

Coming as a climax to a... able day, the colorful blo... it, of the well was comple... satisfactory.

Imperial Oil, in order t... news should have the offi... note of the eye-witness had... vited reporters, photographe... and radio broadcasters to a... end in force and the invitat... was responded to from all part... of the province. Among... large crowd surrounding the... derrick could be found many o... the names prominent in the his... tory of Alberta oil development... with civic and provincial offi... cials and large numbers of th... just curious from all points of... the compass, accompanied by... their children and their dogs.

The day opened with a valu...

(Continued on page 5)

Annual Review Issue Next Week

Next Saturday's Examiner will be the Annual Review Issue.

Special articles will give ...icial reports on the opera-...ns in Alberta and Saskat-...wan during 1946. In ad-... on the summary of events ...ch took place during the ... will be set out.

...re has always been a ...mand for the Annual ... issue, so it would be ... well to place orders ...r news dealer before ...k-end.

... Rigging ... Taber Site

... California re-
...aber-Prov. 64-
... of 15-9-17w1
... early start.
...p. Foremost-
...as at 3,183

...PORT

...o Home
...y this
...3142 ft.
... #26
...on.

MINING OIL FINANCE
Western Examiner
Vol. XXI. No. 42
THE WESTERN EXAMINER, CALGARY, SATURDAY, FEB. 22, 1947
Price 10 Cents

At Birth of New Alberta Oil Field

IMPERIAL LEDUC No. 1 WELL—Discovery for a second major Alberta oil field, blowing out its huge billow ... and heavy smoke when the well was completed as a big producer last week. —Foote by H. Pollard, Calgary

12   *The Canada We Know*

anadians, like most in the western world, breathed a collective sigh of relief at the end of the war. Austerity would be over; now they could get on with the good life. And, apart from a few hiccups, so they did. A brief foreign exchange crisis in 1947 with a ban on imports of luxury goods ended the following year when the United States came up with the Marshall Plan to aid reconstruction in Europe and allowed the money to be spent in Canada as well as south of the border. With the economic dynamo C. D. Howe as minister of reconstruction, the economy was quickly on its feet and American investment started to flow north. By 1947 houses were being built at a rate that outpaced even the number of marriages, the explosion of which was to produce the much-touted baby boom (see page 253).

In 1947 the discovery of large reservoirs of oil in western Canada transformed the economic outlook for the West, and indeed all of Canada, which was at the time using much more oil than was being produced domestically. A single well, drilled at Leduc, just southwest of Edmonton, started it all.

Although small amounts of oil had previously been found in Alberta, notably the Turner Valley field south of Calgary, by the end of the war the flow of oil was dwindling, and oil companies searched almost desperately for more sources. Imperial Oil, one of the major oil companies, had by February 1947 drilled well over a hundred holes, all of which were dry. Then the company drilled a hole at Leduc and found oil in a Devonian reef formation not previously suspected to hold oil in quantity. But it did, and the West would never be the same again.

On 11 February 1947 Imperial became certain that this hole was a wet one. As a public relations stunt they invited dignitaries and the public to come and watch the well "blow," setting the date and time two days hence. It was a calculated risk, for oil wells are not known to blow to any man-made schedule. The result, on 13 February, was a crowd standing around in −20°C weather—waiting. At 1 pm, the predicted time, nothing happened. But the prediction wasn't that bad. At 4 pm, after some, including the mayor of Edmonton, had gone home, there was a rumble like a freight train and oil roared

Above, top.
The Newfoundland delegation to Ottawa poses with members of the federal government in the Parliamentary Railway Committee Room in Ottawa on 25 June 1947. Joey Smallwood is seated at left, Mackenzie King is seated at centre, and Louis St. Laurent is seated second from right.

Above.
Joey Smallwood signs the agreement admitting Newfoundland to confederation with Canada, 11 December 1948. Seated to the right of Smallwood is Albert J. Walsh, chairman of the Newfoundland delegation.

to the surface. For twelve minutes, the oil, initially contaminated with mud, was burned off, creating the stereotypical flare captured by all the newspapers. This one was 15 m high, the belching black smoke much higher.

In 1946, when the drilling of Leduc No. 1 began, Alberta's oil output was 6.7 million barrels a year. Ten years later, it had climbed to 144 million barrels. And Alberta was transformed from a basket case to a powerhouse. Even today, oil remains Alberta's largest industry, accounting for almost a fifth of its economy.

A New Province

The Depression had also made a basket case out of Newfoundland. The island, which had rejected a chance to become a Canadian province in both 1864 and 1869, had become bankrupt and in 1934 had requested that Britain take over; it had been governed by a British-appointed Commission of Government from that date. Considerable British and American investment in the strategically located island during the war had restored its economy somewhat, and at war's end there began a debate over the next course of action. The alternatives were to remain as a colony, to again become independent, to join Canada, or, as an unofficial choice nevertheless supported by significant numbers, to join the United States or at least set up a customs union.

Newfoundland set up a convention to advise the government on its option, and delegations were sent to London and Ottawa to find out which country might offer the best deal. Britain, unable to afford much after the war, could offer only independence, whereas confederation with Canada offered all the new social security that had recently been achieved, including family allowances and unemployment insurance, the latter a big attraction to an often seasonally employed workforce. Joseph Roberts Smallwood, a journalist universally referred to as Joey, took up the torch for the forces of Confederation, getting himself elected to the convention in 1946, where he demonstrated the qualities that would eventually make him one of the most successful popularist politicians Canada has ever known. The merchants of St. John's, fearing that they would be overrun by businesses in Canada, were adamantly against Confederation, arguing instead for the independence that had worked well for them, at least.

A referendum was held on 3 June 1948 with three options on the ballot (everything except union with the United States). When that failed to produce a majority for any option, another referendum was held on 22 June with only the independence and Confederation options on the ballot. This time Confederation obtained 52.3 percent of the votes, a bare majority of 7,000 votes gained from everywhere but St. John's; the rural vote was lured by the dangled carrot of unemployment insurance.

On 11 December the New Canadian prime minister, Louis St. Laurent (he had taken over from King the month before), signed the documents uniting a new province, Newfoundland, to Canada. Newfoundland became Canada's tenth province at midnight on 31 March 1949. The original agreement called for 1 April, but the savvy Smallwood was not going to start off on April Fool's Day, and put the instant of Confederation back a few minutes.

One of the things Newfoundland had to do was change the side of the road on which its citizens drove from the left, as in Britain, to the right, but except in the cities this was a minor inconvenience.

Joey Smallwood was appointed interim premier of the province and won an election the following year, beginning twenty-three uninterrupted years as premier. His efforts to promote industry were not very successful except for the Churchill Falls hydroelectric project in Labrador, which nearly foundered on the negotiation of power transmission through Québec, negotiated only in 1969. Smallwood oversaw a resettlement of many outport communities that were economically unviable. He finally lost power to a Conservative government in 1972, and spent his final years writing a monumental five-volume *Encyclopedia of Newfoundland and Labrador*. With his customary canniness, he knew that the best way to ensure his place in history was to write it himself!

Yet Another War

Canada was slowly but surely cutting the apron strings that tied it to Britain. The post-war governments of Mackenzie King and St. Laurent deliberately dropped references to the "Dominion," the name by which the country was correctly and universally known up till then. Canada is still legally the Dominion of Canada, but virtually no one uses the term any more, so successful has been the expunging of this perceived vestige of colonialism. But Canada had moved into the American sphere of influence and in 1947 signed a North American defence agreement (see page 241). Some redress against what many saw as increasing North

Above.
In September 1948, people on the street in Cornerbrook, Newfoundland, read of Canada's acceptance of their island into Confederation.

Below.
The generally favourable opinion in Canada towards adding Newfoundland to Confederation is reflected in this cartoon from the *Vancouver Sun*, 3 June 1948.

American isolationism came with the creation, in 1949, of the North Atlantic Treaty Organization (NATO), the idea for which had originated with a Canadian diplomat, Escott Reid, then been promoted by his minister, Louis St. Laurent, and the deputy minister, Lester Pearson. It was Canada's first peacetime military defence alliance.

Communist North Korea had been created in 1948 after the end of Japanese occupation of the Korean Peninsula. In June 1950, North Korea crossed the line that had been drawn around the free world and, sponsored by Russia and China, invaded South Korea. With the aid of a United Nations resolution, the United States responded, as did other nations. It took St. Laurent two months to commit Canada to the war; Princess Patricia's Canadian Light Infantry were dispatched to Korea in November and December. Then the Chinese joined the war on the side of the North Koreans and threw huge armies at the Allied troops, pushing them back to about the original border. Rich in manpower but not weapons, the enemy forces often tried to overwhelm by sheer force of numbers. In what became the defining battle of the war for Canadian troops, the Pats held the defensive Hill 677 at Kapyong against a massive Chinese offensive during a general withdrawal, despite being surrounded.

Princess Patricia's Canadian Light Infantry returning from a patrol in Korea, about 1951.

Almost 27,000 Canadian troops served in Korea, and 516 were killed. Only because of its proximity to World War II—with a million Canadian troops and more than 40,000 killed—has the Korean War not received as much attention. Yet by any measure it was a major conflict. Through it Russia and the Communist world learned the important lesson that they could not invade the democracies of the West or anywhere else and expect to get away with it.

Dief the Chief

A chance opportunity resulted in this once well known photograph of a saintly Diefenbaker.

The oil companies planned to export the gas that had been found with oil in Alberta to western American markets, while American gas supplied eastern Canada. C. D. Howe, known now as "minister of everything" because of his power in the St. Laurent government, instead wanted a pipeline across Canada to reduce dependence on American suppliers. But when government financing for a stretch of uneconomic line between Winnipeg and Sudbury came to be debated in Parliament in 1956, the government had to use closure to ram it through in time for construction to start that year. The opposition Conservatives, now led by John George Diefenbaker, exploited the debate to suggest that the Liberals had denied democratic rights, and denigrated Howe as an imperious pro-American. He was indeed originally an American but was in this case trying to protect Canada's position. Nevertheless, when St. Laurent called an election in 1957, Diefenbaker led his Conservative party to an upset victory and formed a minority government. A year later he achieved the largest parliamentary majority of any party ever, with more than 79 percent of the seats.

Considered by many to be one of the twentieth century's finest prime ministers, Diefenbaker was a down-to-earth Prince Albert lawyer with a gift for oratory. His enormous popularity was matched only later in the century by that of Pierre Trudeau; five days before the election even police officers cordoning off a crowd in Calgary had abandoned their task to shake his hand. And then there was "The Vision." John A. Macdonald's vision had been the West; Diefenbaker's was the North. And he followed through. Lester Pearson, now his Liberal opponent after taking over from St. Laurent in 1958, taunted that roads would be built "from igloo to igloo." But in spite of this criticism, Diefenbaker's government opened up Canada's North to an unprecedented degree, building roads and creating the new town of Inuvik in the Mackenzie Delta, which Diefenbaker officially opened in July 1961.

Naturally enough, Diefenbaker—by now universally "Dief the Chief"—was a staunch supporter of farming, and in 1961 his agriculture minister, Alvin Hamilton, concluded an important deal with Communist China to sell that country Canadian grain. The deal was particularly significant because there had been a glut of wheat and barley on the market and nowhere to store the overflowing grain. The United States was upset, for that country's policy was to isolate Red China from world trade. But Diefenbaker didn't care; he didn't get on with the brash new president John F. Kennedy, anyway. Diefenbaker again collided with Kennedy in 1963, during the Cuban Missile Crisis. When a third world war seemed likely, Canada took three days to prepare for engagement, arguing about the previously agreed American command.

Diefenbaker's proudest achievement was his groundbreaking Canadian Bill of Rights, passed in 1960 and endowing all Canadians with the right to life, liberty, and personal security; equality before the law; freedom of religion, speech, assembly, and association; and other rights. Although it applies only to federal law, to the extent that it was not superseded by the Canadian Charter of Rights and Freedoms in 1982 (see page 271) it remains in effect. Like this later charter, it can be overridden by a "notwithstanding" clause, and this was used, once, in 1970, during the October Crisis (see page 265).

No man's popularity lasts forever, and Diefenbaker's declined as precipitously as it had ascended. The economy was going into the downtrend of one of its relentless cycles and necessitated a series of deficit budgets. The Avro Arrow was scrapped (see page 253). Vociferously criticized by the governor of the Bank of Canada, James Coyne, Diefenbaker was forced to introduce a special Act of Parliament to fire him. He was dogged by economic crisis and a dollar that had dropped to what was then a low point—though the 92.5¢ US "Diefenbuck" does not seem so disastrous today—and a debate over nuclear weapons on Canadian soil. An election in 1962 reduced Diefenbaker's government to that of a minority; a further election in 1963 swept Lester Pearson's Liberals to power.

Diefenbaker refused to resign as Conservative leader and led an aggressive Opposition—"we in Opposition are in fact the detergents of democracy," he said in 1964—but in 1967 Diefenbaker was voted out in favour of Robert Stanfield, who had been premier of Nova Scotia. Diefenbaker remained an active MP until his death in 1979.

Above.
John Diefenbaker, Canada's prime minister from 1957 to 1963, with the Canadian Bill of Rights.

Right.
Queen Elizabeth and American president Dwight Eisenhower at the opening of the St. Lawrence Seaway on 26 June 1959. Construction on the seaway had begun in 1954 and was a substantial upgrading of canal facilities that already existed, enabling navigation by large ships from the head of Lake Superior to the Atlantic Ocean.

Milestones of Commercial Aviation

Canadians have come to consider their airlines an essential and integral part of the expansive country in which they live. Now one major airline dominates the skies, Air Canada, but until the end of 1999 there was also Canadian, itself a merging of many smaller airlines.

In 1936 the government finally came to realize the significance of air travel for such a large country and created a new Department of Transport under the ubiquitous minister C. D. Howe, with a mandate to start up a government owned and controlled airline. Canadian Airways, then the largest of the airlines, wanted no part of such an arrangement, and neither did the Canadian Pacific Railway (CPR), so Howe created Trans-Canada Air Lines (TCA) as a completely new company, a wholly owned subsidiary of Canadian National Railways, also government owned.

The first transcontinental flight took place on 30 July 1937, with Howe on board. The Lockheed 12A aircraft took 17 hours 34 minutes, including five stops, to fly from Montréal to Vancouver. The first scheduled transcontinental flights began on 1 April 1939 using the Lockheed 10A, the plane shown below, and the following year a second daily flight was added. In 1943, mainly as a service to fly mail to troops in Europe, transatlantic flights were begun, flown for the government by Trans-Canada, using eight modified Lancaster bombers, called Lancastrians. Up to ten VIP passengers and mail took about twelve and a half hours to fly to Prestwick, Scotland. Although such flights were clearly dangerous in wartime, only one plane was lost over the Atlantic.

The CPR, which had wanted to start an airline but without government control, went on a buying spree, buying up smaller airlines. On 16 May 1942 ten airlines, which notably included Yukon Southern Air Transport, previously owned by bush pilot and aviation pioneer Grant McConachie, were merged into one, called Canadian Pacific Airlines (CPA). McConachie joined CPA and from 1947 until his death in 1965 was the airline's president.

TCA, which had a right of first refusal on all international routes, turned down an opportunity to fly across the Pacific in 1949, and the routes were awarded to CPA. For these routes, later in that year, CPA became the second airline in the world (after BOAC, the British flag-carrier) to order jet aircraft—the British-built Comet. Due to a lack of range, this aircraft was to fly only the Honolulu-to-Sydney leg of the route, but the very first plane crashed while being delivered to Sydney in 1952 and the order was cancelled. This was just as well, for the Comet had an ill-fated history of crashes until it was found that metal fatigue was the problem. After this inauspicious beginning, CPA waited until 1961 to begin flying jets.

Trans-Canada was offered a Canadian-built jet in 1949, the Avro C–102 Jetliner, but turned down the offer as it was thought to be too small. The Jetliner, as a result, was not successful.

CPA started flights to South America in 1955, but was not allowed to compete on the Canadian transcontinental route until 1958, when the airline was allocated a single daily flight; another was permitted in 1967, but not until 1979 was unlimited transcontinental competition allowed.

In 1954 TCA purchased eight Lockheed L1049 Super Constellation aircraft for transcontinental routes. This plane, huge by the standards of the time, carried an amazing sixty-three passengers. Later the same year the airline became the first in North America to purchase a turboprop plane, the Vickers Viscount (shown below).

Above.
A poster advertising jet service across the Pacific, cancelled after the crash of the first Comet en route to Australia.

Below.
A Vickers 757 Viscount turboprop. This one, now at the Canada Aviation Museum in Ottawa, served with Trans-Canada Air Lines from 1957 to 1969. Also shown are two posters, the one on the left announcing that this plane can reach Montréal from Vancouver in just under twelve and a half hours.

By 1956 the airline had fifteen of these popular and quiet planes. Only in February 1960 did TCA acquire its first jet aircraft, the Douglas DC-8. The DC-8 and its Boeing counterpart the 707 (which was introduced in 1958) were to revolutionize air travel worldwide because they could carry so many people in safety and comfort.

On 1 January 1965, just weeks before Canada officially adopted its new maple leaf flag (see page 262), Trans-Canada Air Lines became Air Canada, complete with its distinctive red maple leaf on the rear tail of its aircraft. The name change was to reflect the fact that the airline was now more than just a trans-Canadian one. From 1966 on, Air Canada acquired seventy-two Boeing DC-9s, with the result that by 1974 it was an all-jet airline. In 1971 the first Boeing 747 jumbo was delivered, and in 1982 the first of a new generation of fuel-efficient jets, the Boeing 767.

Canadian Pacific Airlines in 1968 became known as CP Air. In 1979 the airline started the first "no frills" service, from Toronto to Calgary, Edmonton, and Vancouver, with 747s, after receiving permission to fly across the country for the first time. Eastern Provincial Airways merged with CP in 1984, and in April 1986, the airline started a service to Shanghai, China, Canada's the first air connection with that country.

In December 1986 Pacific Western Airlines, until that time a regional airline, purchased CP Air. The combined airline became Canadian Airlines International, with the "a" on the side of its planes made into a company symbol so as to also represent the French *Canadien.* But the company overburdened itself in 1989 when it bought Wardair, a charter and limited schedule airline started by another bush pilot, Max Ward. Wardair had created a niche for itself in a crowded marketplace with the excellence of its in-flight service, using china for meals even in economy class. Canadian tried hard to bring itself up to this standard but ultimately could not afford to. The airline became a financial basket case, and even the buyout of 25 percent of the company by American Airlines in 1992 (the maximum foreign ownership allowed) did not ensure solvency for long. By 1998 Canadian announced it would have to cease operations but in fact held on in hopes of a saviour. Finally, Air Canada obtained government approval for a takeover of Canadian and the two companies merged on 23 December 1999.

In an atmosphere of deregulation many other competitors took wing, especially a jaunty little airline called WestJet, which flies only Boeing 737s to make maintenance easier, but the entire airline industry, in Canada as elsewhere, suffered tremendously with the decline of air traffic after the September 2001 terrorist attacks on the World Trade Center (see page 277). But notwithstanding the rationalization of the airline industry in Canada, more and more people fly each year. In 1931, the first year for which the statistic is available, 7 million passenger-kilometres were flown in Canada. By 1951 this had increased to 929 million, by 1971 to 18,527 million and in 2001 reached 31,750 million, despite the setbacks of that year.

Above.
A Trans-Canada Air Lines Lockheed L1049 Super Constellation built for the transcontinental route and placed in service in 1954.

Below.
Still bearing Canadian colours, Boeing 737 combi *Spirit of Iqaluit* pauses at Norman Wells, N.W.T., in July 2000. Canadian North was owned by Canadian Airlines International until 1998, when the airline was sold to raise cash. It was purchased by NorTerra, itself owned by two aboriginal corporations, one representing the Inuvialuit of the western Arctic and the other the Inuit of Nunavut. The airline remained a feeder to Canadian until its demise. The "combi" designation refers to the fact that the entire front half of the aircraft can be used for passengers or freight according to demand.

The Sad Tale of the Avro Arrow

Canada had played a major role in the training of pilots and manufacture of airplanes during the Second World War, and after the war Canada had an aircraft manufacturer that was amongst the most advanced in the world. It was A. V. Roe, usually just referred to as Avro, of Malton, Ontario. In 1949 the company rolled out the c-102, North America's first passenger jet and the world's second, which flew just two weeks after the British De Havilland 106 Comet.

With the advent of the Cold War, Avro looked forward to a long period of development of military aircraft, and the company attracted top design talent for this purpose. In 1952 the government asked Avro to design a long-range interceptor plane to counteract the threat of Soviet supersonic bombers. The design selected was the CF-105 Arrow. The first prototype was rolled out in 1957. It was widely recognized as the most advanced interceptor fighter plane of its time. No American plane, despite various claims to the contrary, had the capabilities of the Arrow. It could be airborne in 60 seconds and could fly at speeds up to 2 453 km per hour (Mach 2) at heights up to 17 830 m.

But on the very same day that the first Arrow appeared, the Soviet Union launched Sputnik, the first satellite, and there was an immediate concern that the Russians would now have the capability of launching intercontinental ballistic missiles (ICBMs) rather than bombers in any attack on North America. Why then would Canada continue with an interceptor? Better to buy Boeing's Bomarc missiles, a solution of course promoted by the United States. The Diefenbaker government was persuaded and, citing cost overruns, cancelled the entire Arrow project.

On the afternoon of 20 February 1959 about 14,000 employees of Avro, most of them highly skilled, learned over the company's public address system that they had lost their jobs. With the announcement Canada lost one of its most promising industries. Many of the Avro engineers went south and were quickly snapped up by American aerospace companies; some joined the U.S. space program.

According to James Floyd, one of the Arrow's designers, instructions were received "from the government" not only to halt testing of the plane, but to utterly destroy all five prototypes, all engines, all parts and all drawings, technical data, even models and designs. It was as though someone felt it necessary to completely erase all evidence of the very existence of the Avro Arrow. There is an ongoing mystery as to who actually was responsible for the destruction order, and why. Fred Smye, the head of Avro Aircraft, initially refused to carry out the order, but the planes were technically government property and "the government" threatened to send in the army to carry out the task if Avro did not; at this Smye capitulated and complied. The destruction was an absurd waste of advanced Canadian technology and years of accumulated know-how, which destroyed the pre-eminence of Canadian aerospace technology. All that survives today of the Avro Arrow are one nose piece, some wingtips, and a few other parts; these are in the Canada Aviation Museum in Ottawa.

Above.
The sleek, aerodynamic lines of the the Avro Arrow are apparent in this drawing of the plane in flight. The streamlined look was partly due to the fact that all the plane's armaments were concealed inside the outer skin, unlike any other fighter plane at the time.

Below.
Test pilot Spud Potocki enters the cockpit of one of the prototype Avro Arrows prior to a test flight in 1958. Potocki was the only test pilot to fly all five prototype aircraft.

Radio and Television

Radio was essentially a novelty until the 1920s, when many small radio stations sprang up. Companies such as Canadian National Railways, Canadian Pacific Railway, and Imperial Oil produced radio programming during this decade, but by 1929 most Canadians who listened to their radio were tuned to American stations. The proximity to the United States was to prove an ongoing problem for any government that wanted to encourage home-grown Canadian programming both in radio and later in television.

In 1932 a radio network monopoly was granted to a new Canadian Radio Broadcasting Commission, which in 1936 became the Canadian Broadcasting Corporation (CBC).

In 1952 the invention that was to change the way Canadians looked at the world arrived—just. The first televisions were black and white, received transmissions with an antenna, and were live for only forty hours a week, if you were lucky. But often the view looked more like a Canadian blizzard.

The first Canadian television programming went on the air in Montréal on 6 September 1952, followed two days later by Toronto, where, after a technician decided to polish the CBC logo seconds before broadcasting began, the first broadcast image most of English Canada saw was upside down. About 100,000 Canadians had televisions when broadcasting began, having bought them in anticipation. A set cost about $400, representing about a month and a half's work for the average person at the time. On 11 October the first hockey game was broadcast by CBC from Montréal, where the play was covered by just three cameras: one on the play, one on the goal, and the other on wide angle.

Television broadcasting began in Ottawa and Vancouver the following year, and also in Sudbury, Ontario, where the first private CBC affiliate station opened. By 1958 a coast-to-coast microwave network had been completed—the longest in the world—allowing the first nationwide broadcast on 1 July. Well, not quite nationwide. There were still huge swaths of rural areas, particularly in the North, that were not served. It was not until 1967, for instance, that Yellowknife first got television, and this was a transmitter and playback machine that used four hours' worth of taped programs, flown in each day from the south. Whole communities had to pretend they didn't know who won the hockey game the night before. It was 1973 before the first live broadcast was beamed to the North, courtesy of the new *Anik-A1* satellite (see page 275).

In 1966 Canada became the third country in the world, after the United States and Japan, to introduce colour television. Even more important than this—for some—was the introduction that year of instant replays for a developing Canadian institution, *Hockey Night in Canada.*

In 1961 another television network, CTV, began, with second stations in the larger cities, and in 1968 the CRTC (now the Canadian Radio-television and Telecommunications Commission) was set up to regulate broadcasting. Today the station universe has grown to over a hundred and many households have cable or satellite reception. Almost every Canadian household—over 98 percent of them—has at least one television.

An early 1950s-era television displays a scene from 1925 on a Canadian National Railways radio car. The railway was the first radio network broadcaster. The number of Canadian households with a television grew from 373,000 in 1953 to 2.5 million by 1957 and to 4.75 million (94.5 percent of the total) by 1967.

Boom and Burbs

In 1946, immediately after the war, Canada's total population stood at 12.2 million people. Ten years later the population reached 16 million, and by 1966, 20 million. The country added 7.7 million people in twenty years, an increase higher than the total population of the country in 1913, after the immigration boom at the beginning of the twentieth century.

There were two main causes of this sudden phenomenal growth: increased immigration and a rising birth rate that gave rise to the so-called baby boom. Troops returning from the war had delayed having children, the economy boomed in the fifties, and there was a reduction in the workforce participation rate by women, as they returned to the traditional role of home-maker. It was widely believed at that time that women should be at home if they had children, and this attitude was encouraged not least by the government, which did such things as remove tax concessions for families where the woman worked, rules that had been changed during the war for precisely the opposite reason—to encourage women to get into the labour force and the war effort. Daycare centres set up during the war were closed.

About 2.5 million immigrants came to Canada in the twenty-year period 1946–66. Most still came from Britain or the rest of Europe, a situation that

| | M | | | Before 1901 | | F |

1966-71
✴ *1961-66*
✴ *1956-61*
✴ *1951-56*
✴ *1946-51*
1941-46
1936-41
1931-36
1926-31
1921-26
1916-21
1911-16
1906-11
1901-06
Before 1901

Above.
The baby boom, as illustrated by the 1971 census. The graph shows total population, male on the left and female on the right, by five-year age groups, with the birthdate range of each cohort. The years marked by asterisks are those that contained the baby boom, 1947–63.

Below.
The brave . . . and the not so sure. Third graders line up for their polio shots at a Vancouver school in 1955.

The pair of photographs above documents one case of the remarkable growth of suburbia after the war. The photographs are of Lawrence Avenue (running east towards Toronto, away from the camera) at Markham Road in Scarborough. The top image was taken in November 1953 while the one below was taken in 1969, just sixteen years later.

Above.
The construction of a subway in Toronto to service the expanding city created growth of its own wherever a station was built, but here the replacement housing was higher-density apartments. This pair of photographs shows Yonge Street, looking north to St. Clair and Eglinton Avenues, in 1951, with the swath cut by the subway under construction most evident, and in 1973, twenty-two years later.

would not change until the mid-1980s. They included war brides, Polish veterans, and people who had been driven from their homes during the war and found them under Communist rule afterwards, to which the term *displaced persons,* or simply DPS, was applied, sometimes pejoratively. In 1956 some 3,500 refugees from the Hungarian Revolution found haven in Canada.

Canada took in many refugees. In 1959, World Refugee Year, a new minister of citizenship and immigration, Ellen Fairclough—who in 1957 had become the first woman to be appointed to the federal cabinet—pushed the existing rules somewhat to permit the entry of some ill refugees who would not normally have been allowed into the country. That year some 6,912 refugees were admitted. Later (1969) Canada signed an international convention on refugees. Noteworthy admissions of refugees to Canada were Tibetans, in 1971 and 1972; Ugandans fleeing the Amin regime in that country in 1972 and 1973; Chileans in 1973; and about 60,000 "boat people" from Vietnam, Laos, and Cambodia in 1979 and 1980.

Although the baby boom ended about 1963, the rate of immigration continued to climb, and in addition the countries of origin of immigrants began to change. Up until 1962 Canada gave considerable preference to white immigrants. Most were not banned, but the regulations made it effectively much harder to qualify as an immigrant if you were not white. Ellen Fairclough and the Diefenbaker government had removed almost all racially discriminative regulations in 1962. Remaining racial prejudices (regarding sponsoring of relatives) were completely removed five years later. It took Australia until 1973 and the United States until 1978 to do the same thing. The result was a growth in the number of immigrants from Asia, very slow at first, until in 1977 Asian immigration for the first time outnumbered immigration from Europe. By 1997, the year Hong Kong reverted to China, Asian immigration was three and a half times greater than European immigration, and formed about 64 percent of total immigration, which by 2004 was typically between 200,000 and 250,000 persons each year.

Since the Second World War almost all of Canada's immigrants have not been farmers as their predecessors were, and have headed directly to cities and towns. Coupled with the high birth rate, the inevitable result was an explosion of urbanization across the country. Jobs were plentiful, money for mortgages available, and the desire for home ownership strong. And for most Canadians, new and not so new, a home meant a house. Builders were happy to oblige and cities began to sprawl. The scene in Scarborough, Ontario, shown here, is typical: in 1953 an idyllic pastoral scene (*far left, top*), by 1973 (*far left, bottom*) a developed suburb. In the census of 1951 Scarborough had 56,292 people; by the 1961 census this had grown almost four-fold to 217,286, and by 1971 there were 334,000 people residing in the suburb. Today over 600,000 people live in the same area, which was incorporated into the City of Toronto in 2000.

The new suburbs had a different feel to the older city centres. They were viewed as an alternative to the dirt and grime of the inner city. Almost everyone was "middle class,"

Canadian Citizenship

Despite the emergence of Canada as an independent nation, until 1947 there was no legal Canadian citizenship. On the initiative of cabinet minister Paul Martin Sr., whose visit to a military cemetery at Dieppe had caused him to consider what made a Canadian soldier, a new Citizenship Act was passed in June 1946 and came into force on 1 January 1947. On 3 January Mackenzie King became the first Canadian citizen along with others, notably the Armenian-born photographer Yousuf Karsh. Canada was the first Commonwealth country to create its own class of citizenship separate from that of Britain.

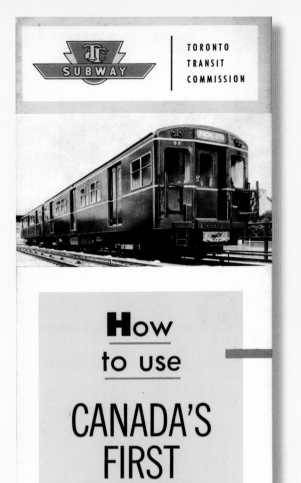

TORONTO TRANSIT COMMISSION

How to use CANADA'S FIRST SUBWAY

vetted by the cost of home ownership, and children grew up surrounded by children of similar economic circumstances from families just like theirs. It was the home of the traditional nuclear family in its heyday.

Toronto grew even faster than American cities such as Los Angeles, adding 50,000 people a year and creating a demand for 20 km² of new suburbs each year. And once you had your house in the suburbs there was the problem of getting to and from your job, likely in the city. Car ownership took off, and with it the demand for better roads, perhaps even freeways. The number of cars on Canadian roads, which was about 2 million in 1950, more than doubled to 4.3 million a decade later.

Toronto had an early solution for its growing city. In 1949 work began on the first subway anywhere in Canada, a line that more or less followed Yonge Street north from Union Station to Eglinton Avenue, a distance of just over 6 km, and was underground for the southernmost 2 km. Trolley and diesel buses connected with the Eglinton station. Modern central Toronto has been shaped by the subway, as the photographs on page 254 demonstrate. The Toronto subway has been added to incrementally over the years so that it is now a 55-km-long system. Other cities adopted rapid transit much later. Montréal in 1966 opened a similar "heavy rail" system, while other cities have adopted so-called light rapid transit (LRT), with lower capacities deemed adequate for their needs. Edmonton began in 1978 with a short line for the Commonwealth Games; Calgary built a tram-like light rapid transit system that opened in 1981; Vancouver's SkyTrain system, full trains operated

Left, top.
In 1954 the subway was such a novel concept that an instruction pamphlet was published to show people how to use it.

Left.
Yonge Street being dug up in 1950 for the construction of the subway. This "cut and cover" method of construction was much cheaper than boring tunnels, as the line did not need to be very deep. The street provided a ready-to-use right-of-way.

Above, centre.
The Canadian-built 1954 Aero Willys automobile.

by computers, opened in 1986 in time for Expo. Other cities stuck to buses, but some gave them special reserved and grade-separated roadways to run on, as in Ottawa's Transitway, created in 1983 and completed in 1995.

In the late 1950s and 1960s most large cities started planning freeway systems, acknowledging the incredible growth in car ownership. The 401 through Toronto was originally intended to bypass the city altogether, but by the time it was completed in 1956 the suburbs had leapfrogged right over it. During the next seven years much of it was expanded to twelve lanes. In 1954 Vancouver completed what was intended to be the first section of a massive freeway system, the Granville Street Bridge over False Creek. But, in the mid-sixties, residents, especially those whose houses were in the paths of proposed freeways, began to organize, and the politicians came to realize that not everyone was in favour of their grandiose plans. The protesters included many young people, the leading edge of the baby boom by this time in their teens, who had come to appreciate that if they stuck together, they could fight city hall—and much more. In Toronto the Spadina Expressway, which was planned to reach the downtown from the 401 to the north, sparked protest rallies. "Think People," "People Not Pollution," "Stop Spadina!" read the signs. And the politicians heard. "People power" worked. Construction of the Spadina Expressway was halted in 1971, and the completed stretch was renamed the W. R. Allen *Road.* In 1964, work began to extend the Gardiner Expressway, an elevated freeway that had been built along the Toronto waterfront in the fifties, eastwards to connect with the 401. But the project was in the wrong time and place. Suddenly it became unfashionable to raze whole neighbourhoods for the benefit of the polluting automobile. The extension was cancelled, but not before 1.3 km of it had been built. This section sat unused for thirty-seven years before it was dismantled in 2001.

In Vancouver several proposals to build a freeway along the waterfront and through Chinatown to the downtown attracted similar attention in 1969 and 1972 with the same result as Spadina—cancellation. The decision is credited with saving Vancouver from the inner-city decline that has affected most American cities, where the automobile was—and still is—king. Indeed, Canadian inner cities are today generally much more liveable than their American counterparts because of a fine balance between the automobile and transit.

Above.
Like an arrow pointed straight at the heart of downtown, Vancouver's Granville Street Bridge, a multi-lane structure built to freeway standards in 1954, was intended as the first part of an extensive freeway network that never materialized.

Below.
The Second Narrows Bridge, under construction in 1958 to carry the Trans-Canada Highway across Vancouver Harbour, collapsed, killing eighteen men.

Two inventions that sought to control the increasing flow of automobiles. One of the first radar speed trap instruments (*left*), first used in the sixties, and the Harger Drunkometer (*right*), the first Breathalyzer kit to be used in Canada, in 1969. Both of these are now in the Toronto Police Museum.

Connecting Canada

The road between Golden, B.C., and Lake Louise, Alberta, sometime in the fifties when it was a Parks Branch road. The route became part of the Trans-Canada Highway. The mountain is Mount Stephen.

Until 1942, it was not possible to drive an automobile right across Canada without resorting to the railways. The first automobile to cross the country was a 1912 Reo Special touring car driven by English writer Thomas Wilby accompanied by Jack Haney, a mechanic employed at the Reo Motor Car Company of St. Catharines, Ontario. The pair took fifty-three days in 1912 to cross the country, hitching rides on freight trains when necessary and even bumping along the sleepered track itself at one point. A Model T driven by good roads activist Perry Doolittle crossed Canada on a trip sponsored by the Ford Motor Company in 1925. For driving on tracks, Doolittle replaced the car's wheels with flanged railway wheels, as had been done in 1904 on the first car to cross the Rockies (see page 217).

Many proposals had been put forward for a national road, but none had come to anything. In 1930 the Trans-Canada Highway was mentioned for the first time officially in an Unemployment Relief Act. But work was sporadic and the road was viewed more as a make-work project than anything else. The federal government wanted the gaps in the road filled in. By the end of the thirties, there were two remaining gaps in the transcontinental road. They were at Big Bend, 305 km following the Columbia River between Golden and Revelstoke, B.C., and a 547-km gap in northern Ontario between Nipigon and Geraldton. The former was closed in June 1940 and the latter in October 1942, both largely for strategic wartime uses. At that time only the section from Halifax to Ottawa was paved; the rest was at best gravel. There was little acclaim when the gaps were finally closed; by then the public expected better roads altogether. So arduous still was a cross-country trip that it was not until 1946 that R.A. Macfarlane and Kenneth MacGillivray claimed the Todd Medal—which had been offered originally before the First World War—for driving across Canada on their own tires. The trip took them a respectable ten days.

One barrier to the construction of a federally sponsored and coordinated highway across Canada was that under the British North America Act of 1867, roads, unlike railways, were a provincial responsibility. The legislators of the day could see the national significance of railways, but roads at the time were all local and used by horse-drawn vehicles. Who then could have foreseen the emergence of the automobile? As a result the federal

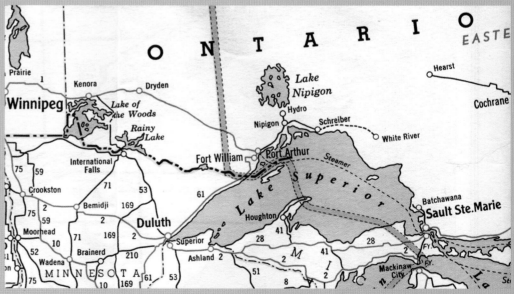

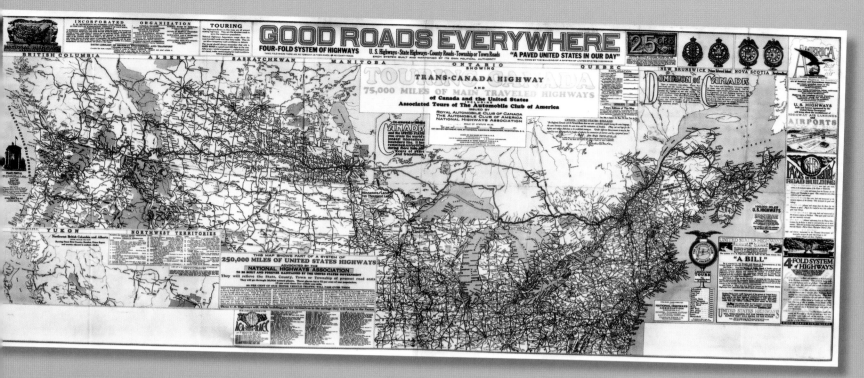

government's role was to get agreement with the provinces, finance roads, set standards, and use persuasion—backed by money—to get the route required.

In 1948 the federal government finally decided that a paved trans-Canada road was needed for economic development, and temporarily rising unemployment at the end of the decade persuaded them that now was the right time to proceed. Robert Winters, minister of reconstruction and a protegé of C. D. Howe, called a federal-provincial conference in December 1948 at which general agreement was reached. In December 1949 the Trans-Canada Highway Act was passed, and after another conference that month, work started on the highway in the summer of 1950.

The act provided for the federal government to give financial assistance to the provinces in return for construction to federally approved standards. The actual routing of the road had to be negotiated, and there were some difficulties here, because the national view of such a road sometimes differed from the local. The original concept had the road ending in the east in Halifax. However, after Newfoundland joined Canada in 1949 the road would now have to end in St. John's, completely bypassing Halifax and involving a road northwards through Cape Breton Island, where the economic benefits were less apparent to Nova Scotia. Most of the road was to be upgraded from existing substandard surfaces, but some new road would also have to be constructed. Perhaps the most notable was a road stretching clear across the interior of Newfoundland where before there had been no road at all.

New road was also constructed in British Columbia, where the long diversion of the Big Bend Highway was cut off by a new road through the Selkirk Mountains at Rogers Pass, the pass surveyed in 1884 by Major Rogers for the Canadian Pacific Railway (see page 162). And it was here that the official opening ceremonies for the Trans-Canada Highway were held on 3 September 1962, presided over by a jubilant Prime Minister John Diefenbaker. The official opening was premature, for the road was not yet completed everywhere—especially in Newfoundland, where premier Joey Smallwood called the opening "deceit, humbug, and bluff." It was 1966 before the road was fully paved right across Canada. It was—and is—the longest national highway in the world.

Above.
With increasing numbers of automobiles, demand for decent roads grew. The Canadian Good Roads Association was formed in 1912. This map was published by its American equivalent, the National Good Roads Association, proposing a route for a Trans-Canada Highway as early as 1928. Much of the route is significantly different from that built, and does not include Newfoundland, separate from Canada in 1928.

Left, bottom.
This was the reality in 1937, as shown on a motoring map from that year. A connection across Lake Superior was provided by steamer.

Below.
Construction of the Trans-Canada Highway in the Fraser Canyon in 1952. Cars pick their way carefully through the construction site. The difficulties of building a road in such country are manifestly apparent.

Canada the Peacekeeper

Below.
Canadian soldiers patrol the border between Israel and Egypt in 1962 as part of a United Nations peacekeeping force.

Right.
Lester Pearson with his Nobel Peace Prize at the presentation ceremony in Oslo in 1957.

In 1963, John Diefenbaker's Conservative government was defeated at the polls and was replaced by a Liberal government under its leader since 1958 (when he defeated Paul Martin Sr. for the leadership), Lester Bowles Pearson, often known as "Mike." Pearson had become popular for his work as an international statesman.

In July 1956 Egypt had nationalized the Suez Canal, a British and French commercial venture since it was completed in 1869, but from which the British had withdrawn military protection two years before. Britain and France made a secret deal with Israel to attack Egypt; when Israel did so, Britain ordered both Israel and Egypt to withdraw so that British and French troops could again occupy the canal zone. Egypt, however, refused to withdraw and Britain and France attacked, bombing the canal and landing paratroopers. But they found little international support and were pressured by the United States, and threats from the Soviet Union, to withdraw.

Canada's Lester Pearson, then secretary of state for External Affairs, with the help of others won support for deployment of a peacekeeping army, the United Nations Emergency Force. This included Canadian troops, and the force was sent to Egypt in late 1956. Pearson won the Nobel Peace Prize for his efforts, the only Canadian ever to win the award. Since then Canada has sent UN-sponsored peacekeeping troops to many countries, notably Cyprus in 1964 to keep warring Turkish and Greek Cypriots apart, and Croatia and Bosnia in the late 1990s to maintain peace in the former Yugoslavia.

UNEF 1 598

A Not-So-Quiet Revolution

In Québec, a radical nationalism was beginning to surface. Back in the late forties, Maurice Duplessis's Union Nationale party, formed in the Depression and once a reform movement, had turned itself into a nationalist party, adopting the blue fleur-de-lis flag in 1948. But Duplessis ran a harsh regime and often ran roughshod over the rights of its citizens. In 1949, a strike at Asbestos was suppressed with violence from provincial police at Duplessis's behest. Duplessis died in 1959 and the Union Nationale lost an election in 1960 to the Liberals under Jean Lesage, whose minister of natural resources was René Lévesque.

Lesage began implementing a program of extensive reforms that became known as le Révolution tranquille, the Quiet Revolution. The role of the Church in the education system was much reduced, electricity companies across the province were nationalized, creating Hydro-Québec, women's legal rights were brought up-to-date, and the Québec Pension Plan was created, among other reforms.

But this progress was not sufficient for some. Twelve days after Pearson became prime minister in 1963 a night watchman, Wilfrid O'Neill, was killed in Montréal by a terrorist bomb. Then mailbox bombs throughout the upscale English neighbourhood of Westmount exploded at night. The city felt it was under attack. A bomb disposal expert was severely injured when another bomb went off in his hands as he tried to dismantle it. The bombs were the work of a new extremist terrorist group called the Front de Libération du Québec—the FLQ.

The FLQ was a small group of ultra-nationalists willing to go to any lengths to obtain independence for Québec. They achieved little, but the violence was a wake-up call for Canada. Lesage and Lévesque warned that Canada must find a way to "keep Québec in" Confederation. In June 1963, Pearson's new federal government established a royal commission on bilingualism and biculturalism, and committed to improve the status of the French language in the federal government. This, predictably, raised the ire of many in English Canada, but also was rejected by René Lévesque and others in Québec as unworkable. It was the classic Canadian dilemma. This was the environment in which Canada gained its new flag, after extensive and often rancorous debate (see next page). After an election in November 1965, Pearson took the opportunity to increase the francophone component in his cabinet, and he brought in Gérard Pelletier, Jean Marchand, and Pierre Trudeau.

When in the centennial year of 1967 Canada held Expo 67 in Montréal, one of the visitors was the president of France, General Charles de Gaulle. On 24 July he stood on the balcony of Montréal's city hall and after a few "vives" trumpeted "Vive le Québec *libre.*" English Canada was stunned. Pearson told him in no uncertain terms that his speech was unacceptable. De Gaulle cut short his visit and went home. But many Québécois were pleased. The incident underlined— as if it needed underlining—the Canadian dichotomy once more.

Lester Pearson retired in 1968. His government had introduced the Canada Pension Plan and a universal medicare program (see page 272) and unified the armed forces. It had also made the first steps towards an officially bilingual Canada. The next step in this direction would be made by Pearson's successor, Pierre Elliott Trudeau.

Above.
The fleur-de-lis flag, created in 1948, flies from the Québec legislature.

Below, top.
A revolution of a different kind: Toronto's main traffic computer, about 1967, a monstrous UNIVAC with the equivalent of only 256K RAM and a 6MB hard drive yet costing an astronomical $1.5 million.

Below, bottom.
Habitat, a demonstration housing project created for Expo 67 in Montréal.

Our Maple Leaf Flag

Flags are a peculiar national emblem. Every country has one, and whether used for rallying around on the battlefield or marking a country's prowess at the Olympics, a flag has become essential equipment for any country wishing to call itself a nation. Before 1763, Canada had only the royal coat of arms of France (see page 40), and the pure white flag of the French kings was used in battle. After the arrival of the British, that country's Union Jack was used in Canada, but by the War of 1812 it had been supplanted for many purposes by the Red Ensign. Originally a flag of the merchant marine, the Red Ensign became Canada's flag by usage rather than official decree. The official flag was still the Union Jack of Britain, although in 1945 a federal Order-in-Council mandated the flying of the Red Ensign on all government buildings, both at home and abroad.

This was the situation until 1965, although failed attempts had been made to introduce a distinct Canadian flag in 1921, during William Lyon Mackenzie King's first government, and again during his last, in 1946.

Lester Pearson was responsible for initiating the process that produced a new flag for Canada. When Canadian peacekeepers had been sent to Egypt in 1957 following the Suez crisis of the previous year (see page 260), Pearson had been dismayed to find that the Egyptians objected to Canadian troops because they looked too much like British troops. One of the reasons was their Union Jack–daubed Red Ensign. As leader of the Opposition in 1960 he had raised the issue only to have it rejected out-of-hand by John Diefenbaker. As prime minister Pearson resolved to do something about it, and so, in June 1964, he introduced his choice for a new flag design—immediately dubbed the "Pearson pennant"—into Parliament. This was the three-maple-leaf design with blue stripes shown at left.

As might be expected with such an emotional issue, the proposed change caused an uproar. The result was that the flag design was referred to a fifteen-person all-party committee. During its deliberations, in October 1964, it happened that Queen Elizabeth II was visiting Canada, and when she was in Québec, there were demonstrations for Québec independence, heightening the necessity of arriving at a flag design that was not overly symbolic of one previous colonial power. Pearson certainly had always wanted a flag that had no reference to either Britain or France. Diefenbaker, a staunch and vociferous opponent of any new flag, wanted the precise opposite, a flag that had the symbol of Britain front and centre.

The flag committee chose three finalist designs, shown here, and one final recommendation—the red and white maple leaf design that became our national flag. After a long debate and 250 speeches in the Commons, the committee's recommendation was accepted by a vote at two in the morning on 15 December 1964. On 28 January a royal proclamation was signed, and the red Maple Leaf replaced the Red Ensign on 15 February 1965.

And the winner is . . . Prime Minister Lester Pearson displays the winning flag design to the press late in 1964. The three finalists are shown below. The top one, the "Pearson pennant," was Pearson's favourite, but detractors thought it looked too much like a Liberal party flag. The bottom one was an attempt to recognize the French and English "founding races"; the middle one, of course, was the winner.

The Red Ensign is lowered and the new Maple Leaf flag simultaneously raised aboard HMCS *Fraser,* at sea on 15 February 1965.

Trudeaumania

Lester Pearson was succeeded in April 1968 by Pierre Elliott Trudeau, who promptly called an election, winning a majority government handily. Trudeau, a bachelor, was wildly popular in the country and was mobbed at every turn. He was in the right place at the right time. The leading edge of the baby boom could now vote and Canada was a place of young people—at the 1971 census, 64 percent of the population was under thirty—and they liked his style; Trudeau was a habitual flaunter of convention, and he appealed to the flower power set of the sixties. "Trudeaumania" made his jokes headlines, his pranks a front-page feature, and everything he did a "happening." And Trudeau was happy to act the part.

Trudeau was from the first a staunch supporter of human rights. He would, he told Canadians, do his best to create what he called a "Just Society." As minister of justice under Pearson he had already reformed Canada's divorce laws and liberalized the laws governing abortion and homosexuality, famously stating that "the state has no place in the bedrooms of the nation."

Under Trudeau's administration many leaps forward would be made, symbolic but also encouraging of a larger societal tide. Notable are the appointment of the first female lieutenant-governor (Pauline McGibbon in Ontario in 1974) and the first native lieutenant-governor (Ralph Steinhauer in Alberta in 1974); the naming of the first Inuit to sit in Parliament (Willy Adams to the Senate in 1977); the appointment of the first female to the Supreme Court (Bertha Wilson in 1982) and the first female governor general of Canada (Jeanne Sauvé in 1984). Add to this record the improvement of social welfare (see page 272), the

Above.
Pierre Trudeau makes a point with his famous finger in this classic 1980 photograph by official photographer Jean-Marc Carisse.

Left.
Prime ministers all. Lester Pearson (right) and three of his ministers in 1967, *left to right,* Pierre Trudeau, John Turner, and Jean Chrétien.

Left.
An ardent Trudeau supporter displays her allegiance in September or October 1972. Despite the enthusiasm, the Liberals managed only a bare minority government in the election of that year, sustained by the support of the New Democratic Party.

Below.
Pierre Trudeau at the Liberal convention in 1968 that elected him leader and prime minister. The other candidates were Robert Winters (see page 259) and John Turner.

abolition of capital punishment in 1976, and the embedding of the Canadian Charter of Rights and Freedoms in the 1982 Constitution and there can be no doubt Canada emerged from its tryst with Trudeau a kinder, gentler, and fairer place.

Despite Trudeau's trademark nonchalant disregard for those who did not agree with him—famously much of the "alienated" West and hallmarked by his celebrated "one-finger salute" to some protestors who waved their signs in his face at Salmon Arm in 1982—many adored his flippantly cerebral style.

Trudeau's first major legislation was the Official Languages Act of 1969, which implemented the recommendation of the Royal Commission on Bilingualism and Biculturalism, a much-misunderstood law that gained him friends in the East while increasing "western alienation" in a West that thought *it* was now the one not understood. But Trudeau, who understood better than most the duality required to govern Canada, was, as usual, unfazed. Two years later he introduced a policy of multiculturalism within the bilingual framework, a move shrewdly calculated to persuade those of neither English nor French language origins—mainly in the West—to accept bilingualism.

In October 1970 came Trudeau's first real test. The Front de Libération du Québec kidnapped James Cross, the British trade commissioner in Montréal, and demanded the freeing of a number of FLQ prisoners languishing in a Québec jail, the payment of $500,000, and the reading of an FLQ manifesto on Radio-Canada. The latter was done, but it made no difference; a second FLQ group kidnapped the Québec minister of labour and immigration, Pierre Laporte.

Five days later, on 15 October, the Québec government of Robert Bourassa requested the assistance of the armed forces. The following day Trudeau proclaimed the existence of "a state of apprehended insurrection," under the War Measures Act, and moved troops into Montréal to patrol the streets, man roadblocks, and guard government buildings, the latter also being done in Ottawa. The sight of the army on the streets in Canada stunned most Canadians. Asked about it by a television reporter, Trudeau made his determination clear: "There are a lot of bleeding hearts around here who just don't like to see people with helmets and guns," he said. "All I can say is, go on and bleed, but it is more important to keep law and order in the society than to be worried about weak-kneed people." Later he was asked how far he would go. "Just watch me," he snapped.

On 17 October the body of Pierre Laporte was found in a car trunk. Close to five hundred people were rounded up and held without warrant, as the War Measures Act allows, but the FLQ turned out to be much smaller than anyone thought at the time—just two groups of about a dozen people each. There was no more violence. James Cross was discovered and his release negotiated in return for safe passage to Cuba for his abductors. The murderers of Pierre Laporte were arrested and served jail sentences for their crime. Everyone else who had been arrested was eventually released without charges being laid.

It is still not clear what prompted Trudeau, the committed libertarian, to order the suspension of civil liberties by invoking the War Measures Act. John Turner, who was minister of justice, maintained it was to reverse "an erosion of public will" in Québec. Jean-Luc Pepin, then minister of industry, told a CBC documentary in 1975 that it was because Trudeau, his cabinet, and a small group in the civil service thought themselves to be revolutionaries as well, "making the civil service, kicking and screaming all the way, bilingual." But the Canadian public supported Trudeau all the way in 1970, of that there is no doubt.

If not revolutionary, there was certainly centralization of power in the prime minister's office. This concentration of power annoyed many and gave Trudeau's enemies much to snipe at. It was probably the principal cause of the Liberals nearly losing power in the election of 1972; as a minority government they only held on to it through an alliance with the NDP, although another election in 1974 restored Trudeau and the Liberals to a majority.

On 28 September 1972, in the midst of that year's election campaign, most Canadians had their minds on something completely different. Two out of every three watched the final pivotal game of the Russia-Canada hockey series, being played in Moscow (see page 268).

The seventies were for many a period of peace and love, a continuation of the flower power of the sixties, in stark contrast to the United States, which was fighting a war in Vietnam. Many draft dodgers fled to Canada. It was the time of "hippies"—really a time of revolt against societal norms—and a growing concern for the environment. Greenpeace was founded in 1970, initially to protest nuclear testing in the Pacific, but the movement grew to encompass an activist approach to most environmental issues. Fashions changed. Women's skirts got shorter, men's

hair longer. And everything, it seemed, was orange, avocado, or gold, the most popular colours of the seventies.

One of the biggest concerns of ordinary Canadians during the seventies was inflation. It was fuelled by the world price of oil, which as a result of the deliberate policy of OPEC, the Organization of Petroleum Exporting Countries, in 1972 shot up from about $2 US a barrel to $16 US a barrel and then continued to rise, doubling again in 1979 as a result of the Iraq-Iran war to an ultimate high of $40 US a barrel. Inflation was at 2.9 percent in 1971; a decade later it was 12.4 percent. Mortgage rates went up, reaching 18 per cent in 1981, although in that year housing prices, which had ballooned more than inflation, collapsed. In 1975 the Trudeau government brought in wage and price controls to attempt to hold down spiralling inflation by allowing only minimal wage increases. Needless the say, the measure was not popular. The government's first response to high fuel prices came in 1972, when it announced that an oil pipeline would be extended east of Montréal, and in 1975, it created Petro-Canada, a Crown corporation. The federal government subsidized imported oil—with a budget deficit— but Alberta had to sell oil to the rest of Canada at lower than world prices, and the province was outraged. "Let the Eastern Bastards Freeze in the Dark" proclaimed the bumper stickers. Then in 1981 came the much-vilified National Energy Policy. It was a typical Canadian compromise: energy prices were allowed to increase and Alberta got an increase in oil prices, but not to world levels.

In 1968, several separatist parties in Québec had come together to form the Parti Québécois under René Lévesque, who left the Liberal government of Jean Lesage. A clever

Above, left.
Troops guard Québec provincial police headquarters in Montréal at the height of the October Crisis on 15 October 1970 while curious kids look on.

Above, right.
The prime minister with Beatle John Lennon and his wife Yoko Ono in December 1969. Lennon said afterwards: "If all politicians were like Mr. Trudeau, there would be world peace."

Left.
A "hippie" family bathe in the waters of English Bay in Vancouver in 1971 in this award-winning photograph by *Vancouver Sun* photographer Glenn Baglo that sums up the flower power generation in a single image.

Right, centre.
Trudeau walks the streets with Chinese leader Deng Xiaoping (left) in 1973, during his groundbreaking visit to China.

Right, bottom.
The typical Trudeau style. This is a famous photograph of Trudeau doing a pirouette behind Queen Elizabeth at Buckingham Palace during a visit in 1977.

He Shoots!—He Scores!

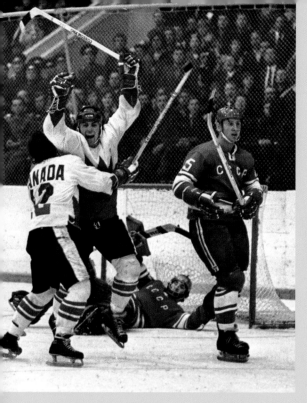

Above.
Paul Henderson reacts after scoring the winning goal in Russia in 1972.

Below.
The McGill University Hockey Club, founded in 1879, was Canada's first organized team. Here McGill students play hockey in 1904. The goal was netless and there was an almost complete lack of protective gear.

The final game of the Russia-Canada hockey series being played in Moscow on 28 September 1972 was played when it was daytime in Canada, causing streets to be empty, school classes to be cancelled, and stores and offices quietened. The series was the first time the Soviets, who had dominated the sport in recent years, had played a professional team of Canada's best players. The series was tied, and then the game was tied. With thirty-four seconds to go Paul Henderson scored the winning goal for Canada, and the whole country cheered. And continued to cheer; it seems that Henderson's famous goal is easily the most remembered in hockey history. In 1999, Canadian Press voted Henderson's goal the sport moment of the century and the team as Canada's Team of the Century.

More important, perhaps, was the effect on the Russians. They had visited Canada, seen the good life. The beginnings of the whole *perestroika* movement in Russia (reform and restructuring under the leadership of Mikhail Gorbachev from about 1985 to 1991) have been attributed by some to this 1972 hockey series.

Hockey is Canada's favourite sport, but its origins have been a contentious issue for many years. The first mention of hockey played on ice was in a letter written by the Arctic explorer John Franklin in November 1825, when he was encamped on the shores of Great Bear Lake at Fort Franklin, now Déline (see page 112). Before the recent rediscovery of a reference to this letter there was an ongoing battle for the "birthplace of hockey" between Kingston, where a British army officer wrote in his diary that he had learned to skate and play hockey on the ice in 1843, and Windsor, Nova Scotia, which based its claim on an 1844 novel that refers to a fictional game of "hurley."

Hockey as we know it today began in Montréal in 1875, when rules for the game were created by J. G. A. Creighton, a student at McGill University. A puck was substituted for a ball to give more control. The first organized hockey club was formed in 1879, and the first association of clubs in 1886, with Québec, Montréal, and Ottawa. In 1893 Governor General Lord Stanley donated a trophy, and the first Stanley Cup game was played that year.

strategy was devised to attract voters wary of independence: there would first have to be a referendum before any separation could occur. Not only that, Québec separation would take the form of sovereignty-association, a smoke-and-mirrors term that implied continued Canadian benefits. Whether the rest of Canada would allow any such an arrangement was both doubtful and unclear and, as far as the PQ was concerned, irrelevant.

In 1976, just months after the nationally evocative spectacle of the summer Olympics had been staged in Montréal, Lévesque's party won election, putting both Trudeau, who had not expected it, and the country, which had not thought much about it, into a tizzy. Trudeau was, it seems, very concerned about the PQ win. He wrote to Thomas Enders, the U.S. ambassador, two days after the election to warn of the possible emergence of a "radical state" supported by hostile outside powers, considered possible at the time in light of what had happened in Cuba; this was only fourteen years after the Cuban Missile Crisis.

The new PQ government soon undid some of what Trudeau was trying to achieve at the federal level by passing Bill 101, making the French language the sole official language of the province, to be used in all government and business, especially on signs. Then on 20 May 1980 came the promised referendum on sovereignty-association. The *non* side was officially led by Claude Ryan, the Québec Liberal leader, but when the campaign began to falter, Trudeau assigned his minister of justice Jean Chrétien to muster the federal forces against the *oui* vote. The result was almost 60 percent *non*. Although there are no separate figures, it is thought that even among the francophone vote, the result was still less than the magic 50 percent. Canada was safe again, at least for a while.

For nine months between May 1979 and February 1980, Trudeau and the Liberals had been out of office after losing an election.

km °C kg mm litre g ha

The Metric System

Metric measurement, legal in Canada since 1871, was not implemented for a hundred years. Responding to industry requests, Trudeau's government recognized the Système international d'unités (SI), a modern form of the metric system, in 1971. Weather forecasts were the first to go metric, with °C being used from April 1975; rain and snow in mm followed in September. Road signs were changed over from miles to km in September 1977, and in January 1979 gas stations started selling gas in litres. Despite delays due to some opposition, all stores and scales had to be changed to kg and grams by 1983, as did product labels.

km °C kg mm litre g ha

Below.
The media go wild over René Lévesque on the night of the election victory of his Parti Québécois, 15 November 1976.

Above.
The power of an image: this famous photograph of Conservative opposition leader Robert Stanfield is credited with losing his party the election of 1974. "Stanfield fumbles!" screamed the headlines the next day. Trudeau in his *Memoirs* referred to Stanfield as "a quiet, decent man who perhaps entered politics at a time when his virtues were not appreciated." When he died in December 2003, Stanfield was lauded as "the best prime minister Canada never had."

The Constitution Act was proclaimed with the signature of Queen Elizabeth on 17 April 1982. A beaming Trudeau looks on. Behind him are (*left*) André Ouellet, Registrar-General, and Gerald Regan, once premier of Nova Scotia and in 1982 minister of labour; to the right of the Queen are clerk of the privy council and cabinet secretary Michael Pitfield and (*with hand on the table*) deputy clerk of the privy council Michael Kirby, both Trudeau's closest aides.

Joe Clark—"Joe Who?" joked the newspapers—had succeeded Robert Stanfield as Conservative leader in 1976. He led a government that fell seven months after its election on a non-confidence vote in the Commons over a tough budget that included a new gas tax. In the ensuing election Trudeau and the Liberals were re-elected largely on the promise of cheaper gasoline. Trudeau also messed up budgets: the 1981 budget of Finance Minister Allan MacEachen was a disaster and many measures he introduced had to be withdrawn, but the Liberals had the political skill to avoid having to go to the country over it.

In March 1981 a newly elected American president, Ronald Reagan, visited Ottawa. Reagan did not think much of the cerebral Trudeau, but the feeling was mutual. "My children found him entertaining," Trudeau wrote in his *Memoirs*.

Trudeau had long wanted to repatriate the Canadian Constitution to Canada. The British North America Act still resided in Westminster, and it was grating to have constitutional amendments controlled, however nominally, by another country. Trudeau had tried as early as 1971 to reach agreement on a new constitution. The Victoria Charter had been agreed to by all the premiers, but Robert Bourassa of Québec had changed his mind; he maintained that he had never agreed in the first place. Other attempts to find a consensus with the provinces had continued in 1978 and 1979 with no success.

In speeches made by Trudeau during the Québec referendum he had promised to "take action to renew the Constitution," and when René Lévesque conceded defeat for the *non* side he demanded that Trudeau fulfill his promise. The prime minister was pleased to oblige.

Trudeau wanted to entrench a Charter of Rights and Freedoms in the Constitution and for this he needed the support of a majority of the provinces. Getting this agreement proved elusive. A conference was held in September 1980, but it was acrimonious. Lévesque somehow got hold of the federal government's secret negotiating strategy and circulated it. The conference, not unexpectedly, failed, and on 2 October Trudeau announced that the federal government would make a unilateral request to Britain for the patriation of the BNA Act. This was ruled on by the courts in Spetember 1981 and found to be legal, though offending to legal convention. In any case, although this would have brought home the Constitution it would not have allowed any changes to it. But the threat of unilateral action did bring the provinces back to the bargaining table.

Another conference was held in November 1981. It was getting nowhere until three attorneys general, the federal Jean Chrétien, Saskatchewans's Roy Romanow, and Ontario's Roy McMurtry, worked out a last-night compromise that was agreed to by all—except Lévesque. Indeed, he had been sleeping in his hotel room across the Ottawa River while all this was going on and was furious to be presented with a *fait accompli* the next morning. Lévesque complained bitterly about this "night of the long knives," as he called it, but in truth he had simply been outmanoeuvred.

Apart from some clauses affecting native peoples and women, which were added in the following few weeks, the deal was done. The British Parliament passed the new Constitution Act, and it was proclaimed by the signature of Queen Elizabeth on Parliament Hill on 17 April 1982. Canada was now, in legal nicety and well as in fact, independent. And the new Canadian Charter of Rights and Freedoms in the act ushered in a new era of court-decided rights. The compromise, the "notwithstanding" clause that allows legislation to violate the charter if expressly stated in the law, has in fact rarely been invoked, for no elected body wants to advertise its violation, although Québec did initially pass some blanket legislation invoking it for every Québec law. One of the first rulings under the new charter came in 1984 when the Supreme Court of Canada ruled invalid some of the sections regarding education in Québec's language Bill 101.

As one of the world's elder statesmen and respected abroad—other than in the United States—more than in Canada, Pierre Trudeau spent his last two years as prime minister attempting to right world wrongs: he began what he called a "North-South" dialogue between richer and poorer countries, and tried to get other world leaders to reduce the level of nuclear weapons to lower Cold War tensions. For the latter he was awarded the Albert Einstein Peace Prize. In February 1984, perhaps sensing a coming electoral defeat, Trudeau took a "walk in the snow" and announced his retirement. He left office in June and was succeeded by John Turner.

Above.
Trudeau with Lévesque and Chrétien at the 1981 constitutional conference.

Below.
Canada's Constitution: the document proclaiming the act signed by Queen Elizabeth on 17 April 1982. This is one of two documents signed during the ceremony shown in the photograph at left. Notice that some of the words ares smudged; this was due to a slight drizzle at the time of signing.

The Well-Being of Canada

In 1980 the nation was captivated by a twenty-two-year-old from British Columbia who, having already lost a leg to cancer, was now running across Canada to raise money for cancer research on his "Marathon of Hope." Terry Fox made it from St. John's to Thunder Bay before having to give up due to the spread of cancer to his lungs. He died ten months later, but his memory lives on in the vast amounts of money raised in his name for cancer research through annual Terry Fox runs in every part of the country. This award-winning photograph was taken by Peter Martin of Canadian Press.

Beginning in 1985 Rick Hansen made a similar trek, inspired by his friend Terry Fox. In 34 countries he covered a distance equivalent to around the world in a wheelchair, this time for spinal cord research, wearing out 117 wheelchair tires in the process.

Canada has one of the most comprehensive social safety nets of any country in the world. Most of it came into being as the result of a desire to ensure that the Depression did not return with the soldiers from the Second World War. The net includes a diverse range of benefits including old-age pensions, insurance against unemployment, universal medical care, and a welfare system for those in desperate straits.

Old-age pensions began in 1927, but had a strict means test widely regarded as humiliating. In 1951 universal old-age pensions were introduced but this required an amendment to the British North America Act. An additional scheme, funded by current workers, was added in 1966. This was the Canada Pension Plan, or CPP. In Québec, which opted to operate its own scheme, it was the Québec Pension Plan, or QPP. These plans had to be revamped in 1997 to accommodate the approaching retirement of the baby boomers.

Unemployment insurance first appeared in 1940. A far-sighted William Lyon Mackenzie King initiated the scheme when there was almost no employment so as to build up funds for possible use later. In 1945 family allowances were introduced, following one of the recommendations of a 1943 report by Leonard Marsh for post-war reconstruction. Family allowances were replaced by child tax credits in 1992 as a cost-saving measure.

Hospital insurance and medical care insurance were first initiated in Canada in Saskatchewan by social crusader Tommy Douglas, the province's premier from 1944 to 1961. Insurance to pay for hospitalization had been introduced in Saskatchewan in 1945. In 1957 the federal government agreed to share the costs, and as a result, by 1961 all provinces had hospital insurance. Medical insurance had a more turbulent birth. It came into force in Saskatchewan in July 1962 and immediately sparked a strike by the province's doctors. The government rushed in doctors from other provinces and even from Britain, and some adroit manoeuvring by Douglas and his advisors produced a compromise amendment that allowed doctors to practise outside the plan if they wished; the strike ended after a month of dissension. Within a few years, most Saskatchewan doctors were operating within the medical insurance plan voluntarily. The federal government passed the Medical Care Act in 1966, allowing it to contribute to provincial plans provided they gave universal coverage; by 1971 all provinces were participating. In 1984, to deal with an erosion of universality due to hospital user fees and extra billing, the Canada Health Act was passed, requiring universality without any additional costs as a condition of receiving federal funding.

Welfare, a provincial responsibility, was shored up in 1966 by the passing of the Canada Assistance Act, a cost-sharing program. Nevertheless, charitable help continues; the soup kitchens of the thirties have metamorphosed into the food banks of today.

Modern Canada is one of the healthiest countries in the world in which to live. Canadians often do not realize that their country leads the world in the promotion of healthful living. This is the result

of a deliberate government policy initiated in the 1970s by Marc Lalonde, then minister of health under Pierre Trudeau. In 1974 he published a significant policy document called *A New Perspective on the Health of Canadians* in which he advocated the active promotion of healthy lifestyles as a way of containing the rising costs of health care, at the time rising between 12 and 16 percent a year. If unchecked, he noted, health care costs would soon rise beyond the capacity of society to finance them, a refrain that seems as familiar now as then. Lalonde wanted to moderate what he called self-imposed risks to health. He proposed an attack on "sedentary living, smoking, over-eating, driving while impaired by alcohol, drug abuse, and failure to wear seat belts."

Lalonde's document has been seen as controversial by some, as an unwarranted intrusion by government into private affairs. But all Lalonde was trying to do was promote health rather than impose it. He might *suggest* running a mile, but no one was going to *make* anybody run. It was, however, a radical change, from helping those in poor health to trying to stop them from becoming ill in the first place. But Lalonde realized that in order to have an effect, the government had to be unequivocal in its advice, even if not 100 percent accurate, and this inevitably permitted attacks from critics, most notably those supporting the tobacco industry. The connection between smoking and cancer has been attacked for years. For while we have seen programs such as Participaction—to encourage exercise—the federal government has also since the seventies progressively hindered tobacco companies from advertising or otherwise promoting their product, and this has caused a significant drop in the number of smokers. Public attitudes to smoking have been radically changed; what used to be perfectly acceptable now is not, and smokers huddle outside in doorways to get their daily puff. Smoking, banned in all government buildings, is now banned in most private ones as well—the public demands it. It is a measure of the success of the so-called "Lalonde Doctrine" that its opponents have become apoplectic in their denouncing of his methods, but time has proven them to work.

Humphrey Bogart posed for Yousuf Karsh in 1946, and the master Ottawa photographer took this classic and stunning image that shows well the quality for which Karsh became famous. Then it was perfectly acceptable for Bogart—who thousands of young people could be expected to emulate—to be shown smoking a cigarette. Now, as a result of deliberate policy begun by Marc Lalonde when he was minister of health in the 1970s, and adopted to some extent by many countries, smoking is largely unacceptable. In 2000 the Canadian government made it mandatory for cigarette packages to cover half of their area with graphic health warnings, an expansion of the earlier policy of smaller, non-graphic warnings, and three examples are shown in Bogart's cigarette smoke. (The cigarette packages have been digitally altered to hide the manufacturers' brand names on the lower part of the package.) A 2003 University of Waterloo study showed that the warnings had been effective. And a footnote: Humphrey Bogart died in 1957 at the age of only 58—from cancer.

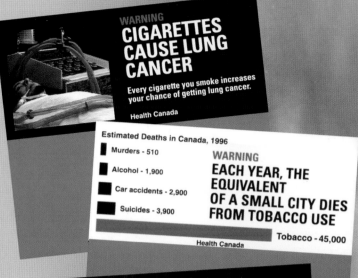

WARNING
CIGARETTES CAUSE LUNG CANCER
Every cigarette you smoke increases your chance of getting lung cancer.
Health Canada

Estimated Deaths in Canada, 1996
Murders - 510
Alcohol - 1,900
Car accidents - 2,900
Suicides - 3,900
Tobacco - 45,000

WARNING
EACH YEAR, THE EQUIVALENT OF A SMALL CITY DIES FROM TOBACCO USE
Health Canada

WARNING
CIGARETTES HURT BABIES
Tobacco use during pregnancy reduces the growth of babies during pregnancy. These smaller babies may not catch up in growth after birth and the risks of infant illness, disability and death are increased.
Health Canada

Taxing Times

John Turner did not last long. He called an election nine days after becoming prime minister and lost it to the new Conservative leader, Brian Mulroney, who achieved the highest absolute majority ever, 211 of the 282 seats in the Commons. It is perhaps unfortunate that Mulroney is most remembered today—by the average person at least—for something Canadians cannot escape, day after day. This is the Goods and Services Tax, the GST. This 7 percent tax, introduced by the Mulroney government in January 1991, is so reviled because as an add-on it is always so visible. It replaced a similar, though less inclusive, manufacturer's sales tax, which had the political advantage of being hidden, embedded in the price at the till. (Three Maritime provinces since 1997 have had the Harmonized Sales Tax, or HST, a combination of provincial sales tax and the GST.) Ultimately the Conservatives paid the price, losing the election of 1993 to Jean Chrétien, Liberal leader since Turner's resignation in 1990.

Another Mulroney legacy is the North American Free Trade Agreement, NAFTA. An entire election, in 1988, was fought essentially over this one issue, and it turned out to be the first time Canadians had voted explicitly for free trade with the United States. Many of the forecasted benefits to Canada evaporated when Mexico also joined the economic union, but it did result in a freer border, as most goods manufactured in either country flow duty-free across it.

The Mulroney government made two attempts to accommodate Québec, the only province not to sign the 1982 Constitution (although equally bound by it). First there was the Meech Lake Accord, reached in 1987. But provincial legislatures were given three years to ratify it, and opinions—and governments—changed. In 1990 the legislatures of Newfoundland and Manitoba turned it down. The second attempt was the Charlottetown Accord of 1992, which attempted to recognize Québec as a "distinct society." The accord was put to the Canadian people as a referendum on 26 October 1992. Some 54 percent voted against it. In 1993 an increasingly unpopular Mulroney handed over the reins of government to Kim Campbell, Mulroney's minister of defence. She had the disinction of becoming Canada's first female prime minister, but she lasted only fifteen weeks, for the election she had to call wiped out the Conservative party. Campbell lost her own seat and the party of John A. Macdonald was reduced to only two seats in the Commons, not enough for even official party status.

Part of the reason for this was the rise of other parties, the right-wing Reform Party, created by Preston Manning in 1987, later the Canadian Alliance (which in 2004 merged with the Conservatives); and the Bloc Québécois, created by disillusioned Conservative minister Lucien Bouchard after the failure of the Meech Lake Accord, which won enough seats to become the official Opposition. It struck many people as peculiar that a separatist party could be the Opposition, a government-in-waiting that in this case could never become the government.

Jean Chrétien, a trusted lieutenant of Pierre Trudeau during the time that considerable ongoing budget deficits were routine, set himself the task of reducing the deficits, which was achieved with the help of his finance minister Paul Martin. He also had to deal with another Québec referendum in 1995. This time it was orchestrated by Québec premier Jacques Parizeau, who had refused to accept the

Above.
Brian Mulroney and his wife, Mila, meet with Pierre Trudeau in 1984.

Below.
Two solitudes. Québec Premier Lucien Bouchard (*left*) and Prime Minister Jean Chrétien seem to be studiously ignoring each other in this 1996 photograph. Both are francophones, but have radically different views of Canada. Bouchard became premier of Québec in 1996 when Jacques Parizeau resigned following the defeat of the *oui* vote in the 1995 referendum. He retired in 2001.

Canada in Space

Canada became the third nation in space with the launch by the defence department in 1962 of *Alouette 1*, a satellite for radio research, but the first commercial satellite was *Anik-A1,* launched in 1972, which carried television programs to northern Canada. *Anik* means "little brother" in Inuktitut. Canada was the first country in the world to use a satellite for domestic television broadcasting. The method was ideally suited to the necessity of covering a vast, sparsely populated land.

Perhaps Canada's most well known contribution to the space program was the development of the Canadarm, technically the Shuttle Remote Manipulator System (SRMS). It is 6 m long, functions like a human arm, and is controlled from inside the shuttle. The first one was deployed on the second space shuttle mission in November 1981. A more recent improved arm has been developed for the building of the International Space Station and was delivered in April 2001 by astronaut Chris Hadfield on the space shuttle *Endeavor*.

Marc Garneau was the first Canadian in space, in 1984, and has since flown twice more, in 1996 and 2000; Roberta Bondar became the first Canadian woman in space eight years later. Canadian astronauts remain a small select group. The Canadian Space Agency was created in 1986 to coordinate most Canadian space activities.

Information from satellites is used in many fields. RADARSAT, which can gather information regardless of clouds or darkness because it uses radar wavelengths rather than visible light, was a Canadian development, and was launched in 1991. An improved version was launched in 2001. RADARSAT is used to detect the state of sea ice on the northern and eastern coasts of Canada, giving a comprehensive view that would be impossible by any other means. What would the Arctic explorers trying to find a Northwest Passage in the nineteenth century have given for such information!

A satellite-map of part of the Canadian Arctic from RADARSAT. It shows the state of the sea ice on 30 July 2002.

Above and below.
One of the conditions under which Prince Edward Island entered Confederation in 1873 was that year-round steam communication be maintained with the mainland, at the Dominion's expense. Ferries had been operating across the ice-choked Durham Strait to the island since 1917. In 1992 a private consortium proposed to build and finance a bridge. The federal government jumped at the idea, and a plebiscite was held by the province which gained a 59.4 percent approval in 1993. Construction started in 1994. A special huge floating crane lifted forty-four main spans into position from the water. The last span was completed on 19 November 1996 and the bridge opened to traffic on 31 May 1997. Confederation Bridge is the longest in the world over waters subject to ice. It spans 13 km across Northumberland Strait. These photographs were taken as the bridge neared completion in August 1996.

defeat of the *oui* vote in the 1980 referendum, and in the last few weeks of the campaign by Bouchard. And he came within a hair's breadth of winning. He had even prepared a speech proclaiming independence. As it was he lost to a 50.56 *non* vote, close enough to spark many charges of irregularities and demands for recounts. Canada had never been so close to disintegrating. The Chrétien government thought that the question asked in Québec was ambiguous and referred the whole matter of the legality of unilateral secession to the Supreme Court, which ruled in 1998 that this was not a right under international law, and also that any question asked in a referendum must be clear and unambiguous. These principles were reiterated in a law passed in 2000 called the Clarity Act. With the election of a non-separatist Liberal government under Jean Charest in Québec in 2003 the separation question disappeared, but it will no doubt resurface in future. Chrétien retired in December 2003, after announcing his intention sixteen months earlier, and was succeeded by Paul Martin.

Canada gained a new territory in 1999, by the division of the Northwest Territories into two. The new eastern part was named Nunavut. It had only 25,000 people, and 21,000 of them were Inuit. Nunavut Tunnagavit, an Inuit-owned corporation for economic development, received $1.6 billion from the federal government as settlement for Inuit land claims. A start has been made elsewhere in recognizing the rights of our first residents, who were in Canada long before anyone else. Some 2 000 km^2 of land on the northern coast of British Columbia has been given back to the Nisga'a of that region and native governance recognized as another level of government, equivalent to municipal in powers. This settlement was long-sought and brought to the surface another problem, that of competing land claims in overlapping areas, requiring a Solomon-like wisdom to adjudicate.

Canada continues to change. In 2000 Pierre Trudeau died, saddened by the loss of one of his sons in a wilderness accident, and a nation mourned the architect of so much that we today take for granted as particularly Canadian. Trudeau in death touched, it seemed, more people than he had in life; thousands came out to pay their respects as his funeral train passed, in a spectacle not seen since the death of John A. Macdonald over a hundred years before.

And then, on Tuesday, 11 September 2001, the unthinkable happened: fortress North America was attacked on its own turf. Two planes hijacked by terrorists flew into the twin towers of the massive World Trade Center in New York, killing thousands. Another crashed into the Pentagon in Washington. In an instant, the United States, and the world, changed. In a longer view, the event will likely come to be seen as the beginning of a new era. In the shorter term it sparked the American invasions of first Afghanistan and then Iraq.

Canada, like much of the western world, has been going through the pains of economic globalization in recent years. Many have lost jobs through mergers and rationalizations. Some have promoted a new economic nationalism, but the country cannot isolate itself from these worldwide trends, and people adapt.

The British connection still survives, but fewer and fewer really care. Deputy prime minister John Manley openly stated his republican opinions while the Queen was visiting in 2002 and was promptly roundly criticized for his rudeness rather than what he said. British-originated democratic institutions, however, continue to serve us well—though there are rumblings about the relevance of the Senate from time to time. Canada has become a multicultural, kinder, more tolerant America. The country was rated the best in the world in which to live by the United Nations Development ment Programme all through the 1990s and remains at or near the top. And there is good reason for this: Canada's environment is the envy of much of the world and its diverse, generally well educated people can compete anywhere.

Despite earlier prejudices and mistakes, Canada now has a unique record of acceptance of diversity that, with an increasingly global society, may in future prove to be a model for the rest of the world. As a place of relative tolerance, with a progressive social environment often not appreciated by its citizens until they travel abroad, Canada has become a great place to live. We can all be proud to call ourselves Canadians.

Above.

After the terrorist attacks of 11 September 2001—9/11—American airspace was shut down. All incoming flights had to divert. Canada implemented Emergency Security Control of Air Traffic (ESCAT), a wartime measure that permitted only designated aircraft to be in the air. Canada provided an emergency haven for 239 international incoming aircraft. They landed in many places. The largest numbers went to Halifax, shown above, which received 47 aircraft. Gander received 38, Vancouver 34, St. Johns 21, and Winnipeg 15. In many of the smaller airports, notably Gander, there were simply not enough hotel facilities to accommodate all the passengers and many residents opened their houses—and their hearts.

Below.

This cartoon by noted editorial cartoonist Allan Beaton from the now defunct Toronto *Telegram* was published on 15 July 1963, and brilliantly depicted Canadian culture as all things to all people. Canada as a nation remains so diverse that some lament the lack of nationalism of its people, but this very diversity is also a major strength.

Image Credits

Half-title page (1)
: NAC PA-041785

Title pages (2–3)
: *Montréal from Custom House looking east,* QC, c.1878, William Notman, McCord Museum of Canadian History, Montréal, II-61339.0.1

6 Canadian Museum of Civilization, Derek Hayes photo

7 Derek Hayes photo

8t, 8b Cartier-Brébeuf National Historic Site, Québec, Derek Hayes photos

9t Fort William, Thunder Bay, Derek Hayes photo

9b Château Ramezay, Montréal, Derek Hayes photo

10 Manitoba Museum, Winnipeg, Derek Hayes photo

11t NAC C-030923

11b From John Ross, *Narrative of a Second Voyage in Search of a North-West Passage,* 1835

12t Library of Congress

12b George Dawson photo, Geological Survey of Canada Collection, NAC C-037756

13 Yuquot, BC, Derek Hayes photo

14 Canadian Museum of Civilization, Derek Hayes photo

14–15 Parks Canada National Photo Collection, Hull, Québec, © Parks Canada

15 Det Kongelige Bibliotek, Copenhagen, Denmark, gl.kgl.saml 2881 4° (10v)

16t From map by Diego Gutiérrez, 1562, Library of Congress G3290 1562 .G7 vault oversize

16b Bibliotheca Estense, Modena, Italy

17 Ernest Board, 1906, Bristol City Museum and Art Gallery/ Bridgeman Art Gallery BAG 2072

18 George Agnew Reid, NAC C-096999

20t Théophile Hamel, NAC C-011226

20b British Library Add. MS 5413

21 NAC C-010522

22–23 British Library Add. MS 24065

24t NAC C-028389

24b Derek Hayes photo

25t Derek Hayes photo

25c From Samuel de Champlain, *Les Voyages du Sieur de Champlain,* 1613

25b Derek Hayes photo

26t Henri Beau, NAC C-010574

26c From Samuel de Champlain, *Les Voyages du Sieur de Champlain,* 1613

26–27 Derek Hayes photo

27t Charles Jefferys, NAC C-073716

27c From Samuel de Champlain, *Les Voyages du Sieur de Champlain,* 1613

28 Parks Canada, Halifax, and Kiyoko Grenier Sago, artist/designer

29 NAC

30 McGill University Library

31 Derek Hayes photo

32 Frank Hennessey (attrib.), NAC C-045483

33 Francesco Giuseppe Bressani, NAC NMC 194824

34t Château Ramezay, Montréal

34c NAC C-020126

34b NAC C-006325

35t J. D. Kelly, NAC C-007962

35b Derek Hayes photo

36 NAC NMC 2711

36 inset NAC C-006022

37 Service Historique de la Marine, Vincennes, France, Receuil 66, 12–15

38 Centre des archives d'outre-mer, Aix-en-Provence, France, Archives nationales C11A 19, fol. 43 recto (left) and 44 recto (right)

39 Winkworth Collection, NAC e-001201229

40t Canadian War Museum, Derek Hayes photo

40–41 *Fort Chambly, near Montréal,* QC, 1863, William Notman, McCord Museum of Canadian History, Montréal, I-8139

42 Hudson's Bay Company Archives, G2/5

44 Cornelius Ketel, Bodleian Library, Oxford, U.K.

45t Private collection

45b Abraham Ortelius, *Theatrum Orbis Terrarum,* 1570, Library of Congress G 1006 .T5 1570b vault

46t NAC NMC 26825

46b Augustine Fitzhugh, 1693: British Library Add MS 5414, No 30.

47t NAC C-028555

47b Stewart Museum at the Fort, Montréal

48 Derek Hayes

49 From Jens Munk, *Danish Arctic Voyages,* Hakluyt Society, London, 1896

50t Private collection

50c Norman Wilkinson, Hudson's Bay Company Archives, P446

50b Manitoba Museum, Derek Hayes photo

51t Map by John Thomson, 1817, private collection

51t inset From the Hudson's Bay Company Corporate Collection, Toronto

51b Hudson's Bay Company Archives, P425

52t Norman Wilkinson, Hudson's Bay Company Archives, P401

52b NAC C-02626

53 *A general Plan of Annapolis Royal,* 1753, Library of Congress G3424 .A45 1753 .H3 vault

53 inset Fort Anne National Historic Site, Derek Hayes photo

54 British Library, MS map in Arthur Dobbs, *Account of Hudson's Bay,* 1744, 213 c.11

55 Derek Hayes

56 H. Stevens, NAC C-001090

58 Fortress of Louisbourg Photo Archives, with permission of the artist, Lewis Parker

59t NAC C-40575

59b NAC NMC 500

60t, 60b Thomas Jefferys, NAC NMC 1012

61t Thomas Jefferys, NAC NMC 1012

61b Charles Jefferys, NAC C-000125

62 National Library of Canada.

63 Canadian Museum of Civilization, CPM 1999.185

64t Louis Franquet, NAC NMC 709

64b Charles Jefferys, NAC C-073709

65 Parks Canada, Halifax, with permission of the artist, Lewis Parker

66 Louisbourg National Historic Site, Derek Hayes photo

67t Charles Jefferys, NAC C-073711

67b Richard Paton, NAC C-143388

68 Library of Congress G3424 .L6 S26 1758 .B6 vault

69 NAC C-005907

70 NAC C-027665

70–71 Dominic Serres and Samuel Scott, NAC C-004291

72 NAC NMC 97970

73 Clockwise from top left: NAC C-146565; C-003916; C-121919; C-002834; C-018720

74 NAC C-146340

75 James Barry, NAC Winkworth Collection e-000756717

76t	NAC C-000350	113b	Samuel Gurney Cresswell, NAC C-041019
76b	Château Ramezay, Montréal	114	Charles Beauclerk, NAC C-000392
77t	Adam Sheriff Scott, NAC C-011043	116	NAC C-011811
77bl	NAC C-147536	117t	Charles Jefferys, NAC C-073703
77br	Sir Joshua Reynolds, National Gallery of Canada 8004	117b	Thomas Burrowes, Archives of Ontario AO 5517
78	John Christian Schetky King, NAC C-041824	118t	Henrietta Hamilton, NAC C-087698
80	NAC NMC 21404	118cr	NAC NMC 27
81	Mabel B. Messer, NAC C-002833	118b	Newfoundland Museum, St. John's
82t	NAC C-003490	119t	Private collection
82b	William Faden, NAC NMC 55019	119b	NAC C-052855
83t	NAC C-005415	120	Pierrette and Jacqueline Boulet collection, College Jésus–Marie, Sillery, Québec, 124/1F/PR-6/ic-188, and Parks Canada, Québec
83b	Derek Hayes photo	121t	NAC C-013656
84–85	Winkworth Collection, NAC e-000996055	121b	NAC PA-136924
85t	Derek Hayes photo	122	James Cockburn, Winkworth Collection, NAC e-000756742
85b	Archives of Ontario AO 1316	123t	Bibliothèque national de Québec
86	James Peachey, NAC	123b	Château Ramezay, Montréal
87t	John Forster, NAC C-008111	124	NAC
87b	NAC Upper Canada, Submissions to Executive Council on State Matters, 1791–1841, RG 1, E 3, Vol. 100, p. 98	125t	Charles Beauclerk, NAC C-000393
88t	NAC C-114468	125b	Charles Beauclerk, NAC C-000396
88b	NAC NMC 4800	126t	NAC C-011095
89t	NAC RG 10, Vol. 1841, IT 039 (front and back)	126b	Mackenzie House, Toronto
89b	NAC	127	NAC C-041467
90t	George Theodore Berthon (1806–92), *Portrait of Major-General Sir Isaac Brock, K.B.,* Government of Ontario Art Collection, 694158	128	NAC
90b	NAC C-054666	129	NAC C-004788
91	NAC C-000273	130	NAC C-013392
92t	Fort York, Derek Hayes photo	131t	Derek Hayes photo
92cl	Fort York, Derek Hayes photo	131c	NAC C-005456
92cr	Toronto Public Library, Jarvis Papers, S125.B65/67	131b	*Report on the Affairs of British North America,* Lord Durham, 1839
92b	Owen Staples, Toronto Public Library	132	Samuel McLaughlin, NAC C-018371
93	Peter Rindlisbacher	134t	NAC C-042253
94–95	Peter Rindlisbacher	134b	Joseph Légaré, *The Burning of the Parliament Building in Montréal,* McCord Museum of Canadian History, Montréal, M11588
96t	NAC C-041031	135t	John Wilson Bengough, *Punch-in-Canada,* 1849
96b	Derek Hayes photo	135b	NAC C-005332
97t	NAC C-115678	136t	Archives of Ontario AO-6253
97b	NAC NMC 6852	136b	Museum London, London, ON
98	NAC PA-135819	137t	Josiah Henson, 1830
99	Hudson's Bay Company Archives, E.2-2, folio 12	137b	Archives of Ontario AO-4333
100t	Hudson's Bay Company Archives, P167, T7887	138t	Henry Warre, 1845; print of original painting
100b	James Ford Bell Library, University of Minnesota	138b	Winkworth Collection, NAC e-000996134
101t	Private collection	139t	British Columbia Archives A-01229
101b	Fort Carleton, Saskatchewan, Derek Hayes photo	139b	British Columbia Archives A-03787
102t	Grand Portage Historic Site, Derek Hayes photo	140t	Canadian Railway Museum, Montréal, Derek Hayes photo
102c	NAC C-002477	140b	Winkworth Collection, NAC e-000996083
102b	Public Record Office, U.K., CO 700 America North and South 49	141t	Museum of Industry, Stellarton, NS, Derek Hayes photo
103	Arthur Heming (1870–1940), *Mackenzie Crossing the Rockies,* Government of Ontario Art Collection, 619815	141b	Canadian National Collection, 16257, Canada Museum of Science and Technology, Ottawa. Photo is c.1875.
104t	National Maritime Museum, Greenwich, U.K.	142–43	NAC C-000733
104cr	From James Cook, *Voyage to the Pacific Ocean,* 1784	143t	NAC C-000773
104b	José Cardero	144t	NAC C-006350
105	Harry Heine	144b	Cartier House National Historic Site, Montréal, Derek Hayes photo
106	Yuquot, BC, Derek Hayes photo	145l	NAC Government Archives Division, RG 2, Vol. 5354
107	United Kingdom Hydrographic Office, 228 on 82	145r	*Globe,* 1 July 1867
108t	British Columbia Archives PDP-02258	146	NAC C-018737
108b	John Innes, Manitoba Museum	147t	NAC C-021543
109t	Hudson's Bay Company Archives, P378	147b	NAC C-015021
109b	NAC C-8714	148l	NAC C-013493
110t	Hudson's Bay Company Archives, P206	148r	Canada's Penitentiary Museum, Kingston, Derek Hayes photo
110b	Arthur Heming, from Edwin Guillet, *Early Life in Upper Canada,* 1933	149t	Canada's Penitentiary Museum, Kingston, Derek Hayes photo
111t	Peter Rindisbacher, NAC C-001904	149b	Canada's Penitentiary Museum, Kingston, Derek Hayes photo
111b	From Anon., *Recent Polar Voyages,* 1877	150	NAC C-001875
112t	NAC C-004530	151	NAC C-006792
112b	Thomas Mitchell, NAC C-052573	152t	NAC C-002048
113t	NAC PA-147732	152b	NAC NMC 7064

153t   *Canadian Illustrated News*, 1870
153b   Lionel Stephenson, NAC C-042288
154   National Library of Canada
155t   Derek Hayes photo
155b   Edward Roper, Winkworth Collection, NAC e-000756685
156t   NAC C-017335
156b   City of Vancouver Archives 17–44, BC Telephone Co. Collection
157   NAC PA-026439
158t   George Caitlin, NAC C-100014
158b   Glenbow NA-550-18
159t   Glenbow NA-354-23
159b   Glenbow NA-659-16
160   Edward Roper, Winkworth Collection, NAC e-000756687
161t   NAC C-006393
161c   NAC PA-066576
161b   NAC PA-143155
162–63 British Columbia Archives A-01009
164t   NAC NMC 11868
164b   National Library of Canada C-022248
165t   Fort Battleford National Historic Site, Derek Hayes photo
165b   Robinson Wadmore, Winkworth Collection, NAC e-000996489
166   NAC C-002424
167t   James Peters photo, NAC C-003463
167c   James Peters photo, NAC C-003451
167b   NAC C-002769
168t   Saskatchewan Archives Board, RB-741a
168b   NAC C-001879
169   Canadian War Museum, Derek Hayes photo
169 inset   NAC C-031378
170   Ernest Brown photo, Provincial Archives of Alberta, B. 993
171   Ernest Brown photo, Provincial Archives of Alberta, B. 4233
172t   City of Toronto Archives, William James Fonds, Fonds 1244, Item 2
172b   NAC Winkworth Collection e-000756697
173   Ernest Brown photo, Provincial Archives of Alberta, B.3127
174t   *Saturday Night*, 1896
174–75 NAC C-024322
175t   NAC PA-171896
176t   NAC C-006536
176b   NAC C-007126
177t   NAC PA-013522
177b   NAC C-007983
178t   Private collection
178–79 NAC C-004490
180   NAC C-014063
181t   Front cover, Otto Sverdrup, *Nyt Land*, 1903
181cl   From Otto Sverdrup, *Nyt Land*, 1903
181cr   From Roald Amundsen, *Nordvest-Passagen*, 1908
181b   From Roald Amundsen, *Nordvest-Passagen*, 1908
182   Archives of Ontario AO 6252
183t   NAC PA-027942
183c   NAC
183b   Western Development Museum, North Battleford, Derek Hayes photo
184t   Farm Museum, Milton, ON
184–85 NAC PA-038667
185t   Glenbow NA-919-49
186t   NAC C-056088
186–87 Glenbow NA-984-2
187t   Glenbow NA-789-21
187b   Canada Agriculture Museum, Ottawa
188t   Montreal *Daily Star*, 15 November 1901; Glenbow NA-3683-3
188b   Vancouver Public Library
189t   NAC PA-041785
189b   NAC PA-010401
190t   Eaton's Archives, Archives of Ontario
190c   Ronald Whistance-Smith

190b   Archives of Ontario AO 4467
191t   1905 Eaton's catalogue
191b   1926–27 Eaton's catalogue
192t   Author's collection
192b   Glenbow NA-3639-1
193t   Author's collection (all stamps)
193cl   NAC C-053695
193bl   Canadian Museum of Civilization/Museé J. Armand Bombardier
193br   NAC PA-061702
194t   Winkworth Collection, NAC e-000756702
194b   NAC PA-130297
195   Isaac Erb, Wilson Studios, Saint John. Untraced by New Brunswick Archives
196t   NAC C-009766
196b   NAC PA-109498
197t   NAC C-003623
197b   NAC PA-135835
198t   Provincial Archives of Alberta A2017
198–99 Glenbow NA-303-42
200   NAC PA-030814
202   NAC PA-022731
203t   Musée de la civilisation, Québec, 88-1330
203b   Glenbow ND-3-101
204t   Louis Weirter, Canadian War Museum 8931
204b   Richard Jack, Canadian War Museum 8178
205   NAC PA-003133
206t   From William Bishop, *Winged Warfare*, 1918
206b   From William Bishop, *Winged Warfare*, 1918
207t   Canada Aviation Museum, Derek Hayes photo
207cr   NAC PA-172313
207bl   From William Bishop, *Winged Warfare*, 1918
207br   *Varsity Magazine Supplement*, 1917
208–9   Three sections, left to right: NAC C-019944, C-019953, C-019948
208b   NAC C-001833
209b   NAC PA-022995
210   Newspaper NAC; photo Provincial Archives of Manitoba, Neg. No. N2762, Foote Collection Item 1696
211t   NAC PA-127295
211b   Left to right: Glenbow NA-273-3; NA-2204-12; NA-825-1; NA-2607-1; NAC PA-03212
212   Archives of Ontario F1194, S15000, AO 3001
213t   NAC PA-069901
213b   Glenbow NA-1639-1
214t   NAC C-020260
214–15 NAC PA-121928
215t   Canada Aviation Museum, Derek Hayes photo
216   Canada Aviation Museum 6914
217t   Western Development Museum, Saskatoon, Derek Hayes photo
217b   Vancouver Public Library
218t   Vancouver Public Library
218b   Provincial Archives of Alberta A8996
219t   J. J. Talman Regional Collection, D. B. Weldon Library, University of Western Ontario, London, ON
219b   *Saturday Night*, 1933
221   Lawren Harris, National Gallery of Canada 3708
222   NAC C-087430
224t   Glenbow NB-16-207
224b   Saskatchewan Archives Board R-A4822
225   NAC C-029399
226   Leonard Frank photo, City of Vancouver Archives, City P21
227t   Fred Davis photo, *Toronto Star*
227b   NAC C-002178
228   Claude Detloff photo, City of Vancouver Archives LP 109, with permission of Joan Macpherson
229t   Ronald Whistance-Smith
229b   NAC PA-115129

230t   NAC C-027650
230b   NAC C-087120
231t   NAC PA-037467
231b   NAC C-046350
232t   Canadian War Museum, Derek Hayes photo
232b   NAC Z8471-11
233t   Canadian Pacific Archives 4616
233b   Toronto Public Library
234t   Canadian War Museum, Ottawa, Derek Hayes photo
234b   Centre for Newfoundland Studies, Memorial University of Newfoundland, St. John's
235   NAC PA-112993
236t   NAC PA-191375
236b   NAC C-021529
237   Orville Fisher, Canadian War Museum 12469
238t   NAC PA-132651
238c   NAC PA-137013
238br   NAC C-024354
239t   *Saturday Night*, 1944
239b   NAC PA-144181
240   Jack Lindsay photo
241   Attributed to Canadian Press but not found.
242tr   Glenbow NA-789-79
242bl   Glenbow NA-789-80
243   Provincial Archives of Alberta P2733
244t   NAC PA-128073
244b   NAC PA-128080
245t   NAC PA-128007
245b   George Doubt, *Vancouver Sun*, 3 June 1948
246t   NAC PA-115034
246b   Diefenbaker Centre, Saskatoon
247t   NAC PA-112659
247b   NAC PA-121473
248t   Air Canada
248b   Canada Aviation Museum, Derek Hayes photo
249t   Peter Ewart, designer; Canadian Pacific Railway Archives, a65311
249bl   Private collection
249b   Canada Aviation Museum, Derek Hayes photo
249br   Private collection
250t   Air Canada
250b   Derek Hayes photo
251t   NAC PA-111546
251b   Avro Canada, L. Wilkinson photo. Photo is from Canada Aviation Museum, but I regret I have not been able to locate Mr Wilkinson.
252   Television: author's collection; onscreen image: Vancouver Public Library
253t   Derek Hayes with data from Statistics Canada
253b   Vancouver Public Library 41563
254tl, 254bl   Scarborough Archives, Schofield Collection, ES6-19 (1953, actually November 1954) and ES27-617 (1969)
254tr, 254br   City of Toronto Archives, Series 35, File 1, 1951 and 1973. Both Northway Survey Corporation photos.
255t   NAC PA-124953
255c   NAC PA-181041
256t   Author's collection
256b   City of Toronto Archives, Fonds 1128, Series 381, File 4, Item 5985-8
257t   NAC PA-111266
257c   Author's collection
257bl   Toronto Police Museum, Derek Hayes photo
257bc   Toronto Police Museum, Derek Hayes photo
257br   Vancouver Public Library 3042
258l   British Columbia Archives D-02736
258r   *Western Canada Road Map*, Imperial Oil, 1937, author's collection
259t   NAC Record No. 193840, Acc. No. 2002-00535-4
259b   NAC PA-191901
260c   NAC C-094168

260b   NAC PA-122737
261t   Derek Hayes photo
261c   City of Toronto Archives, Series 4, Box 48158, Image 251
261b   Derek Hayes photo
262t   NAC PA-136153
262b   Flag designs, top to bottom: NAC C-149463; C-149464; C-149462
263   Courtesy Department of National Defence. Neg. O-15930-115
264t   Jean-Marc Carisse photo
264b   Duncan Cameron photo, NAC PA-117107
265t   Duncan Cameron photo, NAC PA-175935
265b   Duncan Cameron photo, NAC PA-111213
266   Glenn Baglo photo, *Vancouver Sun*
267tl   NAC PA-129838, Bird/Montreal *Star*
267tr   NAC PA-110805
267c   NAC PA-136978
267b   Doug Ball photo, Canadian Press 3279526
268t   Frank Lennon, *Toronto Star*
268b   NAC C-017831
269t   Doug Ball photo, Canadian Press 258554
269b   NAC PA-180518
270   Robert Cooper photo, NAC PA-141503
271t   NAC PA-201930
271b   Constitution Proclamation, NAC RG68, Vol. 886
272   Peter Martin photo, Canadian Press 1706745
273t   Department of Health and Welfare
273b   Yousef Karsh photo, NAC PA-212506
274t   NAC PA-152416
274b   Shaun Best photo, Reuters
275t   NASA #STS 100, 331-035
275c   *Annual Arctic Ice Atlas*, Winter 2001. RADARSAT image, Environment Canada, 30 July 2002. National Library of Canada
275b   Canadian Space Agency
276t   Derek Hayes photo
276b   Derek Hayes photo
277t   Tim Krochak photo, Halifax *Chronicle-Herald*/Canadian Press 2657325
277b   *The World of Allan Beaton*, Toronto *Telegram*, 1967
281   Orville Fisher, British Columbia Archives PDP 02286
286   Canadian Currency Museum, Ottawa
287   Canadian Currency Museum, Ottawa

Vancouver as some Utopian worker's paradise, a 1939 painting by Orville Fisher. Never mind that the North Shore mountains are not seen behind the Marine Building so clearly depicted (top left), but across the harbour. Never mind that the new City Hall (the building with the clock) is not even near the waterfront at all. This is an idealized composite, a none the less brilliant painting in a style very much at the forefront of its time.

Further Reading

Abbott, Elizabeth (editor). *Chronicle of Canada.* Montréal: Chronicle Publications, 1990.

Amyot, Chantal, et al. *Special Delivery: Canada's Postal Heritage.* Fredericton: Goose Lane; Hull: Canadian Museum of Civilization, 2000.

Anderson, Fred. *Crucible of War: The Seven Years' War and the Fate of Empire in British North America, 1754–1766.* New York: Knopf, 2000.

Archbold, Rick. *I Stand for Canada: The Story of the Maple Leaf Flag.* Toronto: Macfarlane Walter & Ross, 2002.

Armstrong, John Griffith. *The Halifax Explosion and the Royal Canadian Navy: Inquiry and Intrigue.* Vancouver: UBC Press, 2002.

Baird, Donal M. *The Story of Firefighting in Canada.* Erin, Ontario: Boston Mills, 1986.

Baum, Daniel J., and Penelope Mallette. *Times Past: 1933.* Toronto: IPI, 1999.

Bliss, J. M. *Canadian History in Documents, 1763–1966.* Toronto: Ryerson/McGraw, 1966.

Blatherwick, John. *A History of Airlines in Canada.* Toronto: Unitrade, 1989.

Bothwell, Robert, and J. L. Granatstein. *Our Century: The Canadian Journey.* Toronto: McArthur, 2000.

Brown, Robert Craig, and Ramsay Cook. *Canada 1896–1921: A Nation Transformed.* Toronto: McClelland & Stewart, 1994.

Bruce, Jean. *The Last Best West.* Toronto: Fitzhenry & Whiteside, 1976.

——. *After the War.* Toronto: Fitzhenry & Whiteside, 1982.

Careless, J. M. S. *The Union of the Canadas: The Growth of Canadian Institutions 1841–1857.* Toronto: McClelland & Stewart, 1967.

——. *Canada: A Celebration of Our Heritage.* Toronto: Heritage, 1994.

Carrigan, D. Owen. *Crime and Punishment in Canada: A History.* Toronto: McClelland & Stewart, 1991.

Cavell, Edward. *Sometimes a Great Nation: A Photo Album of Canada, 1850–1925.* No location: Altitude, no date (1984).

Cell, Gillian T. *Newfoundland Discovered: English Attempts at Colonisation.* London: Hakluyt Society, 1982.

Collins, Robert. *A Great Way to Go: The Automobile in Canada.* Toronto: Ryerson, 1969.

Conrad, Margaret, et al. *History of the Canadian Peoples: Beginnings to 1867.* Toronto: Copp Clark, 1998.

Cook, Ramsay (general editor). *Dictionary of Canadian Biography.* Vols. 1–14 on CD. Original print publication 1966–98. Toronto/Québec: University of Toronto/Université de Laval, 2000.

Craig, Gerald M. *Upper Canada: The Formative Years 1784–1841.* Toronto: McClelland & Stewart, 1984.

Creighton, Donald. *Canada's First Century.* Toronto: Macmillan, 1970.

——. *The Forked Road: Canada 1939–1957.* Toronto: McClelland & Stewart, 1976.

Dickason, Olive Patricia. *Canada's First Nations: A History of Founding Peoples from Earliest Times.* Don Mills, Ontario: Oxford University Press, 1997.

Duffy, Dennis, and Carol Crane (compiled and edited). *The Magnificent Distances: Early Aviation in British Columbia, 1910–1940.* Sound Heritage Series Number 28. Victoria: Provincial Archives of British Columbia, c.1980

Eccles, W. J. *Canada under Louis XIV, 1663–1701.* Toronto: McClelland & Stewart, 1964.

——. *France in America.* Toronto: Fitzhenry & Whiteside, 1972.

——. *The Canadian Frontier 1534–1760.* Albuquerque: University of New Mexico Press, 1983.

Filey, Mike. *The TTC Story: The First Seventy-five Years.* Toronto: Dundurn, 1996.

Finkel, Alvin, and Margaret Conrad. *History of the Canadian Peoples: 1867 to the Present.* Toronto: Copp Clark, 1998.

Fitzgerald, Jack. *Newfoundland Disasters.* St. John's: Jesperson, 1984.

Floyd, James. "Post Cancellation Consequences" (of cancellation of the Avro Arrow). Speech at the Aerospace Heritage Foundation of Canada event to commemorate the fortieth aniversay of the first flight of the Arrow. Reported at: http://www3.sympatico.ca/mkostiuk/speech.html#Floyd

Gillmor, Don, and Pierre Turgeon. *Canada: A People's History,* vol. 1. Toronto: McClelland & Stewart, 2000.

Gillmor, Don, et al. *Canada: A People's History,* vol. 2. Toronto: McClelland & Stewart, 2001.

Greenhill, Ralph. *Early Photography in Canada.* Toronto: Oxford University Press, 1965.

Guillet, Edwin C. *The Story of Canadian Roads.* Toronto: University of Toronto Press, 1966.

Harris, Beth, and R. G. P. Colgrove. *Lawren Harris.* Toronto: Macmillan, 1969.

Havard, Gilles. *The Great Peace of Montreal of 1701: French-Native Diplomacy in the Seventeenth Century.* Montréal: McGill-Queen's University Press, 2001.

Hayes, Derek. *Historical Atlas of British Columbia and the Pacific Northwest.* Vancouver: Cavendish, 1999.

——. *First Crossing: Alexander Mackenzie, His Expedition across North America and the Opening of a Continent.* Vancouver: Douglas & McIntyre, 2001.

——. *Historical Atlas of the North Pacific Ocean.* Vancouver: Douglas & McIntyre, 2001.

——. *Historical Atlas of Canada: Canada's History Illustrated with Original Maps.* Vancouver: Douglas & McIntyre; Seattle: University of Washington, 2002.

——. *Historical Atlas of the Arctic.* Vancouver: Douglas & McIntyre; Seattle: University of Washington, 2003.

Hitsman, J. Mackay, updated by Donald Graves. *The Incredible War of 1812: A Military History.* Toronto: Robin Brass Studio, 1999.

Kalman, Harold. *A Concise History of Canadian Architecture.* Don Mills, Ontario: Oxford University Press, 2000.

King, William Lyon Mackenzie. Diaries. Library and Archives of Canada. Online at http://king.collectionscanada.ca/EN/default.asp

Knowles, Valerie. *Forging Our Legacy: Canadian Citizenship and Immigration, 1900–1977.* Ottawa: Citizenship and Immigration Canada, 2000.

Lalonde, Marc. *A New Perspective on the Health of Canadians: A Working Document.* Ottawa: Government of Canada, 1974.

Lillard, Charles. *Seven Shillings a Year: The History of Vancouver Island.* Ganges, B.C.: Horsdal & Schubart, 1986.

Macbeth, Jack. *Ready, Aye, Ready: An Illustrated History of the Royal Canadian Navy.* Toronto: Key Porter, [1989].

McLennan, J. S. *Louisbourg: From Its Foundation to Its Fall.* Halifax: Book Room, 1979.

McNaught, Kenneth. *The Penguin History of Canada.* Toronto: Penguin, 1988.

Marsh, James (editor-in-chief). *The Canadian Encyclopedia: Year 2000 Edition.* Toronto: McClelland & Stewart, 1999.

Milberry, Larry. *Aviation in Canada.* Toronto: McGraw-Hill Ryerson, 1979.

——. *Canada's Air Force at War and Peace.* 3 vols. Toronto: Canav, 2000.

Miller, J. R. *Skyscrapers Hide the Heavens: A History of Indian-White Relations in Canada.* Toronto: University of Toronto Press, 1989.

Monaghan, David W. *Canada's "New Main Street": The Trans-Canada Highway as Idea and Reality 1912–1956.* Ottawa: Canada Science and Technology Museum, 2002.

Monnon, Mary Ann. *Miracles and Mysteries: The Halifax Explosion December 6, 1917.* Halifax: Nimbus, 1977.

Morton, Desmond. *A Military History of Canada: From Champlain to Kosovo.* Toronto: McClelland & Stewart, 1999.

——. *A Short History of Canada.* Toronto: McClelland & Stewart, 2001.

Muckle, Robert J. *The First Nations of British Columbia.* Vancouver: UBC Press, 1998.

Murray, Joan. *Canadian Art in the Twentieth Century.* Toronto: Dundurn, 1999.

Oliver, Dean F., and Laura Brandon. *Canvas of War: Painting the Canadian Experience 1914 to 1945.* Vancouver: Douglas & McIntyre; Ottawa: Canadian War Museum, 2000.

Pigott, Peter. *Flying Colours: A History of Commercial Aviation in Canada.* Vancouver: Douglas & McIntyre, 1997.

——. *Wings Across Canada: An Illustrated History of Canadian Aviation.* Toronto: Hounslow, 2002.

Prowse, D. W. *A History of Newfoundland From the English, Colonial, and Foreign Records.* London: Eyre & Spottiswoode, 1896.

Rawlyk, George A. *Yankees at Louisbourg: The Story of the First Siege 1745.* Wreck Cove, N.S.: Breton Books, 1999.

Ray, Arthur J. *I Haved Lived Here Since the World Began: An Illustrated History of Canada's Native People.* Toronto: Lester Publishing/Key Porter, 1996.

Smith, Philip. *It Seems Like Only Yesterday: Air Canada, The First 50 Years.* Toronto: McClelland & Stewart, 1986.

Statistics Canada. *Aviation in Canada: Historical and Statistical Perspectives on Civil Aviation.* Ottawa: Statistics Canada, 1986.

Sterne, Netta. *Fraser Gold 1858: The Founding of British Columbia.* Pullman, Washington: Washington State University Press, 1998.

Stevens, G. R. *History of the Canadian National Railways.* New York: Macmillan, 1973.

Thompson, John Herd, with Allan Seager. *Canada 1922–1939: Decades of Discord.* Toronto: McClelland & Stewart, 1994.

Trudeau, Pierre Elliott. *Memoirs.* Toronto: McClelland & Stewart, 1993.

Turner, Wesley B. *The War of 1812: The War That Both Sides Won.* Toronto: Dundurn, 2000.

Waite, P. B. *The Charlottetown Conference.* Historical Booklet No. 15. Ottawa: Canadian Historical Association, 1970.

——. *Canada 1874–1896: Arduous Destiny.* Toronto: McClelland & Stewart, 1988.

——. *John A. Macdonald.* Markham, Ontario: Fitzhenry & Whiteside, 1999.

The small change and the large bill. Above is a 25 cent note from 1900, while opposite is a $50,000 note that was in use between 1918 and 1935—but only by banks. They used it to exchange large sums of money in the days long before electronic transfers.